The Total Work of Art

'*The Total Work of Art: From Bayreuth to Cyberspace* is an outstanding accomplishment. Matt Smith has written an original and provocative analysis that "fast forwards" the Gesamtkunstwerk into the 20th and 21st centuries, demonstrating how the project of creating a total work of art has been taken up by very different artists working not only in theater but also film, theme parks, experimental happenings, and digital media. This work will recast how scholars approach the total work of art and help stimulate new research across several fields.'

Jon McKenzie, *University of Wisconsin-Milwaukee, USA*

'In this groundbreaking study, Matthew Smith shows us that the ideal of a total work of art was the driving engine behind the greatest accomplishments and the scariest fantasies of modern culture. Weaving Wagner, Warhol, and virtual reality into a rich and compelling narrative, *The Total Work of Art* is theater studies at its best. This book, written with precision and flair, should be required reading for anyone interested in theater history. And who knows, it just might serve as a blueprint for the theater of the future.'

Martin Puchner, *Columbia University, USA*

Richard Wagner, Oskar Schlemmer, Bertolt Brecht, Leni Riefenstahl, Walt Disney, Andy Warhol, Bill Gates: these disparate figures all represent important stages in the development of the total work of art. Impacting fields of theatre, architecture, music, literature and film, the tradition of the total work of art has exerted tremendous influence on modern culture, in a way that has so far been only partially understood.

The tradition of the total work of art has been studied primarily as a branch of the history of opera. This wide-ranging study, however, stresses the connection between the total work of art and developments in mass culture. Comparing Bayreuth and Disneyland, the Crystal Palace and the Bauhaus Totaltheater, Brecht's Epic Theatre and Riefenstahl's *Triumph of the Will*, Matthew Smith finds that the total work of art has as much to do with mass media as with high art, with commercial spectacle as with music drama.

The Total Work of Art will be of interest to students and scholars across a broad range of disciplines, including theatre and performance studies, history of art, music history, cultural studies, and comparative modernism.

Matthew Wilson Smith is Assistant Professor of English at Boston University.

The Total Work of Art

From Bayreuth to Cyberspace

Matthew Wilson Smith

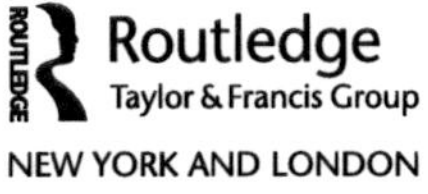

NEW YORK AND LONDON

First published 2007
by Routledge
270 Madison Avenue, New York, NY 10016

Simultaneously published in the UK
by Routledge
2 Park Square, Milton Park, Abingdon, Oxon OX14 4RN

Transferred to Digital Printing 2008

Routledge is an imprint of the Taylor & Francis Group, an informa business

© 2007 Matthew Wilson Smith

Typeset in Baskerville and Gill Sans by
Book Now Ltd, London
Printed and bound in Great Britain by
CPI Antony Rowe, Chippenham, Wiltshire

Library of Congress Cataloging in Publication Data
Smith, Matthew Wilson.
The total work of art: from Bayreuth to cyberspace/by Matthew
Wilson Smith.
    p. cm.
Includes bibliographical references and index.
1. Aesthetics. 2. Performing arts. 3. Popular culture. 4. Mass
media. 5. Art–History. I. Title.

BH39.S5527 2007
700.1–dc22   2006029612

British Library Cataloguing in Publication Data
A catalogue record for this book is available from the British Library

ISBN10: 0–415–97795–9 (hbk)
ISBN10: 0–415–97796–7 (pbk)
ISBN10: 0–203–96316–4 (ebk)

ISBN13: 978–0–415–97795–1 (hbk)
ISBN13: 978–0–415–97796–8 (pbk)
ISBN13: 978–0–203–96316–6 (ebk)

For my parents

Contents

Illustrations

Figures

Tables

Acknowledgments

No one writes alone. My first thanks go to Andreas Huyssen and Martin Meisel, who have been there from the beginning. With their different backgrounds, different approaches, and equally brilliant minds, Martin and Andreas proved the perfect bifocal lens through which to view the history of the total work of art. I am deeply in the debt of these two great scholars. I am also grateful to the many friends, mentors, and colleagues who shared ideas, corrected mistakes, and offered encouragement. Particularly invaluable were Arnold Aronson, Mara de Gennaro, Elinor Fuchs, Julie Stone Peters, Martin Puchner, John Paul Riquelme, and the members of the Columbia Theatre Colloquium. Special thanks also to Ivan Ascher, Silvia Beier, Julia Prewitt Brown, Justin Campbell, Bill Carroll, Joyce Chopra, Amanda Claybaugh, Bonnie Costello, Gregory Fletcher, Sheila Ghose, Darren Gobert, Tom Dale Keever, Laura Korobkin, Tara McGann, Ellen McKay, Susan Mizruchi, Lee Monk, Anita Patterson, Elizabeth Ruf, Laurence Senelick, Jim Siemon, Doug Smith, Erin Snyder, Shilarna Stokes, Sean Sullivan, Rosanna Warren, James Winn, my wonderful colleagues in the English Department at Boston University, and the past and present members of the Tertulia Junior Faculty Colloquium. I have depended upon their aid and encouragement.

Sections of this manuscript were presented at the American Society for Theatre Research, the American Comparative Literature Society, the Modern Language Association, Performance Studies International, the Columbia Historical Musicology Colloquium, the Tertulia Colloquium at Boston University, the American Studies University Seminar at Columbia University, and the Paradigma Conference at the University of Mainz. I am indebted to the members and organizers of those panels, not all of whom I can name here, as well as to the audience respondents. I am additionally grateful to the students, both at BU and Columbia, in my graduate seminars on American spectacle. A particular note of thanks goes to Stephanie Byttebier and Cara Norris, who assisted me in editing the manuscript.

I owe a further debt of thanks to Bill Germano, a great intellectual and a master editor. Bill's support and advice was crucial in the transformation of my project into the present book. My heartfelt thanks to Talia Rodgers and Minh Ha Duong as well, for ably picking up the thread and guiding the book through to publication.

My parents, Patrick and Elisabeth, have always supported my twin interests in theatre and in scholarship. They have stood solidly behind me throughout this process, for which I cannot thank them enough. I dedicate this book to them.

Last but not least, how can I thank Sarah Rose Cole, who has been equally unwavering in every way? Sarah has never ceased to believe in this book, and has read and re-read drafts with a care that goes far beyond both the call of duty and the demands of affection. She has my gratitude and my love.

Visual and textual credits

The cover image and Figures 2.1 through 2.6 come courtesy of the National Archives of the Richard-Wagner-Foundation, Bayreuth. Figure 3.7 comes courtesy of University of California Press. Figure 5.1 comes courtesy of the Theaterwissenschafliche Sammlung at the Universität zu Köln. Figure 5.2 comes courtesy of Photofest. Figure 6.1 comes courtesy of the Anaheim Public Library. Figures 7.1 through 7.3 come courtesy of Artists Rights Society. Figures 8.1 through 8.6 come courtesy of the artists. The author wishes to thank all of these sources for their cooperation.

Sections of this book have previously appeared in two articles:

"Schlemmer, Moholy-Nagy, and the Search for an Absolute Stage."(Yale) *Theater* 32:3 (Fall, 2002): 87–101.

"Bayreuth, Disneyland, and the Return to Nature." *Land/Scape/Theater*. Eds Una Chaudhuri and Elinor Fuchs. Ann Arbor: University of Michigan Press, 2002.

Introduction

Das Rheingold, the prelude to Wagner's vast *Ring* cycle, ends with the gods ascending a rainbow bridge to their new stronghold of Walhall. The price of paradise was high: a mountain of gold topped by a ring of power. "From morning to night, / in anguish and angst, / it wasn't won sweetly!" recalls Wotan, before assuring the gods that the pain has brought a just reward: "now we shall be secure." Wotan's assurances blend with six harps, which in turn give way to the Walhall leitmotif. Played by 13 brass instruments – trumpets, trombones, bass trumpets, contrabass tuba, contrabass trombone, and the specially designed "Wagner tubas" – the Walhall motif is the sound and fury of imperial triumph.

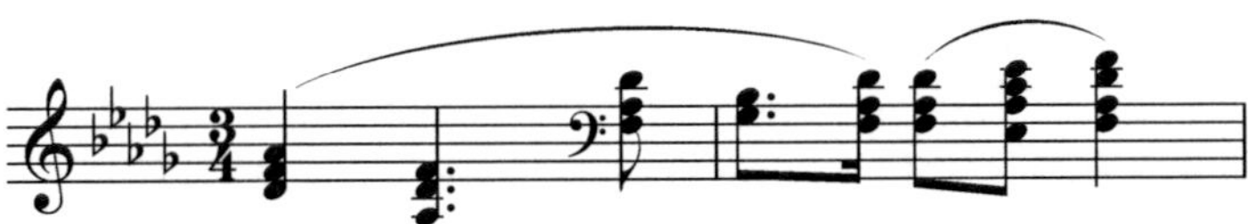

But there are cracks in the edifice, even in this first moment of completion. To begin with, the Walhall motif is uncomfortably close to another already introduced in the preceding scene: the motif of Arrogance.[1]

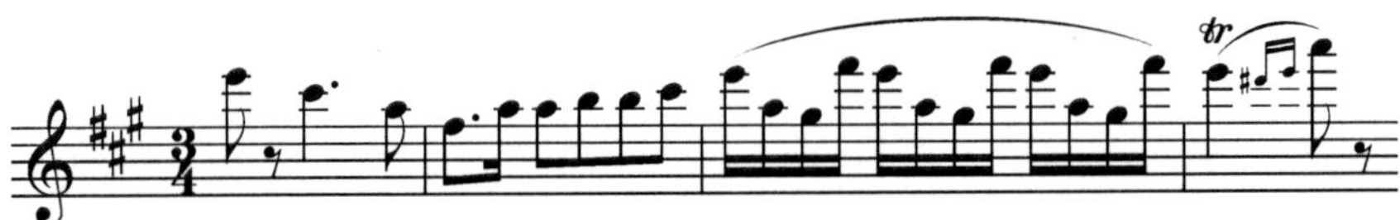

Wagner interweaves the themes still further. As Wotan sings the security of his new stronghold, we hear once more a motif already introduced in Scene 1: the motif of Crisis, pounded out on the kettledrum.

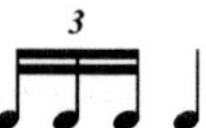

The irony of this moment of triumph is entirely missed by the gods. Only Loge, half-god and trickster, seems aware of the truth. "They rush straight to their end," he laughs. "And they think that they'll live forever."

Turning from the gods of myth to the gods of history, we find that Loge has not stopped laughing. He needs only to turn on the television these days to find our Walhalls and our rainbow bridges. Consider the following spots: a series of multicultural businesspeople harmonizing to the rock anthem "We Are the Champions"; entrepreneurs connecting via the Internet over the Beatles' refrain "Come together / right now / over me"; an executive floating through a high-tech funhouse that cuts suddenly to the slogan, "Dreams Made Real"; the Cisco Systems slogan "Are You Ready?" repeated time and again, by voice and (a Brechtian touch?) placard, from Brooklyn to Bangkok. "Now Anything's Possible," announces a Time Warner advertisement, as Coca-Cola releases a juice mix called "Fruitopia" and Nike plays the Beatles' "Revolution 9" (and, after an outcry, John Lennon's "Instant Karma!") to sell its sneakers. Meanwhile respected political theorists proclaim an "End to History" while policy makers await an "An End to Evil" and crusades are launched on behalf of new world orders.[2] Thus the voices rhapsodize as we ascend to our magic kingdoms, thus assemble the elements of what *Village Voice* critic J. Hoberman calls the "sub-Wagnerian, self-flattering gesamtkunstwerk that constitutes American social spectacle." Shall we come together? Right now? Are you ready?

Next to the barbaric yawps of establishment supermen, the voice of the artistic community has been remarkably garbled. At a recent New York exhibition of work by young Berlin artists, I found little beyond the by-now-familiar array of gestures that might once have been labeled "avant-garde": a film loop of a screaming woman being covered with artificial blood; a violently swaying fan hanging from the ceiling by a cord; a mutilated van filled with odd bits of garbage. These were works marked by an almost poignant aimlessness, a yearning for a lost and almost mythic age when making it new meant something, when rebels had causes or at least fresh styles. Though the works were almost uniformly dark, they lacked the absolute, desperate sort of blackness that produces visions of utopia in the negative: there were no next-generation Samuel Becketts here, no Joseph Beuyses, no Anselm Kiefers. If there was, on the other hand, any utopian imagination, it was to be found in the entrance lobby, where German house-music was playing, rave 'zines were spread out on tables, and colorful t-shirts hung from racks, available for purchase by the public. The enormous promise and delight of what Ernst Bloch called the "*Jetztzeit*" ("Now-time") could be expressed artistically, it seems, only when hitched to the commodity form. And so a sad dichotomy presented itself, one that I have witnessed time and again in contemporary art galleries and theatres and concert halls: to the art-world is ceded the labor of disenchantment and the gestures of *ennui*, while to the commercial world (and the museum gift shop) is granted the far more lucrative business of dreaming.

The mass-cultural and the avant-garde, as Adorno famously remarked, "are the torn halves of an integral freedom, to which, however, they do not add up" ("Correspondence" 66). The history of the total work of art (or *Gesamtkunstwerk*) is inseparable from the history of this dialectical relation.[3] From its very outset, the total work of art has been marked by clashes between mechanical and organic form, technology and technophobia, mass reproduction and the aura of originality, individual genius and the *Volk*, commerce and communism. The first key to understanding the history of the form is to understand that these contradictory impulses are not markers of some vague or hopelessly ambiguous lineage but rather opposing elements of an internal dialectic. In other words, the history of the *Gesamtkunstwerk* is, to a large degree, the history of un-reconciled dialectical struggles performed under the sign of aesthetic totality. This dynamic internal opposition became far more pronounced in the wake of the failed revolutions of 1848–9, the period when the Romantic premonitions of Schiller's *Aesthetic Education* blossomed into the explicit theorization of the total work of art in Wagner's Zurich writings, to be followed by its (at least partial) realization in the music-dramas.

This study will begin, then, with that turning-point in the history of Western aesthetics, Schiller's *Aesthetic Education*, which combined Kant's conception of organic form with a narrative of redemption by means of art. Rooted in Romantic theory on one hand, the *Gesamtkunstwerk* was inextricably linked to structural transformations of the mid-nineteenth century on the other. These transformations included the development of new technologies, the increased dominance of mass media, and the dissolution of the bourgeois public sphere. One result of these historical transformations is that, from its origin, the total work of art has been a divided form. This division may be expressed by means of two competing festival sites: the Crystal Palace, and the Festspielhaus ("festival theatre") at Bayreuth. The first of these festival sites anticipated what I call the *crystalline Gesamtkunstwerk*, a form that exposes and celebrates the outward signs of mechanical production while simultaneously attempting to integrate those signs of production into a pseudo-organic totality. The second embodied what I call the *iconic Gesamtkunstwerk*, a pseudo-organic form that attempts to utterly conceal even the outward signs of the production on which it relies, and which particularly appeals to "folk," myth, and intuition.

While the iconic *Gesamtkunstwerk* seeks to bury all outward signs of mechanical production, it nevertheless relies heavily upon mechanization for its pseudo-organic effects. Scholars have traditionally viewed Wagner's relationship to technology and industrialization, on the rare occasions when they have examined it at all, as almost entirely negative. Wagner, so the argument goes, launched his work as a radical attack on technology, commerce, mechanization. More rarely examined is the fact that behind Wagner's ferocious attacks on the "mechanized world" lay a profound reliance upon it. This curious contradiction may be found in Wagner's theory as well as his practice. In a dynamic that will prove ironically fruitful for the whole tradition, mechanization would become the means by which the total work of art restores humanity to an Edenic condition. Mechanical production, the disease that the total work of art seeks to cure, also underlies its essential structure. This contradiction was exemplified with particular clarity at the Festspielhaus, which combined an unprecedented reliance upon stage technology with an unprecedented attempt to hide the means of its own production.

A radically different form of the *Gesamtkunstwerk* flowered in the theatrical experiments of the Weimar/Dessau Bauhaus. Where Wagner's performances at Bayreuth hid their mechanical sources of production in order to appear organic, Bauhaus artists such as Oskar Schlemmer and Làszlò Moholy-Nagy reveled in at least the rhetoric of mechanized production. Schlemmer and Moholy-Nagy attempted to create theatrical totality, and recapture organic unity, by turning the stage into a "mechanical organism." Intended as an extension of and retort to the Wagnerian tradition, the Bauhaus theatre ended up relying on techniques of concealment more subtle than those of the Festspielhaus but just as pervasive. This fragile, paradoxical form of crystalline totality was often overshadowed by the much larger totality of the commodity culture of Weimar-era Berlin, and was ultimately extinguished by the totality of Nazi mass spectacle.

A more thoroughgoing response to Wagner would have to wait for the epic theatre techniques of Bertolt Brecht. Towards the end of the Weimar period, Brecht attempted to meet the threat of these emergent totalities by developing a theatrical form that emphatically rejected both iconic and crystalline visions of the *Gesamtkunstwerk*. In order to understand Brecht's technique, however, we need to understand his complex relation to the total work of art. Brecht has generally been viewed as Wagner's foil, his epic theatre the antithesis of the total work of art. But critics have largely overlooked the fact that much of Brecht's theory and practice is surprisingly indebted to the genealogy of the total work of art. What Brecht advocated, at least in certain writings, was not so much the entire elimination of the idea of the total work of art as the discovery of an openly divided and critical mixture of the arts that might still be called a *Gesamtkunstwerk*. Unity, for Brecht, would be found through montage technique rather than any notion of an organic whole. Brecht referred to this contrapuntal unity as a "collective of independent arts," a collective that presages the ideal socialist state. A recurring theme in his aesthetics, especially in the late 1920s and early 1930s, was an attempt to radically reconceive the tradition of the total work of art in the face of its usurpation by two much larger (though not quite separable) totalities: commodity spectacle on one hand, and fascist spectacle on the other.

Leni Riefenstahl's *Triumph of the Will*, at once a documentary film and a work of propaganda, inaugurated a new chapter in the history of the total work of art. While the Wagnerian roots of cinema had been appreciated since at least the early years of the twentieth century, *Triumph of the Will* was the first film to operate as a link in a larger chain of total performance, a chain that forged music-drama, rally, and film into a single, tightly controlled aesthetic state. One leitmotif of this cycle of total performance was Nuremberg, the city that served as an emblem of the Aesthetic State and the reawakening of the nation, via music-drama, rally and film, in the Third Reich. Riefenstahl's film presented the German *Volk* as the grandest total work of art, a seamless harmony of previously disparate elements, orchestrated by a single master conductor. It is also a work that, like Wagner's *Die Meistersinger von Nürnberg*, reminds us of the necessary exclusions of the drive to totality.

The uses to which it had been put under the Third Reich made the *Gesamtkunstwerk* culturally unacceptable throughout much of Europe in the wake of the Second World War. The genre would find new life, however, in the United States. In America, as previously in Germany, the *Gesamtkunstwerk* became a way of forming an ideal political unity and an idealized version of the *völkisch* state. This is most clearly exemplified at Disneyland, which replicated many of the strategies of Bayreuth, the Bauhaus, and Nuremberg. It recalls Bayreuth's strategy of pilgrimage as well as its attempt to forge many cultures into a single, idealized national culture; it also echoes Wagner's iconic form of the *Gesamtkunstwerk*. But if Disneyland is iconic in some respects, it is crystalline in others, and many of its crystalline features recall those of the Bauhaus. Finally, Disney's successful attempt to incorporate his pilgrimage site of Disneyland into a much larger system of interlocking total performance (including movies, radio and television shows, and other elements of mass-produced "folk" culture) marks a new chapter in the evolution of total performance.

The *Gesamtkunstwerk* suffers from two principal neuroses: a fear of absorption from without and a fear of contamination from within. The former, as we shall see throughout this study, generally takes the form of a fear of absorption into the larger totality of mass spectacle. The latter, which we shall also witness time and again, generally takes either the form of a fear of contamination by corrupt bodies of the (racial, sexual, ethnic, class-based) Other – or else, most generally, of contamination of the *Gesamtkunstwerk* by the material body itself. (Indeed, the latter is essentially a subset of the former, with the body read as threateningly marginal to idealist totality.) These troubles, abundantly present at the *Gesamtkunstwerk*'s origin in Wagner's music-dramas and recurrent throughout the subsequent genealogy of the genre, took new shape in Andy Warhol's artwork and performances from roughly 1960 to 1968. Warhol's crystalline performances addressed the first trouble of the *Gesamtkunstwerk* by radically embracing the mass-cultural spectacle that threatened to overwhelm them. Warhol's abandonment of his own art to the commodity spectacle obliterated oppositions between art and commodity even as it resisted both autonomy and intervention as aesthetic options. Making matters more complicated, however, is the fact that Warhol simultaneously embraced and camped on the society of the spectacle, so grotesquely performing the neurosis of bodily contamination as to at least imply critique. It is this sly critique of totality that connects Warhol, through the backdoor as it were, with Brecht.

The next, though perhaps not the final, chapter of the development of mass culture, technology, and the *Gesamtkunstwerk* may be found in cyberspace. At times such virtual worlds recall the strategies of Bayreuth, at times the *Totaltheater*, at times the creations of Disney. In one instance – a creation entitled *Beyond Manzanar* – Brecht's epic theatre reemerges within a virtual world accessed through a computer and 3-D goggles. These creations show that the total work of art is still a potent aesthetic ideal, always intertwined with technology, continuing to blur distinctions between high and mass culture, artwork and commodity spectacle. And yet there is a profound transformation as well, for what cyberspace offers is a kind of unity that is not one of Wagnerian synthesis but of networking, a simultaneous and collective creation that transcends the Kantian opposition between mechanical and organic form. Cyberspace performance, as we shall see, ironically realizes many of the dreams of the total work of art.

Though wide-ranging, this book aims at something less than a total account of the total work of art. To the extent that such an account were even possible, it would yield a book immensely larger than this one, or else one that paid only cursory attention to individual artists and artworks. But my hope has been to produce something shorter than a tome and more probing than a survey. What I hope to offer instead is a set of works and terms and a historical narrative that elucidate the relationship between the total work of art, technology, and mass culture, a relationship that has generally been downplayed or overlooked in favor of the "high art" lineage of the opera house, bourgeois theatre, and concert hall. I have chosen to focus throughout on those works that help me narrate this relationship most clearly. Many artists who were influenced by the *Gesamtkunstwerk* therefore make only brief appearances, or do not appear at all. Rather than say too little about Mallarmé, Strauss, Craig, Reinhardt, Diaghilev – the list could be extended at great length – I have chosen to focus closely on the artists most central to the book's narrative. I hope that future scholars will explore connections between other artists and the history of the *Gesamtkunstwerk* I offer here.

Geography has also been a limiting condition of this study. I have decided to center my discussion, with some exceptions, on German and American artists. The *Gesamtkunstwerk*, as we shall see, is a central aesthetic project in the forging of the modern nation-state, and Germany and the United States are two nations whose battles for national unity were particularly violent in the mid-nineteenth century, and whose aspirations to global dominance have been particularly central to the twentieth. These struggles and these aspirations are inextricably linked to the history of the total work of art. Furthermore, in juxtaposing Germany and the United States, I want to offer a certain historical narrative. This is the narrative of the catastrophe of one imperialist project, deeply rooted in neo-Romantic dreams of totality, and the rise of another, also so rooted. It would overstate the case to say that Germany passes the torch of the *Gesamtkunstwerk* to the United States after 1945, but at least a spark from Nuremberg did surely catch fire in Cold War America. If the total work of art is an aesthetic project that ought to continue to inspire us – and I don't believe that it is, regardless of the form – then we should not imagine the possibilities of its future without first considering its past. Moreover, to the degree that the total work of art continues to shape our culture, we must pay attention to its frequently disturbing history in order to understand our troubled present. And the part of that history I find at once most disturbing and least understood is the line that runs from Bayreuth through Nuremberg to the United States.

While a dialectical account of Wagner's music-dramas was influentially developed in Adorno's *In Search of Wagner*, as well as in remarks by Adorno, Benjamin, Horkheimer, and others, no book-length study of the evolution of the total work of art has been attempted. The most general studies, tellingly, are anthologies: they include *Total Theatre* (1969), edited by E. T. Kirby; *Der Hang zum Gesamtkunstwerk* (1983), published in conjunction with an exhibition organized by Harald Szeemann; and *Wagnerism in European Culture and Politics* (1984), edited by David C. Large and William Weber. Each of these studies has its particular focus. Kirby subsumes the *Gesamtkunstwerk* within a larger field of "total theatre," a very broad term that incorporates performance techniques from Craig to Kabuki. Szeemann *et al.* focus their attention on the European (especially German) avant-garde, excerpts of whose writings make up the bulk of the book. Large and Weber's anthology (the only one of the three to foreground critical essays rather than primary-source materials) particularly stresses the inseparability of artistic and political "Wagnerism," and places the lineage in a broadly international context, but generally overlooks the influence of Wagner on emergent mass media. Alongside these general anthologies, several recent books have explored the total work of art in particular historical periods. Studies such as Boris Groys' *Gesamtkunstwerk Stalin* (1988), Frantisek Deak's *Symbolist Theater* (1993), Jeffrey T. Schnapp's *Staging Fascism* (1996), and Joachim Köhler's *Wagners Hitler* (first published 1997) have shed new light on specific episodes in the history of the *Gesamtkunstwerk*. The necessary limitations of these studies are not signs of weakness but rather indications of the extraordinary range and vitality of the genre's history.

My own book has gone through many stages, but the original impetus was a question that has pursued me ever since I saw my first Bayreuth production in the summer of 1991. The production was *Parsifal*, in Wolfgang Wagner's uninspired staging, redeemed mainly by James Levine's conducting and Waltraud Meier's performance as Kundry. The fall of the Wall, a year and a half previous but still fresh in people's minds, was a popular topic of conversation at intermission. So too, among at least a couple of us, was a far less well publicized event: the creation of the World Wide Web, a child of hypertext and the Internet, which was taking its baby steps in the summer of 1991 and would be released to the public two years later. With the Wall behind us and the Web before us, we were in the midst of a quiet and almost secret revolution – the world was changing, peacefully, quietly, suddenly, irrevocably, and with unfathomable consequences. In that moment, at that sacred and accursed and occasionally ridiculous pilgrimage site, I wondered what the continuing urgency of the Festspielhaus might be. What is Wagner's hold upon us now? The question has never quite left me, although, *pace* Christoph Schlingensief, the *enfant terrible* of a later Bayreuth *Parsifal*, my sense is that the answer has nothing to do with rotting rabbits and everything to do with mass culture, technology, and utopia.[4]

Chapter I

The total work of art in an age of mechanical reproduction

Well, I may not have any money, but I do have a tremendous desire to practice a little artistic terrorism.

Wagner to Liszt, 5 June 1849 (*Briefwechsel* 17)

Defining the *Gesamtkunstwerk*

On one hand: the *Gesamtkunstwerk* is impossible. It is a lantern image, a ghost in glass. Utopia, thus nowhere.

On the other: the *Gesamtkunstwerk* is sensuous and concrete. It takes form in literature, in music, in opera, in painting, in dance, in theatre, in drama, in film, in politics. Baudelaire, Mallarmé, Marinetti, Mann; Wagner, Strauss, Schönberg; Böcklin, Kandinsky, Moholy-Nagy; Diaghilev, Schlemmer, Duncan; Maeterlinck, Meyerhold, Appia, Craig; Gropius, Corbusier, van der Rohe; Eisenstein, Riefenstahl, Disney. Mussolini, Hitler, Stalin.

On one hand: the *Gesamtkunstwerk* is modernity's leviathan. Its worst moments are its moments of entry into the world. Its moments of fullest realization are also the moments of history's greatest horror.

On the other: the *Gesamtkunstwerk* is modernity's polestar. It is an uncompromising wish for a joyful community to be realized in this life, in this world. It is a longing for unity amidst fragmentation, for collectivity amidst alienation. It is inherently restless and potentially revolutionary, and while it is inescapably ideological its longings can never be entirely contained within the bounds of ideology. It is the shape of radical hope.

On one hand and on the other – can both hands be right?

To begin with, how shall we define this term?

The place to start, of course, is with Richard Wagner. Wagner coined and popularized the term in his Zurich writings of 1849–57, principally in his book-length essays *The Artwork of the Future* (1849) and *Opera and Drama* (1851), works written in the shadow of the Dresden uprising of 1849 and imbued with its revolutionary spirit. The most frequent translation of the word is "total work of art," but even this is by no means straightforward: other possibilities include "communal work of art," "collective work of art," "combined work of art," and "unified work of art." Indeed, the concept includes all of these ideas, for it is an art-form as much about collectivity as about unity, about community as about totality.

The aspect of the *Gesamtkunstwerk* most widely understood by scholars and general theatre-goers is the strictly formal. Patrice Pavis, for example, defines it as "a synthesis of music, literature, painting, sculpture, architecture, stage design and other elements" (159). And there is much to be said for this approach, as there is undoubtedly a formally aesthetic aspect to Wagner's discussion of the *Gesamtkunstwerk*. In *The Artwork of the Future*, for instance, he argues that there are three fundamental arts: dance, tone, and poetry. These "are so wondrous closely interlaced with one another … that each of the three partners, unlinked from the united chain and bereft thus of her own life and motion, can only carry on an artificially inbreathed and borrowed life" (1:95/3:67).[1] Having fallen away from their original dance, the "three primeval sisters" now answer to "despotic rules for mechanical movement" (1:95/3:67). Thus is the organic whole degraded into the artificially and mechanically fragmentary. The trouble is worsened by the fact that a cheapened pseudo-synthesis of the three primal arts exists in the form of opera, which, "as the seeming point of reunion of all the three related arts, has become the meeting-place of these sisters' most self-seeking efforts" (1:152/3:120). Opposed to opera, writes Wagner, stands the total work of art, which shall reunite the three arts into their original sacred dance.

The trouble with a formalist approach, however, is that Wagner's aesthetics are always inseparable from his larger political vision. As Wagner stresses throughout the Zurich writings, the *Gesamtkunstwerk* is a social and not simply an artistic dream, and the social dream is essentially a communitarian one. At the end of his discussion of the "three sisters" in Part II of *The Artwork of the Future*, for instance, Wagner emphasizes that the *Gesamtkunstwerk* "cannot arise alone, but only in the fullest harmony with the conditions of our whole life" (1:155/3:71). The *Gesamtkunstwerk* will be a collective, not an individual effort; it will be a *"mutual art-work of the future"* (1:77/3:50) in which "all will participate actively in genius, genius will be communal" (*Sämtliche* 12:264). In his Zurich writings Wagner insists that the *Gesamtkunstwerk* is an "associative work" that "is practically conceivable only in the *fellowship of every artist*" (1:196/3:162). "It is not the lonely spirit, striving by Art for redemption into Nature, that can frame the Art-work of the Future"; he writes, "only the spirit of fellowship, fulfilled by life, can bring this work to pass" (1:88/3:61).[2] When this work does come to pass, all social divisions will be transcended as surely as the divisions between the three arts are harmonized. "*[T]he folk*," writes Wagner, "will no longer be a severed and peculiar class; for in this artwork we shall all be *one*, – heralds and supporters of necessity, knowers of the unconscious, willers of the unwilful, betokeners of nature, – *blissful men*" (1:77/3:50). At last the curse of modern culture will come to an end, and humans will return to harmonious, truly artistic relations with each other and with nature.

> This brotherhood of artist-men will mould its works of art in unison with, in complement and rounding-off of mother nature; accenting every quality and

individual trait evoked by special need, in answer to the special call of nature's individual features, but marching forward from the base of this particularity toward a common pact with common nature – as toward the utmost fullness of man's being.

(1:261–2/3:217)

Wagner's theory of the total work of art is inseparable from this revolutionary vision of an age when commerce, industry, mass production, mechanics – the component parts of the "man-destroying march of culture" (1:55/3:31) – are at last incorporated, annihilated, and transcended in a great *Erhebung* of the human race.

A number of scholars have proven more sensitive to these social and political dimensions of the *Gesamtkunstwerk*. Barry Millington's entry for the *New Grove Dictionary of Opera*, for instance, opens with a description of the formal artistic features of the *Gesamtkunstwerk* in a manner similar to Pavis', but goes on to add that "the reuniting of the constituent parts in the *Gesamtkunstwerk* mirrored the socialist aim of restoring integrity to a fragmented, divided society." By connecting the theory and practice of the total work of art with the nineteenth-century dream of an organically unified state, Millington (as well as Bermbach, Borchmeyer, and Fischer-Lichte, among others[3]) rightly sees the artistic aspirations of the *Gesamtkunstwerk* as inseparable from its political aspirations.

Indeed, the emergence of the modern dream of the organically unified "Aesthetic State" ought to be placed in the context of the dialectics of art and mass culture that emerge at the end of the eighteenth century and come to dominate public discourse by the middle of the nineteenth century. In this endeavor, Adorno's reading of the *Gesamtkunstwerk* in *In Search of Wagner* (1939, pub. 1952) proves esential. Adorno argues that Wagner's attacks on the marketplace conceal a deeper affinity between the attacker and his target. Never far from Wagner's Wahnfried was the world of Second Empire kitsch, with its "fake Gothic castles" and "aggressive dream symbols of the Neo-Gothic boom, ranging from the Bavarian castles of Ludwig to the Berlin restaurant that called itself 'Rheingold'" (123). Adorno's point is not simply that Wagner could not escape the world of commodities and kitsch; his point is that Wagner's theory and practice of the *Gesamtkunstwerk* were fundamentally linked to the culture industry. Through techniques such as the absorption of the spectator into the artwork (which turns the audience into a reified object of calculation), the use of the leitmotif (which leads the audience along through insistent repetition), and the systematic occultation of production (which reveals the traces of labor behind a façade of spontaneous origination), the Wagnerian music-drama echoes many of the strategies of industrial commerce that it attempts to combat. The inseparability of Wagner's theory and practice from nineteenth-century mass culture is ultimately a subset of the larger inseparability, *ab origine*, of modernism from mass culture, a larger inseparability on which Adorno insisted throughout his career.[4]

In *Dialectic of Enlightenment*, Adorno and Horkheimer suggest that television, which "aims at a synthesis of radio and film," should be seen as "derisively fulfilling the Wagnerian dream of the *Gesamtkunstwerk*" (124). Adorno and Horkheimer's point is provocatively hyperbolic, but it expresses more than a kernel of truth. While their reduction of the multiplicity of mass-mediated cultures to a "total" aesthetic system overstates the case, the ongoing influence of the total work of art is far more central to contemporary mass culture than has generally been acknowledged. If Adorno's central claim is so – if the emergence of the sovereign artist and the emergence of the culture industry are simultaneous occurrences, and merged in a single figure who becomes a fountainhead for both, and if the culture industry is somehow an extension of the *Gesamtkunstwerk* – then the *Gesamtkunstwerk* becomes crucially important for understanding the *pas de deux* of high art and mass culture in the twentieth century. The place to begin this investigation is at the root of this dialectic. Let us turn back, then, to the closing years of the eighteenth century.

The Romantic roots of the total work of art

One weakness of Adorno's otherwise indispensable reading of Wagner is that it lacks an account of the Romantic precursors of the *Gesamtkunstwerk*. In *In Search of Wagner*, Adorno argues that "[t]he *Gesamtkunstwerk* is actually unrelated to the Romantic theories of fifty years earlier" (97), which explains the absence of such considerations from his study. Adorno is rightly at pains to emphasize the *Gesamtkunstwerk*'s ties to industrial capitalism, and yet he somewhat overstates the break with late eighteenth-century and early nineteenth-century cultural formations. However much bound up with late nineteenth-century commodity culture Wagner's work may be, the origins of the theory of the total work of art do indeed lie with Romanticism, and more precisely with Romantic idealist aesthetics.

While Adorno overemphasizes the discontinuity of the tradition of the total work of art with earlier theories, others have overemphasized the continuity.[5] To say that the theory of the total work of art has its roots in Romanticism is not to say that the theories and practices of sixteenth- and seventeenth-century music-drama are irrelevant to the history of total theatre. But Renaissance or Baroque theorists never advanced anything like a full-fledged theory of the total artwork; although festival productions such as the Viennese *ludi cesarei* or the Medici *intermedi* may have been lavish multimedia extravaganzas, they were not *Gesamtkunstwerke*. The total work of art is neither a court festival nor a celebration of a particular monarch or regime. As we shall see when we turn to Schiller, the total work of art implies not only an intermingling of art-forms but also an attempt to create an organic synthesis of arts that recovers supposedly original, lost, organic unities: unity of the individual subject, unity of the social body, unity of life and art. The *Gesamtkunstwerk*, as it first takes form in Wagner, is a theory and practice that reaches back to Romanticism in order to combat and appropriate the emergent pressures of mass culture.

If the precursors of the theory of the total work of art lie in German Romanticism, then no single source is so influential as Friedrich Schiller's *Aesthetic Education*. The treatise has correctly been referred to as a "turning-point" in the history of aesthetics and of utopian thought, a transformation of the Kantian idea of taste into a radical imperative to live aesthetically.[6] Though rarely considered in relation to the *Gesamtkunstwerk*, Schiller ought to be given his proper place as its theoretical progenitor. In many of Schiller's aesthetic theories – particularly those of the *Aesthetic Education* – we see, *in utero*, Wagner's theory of the total work of art, and its relationship to industrial production and commodity culture.

Schiller's *Aesthetic Education* was composed, like Wagner's Zurich writings a half-century later, in the wake of failed revolution. It was a failure that encouraged Schiller, like Wagner, to turn to aesthetics as both compensation for political loss (the souring of the French Revolution, in Schiller's case; the defeat of the revolutions of 1848–89, in Wagner's) and hope for future political transformation. Wagner, who read Schiller throughout his life, suggested that Schiller's aesthetic theories, particularly the *Aesthetic Education*, be read as "prelude" to his own (6:116/10:121–2). He praised Schiller in revealing terms: Schiller was the "first," continued Wagner, "to have recognized and described our State-machinery as barbaric and utterly inimical to art" (6:116/10:121–2).

In the Sixth Letter of the *Aesthetic Education*, Schiller argues that organic Greek culture has given way to

> an ingenious clock-work, in which, out of the piecing together of innumerable but lifeless parts, a mechanical kind of collective life ensued. State and Church, laws and customs, were now torn asunder; enjoyment was divorced from labor, the means from the end, the effort from the reward. Everlastingly chained to a single little fragment of the Whole, man himself develops into nothing but a fragment; everlastingly in his ear the monotonous sound of the wheel that he turns, he never develops the harmony of his being, and instead of putting the stamp of humanity upon his own nature, he becomes nothing more than the imprint of his occupation or of his specialized knowledge.
>
> (35)

Modernity (chiefly marked, in Schiller's account, by the division of labor) has torn asunder the basic fabric of social life, until nothing remained but a "single little fragment of the Whole." It thus stands in marked contrast with the "whole organism" of ancient Greek society (35), in which the poles of reason and feeling within each individual were harmonized, as were relations between one citizen and another. But commerce and industry, beginning with the division of labor but gaining steam with the advancement of capitalist production, had replaced unified, organic culture with a mechanized collective life, and the way back toward a lost totality lies through the gate of art.

Schiller's distinction between the "whole organism" of ancient Greek collective life and the "mechanical" nature of modern life recalls not only Winckelmann's grecophilia but also Kant's distinction between mechanism and organism. One of the central innovations of Schiller's *Aesthetic Education* is that it adapts Kant's distinction between organic and mechanical form to a social and historical argument. The ideal state, like the Kantian work of art, is "organic," and the modern condition is "mechanical." Indeed, Schiller uses Kant's own illustration of mechanical form – a watch – to make his point, comparing modernity to an "ingenious clock-work," thus suggesting that the modern individual is living *within* the watch of Kant's illustration. In one sense, Schiller's argument was not original: the Deists had similarly compared the world to a clock. But Schiller's innovation was to ascribe humanity's mechanical condition to historical forces rather than universal laws, and to see in this mechanical condition something infernal. Schiller's clock-work world is neither natural nor necessary nor desirable, but the fragmentation of the human and the antithesis of the beautiful. Schiller's argument thus historicizes and politicizes Kant's notion of mechanical form in *Critique of Judgment*, and places the mechanical allegory of Deism on its head.

While Schiller's historical narrative of humanity's fall from organism into mechanism would prove crucial to Wagner's historical narrative of the total work of art, his idea of the reunion of the separate art-forms would influence Wagner's theory of the "sister-arts." In "On the Use of the Chorus in Tragedy" (1803), Schiller longs for the return of a dramatic form that is unified and idealized in all its parts. Since nature "never comes to sensory perception" but is available only as "an idea of the spirit," it is left to art "to grasp this spirit of the All and bind it into bodily form" ("Über" 243–4). Art performs this function not by bringing nature to sensory perception, which is impossible, but rather by bringing nature "to the powers of the imagination," powers which are "truer than any actuality and more real than any experience." In order to remain uncorrupted by crude "actuality" or haphazard "experience," art must strive toward total idealization. "It follows, then, that the artist cannot use a single element from actuality as he finds it, that his work must be ideal in *all* its parts if it is to have a total reality and correspond to nature" (244).

Schiller ends his *Aesthetic Education* with an evocation of this ideal condition. Turning, in his final Letter, to the millenarian language of the medieval mystic Joachim di Fiore, Schiller associates this state with the glorious "Third Kingdom" of the spirit.[7] The Third Kingdom, Schiller writes, would bring the realm of living form not to isolated individuals but to society as a whole.

> In the midst of the fearful kingdom of forces, and in the midst of the sacred kingdom of laws, the aesthetic impulse to form is at work, unnoticed, on the building of a third joyous kingdom of play and of semblance, in which man is relieved of the shackles of circumstance, and released from all that might be called constraint, alike in the physical and in the moral sphere.
>
> (215)

The kingdom Schiller writes of here he also names "the Aesthetic State," in which "none may appear to the other except as form, or confront him except as an object of free play" (215).[8] The play drive is uniquely able to effect this ideal relation between people because it alone allows communication without fragmentation. While "all other forms of communication divide society," the "aesthetic mode of communication unites society, because it relates to what is common to all" (215). The utopian result is a perfectly free and united state. "In the Aesthetic State everything – even the tool which serves – is a free citizen, having equal rights with the noblest" (219).[9] In the end, even the epitome of the mechanical ("the tool which serves") will become integrated into the organic society.

Taken together, several aspects of Schiller's theory – his dream of an "organic" artistic expression that might help to bring about an Aesthetic State, his extreme privileging of the aesthetic sphere in the realization of this utopian condition, the central role he grants to the populace for the realization of art and the transformation of society – would become central elements of the total work of art. Several decades before Wagner, these aspects of a nascent theory of total art were developed by a number of German Romantics. In *Athenäum Fragment* (116), for instance, Friedrich Schlegel celebrates the collective form and utopian potential of Romantic poetry, which "tries to and should mix and fuse poetry and prose, inspiration and criticism, the poetry of art and the poetry of nature; and make poetry lively and sociable, and life and society poetical." Poetry, for Friedrich Schlegel, does not so much dominate over other arts as inspire them all like a sort of Over-soul, and thus serves as a principal of aesthetic unification. While A. W. Schlegel occasionally agrees with his brother on the universality of poetry, he also emphasizes the collective powers of the Romantic stage, "where the magic of several arts may work as one" (quoted in Kindermann 6:29). F. W. J. Schelling, too, argues that the theatre was capable of "the most perfect combination of all the arts, the unification of poetry and music through song, of poetry and painting through dance" (5:736). Schelling goes beyond Schlegel's celebration of the stage by suggesting that the total theatrical production is the aesthetic expression of a unified people, whom he regards not as a fragmented grouping but as a *Gemeinschaft des Bewusstseins* – a "community of consciousness," unified by collective myth. The artist and theorist Philipp Otto Runge, meanwhile, argues for the predominance of music in the total work of art, writing that music "is that which we call harmony and tranquility in the three other arts." Runge's "music," however, much like Schlegel's "poetry," is more of a universal, unifying spirit than a distinct art-form. Runge believes that the (musically inspired) total artwork would "pull together all the eternally different natural forces into one being" (1:12). While he does not share Schelling's emphasis on the social aspects of total art, he does share Schelling's almost mystical idealism, arguing that the total artwork would perfectly represent the "symbols of God's forces" and thereby "create a representation of the Infinite." Like all Romantic theories of total art, Runge's is transcendental, quasi-religious.

It is from such a charged atmosphere that Wagner's theory of the total work of art will emerge. Far from being unrelated to the Romantic theories of a half-century earlier, the total work of art is inextricably linked to them. It arises from the strange concatenation of Wilhelmine industrial culture and Romantic aesthetics.

The labor of the Nibelungs

Commerce, industry, mass reproduction, mechanism: these are the deadly sins that, according to Wagner, complete humanity's fall from Greece. Though Wagner's thought went through a number of changes over the course of his life – he was by turns a democrat and a monarchist, a Romantic humanist and a cultural reactionary, a radical utopian and a world-renouncing pessimist – on the matter of the relationship between art and industrial capitalism he remained remarkably consistent. As Dieter Borchmeyer has pointed out, Wagner's early revolutionary socialism was just as much an "attempt to free art from the vicious circle of a market mentality, and hence to destroy its mercantile aspect" as was his embrace, later in life, of the monarchical patronage system (*Richard Wagner* 5). In his Zurich writings, Wagner's revulsion with machinery and the marketplace is plainly visible, and his revolutionary politics follow more or less straightforwardly from his diagnosis. By the 1860s, Wagner was seeking a more conservative route to detach art from commercial demands, but his attacks on the marketplace still drive his theory. In *German Art and German Politics* (1867–8), for instance, he looks back longingly to the Grand Duke Carl August's patronage of Goethe, which gave Goethe such freedom from market demands. It is this longing for monarchical patronage that would prompt Wagner to court Ludwig II, and Wagner would ultimately find in Ludwig something like a latter-day Carl August. Wagner's turn to royal patronage was not a compromise of his earlier ideals but a fundamental turn, utopian in its own way, toward a more conservative solution to the old problem of the commodification of art.[10]

Like so many Germans of his time, Wagner saw in ancient Greece a *Gemeinschaft* in which art arose out of the common need of the *Volk*. That Greek utopia has vanished; in its place lies an art enslaved to the "mistress" of *"commerce"* (1:41/3:18). "This is art, as it now fills the civilized world," writes Wagner in "Art and Revolution."

> Its true essence is industry; its ethical aim, the gaining of gold; its ethical purpose, the entertainment of those whose time hangs heavily on their hands. From the heart of our modern society, from the golden calf of wholesale speculation, stalled at the meeting of its crossroads, our art sucks forth its life-juice, borrows a hollow grace from the lifeless relics of the chivalric conventions of mediaeval times, and . . . descends to the depths of the proletariat, enervating, demoralizing, and dehumanizing everything on which it sheds its venom.
>
> (1:42/3:19)

If such is the condition of modern art generally, then the theatre is in an especially sorry state. After offering a list of the various customers each modern artist has to serve (the painter must paint "the repugnant visage of a millionaire," the musician must "compose his music for the banquet-table," and so forth), Wagner argues that the corruptions of the several "sister arts" all culminate in that saddest of figures:

the modern dramatist. The modern dramatist must shoulder "the sufferings of all other artists combined in one," answerable to theatrical institutions that are nothing more than "[i]ndustrial enterprises" and a "mere means for the circulation of money and the production of interest under capital" (1:61–2/3:37*). The modern theatre is for Wagner the ultimate commercial product, the sad synthesis of the commodification of all other branches of art, and thus the *Gesamtkunstwerk* in negative.

Allied to commerce and industry, and equally inimical to art, is mass reproduction. Following the mainstream of German Romantic aesthetics, Wagner stresses that the original Greek folk-poetry was a "live," oral performance, and thereby achieved an effect impossible through instruments of mass reproduction. "The Lyrics of Orpheus," writes Wagner,

> would never have been able to turn the savage beasts to silent, placid adoration, if the singer had but given them some dumb and printed verse to read: their ears must be enthralled by the sonorous notes that came straight from the heart, their carrion-spying eyes be tamed by the proud and graceful movements of the body, – in such a way that they should recognize instinctively in this whole man no longer a mere object for their maw, no mere objective for their feeding-, but for their hearing- and their seeing-powers, – before they could be attuned to duly listen to his moral sentences.
>
> (1:135/3:103*)

Importantly, Wagner juxtaposes the enthralling notes of Orpheus to *printed* verse (*gedruckte Gedichte*), establishing a binary opposition not between speech and writing but between spoken and mass-produced words.[11] The immediate, the auratic word enthralls and tames the wild hearers, opening them up for immersion in art. Wagner elaborates on this argument in his letter to Liszt of April 1851 ("On the '*Goethe-Stiftung*'"). There, Wagner laments the fact that poetry and music have, due to mass reproduction, sunk to the status of mere instruments of exchange. "[T]hrough the medium of the book-trade, [poetry] stretches far and wide, and makes of itself a paper currency; much the same is the case with our literature-music" (3:8/5:6). As difficult as the situation is for the poet and composer, the financial trouble is even more severe for the painter and sculptor, as their work does not lend itself to mass reproduction and is therefore less easily commodifiable. While it is true that "engravings and lithographs" now "circulate … among the public through the art-trade," painting and sculpture are nevertheless more reliant upon the production of "originals" than poems or music. For plastic artists, the "original can only consist of *one* example," rendering such works unattractive to "the money-princes of our time" (3:8/5:6). Wagner's diagnosis of the relation between the unique artwork and the commercial sphere, in other words, is almost precisely the opposite of what we have learned from the last century and a half of the institutionalized art-market. Wagner was entirely right, however, when he argued that modern artists would, generally speaking, not be able to survive by the art-market alone. The solution Wagner offers in "On the *Goethe-Stiftung*" (1851), while practical, is hardly revolutionary: he argues there for the founding of an endowment that might support the arts in place of the old princely patronage system.

Wagner often describes ills such as commerce, industry, and mass reproduction as though they were subsets of a broader category that has come to dominate the modern world. This broader category may be simply called "mechanism." In *Opera and Drama*, Wagner contrasts the organic artwork with what he ironically calls the "masterpiece of mechanism."

> By leading forth his artwork in continuous organic growth, and making our selves organic helpers in that growth, the poet frees his creation from all traces of his handiwork; whereas, should he leave those traces unexpunged, he would set us in that chill of feelingless amazement which takes us when we look upon a masterpiece of mechanism.
>
> (2:337/4:192)

The genuine artwork, in short, is a created object that masquerades as an uncreated one. The "masterpiece of mechanism," by contrast, is precisely the artwork that shows the traces of its creation; as such, it is not really an artwork at all.

In *The Artwork of the Future*, as throughout his Zurich writings, Wagner's distinction between organism and mechanism has explicitly political as well as aesthetic connotations. In this treatise, Wagner identifies "organism" not only with "art," but also with the ideal society; on the other hand, he identifies "mechanism" with luxury, fashion, industry, and the modern marketplace. Wagner asserts that "the mechanical" is "Fashion's invention" and is therefore the antithesis of "the artistic." The mechanical "fares from derivative to derivative, from means to means, to finally bring forth one more mean: the *machine*. Whereas the artistic strikes the very opposite path" (1:85/5:58). The "mechanical" culminates in "the *machine*," whereas "the artistic" springs from "*nature's* self" and culminates in art. "The *machine*," writes Wagner,

> is the cold and heartless ally of luxury-craving men. Through the machine have they at last made even human reason their liege subject; for, led astray from art's discovery, dishonored and disowned, it consumes itself at last in mechanical refinements, in absorption [*Einswerden*] into the machine, instead of in absorption into nature in the art-work.
>
> (1:85/5:58)

Wagner's point here is trenchant: both the machine and the artwork have "absorption" as their aim, but the machine aims to absorb the audience into degraded culture, while the true artwork aims to absorb the audience into nature. "Nature alone," as he writes in *German Art and German Politics*, "supplies a model for aesthetic imitation [*ästhetische Nachbildung*], whereas culture [*Kultur*] can become an object of nothing but mechanical imitation [*mechanische Nachahmung*]" (4:84/ 8:74).[12] Modern *Kultur* not only absorbs the spectator, it reveals itself as something like a coherent whole. But the totality of modern *Kultur* is a "*bad coherence*," a *Zusammenhang* rather than an *Einheit*, springing not from nature but from "un-nature's rule" (1:81/3:54). The artificial coherence of modern culture exhibits itself as a grotesque parody of the organic unity of the total work of art.

There are clear echoes here of Schiller's attacks on mechanism and modernity in the *Aesthetic Education*. Wagner goes beyond Schiller, however, in the specificity of his invectives. Wagner's antisemitic and francophobic rhetoric is inseparable from his hatred of modern mechanization: the Jews and the French are loathsome, in large part, because they are nature's rejects and culture's guardians, purveyors of luxury and fashion against simple human need. French opera, for example, is "pinned together through mechanical expedients" and lacks "the organic structure of genuine artwork" (3:37/5:32). French opera music, similarly, has "been driven to borrowing from the most material mechanism," and thus has sunk to "spiritual penury" (2:102/3:307). The French, too, are mechanical rather than organic in their embrace of "luxury" and "want" rather than genuine inner "need." Parisian culture springs not from true "artistic force" but from mere "technical routine" (3:49/5:44). Most notoriously, Wagner's attacks on "the Jews" often focus on their supposedly mechanical nature. Thus "the Jew" "merely listens to the barest surface of our art, but not to its life-bestowing inner organism" (4:92/5:78). "So long as the separate art of music had a real organic life-need in it, down to the epochs of Mozart and Beethoven, there was nowhere to be found a Jew composer," writes Wagner in *Judaism in Music* (1850), adding that "the Jew" is "entirely foreign" to the "living organism" of music (4:99/5:84). The Jew may be capable of mechanical imitation (in the manner, say, of an industrial book-press) but never of organic creation. Given the fact that Wagner's idealist aesthetics already presuppose that art is essentially imitative (a mechanism pretending to be an organism), the Jew is revealed to be the true artist's evil twin, the rude mechanical who embarrasses by his clumsy attempts at the noble masquerade of art. Thus does Wagner's anti-semitism become not only a social and physiognomical problem but also, as David J. Levin has convincingly shown, an aesthetic one.[13]

For Wagner, as for Schiller, the route back to an organic society lay in the aesthetic sphere. Towards the end of "Art and Revolution," Wagner enjoins the money-bound masses to throw off their chains and forge a new art and a new society:

> You suffering brethren, in every social grade, who brood in hot anger how to flee this slavery to money and become free men: fathom our purpose, and help us to lift up Art to its true dignity, so that we may show you how to raise trade into Art, and the slave of industry to the fair, self-knowing man who cries, with smiles filled with understanding, to sun and stars, to death and to eternity: *You, too, are mine, and I your lord!*
>
> (1:63/3:39*)

Throughout this passage, as indeed throughout all of Wagner's Zurich writings, aesthetic perfection and social emancipation are inseparable. Thus the raising of trade into art, referred to in one clause, is followed quite naturally in the next clause by the raising of the "slave of industry" into a master of all he surveys. Here Wagner embraces the most revolutionary aspects of Schiller's dream of an Aesthetic State, "in which man," as Schiller described it in the *Aesthetic Education,* "is relieved of the shackles of circumstance" (27/215). For Wagner, as for Schiller, this new society would be more than simply a return to Greece; it would be Greece perfected by modern reason. Industrial machinery, previously a curse, would become part of the road to redemption. Where the Greeks had relied on slavery for the maintenance of their freedom (1:50/3:26–7), machines would replace slaves in the new society (1:57/3:33), making human freedom a universal condition. Machines were therefore as necessary to the realization of the ideal state as they were the source of modern society's alienation. Modern society worships the machine as mere "fetish," but after the revolution "free creative man" will make machines its "artificial slaves" (1:57/3:33). "Then will man's whole enfranchised energy proclaim itself as naught but pure *artistic* impulse," artistic impulse freed, as the Greeks never could have been, from reliance upon a system of human oppression. The result will be a people and an artwork – the two really become interchangeable – made equal and free as never before in human history. Wagner would retreat from this radically utopian dream after his turn to Schopenhauer in 1854, much as Schiller himself retreated from political radicalism at the end of the *Aesthetic Education.*[14] But the dream, which Schiller and Wagner shared, held sway throughout the period when Wagner was formulating his notion of the total work of art, and it would recur throughout that tradition. Significantly, Schiller and Wagner were both split, at some times advocating the radical transformation of society, at other times turning away from any hint of political revolution in order to cultivate chosen circles of acolytes and esthetes. We find, in this split, a dialectic that will be central to the history of the total work of art as a whole. Simply put, it is a split between avant-garde and aestheticist approaches to art, both of which will recur and develop throughout the history of the genre.

Structural transformations

The *Gesamtkunstwerk,* then, is strongly related to the Romantic theories of 50 years earlier, and in particular to Schiller's aesthetic writings. We find Schiller's influence in much of Wagner's theoretical writing: in his extreme championing of the "organic" over the "mechanical"; in his attacks on the division of labor; in his almost desperate sense of the loss of social community; in his utopian dream of an "Aesthetic State"; in his desire to recover the past by pushing modernity to its furthest limits; in his spiral vision of revolution, in which ancient Greece is restored at a higher level of achievement. And yet there is a significant break between Schiller's dream of the Aesthetic State and Wagner's dream of the *Gesamtkunstwerk,* and that break has historical roots. Wagner's loathing of mass reproduction, his attacks on mass media, his almost paranoiac sense of omnipresent industrialization and commodification: these are the cultural products of the Second Industrial Revolution, and are inseparable from the dawning of what Guy Debord would come to call a society of the spectacle.[15]

Indeed, several aspects of Wagner's theory of the total work of art need to be read in light of the technological developments and structural transformations of the mid-nineteenth century. Habermas was not the first, but he was certainly one of the most systematic, to link the emergence of mass media with a decay of the bourgeois public sphere (*Öffentlichkeit*), the "sphere which mediates between society and state, in which the public organizes itself as the bearer of public opinion" ("Public" 50). This sphere of public discussion based on private interests was one of the great cultural creations of the bourgeoisie; it was a realm gradually hammered out from centuries of struggle against aristocracy. By roughly 1850 it had already begun its collapse. The crisis came about in large part due to contradictions within the public sphere itself, as its ostensible liberalism and coherence depended on a host of exclusions and repressions. Reformist and revolutionary actions of mid-century exacerbated these contradictions, as the bourgeoisie was forced to acknowledge previously excluded groups ("Public" 54). The expansion of the public body "beyond the bounds of the bourgeoisie," in other words, provoked counter-revolutionary measures, leading to a decline in the public sphere. This decline was further accelerated by the development of mass media aimed at stabilizing the emerging middle classes.[16]

Habermas sees the rise of mass media not only as a consequence of the need to provide ideological coherence to emerging class instabilities, but also as a factor in the decline of the bourgeois family as an institution for the critical debate of public affairs.

> The family lost the function of a "circle of literary propaganda"; already the *Gartenlaube* was the idyllically transfigured form in which the middle-class, small-town family absorbed and on the whole merely imitated the thriving educational tradition of the literary high bourgeois family of the preceding generations. The almanacs of the Muses and poetry journals, whose tradition in Germany started in 1770 with those of Leipzig and Göttingen and continued into the following century with those of Schiller, Chamisso, and Schwab, were displaced around 1850 by a type of literary family periodical that – through successful publishing ventures such as *Westermanns Monatshefte* and the *Gartenlaube* – commercially stabilized a reading culture that had already almost become an ideology.
>
> (*Structural Transformation* 162)

The displacement of literary journals such as Schiller's *Horen* and the Schlegels' *Athenaeum* by mass-market publications such as *Westermanns Monatshefte* and the *Gartenlaube* marks a much broader social transformation in the organization of bourgeois life.

It is a point on which Wagner and Habermas very much agree. In his late essay "Public and Popularity," written for the *Bayreuther Blätter* in 1878, Wagner singled out the *Gartenlaube* as an emblem of the decline of "the public." After excoriating the *Gartenlaube* for refusing to print a correction to a "defamatory article on myself" (because, the editor said, he had to "consider the public"), Wagner confronted the trouble head on. The same people who read the *Gartenlaube*, after all, are the ones buying tickets to his operas. What is this public? Is it good or bad? Most importantly: is it a *Volk*? "[H]ere we have a curious fact," he begins.

> The theatre directors attend to the needs of the public in much the same fashion as the immortal publisher of the *Gartenlaube*, for instance, consulted those of his; with few exceptions, they cannot abide me, just like the editors and reporters of our great political papers: but they find their profit in giving their public my operas … Now, what relation bears the public of the *Gartenlaube* to this other? Which is the genuine article? This or that?
>
> In any case here reigns a great confusion.
>
> (6:53–4/10:62)

A confusion, in fact, that Wagner will never solve. The "curious fact" that the same public is consuming the *Gartenlaube* and consuming the *Ring* is the central trouble of the Wagnerian *Gesamtkunstwerk*, its unavoidable embroilment with commodity culture. Wagner is struggling here with a problem that Schiller saw in much more muted form; in short, Wagner is struggling with the problem of being an "artist of the people" in a mass-mediated society. How to go on believing in "the people" when the people is rapidly becoming the mass? How to claim access to the spirit of the *Volk* when propagandists and marketeers prove more appealing?

Wagner's struggle with the dilemma of art and mass culture was one of the most fruitful sources of his art, and his most ambitious attempt to transcend the problem came with the opening of his festival theatre in 1876. The opening of Wagner's Festspielhaus at Bayreuth marks the most emphatic realization of the theories Wagner had conceived a quarter of a century earlier, for the revolution of art and society by means of the total work of art. The importance of the Festspielhaus is about much more than simply the music-dramas that were performed there. It is about the design and function of the theatre itself, which demanded of its audience a radical reconception of performance, of spectatorship, and of relations between nature and the machine. Bayreuth, as we shall see, is Wagner's ultimate challenge to the modern world of industry and commerce. It is the gauntlet he throws at the feet of the Second Industrial Revolution, but that gauntlet, too, was forged in a factory. It is also the glass he holds up, Perseus-like, to the Crystal Palace, a mirror he hopes will kill by repeating with a difference.

Chapter 2

Total stage
Wagner's Festspielhaus

What we imagined of old fairy tales, of the princess in a glass coffin, of queens and elves who lived in crystal houses – that all seemed to us to have been embodied, powerfully and gigantically, and those feelings have endured over the decades.

(Lessing 10)

Two festivals

Wagner's Festspielhaus was born with an open letter entitled "A Communication to My Friends," at the end of which Wagner announced that he would have "nothing more to do with our theatre of *today*" and dreamt of a new "myth *in three complete dramas*, preceded by a lengthy *prelude*" (1:391/4:343*). This enormous project was *not* to be an opera or series of operas, but a new form for which the inadequate phrase "cycle of music-dramas" would have to suffice. Such a cycle, Wagner argued, would demand a new theatre, built on radically different aesthetic principles from those that governed the opera houses of the day, a theatre intended solely for the realization and permanent exhibition of the artwork of the future. Here was the first suggestion of what would become, a quarter of a century later, the *Ring* cycle at Bayreuth.

The year of the letter's composition, 1851, is intriguing because it coincides with the birth of the other great festival site of the nineteenth century: Joseph Paxton's Crystal Palace in London. Home of the first of the Great Exhibitions and model for glass-and-steel arcades and exhibition halls ever since, the Crystal Palace actually had ties to Germany from its origins: often forgotten is the fact that England's Prince Albert, the political force behind the Palace, was a native of Coburg, a town, as luck would have it, only 45 miles from Bayreuth. The Crystal Palace, like the Festspielhaus, was an expression of a peculiarly nineteenth-century urge for totality, an urge that was inseparable from the emergence of mass culture at mid-century.

The similarities between these two modern festival sites are worth noting. As legions of visitors made their way to the Palace, the site took on the qualities of a mass pilgrimage site. Prices were kept low – a single shilling except on Fridays and

Saturdays – to allow all classes to attend Paxton's "People's Palace."[1] The object of their common journey was a space that transported many back to a land of fairy-tale and fantasy. Like Julius Lessing (see epigraph), Lothar Bucher described the combination of trees and glass in the Palace as having the effect of an "enchanted forest" which makes the space "magical," like "a piece of a summer night's dream in the midnight sun" (quoted in Lessing 7, 10). Charlotte Brontë referred to it as a "marvelous, stirring, bewildering sight – a mixture of a Genii Palace and a mighty Bazaar" (3:241) and Lewis Carroll wrote that "[i]t looks a sort of fairyland" (1:34). Even the worldly-wise W. M. Thackeray succumbed to flights of fancy upon viewing the spectacle, describing the space as a magical world created "by a wizard's rod," "a palace as for a fairy Prince, / A rare pavilion, such as man / Saw never since mankind began, / And built and glazed!" (169). For many, the Crystal Palace offered a return to an age of faerie, to lost childhood and lost community, all restored now through a mechanical system that appeared to operate in harmony with the natural world. At the same time, the Palace married these utopian yearnings to festival performances that included choral concerts, Handel festivals, massed brass bands, and so forth, often consisting of performers numbering in the thousands. Included among these festival entertainments were, as might be expected, performances of Wagner. In 1856 a selection of *Tannhäuser* was played, and by the 1870s Wagner overtures were performed in the Crystal Palace on a regular basis. The "Good Friday Music" from *Parsifal* was given its British premiere at the Palace in 1883, and the death of Wagner that same year provided the occasion for a Wagner Memorial Concert.[2] Paxton's Palace, like Bayreuth after it, was an attempt to reawaken the spirit of folk and festival for modern times. It aimed at a symbolic reunification of a fragmented public sphere and, simultaneously, a reunification of modern culture with the natural landscape.

The structure itself helped to make the point. Architect Joseph Paxton placed his Palace directly over already extant rows of trees in Hyde Park, incorporating them into the design and complementing them with a wide range of new plants. While the distinguishing features of the Palace were its enormous vaulted glass roofs and glass walls, these walls encompassed trees, shrubs, plants, pools, and fountains alongside its mechanical and commodity displays. The cutting edge of industrial building technology was thereby combined with the spectacle of lush and often exotic foliage, as though Eden might be discovered again by passing all the way through the domain of knowledge. In this glass-and-iron garden, the line between nature and commodity was blurred; products, machines, plants and people were transfixed into a new unity wherein nature was commodified, commodity naturalized. Here, as later at Bayreuth, a new unity was sought between humanity and nature. As at Bayreuth again, technology played a central role in the forging of this new unity. And as at Bayreuth a third time, this unity was connected to a project at once global and nationalistic, a project that was meant to embrace all humanity at the same time that it specifically celebrated one national folk as supreme.

Indeed, had Wagner's vision been different, his own festival theatre might well have been housed inside a crystal palace. In 1854 the *Glaspalast* opened in Munich, designed by August von Voigt as a variation on the Crystal Palace, and Ludwig II urged Wagner to erect at least a provisional version of his festival theatre within its crystalline walls.[3] A crucial figure in this plan was Gottfried Semper, the architect and friend of Wagner's who had fought alongside him in the Dresden revolution of 1849, and who, like Wagner, had been forced to flee into exile. Arriving in England in 1850, Semper found work designing national pavilions for the first Great Exhibition, and became entranced by the Crystal Palace, composing several architectural treatises on the importance of unifying technology and industry with art.[4] Returning to Europe in 1855, Semper brought the lessons of the Crystal Palace with him. With Ludwig's encouragement, Semper began plans to set the *Nibelung* Festival of 1865 in the *Glaspalast*. Semper's plans called for a theatre modeled on the Odeon at Pompeii, only larger, made up of a platform and tiers enveloped by a colonnade, overlooking a deep stage. The theatre would occupy a significant section of the middle wing of the exhibition hall. Following Wagner's demands, Semper included a number of theatrical innovations in his design plans that would later be incorporated into the Festspielhaus at Bayreuth, including egalitarian seating, a double proscenium, and a deep orchestra pit that hid the musicians from the sight of the audience. Most importantly, the new festival theatre would join Wagner's artwork of the future to Paxton's palace of the future, Teutonic tragedy to glass-and-steel modernity. Central location, a cultured public, enthusiastic patronage, innovative theatrical design, avant-garde architecture: given Wagner's need for a performance space and his famous taste for extravagance and aesthetic innovation, the offer might seem impossible to refuse. And yet Wagner never embraced the design, and eventually lost interest in Munich altogether as a site for his festival theatre. His choice, instead, was for an unknown, out-of-the-way Franconian town called Bayreuth.

Pilgrims to the mechanical hearth

At first glance, Wagner's choice of Bayreuth as a site for his festival theatre may seem odd. In addition to Ludwig's preference for the culturally rich city of Munich, generous offers were also made for the cash-strapped Wagner to locate his new theatre in Berlin and even Chicago. Bayreuth, on the other hand, was hardly a site on any cultural map. But the reasons behind Wagner's selection reveal both the practical and revolutionary sides of the artist. On the practical side, Wagner appreciated that the town fell within Ludwig's kingdom, that it boasted a large opera house (which Wagner had originally considered using), and that it was far enough from Munich to avoid the machinations of friends and enemies alike. On the revolutionary side, Wagner saw in "little, out-of-the-way, forgotten Bayreuth" (5:328/9:331) the antithesis of all that Munich, Berlin, and Chicago represented: an outpost from which to wage his war on industrialized commercial culture. Writing to Liszt on 15 January 1852, Wagner insisted that the *Ring* could not be performed in a city for a metropolitan audience, "least of all Berlin or Dresden." Its proper setting would be in "some beautiful wilderness" far from "the smoke and revolting industrial smell of our urban civilization." An anti-city, then, intended as a refuge from urban decay and a means of social restoration.

If industrialized, commercialized cities only reflect the fragmentation of modern society back to itself, then Wagner would find a site for his festival theatre that would help the public to rediscover its lost, organic self. Bayreuth's location near the center of the German states appealed to Wagner, who considered the town's geographical centrality to be symbolic of the aspiration of the total work of art. It was an essentially German land that Bayreuth occupied, a "vast Hercynian wild, in which the Romans ne'er set foot" (5:329/9:332). Indeed, the town was so profoundly German that we might "paint a picture of the German character and history, a picture which enlarged would mirror back the German realm itself" (5:330/9:333). The town symbolized Germany despite, and perhaps even because of, the fact that the residents of Bayreuth were not particularly "pure" in their Germanic heritage. Wagner pointed with enthusiasm to the fact that many of its first residents were Slavs, that "many local names still bear alike the Slavic and Germanic stamp," and that "Bayreuth was not left without Romanic culture" (5:330/9:333). Bayreuth's strength lay in its peculiar ability to assimilate multiple cultures into a single German spirit: "here first were Slavs transformed into Germans, without a sacrifice of idiosyncrasy, and amicably shared the fortunes of a common country. Good witness to the German spirit's qualities!" (5:330/9:333). Similarly, the influence of Italian culture was one of assimilation rather than exclusion, as exemplified by the fact that the town was proud of its rococo opera house while the local mayor still insisted upon speaking "honest *German*" to visiting Italian nobility (5:330/9:333). In short, Wagner held Bayreuth to be the mirror and microcosm of Germany at its most essential and a crucible in which the non-Germanic would be Germanized. As such, the town foreshadowed the function of the theatre house, a house that would reflect Germany back to itself at the same time as it threw open its doors to non-Germanic peoples, initiating the wider world into the collective German myth.

Finally, Bayreuth enjoyed the advantage of isolation, which forced visitors to make special, often devotional, journeys to the Festspielhaus and so furthered the site's aspiration to become a cultic center. The distance between Bayreuth and urbanized Germany, Wagner hoped, would necessitate a pilgrim's progress, one that would prepare the visitor to enter into the mythic space and time that Bayreuth offered.[5] The Festspielhaus would function as a site of national and international pilgrimage. It would bind together a people, and also serve as a common destination for a larger *Volk*, a *Volk* currently lost in the hurly-burly of industrialized culture. It is a strategy we might term *retrocartography*; that is, the attempt to return a society to an antique form of marking the landscape.[6] By this strategy, Wagner broke down barriers between audience and spectacle, for the visitors who reembodied this ancient way of being in the landscape would help to realize the more natural society which was the aim of the *Gesamtkunstwerk* itself. Pilgrims to Bayreuth became essentially visitor-actors, participants in a single, great drama of collective reawakening.

Wagner's strategy of retrocartography belongs in the context of a larger turn toward pseudo-medieval culture in the late nineteenth century. "In the closing decades of the nineteenth century," write Elizabeth Emery and Laura Morowitz in their survey of French neo-medievalism, "calls for reviving religious traditions associated with the past – especially the medieval past – flourished and led to widespread organization by the Catholic church of public prayer, religious celebrations and pilgrimages" (143). The revival was not, of course, limited to France, but reflects a broader structural transformation in the second half of the nineteenth century. Habermas has referred to this transformation as a "refeudalization" of the public sphere ("Public" 54) and, while he means this term to apply simply to the transformation of political structures in the period, the term may also be used to apply to the vast range of pseudo-medieval creations that typifies much of late nineteenth-century culture. In size, technological sophistication, and mass-cultural appeal, the mock-medieval creations that emerged from 1850 through the Second Industrial Revolution overshadowed earlier Gothic revivals. Le Sacré Coeur de Montmartre, St Patrick's Cathedral, Neuschwanstein, the Albert Memorial, Pre-Raphaelitism, Collegiate Gothic: late nineteenth-century pseudo-medievalism was an international phenomenon that found its symbolic expression in towering spires and stained glass windows, but also in a revival of medieval habits. Interest in old pilgrimage routes (to Santiago de Compostela, to Rocamadour, to Canterbury, to Walsingham, and so forth) was reawakened, and new pilgrimage routes (to La Salette, to Lourdes, eventually to Fatima) were established. The enthusiasm was not limited to Catholics and spiritual adventurers: sites such as the Festspielhaus and the Crystal Palace exemplified the appeal of the form of secular pilgrimage, pilgrimage organized around art, commodity, technological innovation, nationalism, and the dream of a return to harmony with nature.

If the Festspielhaus attempted to undo industrialization in the approach to the theatre, then this attempt was doubled *within* the theatre, by the performance of the operas themselves. A largely neglected aspect of Wagner's dramaturgy is the importance he attached to landscape painting in the production of his operas. With typical enthusiasm, Wagner called Romantic landscape painting and the natural sciences "the only outcomes of the present which, either from an artistic or a scientific point of view, offer us something of consolation and salvation from madness and impotence" (1:180/3:146–7*). Unlike the painting styles that preceded it, landscape painting restored the broken bond between man and nature and, as such, was capable of lifting her sister arts out of their present state of degeneracy. Wagner was particularly interested in the redemptive power that landscape painting might have over architecture, and expected that landscape painting would "broaden architecture out to a full and lifelike portraiture of nature" (1:176/3:143). Turning his attention to the stage, Wagner concluded that:

> *Landscape painting*, as last and perfected conclusion of all the plastic arts, will become the very soul of architecture; she will teach us so to rear the *stage* for the dramatic artwork of the future that on it, herself imbued with life, she may

> represent the warm *background of nature* for living, no longer counterfeited,
> *man* −.
>
> (1:181/3:147–8*)

In sum, Wagner's dream might be rendered thus: landscape painting, highest of
the plastic arts, will redeem the theatre, pinnacle of architecture, and together they
will set the stage for the music-drama of the future. The fact that Wagner broke
with theatrical tradition by hiring a landscape-painter to make his sets for Bayreuth
is almost beside the point: for Wagner, the whole opera, as realized within the Festspielhaus, functioned as a single landscape painting in sight, sound, and motion.

The Festspielhaus opened on 13 August 1876 to the sound of an E flat so low
that the double basses had to tune their E strings down a semitone to achieve it. In
the fifth bar three bassoons entered on B flat; the fundamental tone is joined by its
dominant. Original Being, peaceful yet static, had been interrupted and transformed, giving birth to the dynamic, harmonious state of nature that Wagner called
"the world's lullaby." The curtain rose to reveal a vista of this Edenic world:

> Greenish gloaming, brighter towards the top, darker below. The upper area is
> filled with swirling seas that flow restlessly from right to left. Towards the
> bottom the waves dissolve into an ever finer, damper mist, so that a space the
> height of a man from the ground appears to be entirely free of water, which
> flows like a train of clouds above the nocturnal bed. Everywhere sheer reefs of
> rock rise up from the depths and mark the boundaries of the stage space; the
> whole ground is broken up into a maze of jagged peaks so that it is nowhere
> completely flat, and on all sides there seem to be deeper gorges within the
> heavy shadows. The orchestra begins while the curtain is still closed.
>
> The curtain is raised. The briny deep at full flood. In the middle of the stage,
> around a reef whose slender point rises up into the denser, brighter twilight
> waters, circles one of the Rhinemaidens with a graceful swimming motion.
>
> (5:200)

The elaborate detail, the attention to shades of color and degrees of motion, the use
of both stark and subtle contrasts, the volcanic dynamism of the scene: altogether a
paradigmatically Romantic landscape. With one important qualification: the scale
of nature here, though grand, was not so large as to overwhelm the actors within it.
We are not in the world of, say, an Albert Bierstadt painting, with its towering
trees, mountains, and ravines, and isolated, passive observers. On the contrary,
Wagner's landscape was built to human proportions: the space beneath the Rhine
is "a man's height from the ground," and the slender rock at center stage is just
wide enough for a Rhinemaiden to swim around.

Other scenes, too, emphasized the harmonious relationship between man and
landscape, a relationship lost to the industrialized world. Take, for instance,
Hunding's hut at the opening of *Die Walküre*, in the middle of which "stands a
mighty ash-tree,"

whose permanent roots spread wide and lose themselves in the ground. The summit of the tree is cut off by a jointed roof, so pierced that the trunk and the boughs branching out on every side pass though it, through openings made exactly to fit. We assume that the top of the tree spreads out above the roof. Around the top of the ash, as central point, a room has been constructed. The walls are of rudely hewn wood, here and there hung with plaited and woven rugs.

$$(6:2)^7$$

In Wagner's description, the branches of the ash-tree have already begun to sprout off from the trunk before the ceiling is reached, indicating a tree of somewhat less than sublime size. Moreover, the interweaving of tree and house is a graceful one: the openings in the roof "exactly fit" the tree branches, and the walls of the house, made of rough-hewn wood, blur the distinction between nature and artifice. It is almost as if these two forms, house and tree, come together to form a single living, breathing entity. This rather modest rendering of nature was echoed in the design model for the original production, which indicates a tree whose trunk is perhaps five feet in diameter, the branches of which are mostly contained within the house itself (Figure 2.1).[8] While Wagner's settings echoed Romantic landscape painting in many respects, they did not push the sublimity of the landscape so far

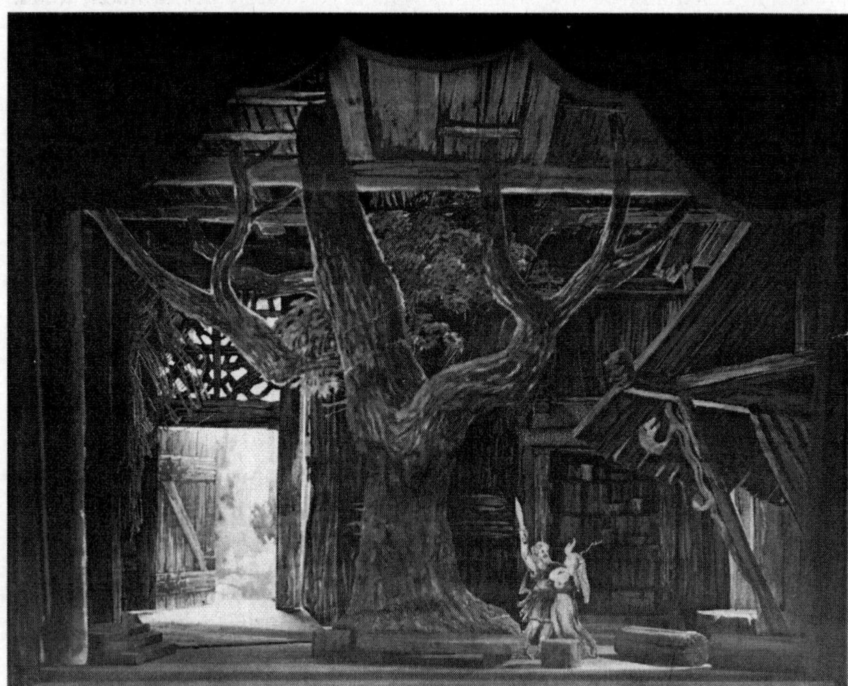

Figure 2.1 Stage model of *Die Walküre*, Act I, at Bayreuth, 1876.

that nature became truly overwhelming to humanity. And just as the sublimity of the landscape was tempered to a human scale, the characters who inhabited Wagner's stage rose to superhuman dimensions. Powerful but not overwhelming nature meets heroic, plus-sized humanity, just as the mighty ash-tree intertwines with the mighty hut.

As with the exterior strategy of retrocartography, pilgrimage played a role in the interior performance of the Festspielhaus as well. Though spectators could not literally walk through the mock-medieval landscapes depicted in Wagner's operas, they could travel across them in their imaginations, and so participate, at least vicariously, in the mythic age of German romance. In *Parsifal*, the only opera written expressly for the Bayreuth stage, this strategy of retrocartography was rendered more forceful by the central role of pilgrimage in the opera itself. Significantly, the reproduction of pilgrimage within the Festspielhaus itself was accomplished by means of innovative technical effects. In a strategy that would become central to the performance of the Festspielhaus, Wagner turned to modern technology in order to undo the debilitating effects of modernity.

For the first act of *Parsifal*, Wagner sought to create the illusion of Gurnemanz and Parsifal's journey into the shrine of the Grail, so that the audience might be "led quite imperceptibly, as if in a dream, along the 'pathless' trails to the Gralsburg" (6:10/10:305). The journey consisted of a pilgrim's progress (through the woods), a liminal crossing (marked by a rising passageway, a gateway, rising trombone tones, and ringing bells), and a transformation in space and time from profane to sacred (Gurnemanz to Parsifal: "*Du sieh'st, mein Sohn, / zum Raum wird hier die Zeit*" – "You see, my son, here time becomes space"). Scenically, the effect of this pilgrimage was produced by means of four long moving dioramas, which were spooled into rollers and gradually unraveled to simulate movement through the forest and into the shrine. Essentially, a four-part, moving Romantic landscape-painting was designed in a manner that trumped even the popular diorama-theatre techniques of Louis Daguerre. The effect of this mechanized landscape painting, at least on enthusiasts, is captured by Felix Weingartner's reactions to the first performances.

> When Gurnemanz prepared to accompany Parsifal to the Gralsburg, a slight dizziness took hold of me. What was happening? It seemed to me as though the house with all the spectators began to move. By means of a backdrop, the scene had begun to transform. The illusion was absolute. One did not walk, one was carried along. "Here time becomes space."
>
> (165)

Thus Wagner's retrocartography reappears, mirrored back to the audience-pilgrims. Parsifal's pilgrimage to Monsalvat doubled the audience's own pilgrimage to the Festspielhaus, thereby reinforcing a medieval sense of the German landscape as well as an identification of Bayreuth with the long-lost Castle of the Grail. Just as Parsifal's pilgrimage to Monsalvat doubled and consecrated the pilgrimage of Wagnerians to Bayreuth, so did Wagnerians see themselves replicated and consecrated as knights before the Holy Grail. When Parsifal returns to Monsalvat to become Grail King, it marks not only the end of the opera, but the end of opera period, and the sacralization of the *Gesamtkunstwerk* in its place.

Through his Festspielhaus, Wagner sought to counter the degrading effects of industrial capitalism through a restoration of the antique relationship between the German people and the German landscape. He did this both in the exterior and the interior performances of his Festspielhaus: that is to say, through the way the Festspielhaus performed as an architectural site in the surrounding landscape, and through the performance of his music-dramas within the Festspielhaus. The harmony Wagner attempted to achieve, however, obscured a deeper dissonance. The threat of mechanization, rebutted on all fronts, welled up again from beneath.

Into the mystic gulf

> Searching,
> no one can see me;
> but I am everywhere,
> hidden from sight.
> (Alberich, *Das Rheingold*, Scene 3)

The harmony that Bayreuth sought to restore rested on two new bifurcations, one of them revealed, the other quite hidden. First the revealed one. Nowhere before Bayreuth was the audience so rigorously separated from the spectacle; most of the architectural innovations of Bayreuth, not to mention the aesthetic innovations of the operas themselves, are intended to serve this separation (Figure 2.2). The theatre house was sparsely adorned both inside and out in order to reduce distraction. Box seats were eliminated and row seats installed, with the seats narrowed and steeply raked in order to allow the whole audience to view the proscenium from roughly equal sightlines.[9] This innovation – essentially merging Greek amphitheatre with proscenium stage design – made the Festspielhaus the first proscenium theatre since ancient Rome designed with the explicit purpose of giving all spectators a clear view of the stage. In sharp contrast to standard practice, Wagner and his designer Carl Brandt sunk the orchestra pit deeply beneath the stage, hiding the musicians from sight. Wagner called this pit the "mystic gulf" ("*mystischer Abgrund*"), from which the music of his works would arise as if by magic, from the navel of the earth (Figure 2.3). Before this pit Wagner placed a second proscenium, which had the dual effect of further obscuring the mystic gulf and of making the actors on stage seem larger and more distant through forced perspective. The stage itself was enormous – almost as large as the auditorium, with cavernous fly space – which allowed a great deal of room for the range of machinery Wagner and Brandt installed to create their theatrical illusions. To light this vast space, Brandt complemented the footlights with gaslights installed behind the second proscenium, an innovative and influential response to the problems of nineteenth-century stage lighting. Finally, and again for the first time in theatre history, house lights were

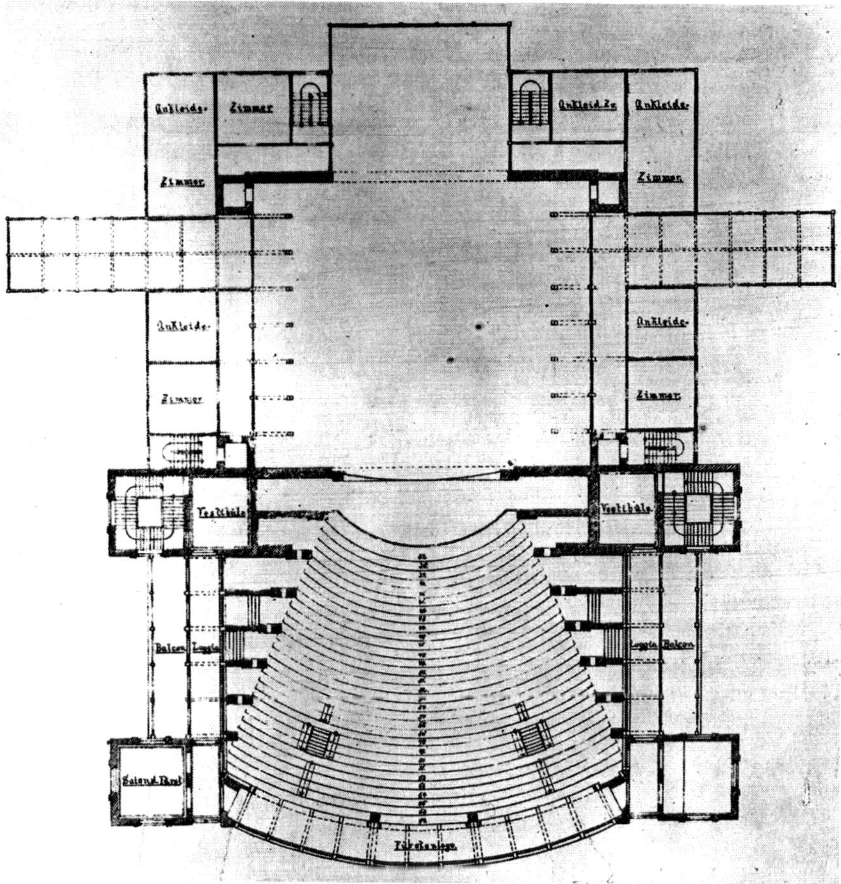

Figure 2.2 Bayreuth Festspielhaus groundplan, 1873.

darkened during all performances, forcing the spectators to direct their entire attention on the work.[10] This last innovation, perhaps Bayreuth's most famous, anticipates not only later theatrical practice but twentieth-century cinemas as well. Taken as a whole, the Festspielhaus may have been the most revolutionary theatre in stage history.

As was typical for Wagner, this was a spiral revolution, carried out for the sake of restoration on a higher plane. The combined effect of all of these innovations would be to restore ancient mysteries to the modern world.

> Between [the spectator] and the picture to be looked at there is nothing plainly visible, merely a floating atmosphere of distance, resulting from the architectural adjustment of two proscenia; whereby the scene is removed as it were

to the unapproachable world of dreams, while the spectral music sounding from the "mystic gulf," like vapors rising from the holy womb of Gaia beneath Pythia's tripod, inspires him with that clairvoyance in which the scenic picture melts into the truest effigy of life itself.

(5:335/9:338)

While recalling ancient mysteries and initiating the audience into a new cult, the mystic gulf also removed the audience from the theatrical spectacle and enforced a strict division of realms, audience versus performance (in Wagner's terms, "reality" versus "ideality"). It separated the zones of audience and performance by "making the spectator imagine [the scene] quite far away" (5:334–5/9:337–8), and thereby reinforced the illusion of a distant dreamworld on stage, entirely removed from the contingencies of everyday life. Wagner intended these techniques at once to separate the audience from the spectacle, and at the same time so entrance the audience that the fundamental distance between spectator and spectacle would be overcome. The mystic gulf thus separated the real from the ideal in order to cause the real to realize itself, its real self, in the ideal: the audience/spectacle opposition at Bayreuth was enforced only for the sake of its elimination.

But this reconciliation between reality and ideality, audience and spectacle, rests upon another, unresolved bifurcation, one which must be repressed in the interest of totality. This bifurcation may be rendered roughly as follows: on one hand, the total work of art, on the other, mechanical production. Along with its concomitants – labor, technology, industry – mechanical production is the *Gesamtkunstwerk*'s inassimilable element, its necessary other, and yet, and therefore, its obsession.

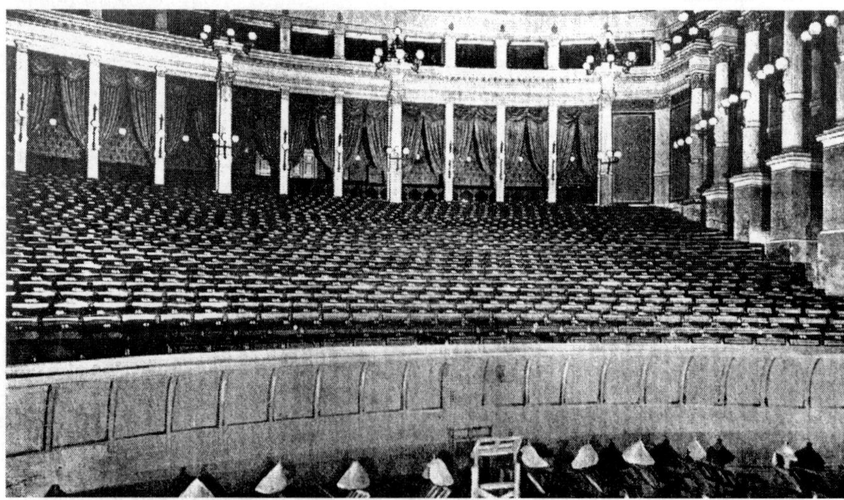

Figure 2.3 The view from the Festspielhaus stage, over the "mystic gulf" and out towards the auditorium.

Wagner may have railed against the mechanization of the modern world, but he placed great stress on the mechanization of his operas. The demand began with the music-dramas themselves, which call for sudden scene changes, swimming Rhinemaidens, flying Valkyries, crags and castles, dwarves and dragons, flames and flood. Wagner intended these spectacles to be presented with a degree of realism only possible through the extensive (and, as it turned out, expensive) use of stage mechanics.[11] The extraordinary scene changes of even the comparatively simple *Rheingold*, for instance – from river basin to mountain heights, down to subterranean workshop, and once more up to the peaks – were masked by clouds of color-lit steam produced by an old locomotive boiler, operated by a railway mechanist (who constantly struggled with the steam, which tended to choke Alberich and warp the instruments in the orchestra pit).[12] Similarly, magic lantern effects made the Ride of the Valkyries come to life, and the dragon Fafner was "a masterpiece of imagination and engineering," as stage director Richard Fricke records in his Bayreuth diary on 22 July 1876. Though many of these techniques drew from the standard arsenal of nineteenth-century scenic illusion, some of the machines had to be invented for the production, such as the exotic contraption Brandt designed for the swimming Rhinemaidens (Figures 2.4 and 2.5).

While Wagner's use of stage technology was undeniably innovative, Friedrich Kittler has recently shifted the question somewhat to look at Wagner's music-dramas in relation to a broader "discourse network" of electronic media. In his

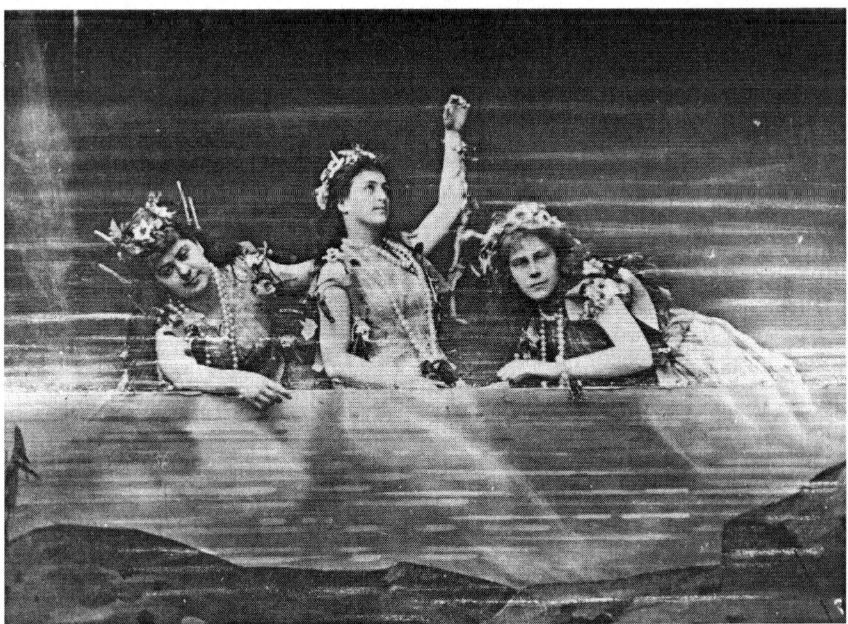

Figure 2.4 The three Rhinemaidens (Minna Lammert as Flosshilde, Lilli Lehmann as Woglinde, Marie Lehmann as Wellgunde) at Bayreuth, 1876.

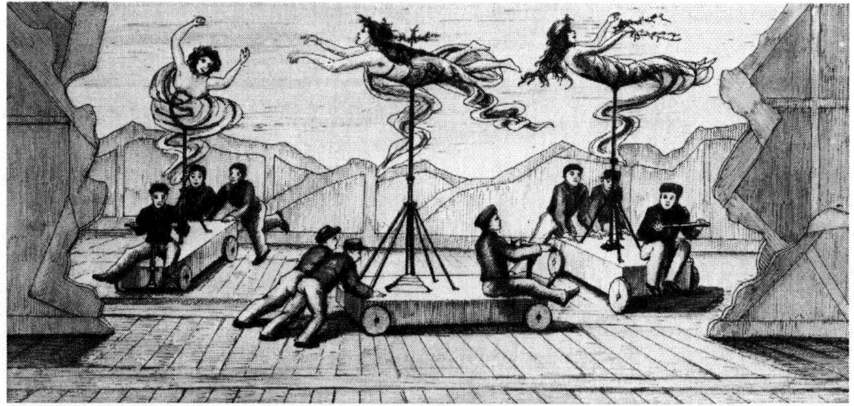

Figure 2.5 Swimming machines for *Das Rheingold* at Bayreuth, 1876.

brief, provocative essay "World-Breath," Kittler argues that Wagnerian performance marks a radical break with traditional arts, and an anticipation of electronic media. Drawing in part from Rudolf Arnheim's *Kritiken und Aufsätze zum Film*, Kittler differentiates sharply between "arts" and "media."[13] Wagnerian performance belongs to the category of media rather than arts, writes Kittler; it is a "machine capable of reproducing sensuous data as such" (216). Wagner's music, similarly, is "a matter of pure dynamics and pure acoustics," thus producing the effect of an electrical amplifier *avant la lettre* (224). Wagner, by this reading, breaks fundamentally with the aesthetic systems that precede him.

> At one fell swoop, reflection and imagination, education and literacy – all of those celebrated psychic faculties necessarily presupposed by classical poetry in order to reach people by means of its pages – became obsolete. For in the revolutionary darkness of the Festspielhaus ... the medium of music-drama began to play with and upon the public's nerves.
>
> (216)

Rather than relating only symbolically to the sensory fields they presuppose, Wagnerian music-dramas *are* those sensory fields in their materiality. At Bayreuth, in other words, the medium is the message.

Kittler's approach is illuminating, and he is certainly right in placing Wagner at the center of the development of modern media. On the other hand, his approach obscures the fact that Wagner is perpetually at odds with the technology he wields. Rather than seeing Wagner as simply a media revolutionary, we ought to understand him as a radically ambiguous figure. On one hand he was a composer whose music-dramas at once play directly on the public's nerves through nonrepresentational uses of "mere" sound and breath (the old cartoon of Wagner hammering directly into the listener's ear, though obviously satiric, captures some of Kittler's point). On the other hand, Wagner was also a composer whose extraordinarily complex motivic systems (to use just one example of his compositional sophistication) reward highly literate, reflective listening practices. Similarly, Wagner was a director who called for cutting-edge technical stage effects while simultaneously advocating decidedly melodramatic modes of acting and painterly stage tableaux. Furthermore, Wagner was an innovator both in performance technology and the concealment of performance technology. To insist on interpreting Wagner's music-dramas "simply as media," therefore, is to overlook the concealment of production at the heart of Wagnerian performance.

In the end, Kittler's essay, for all of its insightfulness, plays Wagner's game in at least one respect. When Kittler insists that Wagner's music-dramas be approached "simply as media," and therefore "be seen with a stupidity that distinguishes Wagnerian heroes, above all Siegfried" (217), he expresses a deeply Wagnerian yearning: a yearning for the audience to return to the condition of the pure fool. Kittler makes a trenchant point about the resemblance between Wagner's music-dramas and twentieth-century media: Wagner's compositions do rely, to an unprecedented degree, on "pure dynamics and pure acoustics," on positive feed-back loops and amplification. But in the Festspielhaus there is always production and its concealment, and so not simplicity but duplicity.

If the Festspielhaus relied heavily on the magic of mechanism, then it relied equally heavily, as Adorno understood, on the techniques of concealment that would bury the machine in shadows. Yet while Kittler's account somewhat down-plays the importance of Wagner's concealment of production, Adorno's account does not quite capture Wagner's own awareness of his reliance upon the instruments of production he so loathed. Nowhere before in aesthetic theory is mechanical production understood to be at once so poisonous and so *central* to an artwork as in Wagner's work. This complex of reliance and disavowal is especially evident in Wagner's prose writings, too often neglected by scholars. Here, for example, is Wagner writing on the importance of hiding the orchestra, in his "Bayreuth" essay from 1873:

> To explain the plan of the festival theatre now in course of erection in Bayreuth I believe I cannot do better than to begin with the need I felt from the first, that of *rendering invisible the technical source of its music*, to wit the orchestra; for this one need led step by step to *a total transformation of the auditorium* of our neo-European theatre.
>
> (5:333/9:336; italics added*)

According to Wagner, then, the need to conceal the orchestra (now understood as machine) from the sight of the spectators was his original step in the "total transformation" of the theatre. To be sure, Wagner's association of the orchestra with a machine is not quite original; it has roots at least as far back as 1783, when J. N. Forkel, Bach's first biographer, compared the orchestra to a clock (1063). And in 1843 Berlioz, who often used mechanical metaphors when describing musical production, went so far as to imagine the orchestra as a "machine endowed with intelligence" (293). For Forkel and for Berlioz, however, the machinical nature of the orchestra was a source of wonder more than horror, of modernity's promise more than its curse, and so did not raise questions of the orchestra's concealment. While the concealment of mechanical production was typical (to varying degrees) of eighteenth- and nineteenth-century stages, and while the orchestra-as-machine metaphor predates Wagner, Bayreuth nevertheless marks a qualitative break with past theory and practice. In no earlier artistic project is the problem of mechanical production so thoroughly developed, or so obsessively worried over, relied upon, reviled, and disguised as it is in Wagner. In no previous artistic project is it so essential.

To expand the point, let us continue to examine Wagner's description of his orchestra as "the technical source of the music" ("*der technischer Herd der Musik*") in the passage just cited. It is a peculiar phrase. In German as in English, "*Herd*" ("hearth") is one of the keywords of folk-ish sentimentality, associated with such phrases as "*Heim und Herd*" ("home and hearth") or "*eigener Herd ist Goldes wert*" ("there's no place like home"). It is an important term in Wagner's music-dramas, suggesting *Gemütlichkeit*, *Gemeinschaft*, and bygone days. In *Tannhäuser*, for example, the Landgraf curses Tannhäuser with the words, "*schmachbefleckt ist unser Herd durch dich*" ("our hearth is disgraced through you"), as though no more damning image than a corrupted hearth could be found. In *Rheingold*, when Loge sneers that "*Haus und Herd behagt mir nicht*" ("home and hearth don't appeal to me"), he reveals himself as the trickster he is. In *Die Walküre*, on the other hand, when Hunding greets Siegmund with "*Heilig ist mein Herd: / heilig sei dir mein Haus!*" ("Sacred is my hearth – sacred shall my house be to you!"), he reveals himself to be a man of homespun honor, if not exactly of charm. But the most revealing of Wagner's many hearth allusions may be in *Siegfried*, which, like *Die Walküre*, opens with a hearth.

At first, Mime's hearth in Act 1 of *Siegfried* seems a place of some domestic comfort: it is the same hearth, after all, that warmed Siegfried's mother back to life, and that warmed Siegfried himself after his birth. But Mime's hearth is a corrupt site as well, for it is the fire to which Siegfried has been enslaved. The hammer-strokes that open the drama, as Mime strikes at the hot iron on his anvil in his vain attempt to forge a sword for Siegfried, recall the chorus of anvils in Alberich's subterranean cavern in Scene 3 of *Rheingold*. The connection is underscored by the repetition of the "anvil leitmotif" – which might be better called the "industry leitmotif" – from the end of Scene 2 of *Rheingold*. In that motif, Wagner's composition imitates the speed, energy, and regularity of mechanical reproduction.

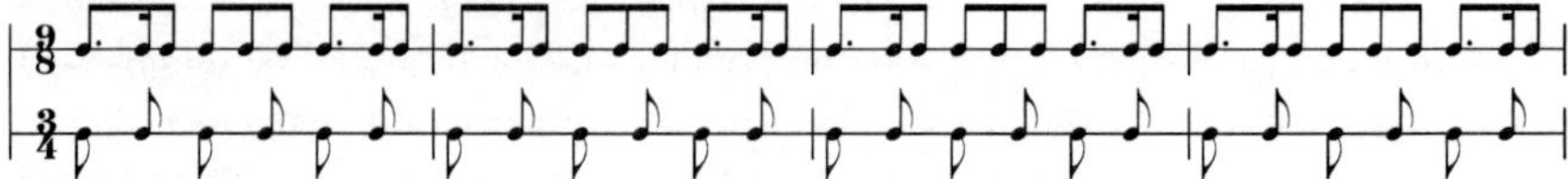

Evoking the industrial labor of the Nibelung slaves, Mime's futile hammering and his lordly treatment of Siegfried illustrate the dangers of the hearth. For *Herd*

here is also *Schmiedeherd*, the hearth a forge, and therefore not far (as the industrial repetition of the motif makes clear) from the factory. But the forge is not rejected; rather, it is testimony to Siegfried's heroism that he uses this instrument of gold-lust and enslavement to forge his sword. In distinction from the hammer-strokes of the Nibelungs, Siegfried's are not routinized and identical but variously spaced and accelerating. They are the blows of the superman rather than the factory worker, as a comparison with the industry leitmotif from the end of Scene 2 of *Rheingold* makes clear.

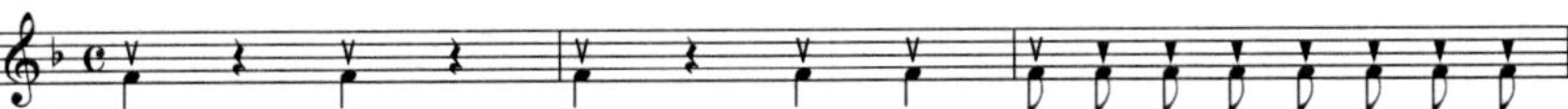

Siegfried has learned how to turn the tools of the industrial master to the ends of Teutonic heroism, how to return, by means of the machine, to the world of pre-industrial myth. The final blow that forges his sword breaks the anvil in two, destroying the seed of industry at the heart of the hearth. If Mime threatens to turn the forge into a factory, then Siegfried smashes the forge back to a warming primeval fire. Siegfried's work is Wagner's too – indeed, it is the fundamental revolutionary labor of the *Gesamtkunstwerk*, according to Wagner – to use the tools of industry to undo the alienating effects of industrialization. Perhaps Wagner's phrase "*technischer Herd der Musik*" ought to be translated more literally, then: not as "technical source of the music" but as "technical *hearth* of the music." For Wagner, the orchestra does the work of the Nibelungs, turning a hearth into a place of industrial production. Small wonder, then, that the orchestra should be buried beneath the stage, for the "mystic gulf" of the Festspielhaus is also Nibelheim.

Given this concept of the orchestra (unusual in any translation), it is even more noteworthy that Wagner's association of the orchestra with technology is placed right beside the injunction that the orchestra must be "render[ed] invisible." A connection is implied between the mechanical nature of the orchestra and the necessity of concealment, a connection that is expanded upon in the passage that follows.

> The reader of my previous essays already knows my views about the concealment of the orchestra, and, even should he not have felt as much before, I hope that a subsequent visit to the opera will have convinced him of my rightness in condemning the constant visibility of the technical apparatus for tone production [*des technischen Apparates der Tonhervorbringung*] as an aggressive nuisance. In my article on Beethoven I explained how fine performances of ideal works of music may make this evil imperceptible at last, through our eyesight being neutralized, as it were, by the rapt subversion of the whole sensorium [*durch die Gewalt der Umstimmung des ganzen Sensitoriums*]. With a dramatic representation, on the contrary, it is a matter of focusing the eye itself upon a picture; and that can be done only by leading it away from any sight of bodies lying in between, such as is done with a technical apparatus [*mit einem technischen Apparate*] for projecting a picture.
>
> (5:333/9:336*)[14]

What Wagner is describing here is a vast performance-machine. And it is, more precisely, a performance-machine ashamed of its status *as* machine. Thus the "mechanism for tone production" becomes an "aggressive nuisance" and an "evil" which must be rendered "imperceptible," and whose "constant visibility" must be "condemned." That the mechanical nature of the total work of art should be a source of discomfort for Wagner follows from the stark dichotomy between mechanism and organism he inherits from Schiller, and stretches to the breaking point. Throughout his writings, as we have seen, Wagner's distinction between organism and mechanism has explicitly political as well as aesthetic connotations. The fact that the *Gesamtkunstwerk* relies so much on mechanics, then, is no small problem for Wagner. The problem is neatly captured by his statement that "the technical apparatus for projecting the picture" is impeded by "any sight of bodies lying in between." Though the purpose of this "technical apparatus" is the reconciliation of humanity and nature, this reconciliation is blocked by the sight of actual living bodies – specifically, by the bodies of the people who operate "the technical apparatus for tone production." For nature and humanity to be reconciled, such producing bodies must be hidden; for the total work of art to succeed, Wagner must rely upon nature's antithesis.

Ironically, in *Opera and Drama* Wagner savages Berlioz for essentially the same problem that he himself eventually struggles with at Bayreuth: that is, the increasing reliance upon hidden technology to realize the natural. In Wagner's account, Berlioz must turn to mechanics to hide the fact that his work is fundamentally "*un*-natural," which only reveals the sham of Berlioz's entire project:

> Berlioz forced his enormous musical intelligence to a hitherto undreamt-of technical power. What he had to say to people was so wonderful, so unwonted, so entirely unnatural, that he could never have said it out in homely, simple words: he needed a huge array of the most complicated machines, in order to proclaim by help of a many-wheeled and delicately adjusted mechanism what a simple human organism could not possibly have uttered – just because it was so quite un-human. We know, now, the supernatural wonders wherewith a priesthood once deluded childlike men into believing that some good god was manifesting himself to them: it was nothing but Mechanism, that ever worked these cheating wonders. Thus to-day again the *super*-natural, just because it is the *un*-natural, can only be brought before a gaping public by the wonders of mechanics [*die Wunder der Mechanik*]; and such a wonder is the secret of the *Berliozian Orchestra*.
>
> (2:76/3:283)

Behind Wagner's attack on Berlioz one senses the fear of a double. Much that he accuses Berlioz of here could be said, with more reason, of Wagner himself. Wagner's music-dramas were at least as reliant upon the wonders of stage technology as Berlioz's operas, and it was not Berlioz, after all, who spoke of the orchestra as a tone-production mechanism, or the drama as a picture-projecting machine, or who thought carefully about how best to enrapture the spectators' "sensorium." Predictably, the terms of Wagner's attack recall the way in which Wagner describes his own project in his "Bayreuth" essay. There, as we have seen, Wagner compares the sounds rising from the "mystic gulf" to "vapors rising from the holy womb of Gaia beneath Pythia's tripod"; here he compares Berlioz's orchestral effects to "the supernatural wonders wherewith a priesthood once deluded childlike men into believing that some good god was manifesting himself to them." Wagner's supposedly fundamental distinction between his own "organic" supernaturalism and Berlioz's "*un*-natural" supernaturalism is hazy at best. One way to make sense of Wagner's attack here is to say that Berlioz's sin lies less in his reliance on technology than in his lack of interest in concealing that reliance. Berlioz's orchestra is *openly* mechanistic; it suffers from a lack of shame.

The business of the Wagnerian *Gesamtkunstwerk* is never complete. The more it aims to realize nature, the more it must utilize the machine, a vicious circle that produces a multiplication of blinders. It is often forgotten, for instance, that the two proscenia Brandt designed to enclose the mystic gulf actually gave birth to a series:

> Now, to mask the blanks immediately in front of our double proscenium, the ingenuity of my present advisor [Brandt] had already hit on the plan of throwing out a third and still broader proscenium. Seized with the excellence of this thought, we soon went further in the same direction, and found that, to do full justice to the idea of an auditorium narrowing in true perspective toward the stage, *we must extend the process to the whole interior, adding proscenium after proscenium until they reached their climax in the crowning gallery, and thus enclosing the entire audience in the vista, no matter where it took its place.*
>
> (5:336/9:339; italics added)

Wagner's account shows how the imperative of concealment produces a multiplication of blinders amid a fear of contamination of the organic by the mechanical. But it suggests, too, that the total work of art, logically extended, places the audience "on the other side" of the proscenium. To enclose the audience "in the vista, no matter where it took its place" is to take another step toward the unification of spectator and spectacle. The audience, Wagner suggests, might now be located *within* the spectacle itself. The enclosure of the entire audience within the vista of the proscenium is an overflowing of the festival out into the auditorium. The festival will not merely take place on stage; it will consume every corner of the theatre; it will encompass the spectators themselves. And in none of Wagner's creations is the dichotomy between audience and participant so sharply challenged as in his last music-drama, *Parsifal*.

Knights of the electric chalice

Parsifal revolves around rituals and rites to such a degree that questions of whether it is an essentially "Christian drama" have been raised ever since the work's premiere at Bayreuth in 1882. *Parsifal* has been read by some as disappointingly Christian, by others as admirably Christian, by still others as faux-Christian.[15] Barry Millington has even argued, against these positions, that *Parsifal* is not "explicitly anything" ("*Parisfal*" 98). The whole debate, however, may be missing the mark. For *Parsifal* is indeed a religious work, but its primary religion is not Christianity but the cult of the *Gesamtkunstwerk*. The circumstances of its composition are important in this regard. *Parsifal* is the only work Wagner wrote expressly for the Bayreuth stage, and he famously intended that it should never be performed anywhere else. There is every evidence that he considered it to be the climax and culmination of his Bayreuth project and, by extension, the fullest realization of his dream of the total work of art. Three years before the opening of Bayreuth, and a decade before the premiere of *Parsifal*, Wagner was already speaking of the Festspielhaus as a holy shrine inspired by the temple of the legendary Grail Knights. In a letter to Ludwig II in August 1873, for instance, Wagner declares that the *Ring* cycle was only a way station on a longer journey, the goal of which was *Parsifal*. *Parsifal*, he writes, would be "the pinnacle of all my achievements" and would answer his need

> to build a Castle of the Grail devoted to art, far removed from the common byways of human activity; for only there, in Monsalvat, can the longed-for deed be revealed to the people, to those who are initiated into its rites, not in those places where God may not show Himself before the idols of the day without His being blasphemed.
>
> (823)

Here Wagner's loathing for modern culture, his love of pilgrimage, his fondness for mythic correspondences, and his taste for occultish rites come into perfect harmony. Correspondences are doubled and redoubled: Monsalvat becomes Festspielhaus, Grail Knights become audience members, and Parsifal's journey becomes – what else but the impossible, longed-for quest of the Wagnerian stage. Parsifal's quest to return the genuine, efficacious Eucharist to the kingdom, and thus to restore the stricken land to wholeness and purity, is Wagner's quest too.

To a degree unusual even for the necessarily exclusionary genre of the *Gesamtkunstwerk*, *Parsifal* makes ritual purification central to its vision of totality. A number of critics have examined *Parsifal*'s rhetoric of cleansing in light of Wagner's antisemitism and embrace of "Aryan Christianity," and the complexity of this rhetoric resists brief analysis.[16] Still, it is important to recall that Wagner's last work revolves around issues of bodily purity. These issues range from the sexual anxieties of its plot (in which the sorcerer Klingsor castrates himself, the Grail King Amfortas loses his Spear after being seduced by the ageless woman Kundry, Klingsor wields the Spear to give Amfortas a wound that will not heal, and the "pure fool" Parsifal attains sanctified manhood by resisting sexual seduction and recapturing the lost Spear), to its interest in blood purity (not even Eucharistic blood can cure Amfortas' corruption until Parsifal returns the Spear), to its utopian vision of the Grail community (ultimately purified in blood and answerable to a single sacred leader), to the ritual function of the drama *Parsifal* itself (intended to consecrate the Bayreuth stage). And a central figure in these purgative rituals is Kundry.

Who is Kundry? She is many things. When we first encounter her, she is a combination of witch and wild woman: "Kundry rushes in, almost staggering; wild clothes tied high; a snakeskin belt hanging low; loose locks of black, fluttering hair; dark brownish-red complexion; piercing black eyes, sometimes wildly blazing, but more often glassy and as rigid as death" (10:326). Throughout the first act, her glassy eyes, screams, laughter, weariness, and manic contortions mark Kundry as a hysteric, thus underscoring the distinctly "feminine" and "Jewish" nature of her illness.[17] Further on in Act 1, we are told that Kundry is a "heathen" and a "sorceress," "burdened with a curse" (10:329). At the opening of Act 2, Klingsor calls her a "nameless creature," "first sorceress," "Rose of Hades," "Herodias," and "Gundryggia" (a wild huntress of Nordic myth) (10:345–6). In her seduction of Parsifal, Kundry performs the dual roles of lover and substitute mother. Finally, toward the end of Act 2, we find an explanation for her many incarnations: she reveals herself as the Wandering Jew, eternally cursed for laughing at Christ. Wagner of course goes sharply against tradition by making the Wandering Jew a woman, but his choice is in fact perfectly appropriate to Kundry's dramatic function as the receptacle of all that which Wagner's *Gesamtkunstwerk* must ultimately exclude. The eternal Woman and the eternal Jew unified in one figure, a cursed thing who must be rejected, broken, and redeemed, and whose last words are "to serve, to serve" before finally falling silent. The ending of *Parsifal* comes, not with Kundry's redemption, but with her death, and the soaring chorus of the all-male, purified Grail community. *Parsifal*'s final apotheosis, with the Spear and Grail unified at the end in an androgynous totality, echoes the unity of masculine and feminine elements that Wagner held to be the grand synthesis of the *Gesamtkunstwerk*.[18] Tellingly, it is an androgyny that can only occur under the sign of the gentile male: Woman must die in order to be raised up and preserved as a symbolic discourse between men, just as the Jew must die in order to be raised up and preserved as a symbolic discourse between Christians. Wagner's final *Gesamtkunstwerk* creates totality through the translation of excluded Others into acceptably symbolic form.[19]

Not only is the *Gesamtkunstwerk* modeled onstage during *Parsifal*, so is the appropriate audience response. The audience's stand-in here is Parsifal himself. Upon first sighting the Grail Castle, Parsifal stands "as if bewitched" (10:339); upon first witnessing Holy Mass, Parsifal "stands still, motionless and silent, clearly overwhelmed by what he has seen" (10:343); when Amfortas cries in pain, Parsifal clutches his own chest "convulsively for a long time" (10:345). When the Grail returns to him in a vision in Act 2, his response is to "fall completely into a trance" (10:358); when the Grail returns one last time at the end of the drama, Parsifal and the Knights are in "rapture" and "ecstasy" (10:375). In such moments, as in his journeys to Monsalvat, Parsifal is not only the hero of the drama; he is the ideal audience member as well. His pure foolishness lies not in an absence of sin (he has abandoned his mother, after all) but lies, rather, in a combination of extreme ignorance and extreme empathy. After the Grail is first revealed, Gurnemantz asks the boy, "Do you understand what you have seen?", to which Parsifal can only shake his head and continue to clutch his heart in empathetic connection with the suffering Amfortas (10:345). Parsifal, like the ideal Bayreuth pilgrim, is all intuition and feeling, always a vision away from a swoon.

More so than any other music-drama, *Parsifal* is about the Wagnerian search for totality. Not that this self-reflexive concern was anything new in Wagner's oeuvre, for several of his music-dramas reflect on the *Gesamtkunstwerk* even as they attempt to realize it. But *Parsifal* surpasses all of Wagner's other work in the extent and centrality of its self-reflection. Wagner dubbed it a *"Bühnenweihfestspiel,"* or "stage-consecration festival play," and the neologism captures some of the peculiarity of *Parsifal* in Wagner's imagination. To begin with, the term raises certain questions: wasn't the Festspielhaus already "consecrated" when Wagner laid the foundation stone? or when workmen raised the roof to the tune of the *Tannhäuser* march? or surely with the inaugural performance of the *Ring*? Most troubling of all: had the Festspielhaus been, for the six years before *Parsifal*, unhallowed ground? Wagner's phrase for *Parsifal* suggests so, and further suggests that there is something very different about this last music-drama.

The difference is incarnation.[20] With *Parsifal*, Wagner's back-to-the-future revolution returns us not to Greek tragedy but to *Quem quaeritis*. In the process, Wagner recovers some of the troubling ambiguities of liturgical drama, ambiguities having to do with the line between speech act and "mere" speech. When is a performance *just* a performance, and when does it transform the world? Which is to say, when are actors just playing that Christ is present, and when is Christ really present? *Parsifal* also raises such questions, and gives us no definite answers. Tellingly, even applause is a vexed question, with some applauding after every act, others only after Acts 2 and 3. On one hand *Parsifal* is clearly a dramatic performance, with tickets, playbills, professional performers, an auditorium, and a proscenium stage. On the other hand, *Parsifal* is a Eucharistic ritual that, particularly at Bayreuth, includes the audience in its community of celebrants. This liturgical aspect of *Parsifal* is what differentiates it most clearly from Wagner's other music-dramas, and what also makes it the fullest realization of his dream of *Gesamtkunstwerk*. *Parsifal* did not simply represent aesthetic and social totality, did not simply exhort the public to realize that totality. *Parsifal* aimed to bring that totality to life here, now, in the theatre itself: to reincarnate Monsalvat as the Festspielhaus. To call itself sacred, and so to make it so. Or, more precisely, to declare that the medium is the message, and that both are sacred. For *Parsifal* recalls medieval liturgical drama in order to move us forward into the realm of media technology, in which a direct correlation is established between sensory data and the materiality they presuppose. The culmination of Wagner's break with classical aesthetics, and embrace of media technology, comes with the unveilings of the Holy Grail.

The Grail unveilings that end Acts 1 and 3 must cause the audience to swoon as Parsifal swoons, and must crown the *Gesamtkunstwerk* as Parsifal himself is crowned. In a letter to Mathilde Wesendonck, Wagner declares himself daunted by the challenge. Describing the "transport, worship, ecstasy," which would be created by "the wondrous presence of the chalice which reddens into soft entrancing radiance," Wagner uncharacteristically doubts his powers of creation: "[a]nd am I to execute a thing like that, to boot? make music for it, too?" (140–1). In the end, Wagner would not rely merely on his musical and poetic skills to enrapture the audience: he would also demand groundbreaking technical effects. In the first Act, as Amfortas raises the Grail above his head, Wagner calls for "a dazzling ray of light" to descend to illuminate the cup (Figure 2.6). The cup is to "glow ever brighter in a brilliant purple light, which softly illuminates everything," until "everyone is immersed in the light of glory" (10:343, 375). At the end of the third act, Wagner calls for essentially the same effect once more. Contemporary accounts testify to the success, as well as the technical sophistication, of the scenes. "A particularly gripping effect is the (electrical) halo originating from the top of the dome and shining down on the new Grail King," writes Bernhard Förster in the 1882 issue of *Zeitschrift für bildende Kunst* (330), describing the Grail itself as "a tall vessel with a half-spherical crystal bowl, which receives its red-glowing illumination by means of electrical light flowing through an almost invisible wire" (329). George Davidson, a member of the Bayreuth Patrons' Association and another observer of the original production of *Parsifal*, offers a more technical description of the Grail-illumination effect.

> I don't think it will take anything away from the experience of future audience members if I tell how the wonderful illumination of the Grail is accomplished. When the boy, who carries the shrine of the Grail ahead of King Amfortas, has placed it on the tabernacle in the middle of the rotunda, an invisible wire

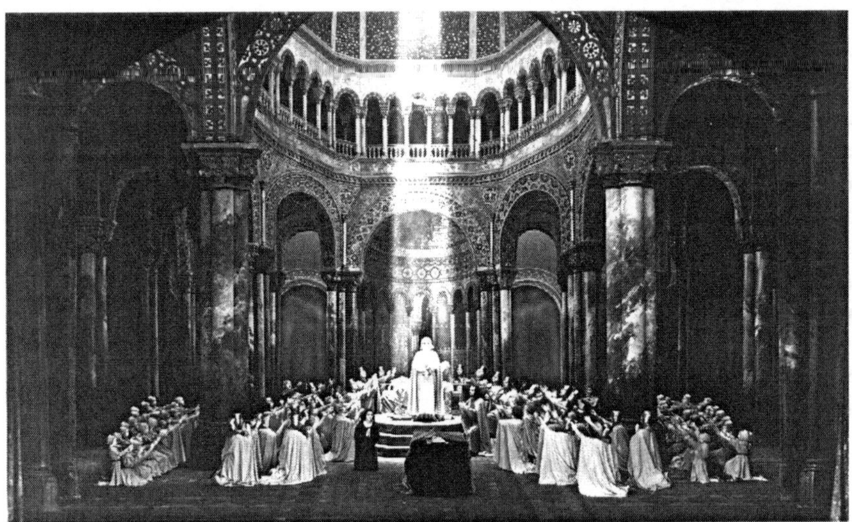

Figure 2.6 Parsifal, Act 3, Bayreuth, 1930 (staging from 1882 production).

connection is established that runs between a small Siemens electrical bulb inside the red chalice and a motor [i.e. a battery] inside the tabernacle. This connection is established by a man who has been placed next to the motor and who is also hidden behind the tabernacle. In this way, the previously dark chalice suddenly glows in a red light, while Amfortas in the first and Parsifal in the last act kneel to pray in front of the uncovered Grail. This incandescence continues when both take the goblet into their hands, raise it slowly, and gently sway it in all directions. The effect remains a wondrous one, even if the means by which it is accomplished are known.

(39)

Writing at a time when the use of electricity was still in its infancy (just a year previous, the Savoy Theatre in London was the first to be lit by electricity), these contemporary observers describe an effect at the cutting edge of stage technology. It is no accident that Wagner reserved the most technologically sophisticated effect of his career for this moment of incarnation. The presence of Christ in the Eucharist coincides with the presence of technology on the Bayreuth stage; indeed, the two share much in common, as both are invisible to the naked eye and yet are felt through their auratic effects. Both maintain a hidden, though real, presence.

In 1882, the year of *Parsifal's* premiere, electric bulbs were the revolution of stagecraft and the avant-garde of everyday life as well. Like will-o'-the-wisps, electric lights were appearing on city streets and in bourgeois homes, to widespread enchantment. Indeed, electricity had long been linked with the sacred in the Romantic imagination. A half-century earlier, in *Versuch einer Witterungslehre* (1825), Goethe had described electricity as a ubiquitous, invisible, and yet vital presence, "the pervading element that accompanies all material existence," and "the soul of the world" (333). Similarly, Novalis had seen in electricity a force that might transcend the boundary between living and dead matter, describing it as "internal light" and "the trace of sensation in the inorganic realm" (483). But these remarks were but premonitions of the cult that bloomed around 1880. Thomas Edison first unveiled the carbon filament lamp (precursor to the modern light bulb) to three thousand awe-struck spectators on New Year's Eve of 1879, then exhibited it to great acclaim at the Paris Electricity Exhibition in 1881, and subsequently at London's Crystal Palace. Electric lights were not only exhibited, they were also used to exhibit. Department-store owners were among the first to seize upon the use of electric lighting for the exhibition of commodities. Two years after the Electricity Exhibition, the Paris Magasin du Printemps installed electric lighting with great success, and was quickly followed by the majority of department stores. Émile Zola's description of the effect of electric lighting at his fictional Parisian department store in *The Ladies' Paradise* (1883) describes the fairytale effects – a Crystal Palace on every block! – such lighting produced.

> It was a white brightness of a blinding fixity, extending like the reverberation of a discolored star, killing the twilight. Then, when all were lighted, there was

a delighted murmur in the crowd, the great show of white goods assumed a fairy splendor beneath this new illumination. It seemed that this colossal orgy of white was also burning, itself becoming a light. The song of the white seemed to soar upward in the inflamed whiteness of an aurora.

(377)

Yet another contemporary vision of electric light transcendent may be seen in the title page of the journal *La Lumière Électrique*, from 1881 (Figure 2.7), which depicts once more a *Parsifal*-like apotheosis.

Electricity not only induced swoons, it cured them. The late nineteenth century was also the great age of electric panaceas. Numerous textbooks on medical electricity were published in the 1870s and 80s, opening up the field for the first time to a wide body of scholars.[21] "In the diagnosis and treatment of serious diseases," begins one popular handbook of the period, "no agent is more generally applicable than electricity" (Ranney 1). Medical batteries, electro-diagnosis, electro-therapeutics, electrolysis, galvano-cautery, electric shock treatment: a new

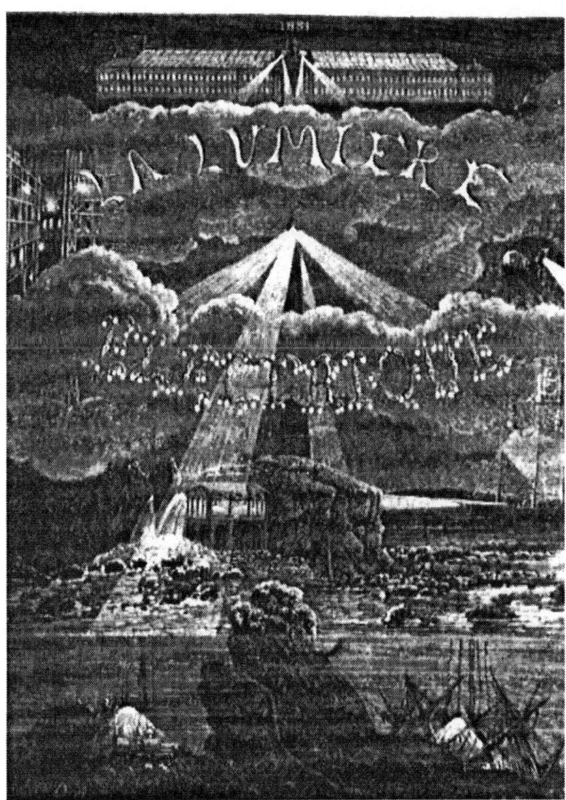

Figure 2.7 *La Lumière Électrique*, cover, 1881.

language was emerging, with remarkable quickness, to describe the curative potentials of electricity. As medicine went, so went commerce. In the name of health, anything (hats, girdles, bathtubs) that could be electrified was electrified. "In the present day," writes Dr G. V. Poore in 1876, "electricity, in its many forms, has again come into fashion, and constant and faradic currents, chain batteries and magnetic belts, are topics of conversation and articles of dress in boudoirs and clubs, as well as in the consulting room of the physician" (107). The curative effects of electricity could be found even in the field of agriculture, where the German scientist Alfred Ritter von Urbanitzky advocated "galvanizing" the land in order to increase crop yields (353). By the 1880s, electricity was widely seen as much more than a new technology: it was a magic and a balm, capable of restoring health to the body and fertility to the land.

This is not to say that *Parsifal* simply sings the body electric. But it is to say that the electric Grail unveilings were more than *coups de théâtre*. Rather, they were transfigurations of technology, transfigurations that unknowingly doubled the form of emergent consumer culture. In these Eucharistic moments, technology was not a mere rhetorical gesture to heighten the effect; in these moments, technology itself was the redeemer in need of redemption. In the Grail unveilings, technology was transformed from emblem of industrial capital into a magic elixir – "The wound," as Parsifal says, "can only be healed by the spear that caused it" (10:375). The irony here is that Wagner could not escape the discourse of commodity culture even when attacking it. For electricity *was* the magic of the *fin de siècle*, and commodity culture was already turning city streets and bourgeois drawing rooms into fairylands. This may have been Wagner's real worry, that industrial capitalism too had an enchanted garden, and that the distance between Klingsor's garden and Monsalvat might not, in the end, be so great.

Parsifal may be the first Eucharist of an emerging society of the spectacle, but it is also more than this: it is a glimpse of a society transformed by mechanized art into utopia. Many scholars have advocated a sharp distinction between Wagner's early music-dramas, which wave the crimson flag of revolt, and his later ones, shrouded in Schopenhauerian black.[22] And yet the later works are just as strongly utopian, in their own way, as were his earlier Zurich writings. With an important difference: impatient of revolution, Wagner at last declared totality, organic community, and real presence in the here and now of *Parsifal*. The transition from his Zurich writings to *Parsifal* therefore marks a transition from a *Gesamtkunstwerk* of hope to a *Gesamtkunstwerk* of presence. Wagner harnessed cutting-edge technology for his numinous stage effects, he conceived of the theatre as a factory, he pioneered the concealment of theatrical production – and he called the result Monsalvat. At the moment of its unveiling, Wagner refers to the Grail as a "crystal chalice" (*Kristallschale*). One wonders whether this chalice was not Wagner's answer to that other great festival space of the nineteenth century, his final retort to the glass palace that was Bayreuth's enemy, its antithesis, and its twin.

The iconic and the crystalline

Wagner's vision of the modern union of society and spectacle, technology and nature was just as totalizing as that of the Crystal Palace, but it flowed in precisely the opposite direction. At Bayreuth, unlike at the Crystal Palace, commerce, industry, and technology would be put to the service of a utopian vision, and yet secretly. For to expose the mechanistic underpinnings of the Wagnerian *Gesamtkunstwerk* would be to concede the incomplete and dependent nature of the supposedly autonomous totality. The stakes were always more than merely aesthetic. Insofar as the Festspielhaus sought to represent and forge the ideal social body, the exposure of the mechanistic process behind this production would mean the fragmentation of that same body, and the reemergence of all those social forces that Wagner sought to reconcile. To expose those forces would be to reopen the Pandora's box of modern culture, releasing once more the monsters of class, specialization, industry, alienation. If the Festspielhaus were to work, the lid of that box had to be kept tightly shut; or rather, it had to be opened in secret, in a darkened room. This is a form of the *Gesamtkunstwerk* we might call *iconic*: a totalizing performance machine that aims to hide the mechanisms of its own production through appeals to nature, to roots, to myth, to blood, to folk. The iconic *Gesamtkunstwerk* is light projected into darkness, is phantasmagoria.

Not so with the Crystal Palace – there the sun shone brilliantly through glass walls. There commodity culture and industrial power were celebrated at the same time as they were made the stuff of fairytale and fantasy. Again harmony with nature was a goal, but this time nature – in the form of ancient elms, tropical palms, exotic gardens – was harmonized with the machine exposed and the marketplace at dead center. The result was a mechanical, mercantile organism, a hybrid of living form, capital, and steel. While perhaps not quite a *Gesamtkunstwerk* itself (falling short of the hyper-controlled form characteristic of the tradition), the Crystal Palace was nevertheless the precursor to an alternate form of the total work of art. It anticipates a form of the *Gesamtkunstwerk* we might call *crystalline*: a totalizing performance that exposes and celebrates symbols of technology and mechanized production (e.g. hyper-rational organization, electronic media, glass-and-steel, gadgetry), while simultaneously hiding real labor beneath the veneer of a supposedly organic unity. The crystalline lies at the origin of the *Gesamtkunstwerk*, and will return throughout its history. Its first realization, as we shall see, lies with the Bauhaus "Theatre of Totality."

It is important to understand that both forms of the *Gesamtkunstwerk*, the iconic and the crystalline, are equally ideological, equally dependent upon the concealment of mechanical production so that the artwork as a whole may shine forth as a pseudo-organic synthesis and a totality. It is equally important to understand that each embodies a longing for human bonding amid alienation, for community recovered through mechanization and technology. The Festspielhaus and the Crystal Palace are two different sides of the same coin, the coin of industrial capital. And they are also two different sides of the same dream, the dream of mass utopia, mediated by the machine.

Chapter 3

Total machine
The Bauhaus theatre

> Today the arts exist in isolation, from which they can be rescued only through the conscious, cooperative effort of all craftsmen ... Let us then create a new guild of craftsmen without the class distinctions that raise an arrogant barrier between craftsman and artist! Together let us desire, conceive, and create the new structure of the future, which will embrace architecture and sculpture and painting in one unity and which will one day rise toward heaven from the hands of a million workers like the crystal symbol of a new faith.
>
> (Gropius, "Program of the Staatliche Bauhaus" 31)

Double evocation

Gropius founded the Bauhaus with a double evocation: an evocation at once of Bayreuth and the Crystal Palace. Accompanied by Lyonel Feininger's woodcut of a crystalline cathedral, Gropius' 1919 manifesto exhorted fellow artists to create a crystalline *Gesamtkunstwerk*, a grand union of art and technology that would restore the splintered whole of society. The vision was at once deeply indebted to German neo-Romanticism and openly celebratory of the revolutionary potential of industrialization. From the Festspielhaus, Gropius took a vision of a society redeemed by total art; from the Great Exhibitions, Gropius took an embrace of industrialization and an almost religious enthusiasm for the possibilities of mass production and mass man.

Where Paxton, Wagner, and Semper had been working between the dusk of the First Industrial Revolution and the dawn of the Second, attempting to incorporate effects they could only roughly comprehend and consequences they could only dimly anticipate, the Weimar/Dessau Bauhaus[1] operated between the dusk of the Second Industrial Revolution and the dawn of the revolution of electronic mass media. Germany had long lagged far behind France, and especially Britain, in industrial production, a historical discontinuity that goes a long way toward explaining Wagner's simultaneously utopian and dystopian, wonder-struck and panicked attitude toward industrialization and technology. From the standpoint of 1919, however, things looked very different. To begin with, Germany's industrial productivity had exploded after nationalization in 1870 and the acquisition of Lorraine in

1871. By the end of the century, Germany was already manufacturing more steel than Britain, and (with the aid of engineers such as Werner von Siemens and cartels such as IG Farben) led the world in electrical and chemical industries. While such industrial developments signaled a brave new world of mass mechanization, they also seemed to many a sign of something far darker, an end not only of community but of civilization itself.

The impact of World War I on Bauhaus ideas of totality can hardly be overstated. The mobilization of vast armies across endless battlefields, the entrenchment of millions along immobile fronts, the unprecedented massacres of massed men, the revolutionary industrialization in weapons manufacturing, the technological innovations of armaments, the use of new communications technologies, the great leap forward of what Eisenhower would come to call the "military-industrial complex": all of these combined to make the Great War into the common crucible of the modern mass. "Man, the individual, existing as a seemingly isolated being, independent (at least seemingly) of social connections, revolving egocentrically around the concept of the self, in fact lies buried beneath a marble slab inscribed 'The Unknown Soldier'": thus Erwin Piscator, looking back a decade after the Armistice (*Political* 186). The response, at least for the *Bauhäusler*, was the despair that gives birth to hope – if apocalypse had descended, millennium must follow. "This is more than just a lost war," wrote Gropius. "A world has come to an end. We must seek a radical solution to our problems" (*Scope* 19). The only radical solution was a total one, one in which sundered parts were integrated again – not, as *völkisch* Romantics would have it, through appeal to primordial sentiment, but through appeal to objective organizational and technological power. Not so much a recovery as a total reengineering of the real.

The Bauhaus theatre, like the work of the Bauhaus generally, was strongly shaped by the lineage of the total work of art, and more particularly by the crystalline *Gesamtkunstwerk*.[2] As with Gropius' inaugural manifesto, the Bauhaus attempted to transcend the opposition between mechanical and organic forms just as it attempted to synthesize Bayreuth and the Crystal Palace: an impossible paradox, but one the Bauhaus theatre struggled mightily to achieve in its fantasy of the "mechanical organism." Particularly in the work of Oskar Schlemmer and Laszlo Moholy-Nagy, the Bauhaus theatre attempted to restore to the mass its lost humanity, and to do so by means of mechanization rendered organic.

Gropius and the crystalline *Gesamtkunstwerk*

Gropius' evocation of the Crystal Palace in "Program of the Staatliche Bauhaus in Weimar" was a direct attack on German classical aesthetics. What Gropius advocated was an artwork that sought to expose the mechanical rather than burying it beneath the veneer of organicism, and thus sought also to expose artists, too, as workers. Or, more precisely, as unabashedly industrialized members of a working collective. And yet, while Gropius attacked classical aesthetics, he never quite cast it aside. On the contrary, he sought to restore a unified Aesthetic State that, in good Romantic style, he found in the mists of antiquity, particularly in the theatres of ancient Athens and the craft guilds of the European Middle Ages. In the 1919 manifesto "New Ideas on Architecture," Gropius writes that:

> [a]ll our works are nothing but splinters. Structures created by practical requirements and necessity do not satisfy the longing for a world of beauty built anew from the bottom up, for the rebirth of that spiritual unity which ascended to the miracle of the Gothic cathedrals.
>
> (Gropius/Taut/Behne 46)

For Gropius, the solution to the splintered soul of the modern world involved the creation of a school that had as its aim "the unified work of art" ("Program" 32) through "[t]he teaching of *organic design*" (24) married to systems of mechanical reproduction. The Bauhaus would be a place where the organic and the mechanical could be rejoined, or, more precisely, where mechanics could be made organic and rendered a crystalline *Gesamtkunstwerk*. By so doing, the artist would not oppose the machine but "overcome its demon" ("Viability" 52) and thereby put mechanics in the service of building the "cathedral of the future." "Art and technology, a new unity!" he declares in 1924. "Technology does not need art, but art very much needs technology" ("Breviary" 76). Though he points back to the Gothic cathedrals as the source of "spiritual unity," Gropius' metaphors indicate a more historically proximate source for the Bauhaus in Bayreuth and the Crystal Palace.

Revolution, of course, demands revolutionary organization, and, in an address to Bauhaus students in 1919, Gropius argues against "large spiritual organizations," advocating instead a set of "small, secret, self-contained societies, lodges" (36). The cultishness of this vision recalls, once more, the cultishness of the *Gesamtkunstwerk* as imagined by the Bayreuth circle; it is a connection Gropius expands upon as his address continues.

> Conspiracies will form which will want to watch over and artistically shape a secret, a nucleus of belief, until from the individual groups a universally great, enduring spiritual-religious idea will rise again, which finally must find its crystalline expression in a great *Gesamtkunstwerk*. And this great total artwork [*Kunstwerk der Gesamtheit*], this cathedral of the future, will then shine with its abundance of light into the smallest objects of everyday life … We artists therefore need the community of spirit of the entire people as much as we need bread. If the signs are correct, then the first indications of a new unity which will follow the chaos are already to be seen.

While beginning in small, cultish circles, the spiritual source and the ultimate aim of this "*Kunstwerk der Gesamtheit*" is the "community of spirit of the entire people." "New, spiritually still untapped strata of the *Volk* are forcing their way up from the depths," writes Gropius for the *Deutscher Revolutions Almanach* in 1919:

Their fresher, undulled instincts are still rooted in nature. It is to them that the future artist will turn, to the original serene soul of the people, which is not afraid of color, the shimmer of gold, sweetness, of finding childlike joy in beauty.

("Baukunst" 314)

While Gropius' founding Bauhaus manifesto of 1919 does not mention the theatre as one of the elements of the "crystal symbol of a new faith," by 1921 Gropius was designing his *Totaltheater*, and by 1922 was declaring "*Bau und Bühne*" ("Building and Stage") the central elements of the Bauhaus. The importance of the theatre as a site for the realization of the total work of art is even attested to by Bauhaus artists who rarely associated with the stage. Wassily Kandinsky, for instance, argues in a 1912 issue of *Der blaue Reiter* that "the gravitational force of the theatre" is uniquely capable of uniting all abstract or pure artistic elements (113). Andreas Weininger envisions a "Spherical Theater" that would unite "all primary media: space, body, line, point, color, light; sound, noise; in a new mechanical synthesis" (89). And Heinz Loew advocates a "Mechanical Stage" that would "bring the apparatus into view in its peculiar and novel beauty, undisguised and as an end in itself" (84). While Gropius' commitment to architecture is well known, less so is Gropius' association of architecture with theatre. In "The Idea and Formation of the State Bauhaus," written on the occasion of the first Bauhaus exhibit in 1923, Gropius argues for the essential relation of the two disciplines of architecture and theatre.

> The work of the stage, as an orchestral unity, is inherently related to architecture; both receive and give to each other mutually. Just as, in the work of building, all members leave their own ego behind in favor of a higher mutual liveliness of the total work of art [*Gesamtwerk*], so too, in the work of the stage, do a variety of artistic problems come together according to this transcending law, to a new, greater unity.
>
> (17)

This "greater unity" of the stage, Gropius writes elsewhere at roughly the same time, finds its "origin" in "an ardent religious desire of the human soul" and "serves … to manifest a transcendent idea" ("Work" 58). Theatre, as much as architecture, could be a grand unifier of all the arts.

Gropius' own involvement with theatre began in 1921, when he designed (together with Adolph Meyer) an extensive renovation and remodeling of the Jena Municipal Theatre. But his most audacious plan was for the so-called "Synthetic '*Totaltheater*'," designed for Erwin Piscator in 1926, though never built.[3] Gropius' design was strongly influenced by such monumental theatres as Georg Fuchs' Munich Art Theatre and Max Reinhardt's Grosses Schauspielhaus, two innovative buildings that were themselves influenced by Wagner's Festspielhaus. Fuchs'

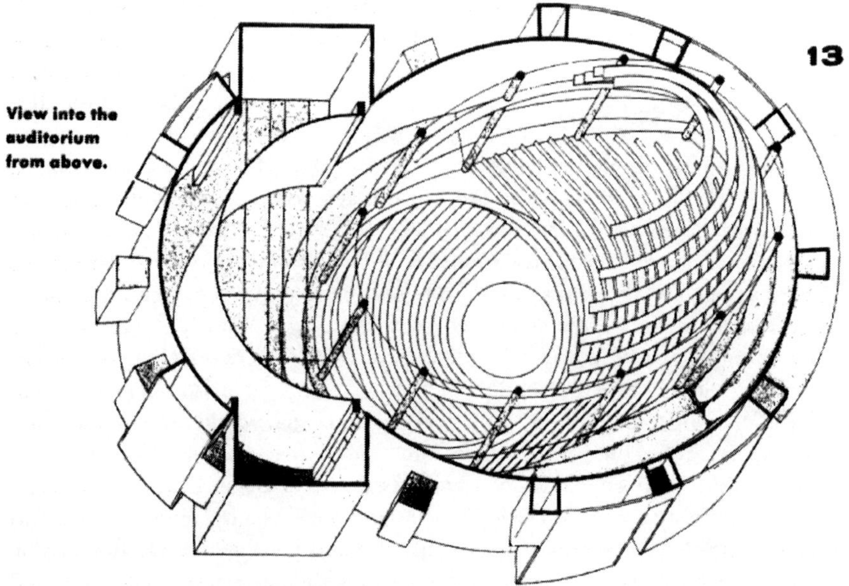

Figure 3.1 Gropius's *Totaltheater* design, 1926.

theatre, which opened in 1907, was a realization of the German critic's call to "re-theatricalize" the arts by uniting them in a revolutionary "theatre of the future." The space featured a sunken orchestra pit and an auditorium much like that of Wagner's Festspielhaus, but then carried Wagner's enthusiasm for pioneering stage effects to a new height, adding an adjustable proscenium, a stage floor divided into sections and mounted on separate elevators, and four colored electric cycloramas at the back wall. Reinhardt's Grosses Schauspielhaus, which opened in 1919, continued this expansion of the Bayreuth idea by combining sophisticated stage mechanics (including an enormous revolving stage) with a gargantuan auditorium (allowing for more than 3500 spectators), and putting them all in the service of Reinhardt's explicitly Wagnerian vision of artistic unification and quasi-religious performance. (With telling irony, the Nazis would continue to utilize the theatre through their "Strength through Joy" program, renaming Reinhardt's creation "Theater des Volkes.")

Borrowing from these forerunners, Gropius imagined a *Totaltheater* that would seat 2000, with mobile platforms that would allow for the theatre space to transform into a wide variety of forms (Figure 3.1). The result would be a recovery of the organic, participatory drama of ancient Greece, a recovery made possible through a heavy reliance on cutting-edge mechanics. "Film projectors," writes Gropius, "were located all round the sides of the theatre, some pointing at the room, so that scenery could be created behind and above the spectators as well, thus giving them the illusion of being totally involved in the drama" ("Erwin" 35).[4] "The reality to which the theatre now aspired," adds Piscator, "was now total instead of fragmentary" ("Theatre of Totality" 64). Such an all-consuming mass theatre, with spotlights and film projectors running alongside rotating platforms and live spectacles, suggests less a unification of the sister arts than a totalization of media space. Piscator insisted that the goal of this totalization was still representation, "a stage-rendering of the totality of the world" (66). And yet, had such a kaleidoscopic multimedia environment ever been completed, it might well have ceded "stage-rendering" to pure media effects, as these were the fundamental stage actions around which the *Totaltheater* was built. Absorption in artistic representation might have given way to absorption in media as media, in light as light, in space as space.

Indeed, as with architecture, the essence of theatre for Gropius lay in space *qua* space, and in the abstract visual and acoustic movements that it encompasses. In his article on "The Work of the Bauhaus Stage," for instance, Gropius writes that:

> The power of [theatre's] effect on the soul of the spectator and auditor is ... dependent on the success of the transformation of the idea into (visually and acoustically) perceivable space. The phenomenon of space is conditioned by finite limitation within infinite free space, by the movement of mechanical and organic bodies within this limited space, and by the oscillations of light and sounds within it.
>
> (58)

If, as Marx argued, capitalism annihilates space through time, then Gropius' ideal stage, like Wagner's, would reverse the process, returning time to space. In this sense, Gropius' insistence on the sacral function of the stage is entirely correct, but not, as Gropius argues, because of theatre's supposed "origin" as "a show for the gods" ("Work" 58). The Bauhaus stage was sacred for much the same reason that Wagner's Festspielhaus was sacred, because of its claim to replace the diachrony of the modern world with the spatial synchrony of the unified work. And yet there are two critical differences between the two projects. The first is that the transition from arts to media, already begun at Bayreuth, is carried through to a much fuller degree in Gropius' vision. The second is that, where Wagner imagined that mechanical bodies would be utterly subordinated to organic totality, Gropius' ideal stage included the movement of mechanical bodies alongside organic ones. On Gropius' crystalline stage, at least in theory, the mechanical would not be submerged beneath the organic.

Schlemmer, Moholy-Nagy, and the organic-mechanical stage

While Gropius' designs for the *Totaltheater* and his championing of "*Bühne und Bau*" ("Stage and Building") in the 1920s were both important for the development of the Bauhaus stage, the Bauhaus artists most involved in the theatre were Oskar Schlemmer and Laszlo Moholy-Nagy. In addition to being attracted to ideas of aesthetic unification and utopian performance, both Schlemmer and Moholy-Nagy embraced a narrative of the fragmentation of modern society by means of commerce and industry, a narrative inherited from the Romantic tradition from Schiller on through Wagner.[5] In *The New Vision* (1928), Moholy-Nagy argues that "[o]ur modern system of production is imposed labor, a senseless pursuit, and, in its social aspects, without plan; its motive is to squeeze our profits to the limit" (15). The alienating conditions of industry have spread so widely throughout society that "not only the working class finds itself in this [tragic] position today; all those caught within the mechanism ... are basically badly off. At best the differences are material ones" ("Education and the Bauhaus" 164). In 1925, Schlemmer laments the fact that:

> [t]his materialistic and practical age has in fact lost the genuine feeling for play and for the miraculous. Utilitarianism has gone a long way in killing it. Amazed at the flood of technological advance, we accept these wonders of utility as being an already perfected art form, while actually they are only prerequisites for its creation.
>
> ("Man" 30–1)

The argument is a familiar one, related to the argument that reason, taken to its furthest point, will provide a way back to the paradise of the Aesthetic State, a theme repeated with variations by Wagner. In a quasi-Futurist mood, Schlemmer celebrates the infinite potential of modernity: "death to the past, to moonlight, and to the soul, thus the present time strides along with the gestures of a conqueror. Reason and science, 'man's greatest powers,' are the regents, and the engineer is the sedate executor of unlimited possibilities" ("Staatliche" 65). "The flood of technological advance" and the "wonders of utility," he writes elsewhere, are in fact "prerequisites for [the] creation" of a "perfected art form" (*Briefe* 31). Moholy-Nagy argues along similar lines, crying "[w]e need Utopians of genius, a new Jules Verne" (*New Vision* 18). The new arts are "not against technological progress but with it," and the path to utopia "lies accordingly not in working against technical advance, but in exploiting it for the benefit of all." "Through technique," he concludes, "man can be freed" ("Education and the Bauhaus" 116). Echoing Schlemmer's almost mystical embrace of mechanics, Moholy-Nagy adds that "this reality of our century is technology – the invention, construction and maintenance of the machine. To be a user of machines is to be of the spirit of this century. It has replaced the transcendental spiritualism of past eras" ("Constructivism and the Proletariat" 185). Or, as Schlemmer expresses it in a passage to be discussed in more detail later, "calculation seizes the transcendent world" ("Staatliche" 66).

For Schlemmer in 1925, the theatre is "an organic link in the total chain of Bauhaus activity" and a "union of the most heterogeneous elements" ("Theater" 81). The theatre, then, is an organic part of the larger organic whole of the Bauhaus arts, and also contains within itself a unified synthesis of separate parts. Moreover, the Bauhaus stage derived its importance from its *aesthetic educational* function, in the Schillerian sense of the phrase. "From the first day of its existence," writes Schlemmer,

> the Bauhaus sensed the impulse for creative theatre; and from that first day the play instinct [*Spieltrieb*] was present. The play instinct, which Schiller in his wonderful and enduring *Letters on the Aesthetic Education of Man* calls the source of man's real creative values … was especially strong at the beginning … of the Bauhaus.
>
> (82)

In defining the stage's importance for the Bauhaus, Schlemmer draws not only from Schiller's notion of the *Spieltrieb*, but also from his notion of theatrical pedagogy. The stage, argues Schlemmer, "should practice 'enchanting pedagogy' and become a Schillerian tribunal … A stage thought of in this fashion could become a powerful regulator at the Bauhaus" (*Briefe* 195). The theatre, for Schlemmer, thus has the "purely" aesthetic function of reviving the play instinct and the pedagogical function of serving as a tribunal and an extension of the classroom. Like Schiller and Wagner, Schlemmer wants the theatre to be simultaneously purposeless and purposeful, an end in itself and a means to that end.

Perhaps the most influential theoretical work of the Bauhaus theatre was Schlemmer's essay "Man and Art Figure," published as part of the anthology *The Theater of the Bauhaus* (*Bühne im Bauhaus*, 1925), edited by Gropius.[6] "Man and Art Figure" develops a complex notion of the relationship between the body and abstraction, mechanism and organism. At the beginning of the essay, Schlemmer identifies mechanization as one of the "emblems" of our time, and describes it as an "inexorable process which now lays claim to every sphere of life and art. Everything which can be mechanized *is* mechanized" (17). The consequence of this universal mechanization is the discovery of mechanization's other, the essentially un-mechanizable. "The result: our recognition of that which can *not* be mechanized" (17). If the process of "inexorable" mechanization is a sort of common crucible into which "every sphere of life" is thrown, then the value of the process lies in what the fire leaves behind: the golden core of existence, the kernel that constitutes, for Schlemmer, the essentially human. The laws that govern this "organic man," writes Schlemmer, "reside in the invisible functions of his inner self: heartbeat, circulation, respiration, the activities of the brain and the nervous system" (25). In other words, the last remnant of "organic man" (25) lies in the materiality of the body. It is not, after all, the *explicit* body that Schlemmer celebrates but rather the *hidden* body, "the invisible functions of the inner self," an amalgam of all the corporeal processes that exist unseen. In the invisible functions of the body, Schlemmer hopes to find a last refuge in the face of universal mechanization.

As Schlemmer's illustrations reveal, the body – whether visible or invisible – is always in danger of being overwhelmed by the geometric space that surrounds it.

The illustrations that accompany Schlemmer's article are revealing in this regard. Figure 3.2, for instance, supposedly demonstrates how the laws of cubical space correspond "to the inherent mathematic of the human body" (23), but in fact it shows little of the sort: the geometric lines Schlemmer sketches here correspond only to the dimensions of the rectangular space in which the human body is placed. Similar features may be found in Schlemmer's costumes, such as the two which aim to show "the functional laws of the human body in their relationship to space" (26) (Figure 3.3) and "the laws of the human body in space" (27) (Figure 3.4), but which would seem to demonstrate more convincingly the subordination of the human body to abstract geometry. The sheer weight and restraining qualities of these costumes, as well as the precision with which Schlemmer's dances are meant to be performed, follow logically from such theoretical conceptions, as does Schlemmer's embrace of Kleist's "*Marionettentheater*" essay. Schlemmer's construction of stage space also follows logically from such conceptions. In his essay "Theater," also printed in *The Theater of the Bauhaus*, Schlemmer describes his technique of stretching "taut wires" across the corners of the "cubical space" of the stage (92). "By adding as many such aerials as we wish," he argues, "we can create a spatial-linear web which will have a decisive influence on the man who moves about within it" (92). As a result of this rigorous geometric subdivision of the stage, the actor becomes "space-bewitched" ("*raumbehext*"), and thus further rendered a human puppet. "The endeavor to free man from his physical bondage and to heighten his freedom of movement beyond his native potential," writes Schlemmer in "Man and Art Figure," "resulted in substituting for the organism the mechanical

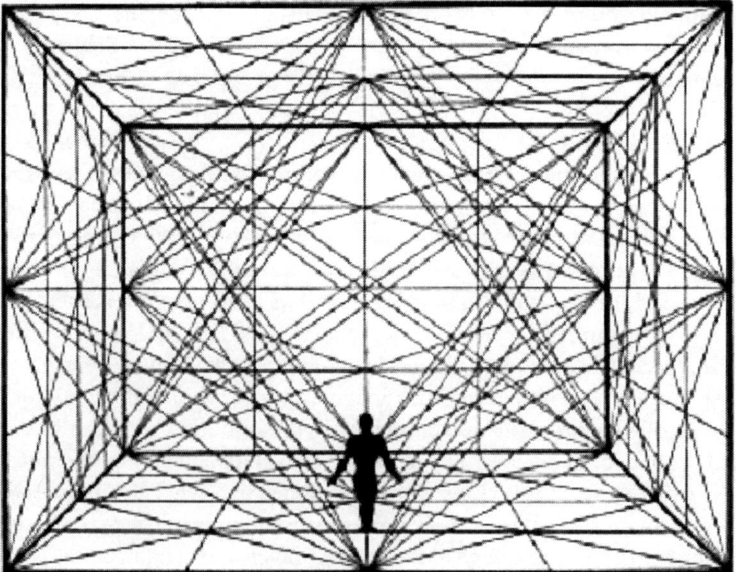

Figure 3.2 Schlemmer's "abstract stage," 1924.

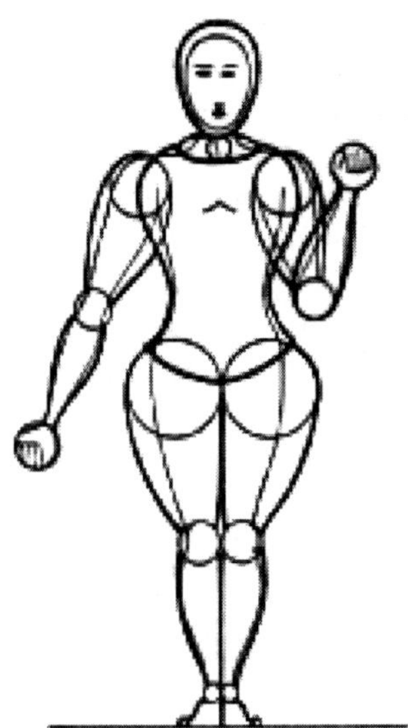

Figure 3.3 Schlemmer's "marionette," 1924.

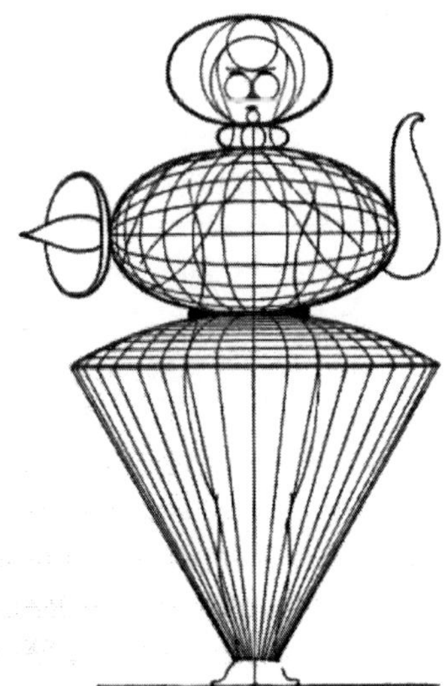

Figure 3.4 Schlemmer's "technical organism," 1924.

human figure: *the automaton and the marionette*" (28). In a peculiar twist of logic, humanity's liberation comes in the form of its elimination, or more precisely in the form of its replacement by the puppet-machine.

Puppets and automata dominate Schlemmer's theatrical imagination. The best-known example is *The Triadic Ballet* (*Das triadische Ballet,* 1922), Schlemmer's most frequently performed theatrical work. The dance is an "apotheosis of the number three" ("Neue" 1068), consisting of three parts, each with its own color scheme (yellow, pink, black), geometric form (square, circle, triangle), and mood (comic-burlesque, festive-solemn, fantastic-transcendental). Schlemmer costumed the dancers to resemble wooden dolls, robots, machine tools, spools, tops, abstract geometric forms, or some combination of all of the above. Their movements are precise and severely restricted (figures trace movements on a grid, a woman in a spiral costume spirals across the floor), though occasionally more humorous combinations appear (a woman in a dress of colored balls dances stiff flamenco steps, a man costumed to recall a jester leaps like a marionette). In the years following the work's premiere, several dance critics expressed concerns about the loss of the human dancer in the face of abstract geometry. The "danger" of *The Triadic Ballet*, according to Ernst Kállai in 1931, was that "the dancer might become merely a puppet completely subordinated to the mechanics of space" (17). Lincoln Kirstein, similarly, wrote that "the work is significant as a now familiar statement of dehumanization, with bankrupt choreography replaced by costume as décor" (214). And yet, despite the precision and restraint of these dances, a certain tension – perhaps unintentional – is maintained between the human body and the demands of automation. The dances fascinate in part because the dancers are *not* marionettes or robots, so the thrill of mimesis as well as technical mastery is continually present. Moreover, the dancers' costumes, made of padded cloth and papier-mâché, succeed only partly in transforming the human body into a mechanical figure; in performance, the papier-mâché shows imperfections and tears, the paint shows cracks, and the padded cloth develops wrinkles along the joints.[7] Tellingly, in a recent production of *The Triadic Ballet*, plastic was substituted for papier-mâché in many of the costumes, giving the dancers a sleeker and more mechanical appearance. When certain original materials (e.g. padded cloth and paint) were used, however, the dancers' bodies emerged more clearly, and a greater tension between the dancers' bodies and the *Übermarionette* ideal resulted. Inevitably, the human body emerges through cracks in the *Kunstfigur*.

Other works by Schlemmer celebrate the automaton with less ambiguity. The "monumental figures" of *The Two Solemn Tragedians* (*Die beiden Pathetiker*), for example, tower above their human counterparts, make "sparse and significant gestures," and speak to orchestral accompaniment through megaphones ("Man" 30). The twin figures look like combinations of pillars, marionettes, and robots (Figure 3.5), and are intended to be "personifications of lofty concepts such as Power and Courage, Truth and Beauty, Law and Freedom" (30). And yet the expression of such transcendent human principles comes not from the human figures below, but from the giant automata who personify their higher selves. It is only a step from this vision of machine-gods to Schlemmer's vision of "the absolute stage" in "Man and Art Figure."

> The stage as the arena for successive and transient action, however, offers form and color in motion, in the first instance in their primary aspect as

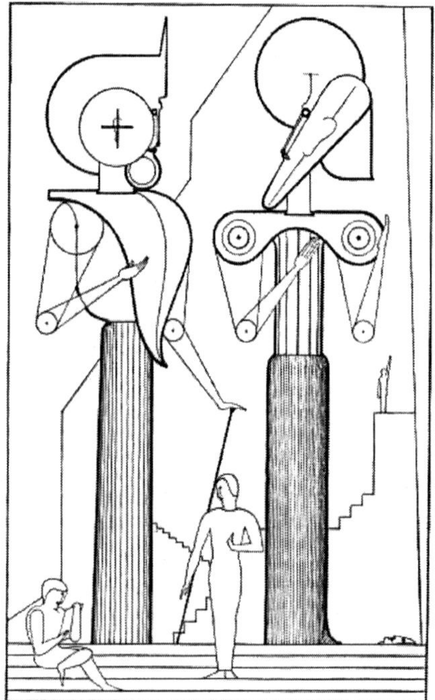

Figure 3.5 Schlemmer's "solemn tragedians," 1924.

separate and individual mobile, uncolored, linear, flat, or plastic forms, but furthermore as fluctuating, mobile space and as transformable architectonic structures. Such kaleidoscopic play, at once infinitely variable and strictly organized, would constitute – theoretically – the *absolute* visual stage [*Schaubühne*]. Man, the animated being, would be banned from this mechanistic organism. He would stand as the "perfect engineer" at the central switchboard, from where he would direct a feast for the eyes.

(22)

Having failed to preserve any trace of the organic body, Schlemmer here dubs the machine itself organic, and bans humanity from the resulting *"Organismus der Mechanik."* As total machine and total organism, Schlemmer's absolute stage is at once externally produced and *sui generis*, simultaneously artifice and nature. Such a perfect synthesis (which suggests, as Schlemmer rightly claims, utopia) must exclude the human, which stands outside it now as a marginal and alien element, at once engineer and waste product.[8]

If anything, Moholy-Nagy advances the notion of theatre as mechanical organism with even greater enthusiasm than Schlemmer. Much like Schlemmer, Moholy-Nagy calls for the replacement of human actors by "equipment … which

is far more capable of executing the *purely mechanical* role of man than man himself"
("Theater" 60). He goes beyond Schlemmer, however, in seeking the total elimination of both representational and causal elements from the Bauhaus stage. In a
radicalization of Gropius' emphasis on the kinetic energies of theatrical "space,"
Moholy-Nagy seeks to transform the stage into an utterly nonrepresentational,
synchronic totality of irreducible media. Moholy-Nagy's stage will forge its unity
through "SIMULTANEOUS, SYNOPTICAL, and SYNACOUSTICAL repro-
duction of thought (with motion pictures, phonographs, loud-speakers), or from
the reproduction of thoughts suggested by a construction of variously MESHING
GEARS" ("Theater" 62). This "TOTAL STAGE ACTION" is to be "a great
dynamic-rhythmic process, which can compress the greatest clashing masses or
accumulations of media – as qualitative and quantitative tensions – into elemental
form" (64). As Moholy-Nagy's language in these passages is intentionally bewildering, it needs a certain degree of attention, particularly as he appears to be
speaking of media in two significantly different ways. In the first passage he
associates media with "reproduction," while in the second he associates it with
"elemental form." Taken together, these two passages suggest that the function of
the total theatre is to "compress" a great variety of (reproductive, mechanical)
media together into a new (elemental, organic) whole. By this means, concludes
Moholy-Nagy, "[t]here will arise an enhanced control over all formative media,
unified in a harmonious effect and built into an organism of perfect equilibrium"
(70). Like Schlemmer, Moholy-Nagy ultimately describes his "Theatre of Totality"
as a sort of mechanical organism, a work at once produced and uncreated.

Moholy-Nagy elaborates on this point when he calls for the marginalization of
causality and "meaning" in the "Theatre of Totality" section of "Theatre, Circus,
Variety." "In the plan of such a theatre," he writes,

> the traditionally "meaningful" and causal interconnections can NOT play the
> major role. In the consideration of stage setting as an *art-form*, we must learn
> from the creative artist that, just as it is impossible to ask what a man (as
> organism) is or stands for, it is inadmissible to ask the same question of a
> contemporary nonobjective picture which likewise is a *Gestaltung*, that is, an
> organism.
>
> In the same way [as a painting], the Theatre of Totality with its multi-
> farious complexities of light, space, plane, form, motion, sound, man – and
> with all the possibilities for varying and combining these elements – must be
> an ORGANISM.
>
> (58–60)

Moholy-Nagy's insistence on the fact that the "Theatre of Totality" is an organism
(the point is emphasized throughout his essay) is more or less predictable given the
dialectic of the total work of art sketched so far. So too is the fact that his insistence
on organicism should become more shrill (note the use of capital letters for
"ORGANISM") as the stage-space becomes more emphatically mechanical.

Architectural historian Manfredo Tafuri has argued that Moholy-Nagy's theatre "no longer has anything in common with Wagner's *Gesamtkunstwerk*," because Moholy-Nagy, unlike Wagner, "relies on the primary means of the various instruments of communication" (104). In other words, Moholy-Nagy (and, one might suppose, Schlemmer) imagines a theatre *about* the medium of the theatre, broken down to its "primary means"; a theatre where the media are the message. There is much to be said for Tafuri's position here. For Moholy-Nagy and Schlemmer both envision theatres in which such primary elements as "light, space, plane, form, motion, sound" are (in theory at least) removed from any system of representation and made to function instead as both media and content. Here, one might imagine, is the birth of a vision of theatre removed from signification, narrative, and mimesis. Here, one might further imagine, is the birth of a tradition that represents a radical break with such representational art-forms as Wagner's music-dramas, and that will eventually lead to the work of such nonrepresentational theatre artists as Robert Wilson and Pina Bausch.[9] One might even view such Bauhaus performances as a forerunner of such multimedia extravaganzas as Andy Warhol's *Exploding Plastic Inevitable* some years later. In such crystalline *Gesamtkunstwerke*, as we shall see when we turn to Warhol in Chapter 7, the symbols of production (lights, camera, action) are put on center stage, put on sale, and made to dance. Bayreuth, it seems, has been left far behind.

Or perhaps not so far behind after all. Even if one sets aside the numerous aesthetic elements that Moholy-Nagy's "Theatre of Totality" and Wagner's *Gesamtkunstwerk* share (organic unity, all-consuming spectacle, breakdown of divisions between spectator and spectacle, reliance on technology, utopian aspirations, etc.) and takes up merely the point of difference Tafuri raises, a certain commonality nevertheless remains. While the emphasis on the "elemental forms" of media in Moholy-Nagy's theatre goes beyond anything in Wagner's work, this emphasis nevertheless finds a precursor in Wagner. As we saw in the last chapter, Wagner's *Gesamtkunstwerke* were revolutionary in part because of their attention to media *as media*. While Kittler has somewhat overstated the case, he is correct in finding that Wagner's compositions already prefigured an avant-garde (and, later, rock) interest in primary media such as sound and breath. In other words, the *Gesamtkunstwerk* was only partially about art-forms even from its origin – even in Wagner, the *Gesamtkunstwerk* was at least in part a matter of unified *media*. But it was left to Schlemmer and Moholy-Nagy to bring this to the fore, to move even more sharply away from the discourse of artistic representation and towards a discourse of media performance. In terms of reliance upon primary means of instruments of communication, and therefore in terms of a shift toward media performance, the difference between Wagner and the Bauhaus theatre is one of degree rather than one of kind. The *Gesamtkunstwerk*, in other words, has never been entirely about the "sister arts," not even from its inception; it has also been about multimedia.

Again, as with Wagner's music-dramas, we ought to acknowledge the importance of the shift to media technology while avoiding the conclusion that media ought to be viewed with Siegfried-like naïveté. While Moholy-Nagy's insistence on the organic nature of the "Theatre of Totality" reflects a compensatory reaction to the increasingly mechanical nature of his theatre, or, more strongly, an attempt to reach edenic wholeness by pushing civilization to its furthest limit, his insistence on the nonrepresentational, media-is-message character of his theatre is a reaction of a different sort. Moholy-Nagy wants us not to inquire into what his "accumulations of media" represent. But the claim that it is "impossible to ask" what the Theatre of Totality "stands for" buries the fact that his theatre does in fact stand for and reflect something, namely the visual codes of Weimar-era urban culture. Though the relationship between the 1920s Bauhaus and mechanical reproduction was generally explicit and affirmative, the relationship between the Bauhaus and commercial culture was highly ambiguous and largely hidden.

Total theatre or total decoration?

With its frequent emphasis on mechanization, totalization, immersion, and control, and its myth of restoration of long-lost unities (whether Greek or medieval) for modern "mass man," the Bauhaus theatre of the 1920s was not entirely divorced from the spirit that gave rise to totalitarianism.[10] Yet the importance of the connection ought not to lead us to ignore another: that between the Bauhaus theatre and commodity culture. To be sure, Nazi spectacle was always bound up with commercial spectacle.[11] And yet the two forms of spectacle remain fundamentally distinct – commercial spectacle thrived, after all, in Weimar Germany to a greater degree than in the Third Reich – and the mutual embrace of the Bauhaus and commodity culture was one of the reasons the school could be successfully transplanted to American soil. Witnesses to the rapid commercialization of the postwar period, *Bauhäusler* such as Moholy-Nagy and Schlemmer shared with many Europeans of the period a sense of terror and fascination in the face of capital.

A representative document of this mood is "The State Bauhaus in Weimar," a comprehensive manifesto composed by Schlemmer for the First Bauhaus Exhibition in Weimar in 1923. This text is often cited because it contains the phrase "cathedral of socialism," which forced it to be withdrawn from distribution, but the real peculiarity of this text lies elsewhere, in a passage somewhat farther on. In this later passage, in apparent contradiction to his "cathedral of socialism" remark, Schlemmer embarks on an extraordinarily breathless hymn to the power of industrialized commerce.

> Mathematics, structure, and mechanization are the elements, and power and money are the dictators of these modern phenomena of steel, concrete, glass, and electricity. Velocity of rigid matter, dematerialization of matter, organization of inorganic matter, all these produce the miracle of abstraction. Based on the laws of nature, these are the achievements of mind in the conquest of nature, based on the power of capital, the work of man against man. The speed and supertension of commercialism make expediency and utility the measure of all effectiveness, and calculation seizes the transcendent world: art

becomes a logarithm. It, long bereft of its name, lives a life after death, in the monument of the cube and in the colored square. Religion is the precise process of thinking, and God is dead.

(65–6)

Schlemmer's analogy – *equivalence* would perhaps be more precise – between cognition, capital, religion, and art, must be seen in the light of the deep ties forged between the Bauhaus and German industrialists, ties actively fostered by Walter Gropius, as well as the commodification, actively sought or not, of the Bauhaus style by the world of Weimar fashion. Perhaps "commodification" really is the wrong word for the commercial uses of Bauhaus creations: *Aufhebung* might be more correct. For, as Schlemmer's text indicates, art in the modern age truly becomes realized only when it enters the "supertension of commercialism," when it is married to "the power of capital."

Schlemmer's conception of the relationship between mechanization, capital, and art is further illuminated by journal notes from roughly the same period. In a journal entry from April 1926, Schlemmer writes:

> No wailing about mechanization, but rather joy about precision!
>
> The artists are ready to transform [*ummünzen*] the dark sides and danger of their mechanical age into the bright side of exact metaphysics. If the artists of today love machines and technology and organization, if they want precision instead of vague and blurry things, so the instinctive salvation from chaos and the yearning for the form of our age is to pour new wine into old skins: to formulate the impulses of the present and of contemporary people to give them a form that is unprecedented and unique.

(*Briefe* 199)

As in "The State Bauhaus," we find here Schlemmer's extraordinary enthusiasm for modern "precision," accompanied by the suggestion that art now finds its proper place amid "machines and technology." But there is also a distinction drawn between the "bright side" of modernity and its "shadow side," wherein the "danger" of the mechanical age lies. The artist serves, here, as a sort of purifying conduit between these two sides, in which the darkness of mechanics is turned into the brightness of "exact metaphysics." More precisely, the artist serves as a money changer: Schlemmer's word for the artist's function is "*ummünzen*," literally "to re-mint." Schlemmer suggests that the purification of the modern world through art is a commercial and a mechanical transaction, a business, in the end, of coinage.

In an essay on Bauhaus education, Moholy-Nagy associates the commercial world more specifically with the world of the Bauhaus stage. Explaining the various workshops of the school, he describes a "third workshop, devoted to the commercial arts." This third workshop, almost certainly inspired by the Great Exhibitions, focuses on:

> [p]lanning fairs, exposition architecture, window display, *and that which is the basis of them all, stage design.* Here again, we develop a new system. Our approach to the theater differs from that of the academic designer. We conceive the stage as an active principle, including and giving form to all human expression: something far more complete than verbal communication can ever be. Using the stage as a laboratory, we work out a means of expression and communication on all possible media: sound, word, color, form, movement and gesture. Here men must return to that earlier stage when their emotional powers, combined with intellectual powers, were more significant in their lives. This will not only rejuvenate their own ideas about the theater, but will serve to create a new radiance and bring back freshness of contact with the public, which the stage has lost.
>
> ("Why" 17; italics added)

The association between the commercial arts ("fairs, exhibition architecture, window display") and the Bauhaus theatre ("communication on all possible media: sound, word, color, form, movement and gesture") is expressed here as a base–superstructure relationship, where the latter serves as the base for the former. The new stage – and, by implication, the new commercial arts that are its superstructure – will return people to an "earlier stage" of being, when emotional faculties were still significant and harmonized with the intellect, and when "freshness of contact with the public" still existed. The Bauhaus artists were of course not alone in their awareness of the connections between the theatre and the emerging world of consumer culture: shop-window designers were often aware of it as well. The designer Herbert N. Casson, for example, writes in 1930 that:

> [w]e are coming now to the apex of technique in the new art of the shop window, [which is] to exhibit in a shop window a scene in which the merchandise appears more or less like an actor in a play. If we want to create a picture-effect, we must bear in mind the theatre as our ideal. Theatre people understand how to arrange people and things effectively, how to form picture-effects impressively. Salespeople do not understand it. For this reason the salesman must, in the matter of his shop window, stick closely to the theatre-space.
>
> (14)

The socialism of Moholy-Nagy, like that of Schlemmer, was always an ambiguous affair, reflecting in its convolutions the uncomfortable relationship of the avant-garde with the capitalist culture from which it first arose and to which it ultimately returned.

In fact, the worlds of the Bauhaus and Weimar-era commodity culture are even more difficult to separate, for the relationship between them ran in both directions: the commercial world increasingly bought, borrowed, and stole from the Bauhaus in the mid-to late 1920s and beyond. While such commercial use was always part of the intent of many Bauhaus artists, the use became increasingly divorced from any corresponding utopian dream (socialist or otherwise) for the transformation of society through the elimination of the distinction between daily life and the institution of art.[12] In part, the acceleration of the commercial uses of Bauhaus style was due to a change in Gropius' management of the school. Starting in 1922, Gropius initiated a series of measures to achieve some sort of financial independence for the Bauhaus, which was always poorly funded by the state.[13] Gropius hoped that through the sale of its workshop products as well as collaboration with German industry, the school would be able to raise enough money to be able to support itself on a semi-independent basis.[14] The strategy eventually proved a success, with the "Bauhaus style" recognized by German industry as a marketable image, and royalties from mass-produced prototypes providing an ongoing subsidy for the support of the school (Gropius, *New* 95). Indeed, by the end of the 1920s the Bauhaus style was well enough absorbed into the fabric of Weimar-era commercial culture that it would be difficult to say where one ended and the other began.

While the transformation of the school into what Schlemmer dubbed a "[h]eadquarters for superior industrial design" (*Letters* 116) was very much Gropius' doing (encouraged by serious financial pressures), the widespread commercial use of Bauhaus style was of course beyond Gropius' control. For, just as Moholy-Nagy drew from the world of commercial spectacle for his theatrical vision, so the world of commercial spectacle also drew from the Bauhaus, sometimes through direct purchase of products, but more often through stylistic imitation. Such commercial usage can easily be seen when comparing, say, Schlemmer's "art-figures" for the stage and Weimar-era mannequins and print-advertisement figures. Consider, for example, the sleek, semi-alien forms of two mannequin designs by Rudolf Belling (Figure 3.6) alongside Schlemmer's stage figures (Figures 3.2 to 3.5). Or consider, again, the figures at the base of Schlemmer's *Two Solemn Tragedians* (Figure 3.5) alongside the cover illustration for a German periodical *"Die Reklame"* ("The Advertisement"), published by the Society of German Advertisers (Figure 3.7).[15] In cases such as these, avant-garde performance and commercial spectacle become the proverbial chicken and egg, the origins of each too deeply intertwined to tease apart.

The shock effects, the breakdown of the spectator/spectacle divide, the unprecedented speed and energy, the "clashing masses or accumulations of media," the seemingly meaningless or at any rate unconnected sequence of events, and yet the sense that "multifarious complexities of light, space, plane, form, motion, sound, man" are all somehow unified into a single *Gestaltung* – all were central features of the Weimar-era urban experience. Techniques of mass ornament, still in their infancy in the nineteenth century, exploded into the world of German urban space between the wars. In Susan Buck-Morss' energetic description, the new urban metropolis of this period "became a landscape of techno-aesthetics, a dazzling, crowd-pleasing dreamworld that provided *total environments to envelop the crowd*" (6; emphasis added). "Cotton 'rises,'" writes Otto Rühle, mesmerized by market fluctuations in 1928, "copper 'falls,' maize is 'lively,' coal is 'slack,' wheat is 'jumpy,' and mineral oil 'shows tendencies.' The things have acquired an independent life, and exhibit human gestures" (325). There is an avant-garde quality to such commodity spectacle, a quality which becomes more vertiginous in the cityscape of Weimar-era Berlin. One contemporary description of 1920s Berlin might as well have been ripped from a Bauhaus theatre essay:

> [c]hains and streams of light accompany and envelop [the bystander], light-architecture rises up, light-shards appear from the fronts of palaces, disappear, appear, sparkling towers grow tall, collapse, grow tall. Flaming wheels thunder, words manifest themselves letter by letter and are obliterated like Belshazzar's Wall, suns burn from mirrored portals.
>
> (Ehrler 25)

Commodity culture, as Thomas Richards has noted, "always turns out to be an exploration of a fantastic realm in which things act, speak, rise, fall, fly, evolve" (11), and the resemblance to avant-garde experiment is not accidental. Images, motions, words "rise up" and "envelop" the spectator, "appear" and "disappear" and "appear" again, "grow tall" and "collapse" and "grow tall" again, all apparently without logic, meaning, causality, reference. In such a world, as Moholy-Nagy would have it, "the traditionally 'meaningful' and causal interconnections can NOT play the major role" – a claim that suggests that the Bauhaus theatre, like Berlin itself, flirted with immersion in pure simulacrum.

The avant-garde-ish experience of Weimer-era urban spectacle – a spectacle described by one contemporary window-display designer as "*Totaldekoration*"[16] – was the *Totaltheater*'s Other, at once its source, its creation, its inspiration, and its enemy. Why its "enemy"? Its enemy because the ubiquitous success of "total decoration" threatened to render "total theatre" not only marginal but irrelevant, an inferior reproduction of a universally available original. Fearing re-absorption into its source, the Bauhaus theatre refused to concede any parentage, indeed any relations outside itself. The irony of the claim, however, is this: it was precisely when the Bauhaus theatre was at its most closed – when it appeared to be a mechanical organism, an autonomous system of clashing media that refused to *mean*, that refused to *stand for*, that reproduced reproduction, that verged on simulacrum – that the Bauhaus theatre was at its most representative, that it pointed most emphatically back to its roots in Weimar mass culture. The Bauhaus theatre was most *mimetic*, in other words, precisely when it was most *hermetic*.

The Bauhaus theatre, and much of the work of the Bauhaus generally, could never resolve the fundamental tension out of which it emerged. On one hand, Schlemmer and Moholy-Nagy presented the theatre as an alternative, possibly even a solution, to the consumer spectacle of Weimar-era culture. On the other hand, the Bauhaus theatre largely reflected that culture back to itself, and thus risked being absorbed by the original that it reproduced. Insofar as it reflected the emergent whirl of capital, electricity, and mechanics, the Bauhaus theatre was in danger of being subsumed by the far more expansive totality of Weimar-era urban experience. Insofar as it mirrored the impersonal energies and reification of consumer society, the Bauhaus theatre also undermined its ability to embody a utopian alternative. The Bauhaus theatre challenged consumer society by presenting an alternative, organic system that would explicitly make use of the instruments of mechanical reproduction. In part because of its insistence on organic totality, it could never really present the alternative its creators hoped for.

The Bauhaus theatre, in other words, represents a further stage in the relationship between mass culture and the total work of art. As we saw in the last two chapters, Wagner struggled mightily to imagine an alternate totality which could stand as a refuge from and a retort to the emerging mass culture of the late nineteenth century. And, as we also saw, that alternate totality was intermeshed from its origins with the very commercial-industrial system it sought to displace. With the Bauhaus theatre, Wagner's troubles returned, but now even his tenuous solution seemed a distant hope. In the face of a far more immersive and ubiquitous commodity spectacle, Schlemmer and Moholy-Nagy were more severely challenged to maintain the autonomous totality, and utopian hope, of their creations than Wagner ever was. In the end, both Bauhaus artists turned to a stage that evacuated humanity entirely, in the desperate hope of complete salvation by the total machine. If Wagner's strategy of occultation of production bears a striking resemblance to the commodity fetish, then the Bauhaus theatre bears a striking resemblance to the ubiquitous spectacle of commodity culture as theorized by Debord. There were already intimations of this spectacle in Wagner, to be sure, but with the Bauhaus theatre this spectacle flowered to an unprecedented degree, and took root in the soil of the avant-garde.

If there was an attempt in the Bauhaus theatre to escape this closed circle of hermetic-mimetic reproduction, it can be found in a largely neglected work of Schlemmer's entitled *The Figural Cabinet* (*Das figurale Kabinett*). The work was first performed in an abbreviated version at the Bauhaus Pfingsten festivals in 1922, and then in its entirety at the Jena State Theatre during the Bauhaus Week of 1923. Schlemmer describes the stage action as:

> [h]alf shooting gallery – half *metaphysicum abstractum*. Medley, i.e., variety of sense and nonsense, methodized by Color, Form, Nature, and Art; Man and Machine, Acoustics and Mechanics …
>
> Slowly the figures march by: the white, yellow, red, blue ball walks; ball becomes pendulum; pendulum swings; clock runs. The Body-like-a-Violin, the Guy in Bright Checks, the Elemental One, the "Better-Class Gent," the Questionable One, Miss Rosy-Red, the Turk. The bodies look for heads, which are moving in opposite direction across the stage. A jerk, a bang, a victory march …
>
> ("Man" 40)

And so on. On one hand it seems a fairly representative example of an *Organismus der Mechanik*, albeit in a comic mode (though even the comic tone was somewhat

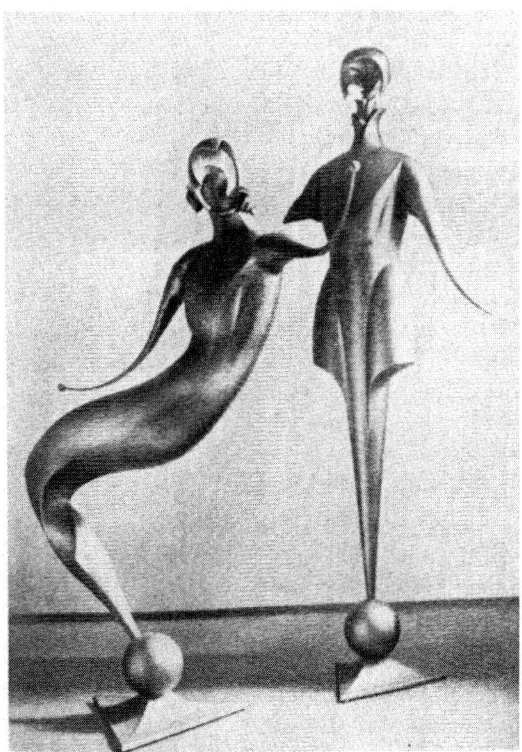

Figure 3.6 Two mannequins by Rudolf Belling, c. 1923.

unexceptional for Schlemmer: *The Triadic Ballet* had comic sections, as did several of his shorter dances such as the *Scenery Dance* [*Kulissentanz*] and the *Building-block Dance* [*Baukastenspiel*]). What distinguishes *The Figural Cabinet*, however, is the playful acknowledgment of its constructed, dependent, and therefore *truly* mechanical nature. In the full production, the play opened as follows: "[t]he master or another figure (in the style of E. T. A. Hoffmann) introduces himself, turns to the cabinet in the background, explains it with gestures, sets parts of it in motion, until at the end the entire cabinet is working" (Schlemmer, "Das figurale Kabinett" 212). In an appendix to the English-language publication of "Man and Art Figure," Schlemmer identifies this Hoffmannesque "master" more precisely: "[i]n the midst [of the action of the play], the Master, E. T. A. Hoffmann's Spalanzani, spooking around, directing, gesticulating, telephoning, shooting himself in the head, and dying a thousand deaths from worry about the function of the functional" (40). The character of Hoffmann's Spalanzani (the creator of the automaton "Olympia" in *Der Sandmann*), here transformed into a parody of a Bauhaus Master ("dying a thousand deaths from worry about the function of the functional"), is a wry

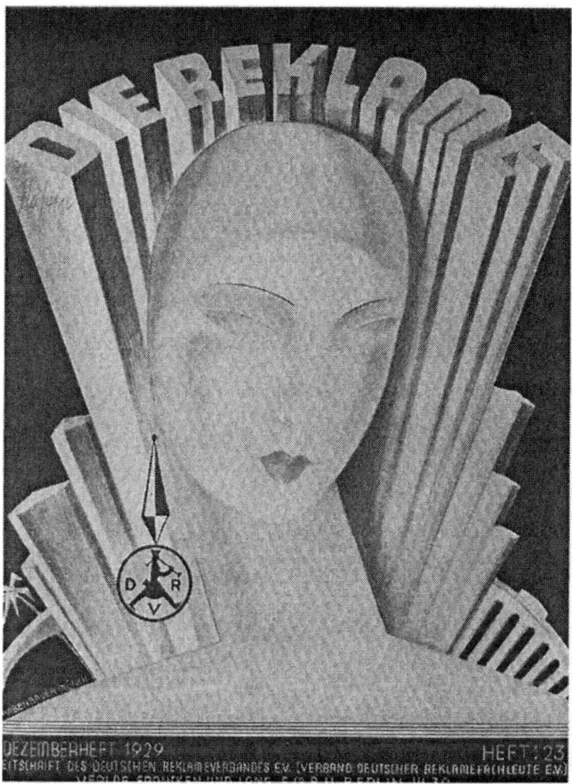

Figure 3.7 Die Reklame ("The Advertisement"), cover, 1929.

representation of the instruments of production behind the total theatre. The presence of Spalanzani reminds us that *The Figural Cabinet* is not in fact a "mechanical organism" but a collection of created machines set in motion for a purpose. We see that Spalanzani has constructed this show, set it running, and remains "spooking around" the stage in his efforts to direct it; we see, too, that he never seems to tire of shooting himself in the head (at the end of the play, he finally succeeds in killing himself).

The Figural Cabinet at once embodies the aspirations of the Bauhaus theatre and satirizes them; it seems that Spalanzani wants to be everywhere and nowhere, all-powerful and powerless, at once omnipresent, omnipotent, invisible, and dead. While his abstract and mechanical creations seem to have organic being, as blue ball "walks" and clock "runs" and bodies look for heads, the Master himself is more or less an automaton who, having brought the mechanical world to life, at last switches himself off for good. With Schlemmer's *Figural Cabinet*, the Bauhaus theatre seems to have wound down to its endpoint, absorbed into the spectacle of

Weimar-era Berlin. The Bauhaus theatre replaced Wagner's vision of an organic work of art with a vision of an organic machine, and yet this crystalline vision failed to resolve the fundamental contradictions of the *Gesamtkunstwerk*. Still wedded to the aesthetics of the organic whole, Schlemmer and Moholy-Nagy inherited Wagner's dream as well as his troubles. Rather than ushering in an age of crystal cathedrals, Schlemmer and Moholy-Nagy's failure underscored the diminishing impact of the avant-garde in an emerging society of spectacle, and its ultimate powerlessness before the truly aestheticized politics of National Socialism. Schlemmer and Moholy-Nagy's failure set the stage, however, for a radically new conception of the total work of art, a reconception that marked an even more radical break with the heritage of Schiller and of Wagner, and dispensed with the promise of organic form altogether. This artistic revolution would not be attempted by Schlemmer or Moholy-Nagy; it would be left to the epic theatre of Bertolt Brecht.

Chapter 4

Total montage

Brecht's reply to Wagner

An alienation of the motor-car takes place if after driving a modern car for a long while we drive an old Model T Ford. Suddenly we hear explosions once more; the motor works on the principle of explosion. We start feeling amazed that such a vehicle, indeed any vehicle not drawn by animal-power, can move; in short, we understand cars, by looking at them as something strange, new, as a triumph of engineering and to that extent something unnatural. Nature, which certainly embraces the motor-car, is suddenly imbued with an element of unnaturalness, and from now on this is an indelible part of the concept [*Begriff*] of nature.

Bertolt Brecht (BOT 144–5/22.1:656–7)[1]

Driving on both sides of the road

A seamless marriage between human and machine, a smoothly humming motor-soul: this was the recurring dream of Schlemmer and Moholy-Nagy. But it was not Brecht's dream. Instead, the cigar-smoking Augsburger presents us with a car as a traveling exercise in dialectics, as a *Lehrstück* in steel, rubber, and upholstery. He presents us with a car as an explosion of contradictions (and this from a Marxist who won his first car by writing a poem in praise of it for an advertising competition!). The car of Brecht's illustration is not a new car – if it were, it might seem to us too natural – but a car whose very obsolescence reveals its inner workings. Its age forces us to pay attention to the mechanics that lie hidden beneath, mechanics rendered suddenly strange. We are forced, in other words, to view the car as *machine*. Pleasure can be had from looking at it this way, though not the same pleasure as might be had with a new car, one whose engine never explodes so conspicuously. No comfort in a "smooth ride," no cozy *Fahrvergnügen* – our pleasure now is one of shock and recollection – we see now (had we ever noticed it before? had we ever really *looked*?) the "triumph of engineering" beneath the hood. And so the old car, by means of its age, becomes new – newer, perhaps, than the factory-fresh models passing by at twice its speed. Our car is clearly mechanical, and yet, strangely, is still a part of nature. It is our concept of nature that must change, must broaden to include the jalopy.

Brecht was never a very good driver, but he understood the nature of cars, which is to say that he grasped their use. Brecht understood, as most of us do, that cars are a means of transport. As metaphors, then – but metaphors for what? In the passage cited above, the car is his epic theatre, jolting its passengers awake with its internal combustions. Elsewhere, as when he writes of "cars that can no longer be driven and are therefore dismantled so that the component parts can be sold" (*BOF* 179/21:488), the metaphorical freight is the market's systematic dismantling of the organic work of art. In both instances, the play of contraries that the automobile embodies – artificial yet natural, mechanical yet organic, useful yet beautiful – allows the auto to serve as an emblem for art. Brecht's old car projects, with the clarity of twin beams of light, the very dialectic that the Festspielhaus sought to hide in darkness, and that the Bauhaus theatre exposed in form but not in fact. His goal was neither the iconic synthesis of the Festspielhaus nor the crystalline unities of the *Totaltheater*, and yet his goal was often inseparable from the dream of the total work of art.

Unity without witchcraft

Brecht has long been understood as Wagner's foil, his *Verfremdungseffekt* ("estrangement effect") the very antithesis of the *Gesamtkunstwerk*.[2] And for good reason: the differences between Wagnerian and Brechtian dramaturgy are legion. Whereas Wagner strove to make his work a total, pseudo-organic whole, Brecht strove for separation of elements and an exposure of the mechanics of production. Whereas Wagner hoped to absorb his audience through appeals to emotion and "spirit," Brecht hoped to estrange his audience through distancing devices and political contradictions. Whereas Wagner aimed to forge a unified *Volk*, Brecht aimed to exacerbate class conflict. The ideal Brechtian audience of the 1920s and 30s could be a cool and distanced one (as in *The Threepenny Opera*), a violently divided one (as in *Mahagonny*), or an active political collective (as in the *Lehrstücke*), but it could not be an assemblage of aesthetes or cultists. Startling the audience out of a condition of mass hypnosis was the first step, for Brecht, in making them an active body.

It is surely no accident that *Rise and Fall of the City of Mahagonny* (*Aufstieg und Fall der Stadt Mahagonny*, 1930), Brecht's most explicitly anti-Wagnerian music-drama, begins with the entry and collapse of a broken-down old truck. With the loss of their transport, the three companions who introduce the play (Willy the Bookie, Trinity Moses, and the Widow Begbick) have lost their last hope of escape. The machine has given up the ghost and left them in a "desolate place," the emptiness of which is underscored by their static dialogue.

> WILLY: What's up? We must go on.
> MOSES: But the truck has broken down.
> WILLY: Then we can't go on.
>
> *Pause.*

MOSES: But we must go on.
WILLY: But there's nothing there but desert.
MOSES: Then we can't go on.

Pause.

WILLY: Then we must go back.
MOSES: But the sheriffs are waiting back there; they know our faces only too
well.
WILLY: Then we can't go back.

They sit on the running-board and light cigarettes.

(Rise 3/2:335)

The companions may begin the scene like Vladimir and Estragon, but they end it, strangely enough, like Wagner's gods. The opera opens with the founding of the new town of Mahagonny, recalling the opening of Wagner's *Ring* cycle, which begins with the founding of Valhalla.[3] It is the first of many parallels between the two works. Mahagonny, like Walhall, is built as a refuge against the turmoil of the outside world, a utopian space which might rise above the ills of (modern) society. As utopias, both Mahagonny and Walhall are cursed from the start, and survive on contradictions (e.g. between the demands of capital and the desire for peace and unity, between the desire for glory and the demands of the law). Both Wotan and Begbick must rely on the aid of others for the realization of their utopian projects. One of their recruits, the tenor (Siegfried in the *Ring*, Paul in *Mahagonny*), is too "wild" to be integrated and therefore exposes the inner contradiction of the civilizing project. Both tenors suffer a similar fate: destruction at the hands of the founder figure. Bernard Shaw famously read the *Ring* as a foundational myth of capitalism, and the same could be said, with still more justification, of *Mahagonny*.

Mahagonny belongs to a period of Brecht's work from roughly 1926 (his turn to Marxism) to 1933 (his exile from Germany), a period that reflects his deepest engagement with the genre of the *Gesamtkunstwerk*. Brecht's theoretical insistence on the independence of artistic elements shaped the entire production of *Mahagonny*. In the original production, according to Brecht,

> [t]he three elements, action, music, and image, appeared together but yet separated: in one scene – which shows how a man eats himself to death – in front of a huge screen, on which could be seen a larger-than-life glutton, the actor (who did not resemble the projected glutton) mimed the suicidal gluttony, accompanied by a chorus who chanted a description of the act. Music, image and the actor performed the same act independently [*selbständig*].
>
> (BOF 13/23:13)

At another moment in the original production, Brecht made use of the projection screen to confront the audience directly with their reaction to the action. The play's climax arrives when Paul is sentenced to death for being unable to pay his debts. At precisely this moment, Brecht interrupted the audience's sympathy with the heroic tenor's plight by flashing the following projection above the stage:

> Execution and death of Paul Ackermann. Many of you might prefer not to see the following execution of Paul Ackermann. But, from our point of view, you wouldn't have paid his debts either. So great is the respect for money in our time.

(2:38)

Such direct confrontations with the audience estranged it from emotional identification with the performance, thus interrupting any "organic" absorption of audience into spectacle.

The separation of stage elements at the premiere of *Mahagonny* famously spilled over into the audience, exacerbating conflicts within the audience itself. Recalling the premiere, Lotte Lenya describes how

> [t]he demonstration started as we were singing the last song, and waving placards – mine said "FOR WEILL," with the whole audience on its feet, cheering and booing and whistling. Brecht had thoughtfully provided us with whistles of our own, little *Trillerpfeifen*, so we stood there whistling defiantly back.

Similarly, the critic Alfred Polgar, in the seats for the premiere, describes an "electrically charged room" in which "contradictions flashed like lightening and awakened further contradictions … spread[ing] from the stage to the auditorium." He particularly mentions, among a host of other outraged bourgeois, "a very large woman, all whooping Valkyrie" who attempts to silence the production by whistling madly through her fingers (32–3). As such descriptions suggest, the proliferation of stage contradictions caught up the audience as well, forcing half-buried tensions to erupt into "war cries" between radically separated parties. The presence of the angry Valkyrie at the first-night riot was predictable. On the subsequent night, the Leipzig authorities required the theatre to keep the houselights on and ring the auditorium with police, requirements that only served to further underscore the anti-Wagnerian aspects of the work, filling the entire auditorium with blazing light and extending the radical separation of elements right out into the audience. The Leipzig Neues Theater had become, for the remainder of the scandalous run, Wagner's Festspielhaus in negative.

In his accompanying "Notes to *Mahagonny*" (1930), Brecht makes clear that the exacerbation of contradictions on the stage and in the auditorium is inextricably linked to a larger attack on the *Gesamtkunstwerk*. The passage is one of his most extended reflections on the total work of art.

When the epic theatre's methods begin to penetrate the opera the first result is a radical *separation of the elements*. The great struggle for supremacy between words, music and production – which always brings up the question "which is the pretext for what?": is the music the pretext for the events on the stage, or are these the pretext for the music? etc. – can simply be by-passed by radically separating the elements. So long as the expression "*Gesamtkunstwerk*" means that the integration is a muddle, so long as the arts are supposed to be "fused" together, the various elements will all be equally degraded, and each will act as a mere "feed" to the rest. The process of fusion extends to the spectator, who gets thrown into the melting pot too and becomes a passive (suffering) part of the *Gesamtkunstwerk*. Witchcraft of this sort must of course be fought against. Whatever is intended to produce hypnosis, is likely to induce sordid intoxication, or creates a fog, has got to be given up.

 Words, music and setting had to become more independent of each other [*mußten mehr Selbständigkeit erhalten*].

(BOT 37–8/24:79*)

Here, Brecht's demand for a "radical separation of the elements" leads as if by necessity to a rejection of the "melting pot" of the *Gesamtkunstwerk*, which he ridicules as "witchcraft." The *Gesamtkunstwerk*, apparently, is the darkness and fog that the epic theatre aims to dispel.

In the face of such obvious hostility, what does it mean to say that Brecht's epic theatre was often inseparable from the total work of art? Let us look at the passage just cited. On closer inspection, Brecht's supposed rejection of the total work of art is more sly than it might first appear. "*So long as* the expression '*Gesamtkunstwerk*' means that the integration is a muddle, *so long as* the arts are supposed to be 'fused' together ..." he writes, using the qualifier *solang* to hold open the possibility that *Gesamtkunstwerk* might mean something else altogether. This may not, then, be quite the total rejection of the total work of art that scholars have generally held it to be. Intriguingly, while Brecht attacks Wagner directly at numerous points in his writing, Brecht states nowhere in any of his theoretical texts that his dramaturgy is an attack on the total work of art per se. What he seems to be suggesting here, in fact, is that the *Gesamtkunstwerk* needs not so much to be discarded as reconceived, such that the integration it offers is real and not merely a phantasmagoric "muddle." But if Brecht is not rejecting the total work of art, then what, precisely, is he embracing?

Further clues may be found in a later text of Brecht's, "On Experimental Theatre" (1939), originally delivered to a group of Stockholm theatre students in 1939. In his theatrical practice, according to Brecht,

[t]he playwright could work out his experiments in uninterrupted collaboration with actor and stage designer; he could influence and be influenced. At the same time the painter and the composer regained their independence, and were able to express their view of the theme by their own artistic means.

In other words, the epic theatre was to be a fully collaborative process, in which independent artists came together into a collective. In such a process, the "*Gesamtkunstwerk* appeared before the spectator as a bundle of separate elements [*das Gesamtkunstwerk trat in getrennten Elementen vor den Zuschauer*]" (*BOT* 134/22.1:556*). Brecht here emphasizes the collaborative nature of the production process in the epic theatre, the fact (or the hope) that scene designer, playwright, director, composer and actor are all independent yet interrelated, influencing and influenced. Beyond this, he suggests that the result of this collaboration is not an anti-*Gesamtkunstwerk* so much as a new form of *Gesamtkunstwerk*, in which the whole appears as "a bundle of separate elements." This is a marked diversion not only from Wagner but even from Gropius, Schlemmer, and Moholy-Nagy. What Brecht is suggesting is a *Gesamtkunstwerk* that dispenses entirely with the claim to be "organic," that dispenses, in short, with an entire tradition of organicist aesthetics from Kant onwards. A *Gesamtkunstwerk* of critical collaboration rather than organic unity.

As is well known, Brecht did not always practice what he preached when it came to collaboration. He tended to work best with artists, such as Caspar Neher and Hanns Eisler, who shared his politics and were relatively comfortable subordinating their aesthetic vision to his. His collaboration with Weill, on the other hand, was always strained, in part due to the fact that the two artists fought bitterly over the relative importance of text and music. With actors, moreover, Brecht could be dictatorial and bullying, less a collaborator than a *Kommandant*. Accounts of Brecht browbeating actors are numerous, and run the course of his career. Similarly numerous are the accounts of Brecht's manipulative treatment of the men, and especially women, who contributed to the work published under his name.[4] And yet it would be a mistake to dismiss Brecht's writings on artistic collaboration as *entirely* theoretical. Brecht wrote most of his operas in close collaboration with the composer (whether Weill or Eisler) and, more strikingly, he included the stage designer (whether Neher, Teo Otto, or Karl von Appen) in the entire development of the production. Indeed, the depth of Brecht's collaboration with his scene designers has little precedent in theatre history, though it would be widely imitated thereafter. Previously, the stage designer (like the lighting and costume designers) was an auxiliary member of the production team, an artist whose work, though important, was limited to the sphere of flats, stage furniture, properties, and so forth. But the Brecht/Neher collaboration marked something new in the history of stage design: the incorporation of the stage designer as an active and roughly equal participant in the development of a new work, attending all rehearsals and influencing the direction of the production. This close director/designer collaboration was a hallmark of Brecht's directing throughout his career. "[Neher's sketches] always lay ready to hand on the director's table, with the scene currently being rehearsed on the top," writes Egon Monk of Brecht's rehearsals of *The Tutor* in 1950. "Nearly all of the blocking of the performances of the Berliner Ensemble go right back to Neher's sketches" (141). Monk's description also offers some insight into the way Brecht and Neher worked when together:

Neher and Brecht next to each other at rehearsal. Both leaning way back, knees pressed up against the seats in front. Brecht appreciatively contemplating his cigar; Neher with his eyebrows raised high up or else curling down over his glasses, more severe. Assistants near and behind them, visitors farther away. They are rehearsing "by interjections." At each interjection Neher or Brecht places the name of the suggestion's originator. "Neher thinks … ", "Besson thinks … ", "Brecht thinks … ", "Monk thinks … ". The interjection is listened to and then tried out. If a detail works, then Brecht giggles with pleasure and Neher gives him a bemused look … This lasts a long time.

(142)

In Monk's account, Brecht and Neher rehearse by applying the epic technique of acting in the third person to themselves. Thus individual feelings are stated as third-person opinions, each of which has to be "listened to" and "tested" with critical distance. The result – and not only in theory – is a collaborative unity of independent elements, rather than a "melting pot" unity of fused parts.

This reconception bears much in common with remarks by Adorno in *In Search of Wagner*. While the main thrust of that text is directed sharply against the *Gesamtkunstwerk*, Adorno makes a rather intriguing suggestion toward the end of the "Music Drama" chapter.

A valid *Gesamtkunstwerk*, purged of its false identity, would have required a collective of specialist planners. Schoenberg … once conceived the utopian idea of a "composer's studio," in which each person would take up the work at the point where another has to give it up. However, collective labor is ruled out for Wagner, not simply by the social situation in the middle of the nineteenth century, but even more radically by the substance of his work, the metaphysics of yearning, rapture and redemption. This makes impossible the only form in which the *Gesamtkunstwerk* could be organized collectively – an antithetical form.

(111–12)

Adorno, like Brecht, suggests here that the *Gesamtkunstwerk* should not be abandoned but re-functioned, transformed into the antithesis of Wagnerism. For Adorno, in 1938 still indebted to Lukácsian dreams of dialectical totality, Schoenberg was a "dialectical composer" who offered a hope that art might preserve the determinate negations of the absent whole.[5] The main trouble with Wagner, then, is not so much the concept of the *Gesamtkunstwerk* itself as the specific shape it took in his music-dramas. "Purged of its false identity," the concept might look something like Schoenberg's "composer's studio" or, on a far grander scale, "a collective of specialist planners" that might constitute the socialist state.

While Adorno would move away from such positive visions of totality in subsequent writings, this interest in creating a unity without false identity remains for Brecht even in his later theoretical work. Brecht's *A Short Organum for the Theatre*

(1948), for instance, argues that theatre is the unified creation of all the artists involved. "Not everything depends on the actor," he writes.

> The "story" is set out, brought forward and shown by the theatre as a whole, by actors, stage designers, mask-makers, costumiers, composers and choreographers. They unite their various arts for the joint operation, without of course sacrificing their independence [*Selbständigkeit*] in the process.
>
> (*BOT* 202/23:94)

The "unit[ing] of various arts" Brecht speaks of here is of course different from Wagner's conception, in *The Artwork of the Future*, of the uniting of the sister arts. But the difference is not a radical one. Brecht, like Wagner, imagines an artwork that overcomes the fragmentation caused by the division of labor, an artwork inseparable from larger political demands. Indeed, Brecht's theatrical vision has much in common with Wagner's. Most broadly, both Brecht and Wagner found the status quo of bourgeois society intolerable. Both argued that the arts played an important role in the support of that order, through entertainment, distraction, the division of the classes, and the creation of artificial desires and mandarin tastes. In Brecht's attacks on "culinary theatre" one hears echoes of Wagner's attacks on grand opera; in his demand for a theatre that responds to the real needs of the people, one hears echoes of Wagner's very similar exhortations. Both lamented the profound social fragmentation and alienation produced by the rise of industrialized capital. Both saw their performances as revolutionary in both artistic and political senses of the word.

Contrapuntal unity

It would be a mistake, then, to read Brecht's call for the radical separation of artistic elements as a rejection of artistic unity. But how might one present a unified work of art without recourse to the hypnotizing tricks of the Festspielhaus? More subtly, how might one present a unified work of art without creating a crystalline *Gesamtkunstwerk* along the lines of the Bauhaus? The place to begin, for Brecht, was a reconsideration of unity. Unity, Brecht found, is often a result of incoherence, jumps, and interruptions. Responding to complaints (chiefly by Berlin critics Herbert Ihering and Alfred Kerr) that Peter Lorre's performance as Galy Gay in *Man Is Man* lacked coherence, Brecht argued that unity of character and type is created "despite, or rather by means of interruptions and jumps" (*BOT* 55/24:49). Significantly, the attack here is not on unity per se, but rather on the illusion of seamless unity. Brecht made much the same point nine years later in his *Arbeitsjournal*, remarking that, while "the progress of the fable is discontinuous" in his theatre, "the unified whole consists of independent parts" (3 August 1940). Again, discontinuity and contradiction are seen as a means to the creation of the "unified whole" rather than a subversion of it. Another eight years later, in the *Short Organum*, Brecht still held much the same position. "The coherence of the [stage] character," he wrote of his plays, "is in fact shown by the way in which its individual qualities contradict one another" (*BOT* 196/23:86). A whole made out of disjointed parts, a totality resulting from independent playlets and contradictory elements: Brecht is speaking here of *montage*. It is this aesthetic principle that Brecht uses not only as an estrangement device but also as a means of achieving a kind of unity through juxtaposition.

Brecht's interest in the aesthetics of montage was profoundly influenced by the emergent medium of film, and more particularly by the "dialectical montage" techniques of Eisenstein that developed alongside Brecht's own, and of which Brecht was very much aware.[6] But then Eisenstein was himself, as is too rarely appreciated, heavily influenced by Wagner.[7] "What most attracted me to Wagner were his opinions on synthetic spectacle which are to be found scattered throughout the great composer's theoretical works," he writes while staging *Die Walküre* at the Bolshoi in 1940.

> The problem of the synthesis of the arts is of vital concern to cinematography … Men, music, light, landscape, color, and motion brought into one integral whole by a single piercing emotion, by a single theme and idea – this is the aim of modern cinematography.
>
> (*Film Essays* 85)

For Eisenstein, it was the particular way in which film brought together sculpture, painting, music, and literature – and fused these various arts through montage – that made film succeed as a *Gesamtkunstwerk* where the theatre had failed. "The cinema," he writes in *Film Form*, "is that genuine and ultimate synthesis of all artistic manifestations that fell to pieces after the peak of Greek culture" (181). Through significant leaps in space and time, and startling juxtapositions of image, sound, and movement, Eisenstein developed a "total cinema" that utilized montage in a manner that sought to expose supposedly fixed, natural entities as in fact fluid, constructed, and alterable. Eisenstein's "dialectical montage," like Brecht's, would produce an artistic unity that would not be an organic unity, that would be directed at stripping away the aura of "naturalness" from socially constructed reality.[8]

What Brecht, like Eisenstein, therefore wished to reject was not aesthetic unity per se, but rather the Wagnerian unity that functions as a great melting pot and that seeks to hide social reality behind a mask of nature. Montage breaks down distinctions between unity and fragmentation, continuity and interruption, such that the terms serve not as antitheses but as mutual aids. Most importantly, it breaks down the old Kantian dichotomy of organism and mechanism. As Peter Bürger has pointed out, the "'fitted' (*montierte*) work calls attention to the fact that it is made up of reality fragments; it breaks through the appearance (*Schein*) of totality" (72). Hence the *papiers collés* montages of Picasso and Braque – and more forcefully, the photo montages of John Heartfield – upend traditional systems of representation by introducing found fragments (e.g. newspaper clippings, bits of woven basket) into the painting. Brecht, particularly in his projects in the late 1920s and early 30s, delighted in such a magpie method of construction. Consider, for instance, his "*Umfunktionierung*" ("changing the function") of John Gay's *The Beggar's Opera* into *The Threepenny Opera* (*Die Dreigroschenoper*). The playbill of the Berlin premiere in 1928 tells much of the story: the work is identified as "Die Dreigroschenoper (The Beggars [sic] Opera): A piece with music in a prologue and eight scenes, after the English by John Gay. (Inserted ballads by François Villon and Rudyard Kipling)." Listed beneath Elisabeth Hauptmann's credit for "translation," Brecht is credited for *Bearbeitung*: "adaptation." It would be difficult for an audience member reading this program to miss the point that the opera constituted a curious hodge-podge of worked and re-worked elements (Gay *and* Villon *and* Kipling?) rather than an organic whole. If *The Threepenny Opera* seems a unified work despite the open exhibition of its process of production, then that unity must be contrapuntal.

The result of this technique is a work that blurs the distinction between mechanical and organic form. Indeed, Brecht occasionally played with the confusion between these two forms, redefining "mechanical" and "organic" along new lines. Consider, for instance, Brecht's discussion of his use of projections in the original staging of *The Mother* (*Die Mutter*, 1932). In his "Notes" to the play, Brecht writes,

> [t]he projections are by no means a mechanical auxiliary [*mechanische Hilfsmittel*] in the sense of a supplement [*Ergänzungen*], and offer no cribsheet. They have no intention of assisting the spectator but aim rather to oppose him; they frustrate his total empathy and interrupt his mechanical assent [*unterbrechen sein mechanisches Mitgehen*]. They render the EFFECT INDIRECT. In this fashion they are organic parts of the work of art [*organische Teile des Kunstwerkes*].
>
> (*Mother* 134/24:151*)

Brecht's conclusion that stage projections (a quintessential estrangement device of the epic theatre) are "organic parts of the work of art" is quite surprising. Were not such devices employed precisely in order to disrupt the conventions of "organic" art? In order to make sense of Brecht's claim, then, we have to recognize the ways in which he is reversing conventional definitions. Brecht uses the adjective *mechanisch* not in its Kantian sense but in the sense of something being done without serious thought (as in the sentence, "Half my students just answer my questions mechanically"). This sense of *mechanisch* goes very strongly against the conventional use of the word in the tradition of the organic work of art. According to Brecht, absorption into an organic work of art is actually a *mechanical* process, in the sense that it is an automatic response unmediated by critical thought. This is the first part of Brecht's ironic reflection on the organic/mechanical dichotomy. The second follows naturally from the first. By mediating the spectacle for the spectator, by rendering the effect of the spectacle "INDIRECT" (*MITTLEBAR*), estrangement devices destroy the seeming naturalness of the artwork. In Kantian terms, estrangement devices would therefore undermine the work's claim to be art at all. For Brecht, however, estrangement devices do more or less the opposite: they become "an organic part of the work of art" *through* their mediation. The Brechtian work of art no longer pretends to be a work of nature, and yet the work becomes, for this very reason, an organic form. Beneath Brecht's anti-Kantian word-play lies not only a profoundly different aesthetic but a profoundly different anthropology as well. Human nature, Brecht suggests, lies less in absorption than in critical thought, less in unmediated assent to a completed whole than in manipulation of independent elements. How separable, in the end, are "mechanism" and "organism" for the tool-producing animal?

Appropriately enough, Brecht's theoretical writings from the 1920s and 30s often contain forms of *greifen* ("to grasp"). A further passage from Brecht's "Notes on *The Mother*" is particularly rife with forms of the word. In order to get a full sense of the repetitions and their significance, it will be necessary to quote the passage at length.

> When we speak of having a "mental grip" [*Begreifen*] of what constitutes a human being, we certainly mean no less than: having some kind of hold [*Griffe*] on him. That "total" view of man, which outlines him for us and is momentarily necessary, nevertheless is inadequate save as an hypothesis for the real and decisive operation of getting a "mental grip" [*Begreifen*], which manipulates him, and for just that purpose requires a "total" view as a kind of situational plan. But even this "total" view is not to be gained without some sort of operational plan; only in conjunction with this can the view be gained and made effective. We can attain a mental grip [*begreifen*] on what constitutes another only when we get some sort of hold [*eingreifen*] on him. Even with ourselves, we have a mental grip [*begreifen*] of ourselves only when we "have hold of" ourselves [*eingreifen*]. The human being appears to be above all a creature used by and useful to human beings, not yet defined to an end. Or in any case it is practical for the Communist organization, the organization that must fight the perverted usage of man by man, to so define him. Thus defined, he appears beyond all his tractability in his totality – as unexpectedly as this may happen.
>
> (*Mother* 149; 24/127)

Brecht's repeated use of the term *greifen* underscores, again, his distance from Kantian ethics. Humans are not to be treated as ends in themselves but as means to an end that is "not yet defined"; above all, humans are tool-makers and tool-users, are graspers and manipulators. Brecht's word-play exposes the degree to which our own thoughts reflect this central utilitarian impulse. We understand ourselves (*begreifen*) only when we take hold of ourselves (*in uns eingreifen*): grasping is the basis of self-knowledge. Moreover – and here Brecht throws a final wrench into the *Gesamtkunstwerk* – it is only through such a utilitarian view of humanity that we find humanity's totality. Tractability is not, as for Kant and Schiller, the enemy of totality but the means to it; an object (either human being or artwork) must be understood as a mechanism in order to be understood as a whole.

Wagner, as we have seen, associated opera production with mechanization to an unprecedented degree. Here, too, Brecht shared more with Wagner than one might expect. While Brecht's remarks in "Notes to *Mahagonny*" on the *Gesamtkunstwerk* are frequently cited, his extensive discussion of the *Apparat* ("apparatus" or "machine") in the essay has been largely overlooked. Brecht uses the term *Apparat* in three senses in the essay: as an amalgam of the dominant cultural forces under capitalism (similar to what Horkheimer and Adorno would refer to as "the culture industry"), as mechanical tools in general, and as the specific tools of film production (camera, film, and so forth). All three of these senses of the term are actually intertwined, however, in that the *Apparat* (in the sense of culture industry) controls the distribution of machine tools, including those of film production. Echoing Wagner's notion of the orchestra as a "mechanism for tone production," Brecht refers to the site of tone production as an "orchestral apparatus" (*Orchesterapparat*) (*BOT* 38/24:80) and, elsewhere, as "music mechanism" or "musical apparatus" (*musikalischen Apparat, Musikapparat*) (*BOT* 82/24:171). For Brecht as for Wagner, the orchestra is mechanical and, as such, is a part of a much broader domination of mechanics over modern life. Not only is the orchestra an *Apparat*, so too is virtually the entire realm of capitalist culture. "Great apparatuses like the opera, the stage, the press, etc., impose their views as it were incognito," writes Brecht.

> For a long time now they have taken the handiwork (music, writing, criticism, etc.) of intellectuals who share in their profits – that is, of men who are economically committed to the prevailing system but are socially near-proletarian – and processed it to make fodder for their public-entertainment machine.
>
> (*BOT* 34/24:74)

Brecht's attack on the "public-entertainment machine" echoes Wagner's attack, which we saw in Chapter 1, on the degradation of modern culture through "absorption into the machine" (1:85/5:58). Capitalist society replicates itself, Brecht argues, with the help of the cultural apparatus.

> Society absorbs via the apparatus whatever it needs in order to reproduce itself. This means that an innovation will pass if it is calculated to rejuvenate existing society, but not if it is going to change it – irrespective of whether the form of the society in question is good or bad.
>
> (*BOT* 34/24:75)

This point implies, for Brecht, a critique of the avant-garde. Thinking that they are somehow able to control or work outside of the apparatus, avant-garde artists have succeeded only in forgetting the dependent nature of their own existence.

> The *avant-garde* don't think of changing the apparatus, because they fancy that they have at their disposal an apparatus which will serve up whatever they

freely invent, transforming itself spontaneously to match their ideas. But they are not in fact free inventors; the apparatus goes on fulfilling its function with or without them; the theatres play every night; the papers come out so many times a day; and they absorb what they need; and all they need is a given amount of stuff.

(BOT 35/24:75)

Again, Brecht's argument here has echoes of Wagner's in *Artwork of the Future*. The argument they share might almost be rendered in the form of a syllogism: since all aspects of cultural production form a single, all-absorbing machine, and since this cultural machine serves to perpetuate the (degraded) conditions of society, therefore mere formal innovation cannot pose an authentic challenge (either aesthetically or politically) to the existing apparatus. If an attack on the apparatus is what is desired, then only a radical attack will do, an attack as much political as aesthetic.

Brecht, in other words, shares with Wagner a commitment to aesthetic unity (albeit unity of a very different type) and a condemnation of the mechanics of culture production. Bearing in mind this connection to Wagner, we can now return to the issue of their distance from one another. After he argues that the dominant mode of cultural production severely restricts the creative potential of artists, Brecht then qualifies the point. "And yet," he muses, "to restrict the individual's freedom of invention is in itself a progressive act." Why should this be so? Brecht continues:

> [t]he individual becomes increasingly drawn into enormous events that are going to change the world. No longer can he simply "express himself." He is brought up short and put into a position where he can fulfill more general tasks. The trouble, however, is that at present the apparatuses do not work for the general good; the means of production do not belong to the producer; and as a result his work amounts to so much merchandise.

(BOT 35/24:76)

Brecht makes two points here, both important to his general theory. First, he argues that the dominance of the "public-entertainment machine" has more than simply a repressive function. Insofar as it undermines the bourgeois conception of the artist (with its emphasis on individuality and self-expression), the cultural apparatus draws the artist "into enormous events that are going to change the world." In other words, the cultural apparatus forces the artist to become explicitly political. Second, Brecht suggests that the trouble with the apparatus lies not in the nature of the apparatus itself but rather in the economic relations that govern its employment. This is a fairly standard Marxist argument, echoing Marx's point that the trouble with capitalist production lies not in the tools themselves but rather in their ownership by a particular class.

The trouble, then, lies not with the machine itself, but rather with the use to which the machine is presently put. Walter Benjamin understands this dimension of Brecht's work when he writes that:

> a writer's production must have the character of a model: it must be able to instruct other writers in their production and, secondly, it must be able to place an improved apparatus at their disposal. This apparatus will be the better, the more consumers it brings in contact with the production process – in short, the more readers or spectators it turns into collaborators. We already possess a model of this kind ... It is Brecht's theatre.
>
> ("Author" 98)

Brecht's theatre, as Benjamin understood, aimed to "bring consumers in contact with the production process" and therefore "place an improved apparatus at their disposal." Brecht could be severely critical of productions that failed to actually engage the audience into the production process, even if the scripts were his own. His comments on the 1935 Theatre Union production of *The Mother* are indicative. "The dangers which the apparatus can present," Brecht writes,

> were shown by the New York production of *Die Mutter*. Its political standpoint puts the Theatre Union in quite a different class from the theatres which had performed the opera *Mahagonny*. Yet the apparatus behaved exactly like a machine for simulating the effects of dope.
>
> (*BOT* 88/22.1:161)

The apparatus can operate as dope-production machine or as collaborative engine; either way, it is not the mechanical nature of the production process that is at fault. Improperly used, the "*Apparat*" could be a fog machine; properly used, it could work as a collaborative engine, a model of a unified collective.

The Lindbergh Flight as Brechtian *Gesamtkunstwerk*

One of the finest, and at the same time most troubling, examples of Brecht's attempt to use the *Apparat* as a collaborative engine may be found in *The Lindbergh Flight* (*Der Lindberghflug*). The work was first performed at the Baden-Baden Music Festival on 27 January 1929, and transmitted to other local auditoria the next day. On 29 January it was broadcast throughout Germany, and was broadcast twice more before 1933 (on 5 December 1929 and 18 March 1930). It is a cross between a radio play and a cantata, made up of 17 sections of verse composed by Brecht. Thirteen of these sections were set to music by Kurt Weill, four by Paul Hindemith, and the resulting score demands a mixed choir, bass and baritone solos, and a tenor (who plays Lindbergh). The music was later revised in a composition by Weill alone; this version opened at the Kross Opera in December 1929. Subsequent performances included an extremely successful version broadcast specifically for schoolchildren, which Brecht entitled *The Flight of the Lindberghs: A Radio Learning Play for Boys and Girls* (*Der Flug der Lindberghs. Ein Radiolehrstück für Knaben und Mädchen*). The plot is a straightforward narration of Lindbergh's transatlantic flight, beginning with an invitation to the audience to join in and proceeding to Lindbergh's presentation of himself and his determination to cross the Atlantic. Lindbergh is then assailed by a series of hazards (fog, snow, and sleep) before landing to the amazement and celebration of the chorus. The allegorical simplicity of this plot suggests a medieval morality play, with dramatic personae (including New York City, the ship *Empress of Scotland*, Scottish fishermen, and a Parisian crowd) as types rather than personalities. Lindbergh, too, is a mere emblem, speaking mostly in exposition and giving little or no evidence of rounded "character." In keeping with the montage form of epic dramaturgy, neither the action nor the music is continuous, and no effort is made to make the transitions seamless. At 13 points in the play, a narrator breaks in and announces the events of the following section, and characters frequently announce their own identities and functions to the audience.

The Lindbergh Flight is a play about an airplane; more significantly, it is a play about mass media and the *Gesamtkunstwerk*. The work opens with a repeated choral invocation of the *Apparat*: "Here is the *Apparat*! Climb in!" ("*Hier ist der Apparat! Steig ein!*"). The *Apparat* to which the chorus refers is generally translated into English as "airplane," but the translation avoids the complexities of the word Brecht employs. Given Brecht's theoretical writings from the period, in addition to the odd word choice here (*Apparat* is not commonly used in order to refer to a plane), we may conclude that the word refers both to Lindbergh's plane and to the larger discourse of the *Apparat* already discussed. In this latter sense, the call "Here is the *Apparat*! Climb in!" is a challenge to the audience to seize the controls of the mass-media apparatus and operate them for their own ends. This point is further emphasized by the placards Brecht used in the original production (Figure 4.1). In Brecht's staging, the orchestra/chorus bears a placard marked "The Radio" (*Das Radio*), while The Flier's placard reads "The Listener" (*Der Hörer*). A large sign along the back wall exhorts the audience to join the performance by singing along loudly with the Flier. The audience, then, both *performs* and *witnesses* a lesson in how to listen to the radio. It *performs* this lesson by actively participating in the work, while it *witnesses* this proper relation by following the Lindbergh character (at once designated as Hero and Listener) as he takes control of the *Apparat* against all odds. "In this way," Brecht writes, "a collaboration develops between participant and *Apparat*" (*BOT* 31/24:87).

"A collaboration between participant and *Apparat*": it is no accident that Lindbergh sings at great length of the tools he carries with him, offering us a laundry list as though it were the stuff of high drama: "2 electrical lamps / 1 rope / 1 role of sewing thread / 1 hunting knife / 4 red torches sealed into tubes / 1 waterproof sack with matches" and so on (3:10). Similarly, the climax of the drama – just before Lindbergh bursts through the clouds over Scotland – takes the form of a dialogue between the Flier and his motor:

Now it's not much further. Now
We must work together,
We two.
Do you have enough oil?
Do you think you have enough gas?
Are you cool enough?
Are you feeling alright?
[THE MOTOR RUNS]
The ice that was bothering you
Is already gone.
The fog, that's my concern,
You do your work.
You just keep running.
[THE MOTOR RUNS]

(3:20)

A similar dialogue emerges when Lindbergh comes closer to Paris, and a chorus cries out in celebration. "Now he's coming!" sings a chorus of Parisians. "A spot appears in the heavens. It's getting bigger. It's an airplane. Now it will land" (3:22).

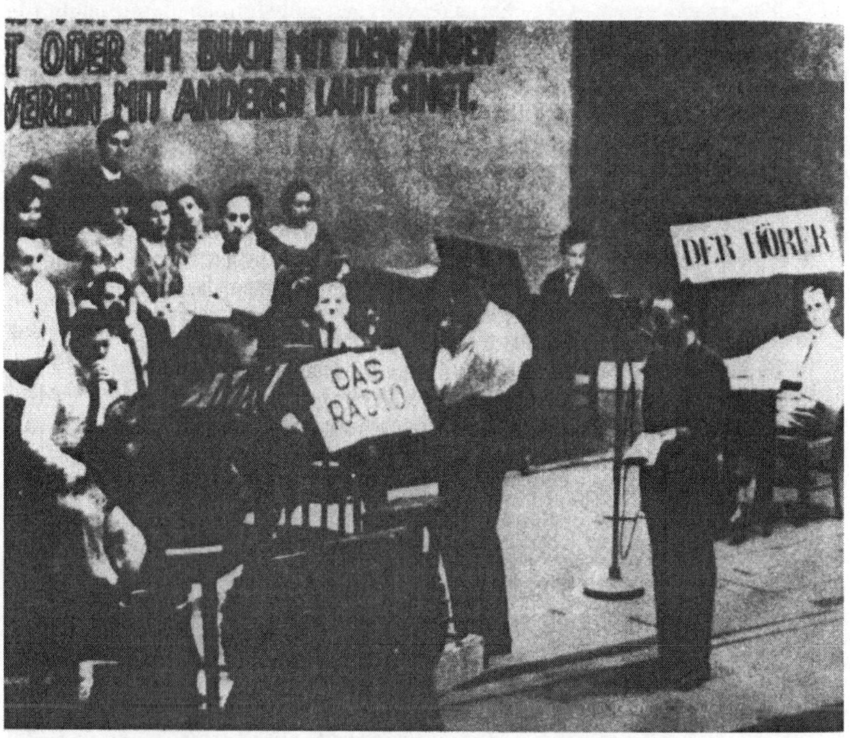

Figure 4.1 Premiere of *Der Lindberghflug*, 1929. Brecht in foreground, to right.

The play of pronouns in this passage again blurs the distinction between pilot and plane. "*Er wird größer*" (lit. "he/it's getting bigger"), for instance, could refer either to the pilot or to the approaching "spot" (*Punkt*) of the airplane.

Not only does *The Lindbergh Flight* blur distinctions between human and machine, it models an ideal union of humanity itself, mediated by mass communications. Lindbergh's flight is reported on through telegraphic exchanges, rendered as song, between the city of New York and the ship *Empress of Scotland*, thus making the whole "wired" world witness to the event. The fact that the telegraph radically expanded the audience of the historical Lindbergh flight is doubled by the fact that radio communications are now radically expanding the audience for Brecht's cantata. In both cases, wireless communications make whole nations a communal chorus to heroic events. Increasingly, Brecht strove to identify the hero of *The Lindbergh Flight* not with an individual but with a mass. Even in its first production, Lindbergh's opening words – "My name is irrelevant" – make it clear that the pilot stands for an Everyman. After the work's premiere, however, Brecht took even greater pains to stress the collective nature of the work. "Only through *joint singing of the 'I' role* (I am so-and-so, I am starting forth, I am not tired, etc.) can we save something of the pedagogical effect" of the performance, he concluded in 1930 (*BOT* 32/24:89*). The change in the protagonist helps to emphasize the point that the true hero is the people, not the individual, the true journey the seizing of the *Apparat*, not the crossing of the Atlantic. In subsequent performances, Brecht replaced the single tenor role with a chorus of "Lindberghs." This chorus was not limited to stage singers but included the audience as a whole, in the studio as well as at home by the radio. For perhaps the first time in the history of mass communications, an audience at home by their radios was expected to sing along as one, to participate in a single, mass cantata. The conclusion of the piece – a triumphant vision of humanity's capacity to lift itself up by means of technology – takes on an even more utopian cast when performed in a manner made possible only by means of mechanics. "For thousands of years everything fell downward, all except for the bird," sing the Lindberghs at the end. "Even the most ancient engravings give us no sign that anyone has ever flown through the air. But we have lifted ourselves up" (3:24). Appropriately enough, Brecht changed the title to *The Flight of the Lindberghs* (*Der Flug der Lindberghs*) in 1930.[9] In the most literal way possible, Brecht emphasizes that Lindbergh is a collective, is all humanity "lifting itself up" by means of mechanics. Like the Wagnerian music-drama, this Brechtian experiment in what Hindemith called *Gemeinschaftsmusik* ("communal music") aimed to both mirror and forge the ideal social collective, the unalienated state.

The Lindbergh Flight is thus a utopian experiment that transcends the distinction between "high art" and "mass culture." On one hand, it responds to a desire for aesthetic unity, while on the other it expresses a desire to make radio a truly participatory mass medium. The legal context is important, as laws over the control of radio were still developing in 1929. It was only six years earlier, in 1923, that the ban on listening to wireless transmissions had been lifted in Germany, and it was only four years earlier that nine radio stations had been permitted to broadcast on a regional basis. Both of these developments had come only in the face of stiff opposition, largely from the *Reichspost*, which feared losing business, but also, intriguingly, from the Berlin Critic's Association, which feared a decline in theatre attendance. While the developments were positive in that they allowed radio to flourish for the first time as a broadcast medium, they were also intended to centralize the medium by placing it under the control of a few state-sponsored outlets. The vast majority of wireless licenses granted in Germany during these years were licenses only to listen, not to broadcast.

"Radio is one-sided when it should be two-," Brecht argued shortly after the Baden-Baden Music Festival.

> It is purely an instrument for distribution, for mere sharing out. So here is a positive suggestion: change this apparatus from distribution over to communication. The radio would be the finest possible communication apparatus in public life, a vast network of pipes.
>
> (*BOT* 52/21:552)

A revolutionary transformation of the *Apparat* of radio, Brecht suggests, would bring it closer to the *Apparat* of the telephone, a medium for communication rather than mere distribution. Further on in the same essay, Brecht specifically connects his views on the proper functioning of the radio with his radio cantata.

> *Der Flug der Lindberghs* is not intended to be of use to the present-day radio but to alter it. The increasing concentration of mechanical means and the increasingly specialized training – tendencies that should be accelerated – call for a kind of resistance by the listener, and for his mobilization and redrafting as a producer.
>
> (*BOT* 32/24:88)[10]

Brecht recognizes – correctly, as the subsequent history of mass media illustrates – that the development of ever more powerful communication technologies demands both "a kind of resistance by the listener" and an effort to turn the listener into a producer. These demands are in the deepest sense political; they are questions of who controls the dominant instruments of communication, and for what end.

And yet Brecht's attempt to rehabilitate radio as a participatory mass medium is curiously unsuccessful. The role of the audience-participants in *The Lindbergh Flight*, as well as in its subsequent variations, is in fact limited to the role of scripted chorus. "We have lifted ourselves up" ("*Wir haben uns erhoben*") sings the audience at the end of the work, but it is by no means clear that it is the chorus that pilots this airplane, even in the variation where Lindbergh is played by the audience. Theirs is not in fact the job of "communication," nor of "resistance," nor even of "production," insofar as these terms imply any real agency on the part of the communicative producer. In terms of audience participation, *The Lindbergh Flight* actually represents a narrower vision than we find in *Mahagonny*, which actively encouraged resistance, struggle, even riot in the auditorium. As a *Lehrstück*, or "didactic play," *The Lindbergh Flight* is intended to function as both message and medium, with the active participation of the radio audience reinforcing the teaching of the work. But instead its performance suggests something quite different: that by "seizing control of the apparatus," the people may be changing their tune, but not their agency.

In part, Brecht is struggling against inherent limitations of the medium of broadcast radio. When Brecht speaks of changing the apparatus of radio "from distribution over to communication," he is attacking the sort of centralization of the medium that had been occurring over the past six years in German law. And there is much to be said for Brecht's attack, for German law (like British and US law) was slow to catch up with the potential of the new medium, and quick to urge its regulation and centralization. Yet there are unavoidable troubles here too, as more equitable and democratic control of broadcast channels could only go so far in transforming a broadcast medium into a dialogic one. Even with more equitable control, and without the demand of private profit, broadcast radio remains a predominantly unidirectional medium operating within an unavoidably limited spectrum. Because the spectrum is not infinite, broadcast radio necessitates some sort of regulation and centralization so as not to degenerate into mere static. In this regard Brecht's metaphor of radio as "a vast network of pipes" is somewhat misleading: pipes can flow in both directions, and new pipes can, at least in theory, always be added alongside old ones. What we discover with *Lindbergh Flight* is that Brecht is hampered by the inherent limitations of his medium. A Listener, even in *Lindbergh Flight*, remains largely a Listener, in a broadcast medium that necessitates control and regulation.

It should be noted that my reading of radio is at odds with that of a number of leftist media critics, ranging from Brecht himself to, more recently, Hans Magnus Enzensberger. "Every transistor radio," Enzensberger has argued,

> is, by nature of its construction, at the same time a potential transmitter; it can interact with other receivers by circuit reversal. The development from a mere distribution medium to a communications medium is technically not a problem. It is consciously prevented for understandable political reasons.
>
> ("Constituents" 64)

The argument is doubtful, however. For one thing, ham radios, walkie-talkies, and other two-way radio transmitter/receivers were legal in many countries for much of the twentieth century (though Germany was more laggard, the United States began issuing radio licenses for amateur transmissions as early as 1912). The fact that they have not proved popular as instruments of mass communication has far more to do with practical limitations of the medium than with political pressures. As anyone who has ever tried to listen in on a crowded frequency can attest, such devices have proven well suited to person-to-person or small-group communication, but far less well suited to interactive mass communication, which can easily overwhelm a frequency or else disintegrate into a jumble of voices. Truly interactive mass communications through independent transmitter/receivers will have to wait until the invention of the Internet – a mass medium that, for all its interactive potential, has hardly found itself at odds with capitalist political economy.

In *Dialectic of Enlightenment*, as we have seen, Adorno and Horkheimer make the suggestion that television is a dangerous new form of the *Gesamtkunstwerk* (124). The suggestion is intriguing because television, like radio, is able to combine highly centralized control with a broadcast medium. This is only partly due to the behavior of mass media under capitalism. A far more important factor, and one which Adorno and Horkheimer both ignore, are the inherent limitations of broadcast radio and television as media. It is no accident that unidirectional media such as broadcast radio and television, rather than inherently multidirectional media such as two-way radios or telephones, become the favored tools of centralized mass spectacle. Broadcast media simply do not lend themselves to the sort of dialogic, dialectical aesthetics Brecht favors. As media theorist Pierre Lévy argues,

> [t]he true break with the pragmatics of communication brought about by writing can't take place with radio or TV because there is simply no place within these instruments of mass distribution for true reciprocity or non-hierarchical interaction among the participants. Rather than giving rise to living interactions among one or more communities, the global context created by the media remains out of reach to those who remain its passive, isolated receivers.
>
> (97)

Brecht attempts to find a way around this problem by synthesizing broadcast radio and theatre, by having a live, participatory component to the production for the home listener. But this synthesis only exacerbates the problem, for it places scripted, simultaneous performance in every kitchen and every union-hall. The questions of who is writing the script, and for what ends, remain un-askable within the context of the mass music-drama itself.

And yet the troubles of *The Lindbergh Flight* do not only stem from limitations of the medium. They also stem from the fact that, in such works (though not by any means in all his works), Brecht remains committed to an aesthetics of totality. His embrace of montage form is radically anti-Wagnerian in many respects (not least of which is its rejection of organicism), but in the end it is a contrapuntal unity and a dialectical totality that Brecht occasionally seeks. It is no surprise, then, that many of the recurring features of the total work of art emerge again in Brecht's cantata. The utopian dream of an Aesthetic State – a state that literally and figuratively sings together – recurs here. So too does the linking of political with aesthetic revolution, the hope that such a utopian state might be modeled, prefigured, and even encouraged by means of a unified artwork. Here, as at Bayreuth, the audience is both the witness of society's potential transfiguration and a crucial agent in the accomplishment of this transfiguration. Further, Wagner's conception of the central importance of the machine for the realization of the total work of art once more emerges in *The Lindbergh Flight*. Indeed, something like Wagner's love–hate relationship with the *Apparat* returns with Brecht's attempt to fight the apparatus of capitalist media with the apparatus of socialist media. It is Brecht's attempt to challenge what Wagner called the "*bad coherence*" (1:81/3:54) of commodified culture by means of the good coherence of the revolutionary artwork. Brecht's dream of an open, collaborative, montage *Gesamtkunstwerk* finds its most daring form in *The Lindbergh Flight*, which takes up the challenge of mass epic performance. But Brecht's most audacious experiment is also, tellingly, his greatest failure.

What Brecht searched for in *The Lindbergh Flight* was a dialectical form of electronically mediated collectivity. In the end, however, the limitations of a broadcast medium combined with the dictates of totalizing aesthetics (even in a montage form) to disable Brecht's airplane before it could really take flight. In *Lindbergh Flight* the "people" are figured more as a mass-mediated chorus than as a genuinely divisive and divided, troubled and troublesome collection of groups that requires an active public sphere rather than a script. Perhaps some of Brecht's recurring admiration for pharaohnic figures of the authoritarian left, not to mention his frequently dictatorial behavior as director and manager, may be traced to this penchant for totality – not the totality of Bayreuth, to be sure, but totality *in a new form*. Alongside its hopefulness, in other words, there is something decidedly dark about *Lindbergh Flight*, something of the cautionary tale. There is the suggestion that mass media, even in revolutionary hands, may end up being worse than a mere instrument for distribution, may be a way of turning the public into a choral mass. With *Lindbergh Flight*, Brecht may have come closer to Riefenstahl than he ever would have wished.

Chapter 5

Total state

Riefenstahl's *Triumph of the Will*

Gentlemen, in one hundred years' time they will be showing a fine color film of the terrible days we are living through. Wouldn't you like to play a part in that film? Hold out now, so that 100 years hence the audience will not hoot and whistle when you appear on screen.

Josef Goebbels, 1945 (quoted in Koepnick 51)

The invisible pilot

The opening images of *Triumph of the Will* (*Triumph des Willens*, 1935) are all of flight. We see first, lifted by Herbert Windt's soaring score, the iron eagle of the Reich, wings spread wide. Successive titles tell us of Germany's Christlike suffering (*Leiden*) and its majestic rebirth (*Wiedergeburt*). The final title card begins with the word "flew" (*flog*):

flog Adolf Hitler
wiederum nach Nürnberg
um heerschau abzuhalten
über seine Getreuen.

Adolf Hitler flew
again to Nuremberg
to review
his faithful followers.

After this title card we are taken into the cockpit of a plane, soaring above the clouds. The implication is clear: Hitler, the first politician to campaign with a plane, is the one who flies, and we are witnessing the Führer flying, the Führer who is also the German Eagle, the Führer who is also an angel, the Führer who is also, as Siegfried Kracauer has noted, the modern Messiah come to save Germany and baptize his *Volk* in the triumphant Aryan Will.

But there is also something peculiar about this opening shot in the cockpit of the plane that is meant to be Hitler's plane. What is peculiar is this: there is a ghost in the plane with us. We begin the shot looking out, from the cockpit, at the clouds. We are sitting to the right, in the co-pilot's seat perhaps. The camera slowly turns leftward, scanning the clouds but also, presumably, looking over towards our pilot, turning to face him. We scan almost the whole of the cabin, we see almost directly to the left of us, but there is nobody there. The joystick waggles back and forth, but we see no hand upon it. Then suddenly, just before we come to the seat to our left, we are torn from the shot and find ourselves looking away again, out into the clouds.

What is going on here? Is there no pilot to this plane? Or are we all, as Brecht would have it, the pilot? Or is the absence meant to imply that Hitler is piloting his own plane into Nuremberg, like George W. Bush in his flight suit? Riefenstahl, who loved rugged men in uniform and in action, would surely see the cinematic potential of a Nordic chin guiding our plane to ground. Was our pilot perhaps too plain for pictures?

On further reflection, the solution to the riddle becomes clear. Riefenstahl cannot show the pilot of this plane because that pilot is of course not Hitler, and Riefenstahl must maintain the illusion that Hitler is always and everywhere the pilot, guiding vast energetic engines with a twitch of his hand, soaring above billowing masses with effortless abandon. To show a pilot to this plane would be to show a man leading the Leader, a flier who is not the Führer. More than this, to show a pilot to the plane would be to show the mechanical underbelly of Hitler's pseudo-organic *Gesamtkunstwerk*, the underbelly that is labor. Not labor transformed into mass ornament (as in the vast troops of spade-wielding "Labor Corps" workers which come later in the film) nor labor transformed into "Strength through Joy" kitsch (as in the happy sausage-wielding cooks of the camp scenes) but labor in the form of one man chauffeuring another man through the air. And the accompanying suggestion, also unmentionable, that the chauffeur is in fact the one in the driver's seat, and might not need the extra baggage.

The medium of film has always owed much to Wagner and the tradition of the *Gesamtkuntwerk*. When the moviehouse was thrust into darkness and the spectators stared forward at images produced by a "technical apparatus for projecting a picture" (Wagner 5:333/9:336), Wagner's proto-cinematic theatrical vision was realized to an extraordinary degree. The indebtedness of the cinema to Wagner was already apparent at least as early as 1910, with words such as *Gesamtkunstwerk*, *Leitmotiv*, and *unendliche Melodie* occasionally employed by film directors, film composers, and film critics to describe the new form.[1] This indebtedness is even more pronounced in Riefenstahl's creation, a work that marks the translation of the iconic *Gesamtkunstwerk* into film. At once fervently in pursuit of "organic" totality and profoundly reliant upon cutting-edge techniques of mechanical production, *Triumph of the Will* must rigorously hide all of the techniques on which it relies. The film is Wagnerian, too, in its utopian evocation of an ecstatic German *Volk*, a *Volk* unified not only through a common Will but also through communal participation in a great artwork. Riefenstahl's film, like the Wagnerian music-drama, operates as a supposedly organic work of art that at once reflects the ideal state and helps to forge it. "High art" versus "folk art," "politics" versus "art," "culture" versus "daily life": all such oppositions are annihilated in the great organic totality evoked at the 1934 Party Convention, and celebrated in *Triumph of the Will*. Set to the pseudo-Wagnerian strains of Windt's score, the directorial vision of Riefenstahl – combined, of course, with the visions of Hitler, Goebbels, and Speer – comes remarkably close to a realization of at least certain aspects of Wagner's dream of the *Gesamtkunstwerk* as first expressed in his Zurich writings. In many ways, *Triumph of the Will* serves as a paradigmatic case of the Nazi *Gesamtkunstwerk*, one that helps to illustrate the troubles of totality suffered by the Nazi state, and the strategies for their resolution.

And yet there is much that is atypical, too, about *Triumph of the Will*. For it is a film that was made at a specific historical moment for specific historical ends, both of which must be considered in order to understand the total performance it offers. And it is a film that raises almost unique questions about the relationship between art and politics, documentary and propaganda, questions that will become central to the history of the total work of art. In order to situate *Triumph of the Will* within the history of the total work of art, we must make sense of both its peculiarity and its broader significance.

A chain of rings

Triumph of the Will was commissioned "by order of the Führer" as a document and a glorification of the *Reichsparteitag*, or Party Convention (literally "Reich's Party Day"), of 1934.[2] It was produced by Riefenstahl's production company, Leni Riefenstahl Studio-Film, a fact that Riefenstahl frequently pointed to as evidence of her creative independence, though she invariably left unmentioned the fact that the film was financed and distributed by Ufa, a German film company closely allied with the Nazi Party. At any rate, Nazi control over the national cinema was such that Riefenstahl's "artistic freedom" was always subject to Party demands. After its release, the film won first prize at the Venice Biennale in 1935, the German National Film Prize (awarded by Goebbels) in 1935, and the Medaille d'Or and the Grand Prix de France in 1937. That judges in Fascist Italy, Nazi Germany, and republican France should all have honored the film speaks volumes about its ambiguities, and audiences have long debated whether the film ought to be understood primarily as a documentary or a propaganda piece. In fact it is both, at once providing an indispensable record of Nazi mass spectacle and manipulating sounds and images so as to sweep the spectator into the arms of the Führer. Far from detracting from the film's function as propaganda, the documentary aspects of the film serve only to support the propagandistic aspects.

More than this: the documentary and the propagandistic aspects of *Triumph of the Will* are so intertwined and mutually supporting that the result becomes a synthesis that transcends them both, an *Aufhebung* of documentary and propaganda into something else entirely. Embroiled in ping-ponging documentary-versus-propaganda debates, film critics have generally missed the larger synthesis, which is the real mark of Riefenstahl's achievement and the crucial point of connection between *Triumph of the Will* and the total work of art. At one extreme, some critics have attempted simply to remove the historical aspects of the film from the film itself. David Hinton, for instance, writes that "[u]nderstanding the historical background of the film is necessary when approaching the film as a document, but it reveals nothing of the nature of Leni Riefenstahl, the filmmaker. For that, the film itself must be studied apart from its historical background" (33). To attempt to study either "the nature of Leni Riefenstahl" or her "film itself" apart from their "historical background" would seem a *reductio ad absurdum* of formalist criticism, and yet Hinton appears to be in earnest. Ken Kelman is more sensitive to the inextricably political nature of Riefenstahl's film aesthetic when he argues that the *Triumph of the Will* comes to

> surpass *Potemkin* as the ultimate in cinema propaganda. This is for one essential reason: *Triumph* is a true documentary, completely made up of 'actual' footage – the ultimate in incontrovertible credibility. The wonderful paradox here is that under any conditions but this absolute reportorial truth, the propaganda itself would be quite incredible.
>
> (162)

Kelman is correct in arguing that *Triumph of the Will* surpasses Sergei Eisenstein's *Potemkin* as "the ultimate in cinema propaganda," but the reason he gives (that it uses "'actual' footage" for propagandistic effect) does not go quite far enough. Kelman's quotation marks around "actual" suggest that he is not fully comfortable with the "incontrovertible credibility" of Riefenstahl's "true documentary," but then the quotation marks disappear in the next sentence, when he writes of the film's "absolute reportorial truth." Rather than shying away from the troubling nature of actuality in Riefenstahl's film, we should embrace it as a key to the whole work.

While it is widely agreed that Riefenstahl rearranged the chronology of the rallies for her film, scholars have debated how much, if any, of *Triumph of the Will* was restaged and reshot.[3] The debate in fact reproduces the old documentary-versus-propaganda question in miniature, and the battle lines are roughly the same. Unsurprisingly, Riefenstahl insisted that none of *Triumph of the Will* was restaged or reshot, aiding her claim that the film was purely objective reportage, barely more than artfully edited newsreel footage.[4] But Riefenstahl's claim is contradicted by the memory of Albert Speer, who writes in *Inside the Third Reich* that some of the film of the rallies was spoiled and so had to be restaged and reshot after the Convention (Speer 62). While Riefenstahl repeatedly denied that this restaging ever occurred, Brian Winston has shown that a close analysis of the film supports Speer's memory (105). Indeed, when they have weighed in on one side or the other, critics have generally sided with Speer and against Riefenstahl, speculating that anything from short speeches (namely those of Streicher, Hess, Rosenberg, and Frank) to longer scenes (namely the "Sprechchor" chants of the Labor Corps, 0:35:20–0:38:50) were at least partially refilmed at a later point. If some restaging occurred, as it almost certainly did, then it would go a long way toward undermining the claim that the rally footage represents "absolute reportorial truth," in Kelman's phrase, or a "pure document," in Riefenstahl's (Riefenstahl, *Cahiers* 46). But it does not necessarily follow that the film is nothing more than propaganda. Kelman is correct when he writes of a fusion, but that fusion does not lie in the marriage of reportorial truth and myth. It lies instead in the disappearance of the opposition between truth and myth in a larger network of performance.

Arguing that "the Convention was planned not only as a spectacular mass meeting, but also as spectacular film propaganda," Kracauer rightly concludes that rally and film cannot be separated. The massive Party involvement in Riefenstahl's film – an involvement mandated and repeatedly reinforced by Hitler himself – ensured that *Triumph of the Will* was a part of the planning of the Convention, and further guaranteed that Riefenstahl would have unprecedented (at least for a "documentary") resources with which to film. Kracauer recalls the sheer size of the film crew employed by Riefenstahl: 30 cameras and a crew of about 120 (301). And yet his numbers are actually conservative, as it seems that the entire crew likely numbered 172, including 29 newsreel cameramen operating their own equipment.[5] Many of Riefenstahl's crew were disguised in SA uniforms so as to better blend into the crowd, and the entire crew was guarded by squads of SA and SS as well as municipal police.[6] In addition to supporting this vast crew, the Party helped Riefenstahl erect an elaborate, pioneering superstructure of filming devices, including cars, fire-truck ladders, roller-skates, airplanes, blimps, camera elevators, and camera dollies. Like Wagner at Bayreuth, Riefenstahl relied upon pioneering technical devices to realize her vision of organic unity. It was always clear that Hitler regarded this film as central to his propaganda efforts, at least as central as the rally itself. Given its subsequent successes and its worldwide audience, its ultimate impact may well have been greater.

Riefenstahl's 1935 book *Hinter den Kulissen des Reichsparteitag-Films* (*Behind the Scenes at the Party Convention Film*) gives us a revealing triptych of photographs.[7] The first shows Hitler leaning over a ground plan for arrangement of troops at the Luitpoldhain Arena, a central rally ground for the Convention. Accompanied by Nazi officials, Riefenstahl looks on. The caption reads: "The preparations for the Party Convention went hand in hand with the preparations for the film production. The Führer described the total picture [*Gesamtbild*] of the plan of assembly" (31). The photograph immediately to the right of this one is similar, but here Speer takes the place of Riefenstahl. "Architect Speer reports on the building construction," reads the caption. A final photograph takes its place below these two. Riefenstahl now surveys the Arena, accompanied by an officer and a man who may be Speer. "The field of Luitpoldhain is still empty, but every meter is allocated for the approaching roll-call and we have to fight for every spot for the film production." As these three photographs and their accompanying captions make clear, Riefensthal's "fight" for position took place within the context of a larger, carefully orchestrated production, a "*Gesamtbild*" in which Speer's designs operated "hand in hand" with Riefenstahl's film, all under the watchful eye of the Führer. Together they would transform the "tremendous symphony of the throng" (11) into "a heroic film of fact" in which the "*Volk* triumphs" by "the Führer's Will" (28). Even the weather participates in this grand totality. "Unfortunately, the sun disappeared behind the clouds," Riefenstahl writes of the day of the Führer's arrival by airplane. "But no – as the Führer comes, the rays break through the clouds: Hitler-weather!" (21). Such statements leave open the question of who the ultimate artist is behind this totalizing production: Riefenstahl? Speer? Hitler? Or perhaps the Triumphant Will itself, parting the clouds for its anointed?

Such questions point to the difficulty in separating documentary from propaganda, or art from reportage, in a film such as *Triumph of the Will*. The supposedly antithetical forms become even more tightly intertwined when we consider the ways in which the film expresses its ideological allegiance through its formal structures. I will discuss some of these formal structures in greater detail later in the chapter, but one that should be mentioned at the outset is the principle of movement. In his wide-ranging discussion of film directors in *Cinema 1: The Movement-Image*, Gilles Deleuze surveys a number of (mostly pre-WWII) directors – Eisenstein, Griffith, Gance, Murnau, Lang, Renoir, Buñuel, Hawks, Stroheim, etc. – but oddly overlooks Riefenstahl.[8] And yet few films – and almost no documentary-style films – are so marked by the dominance of movement as this one. "In 1934, when I made *Triumph of the Will*," remarks Riefenstahl in an interview with Ray Müller,

> newsreels were very static, no movement, no traveling shots. I thought the shots should be made mobile and thus more interesting. That's why my crew began to shoot on roller skates. But above all I needed lots of shots from different camera positions.

The importance of movement may be appreciated in a scene such as the SA and SS review at Luitpoldhain Arena (Scene 14).[9] Though Richard Barsam has argued that the scene derives its effect from Speer's aesthetic vision rather than Riefenstahl's, we can see that Riefenstahl's vision of the movement-image dominates this scene, as indeed it does the film as a whole.[10]

The scene is a typical example of Riefenstahl's use of multiple moving camera angles. It opens with a shot of the German eagle in stone, and already we are in motion, as the camera is panning down to reveal a swastika clutched in the bird's talons. The image dissolves into the next scene, superimposing itself atop endless lines of assembled SA men as it fades away; the Symbol, as Riefenstahl consistently emphasizes by means of such impositions, becomes Spirit, hovering over the masses and guiding them. Through the long military ranks walk three figures (Hitler, Lutze, Himmler) toward the War Memorial, forming a mobile wedge within still columns. Again Riefenstahl sets her own cameras in motion, dancing with the mass ornaments of Speer's creation. We are at a full long angle behind the three figures, viewing them from an enormous height, looking out toward the Memorial. Now we are behind the Memorial itself, at a long angle on the opposite side of the vast field, with Hitler, Lutze, and Himmler approaching us, and, more than this, we are moving horizontally. And now we are at a close-up angle, hovering almost directly above the Memorial, panning down upon the three figures approaching us. Soon a parade of flags enters the arena, the movement of which is doubled by the simultaneous movement of Riefenstahl's horizontal and vertical tracking shots (created with the aid of dollies and an elevator on a 140-foot tower). And so on, with the camera constantly shifting position, always in motion.

The point here is not simply that Riefenstahl was a pioneer in the use of mobile film techniques. The greater point is that Riefenstahl's techniques do two things, both of which are ideologically loaded. First, her techniques carry the viewer away in a sea of movement which is a visual and aural expression of *the* Movement: active, dynamic, political, aesthetic, youthful, disorienting, vertiginous, muscular, impersonal, obedient to some mysterious Will, sublimely greater than oneself. Second, her techniques profoundly disorient the viewer, rendering the viewer's subject-position not only multiple but virtually ubiquitous. The viewer of *Triumph of the Will* is simultaneously everywhere and nowhere, recalling Jonathan Crary's observations about the use of movement in *The Great Train Robbery*. Observing that that film consists of processes "of perpetual displacement and re-creation of positions and relations," Crary concludes that:

> [i]t is hardly a question of a mobile point of view, but instead the serial reconfiguration of a kinesthetic constellation of moving forces, in which the idea of a coherent subject position is as irrelevant as the idea of Cartesian coordinates in a kaleidoscope.
>
> (347)

The same may be said of *Triumph of the Will*, which even more wildly disorients the viewer by means of displacements of position and movement of elements. It is not merely that the viewer's position in *Triumph of the Will* is constantly shifting, but that there is no coherent position or set of positions at all. To put the matter another way, it is not so much that the viewer is a cork bobbing in a moving ocean as it is that the viewer and the ocean are moving independently, creating a whirlpool of cross-currents. Thus is Moholy-Nagy's "great dynamic-rhythmic process, which can compress the greatest clashing masses or accumulations of media" given "elemental form" beyond anything imagined by the Bauhaus ("Theater" 64). Speer may have offered his own vision of "dynamic-rhythmic" *Totaltheater* in the rallies, but Riefenstahl transforms Speer's vision into *Totalfilm*.

Amidst this totalizing flux, Riefenstahl offers the viewer a rock of salvation. The shots of moving masses are repeatedly intercut, in Scene 14 and elsewhere, with shots of Hitler standing alone on a podium. He stands motionless, with his hands folded across his chest for further stability. In his own body, he is the "fixed pole" to which he refers in his closing address ("The German people are happy in the knowledge that the constantly changing leadership has now been replaced by a fixed pole"). At the same time, he is generally filmed from beneath, often with nothing behind him but sky. The angle – Riefenstahl's favorite for Hitler – at once raises Hitler up as a god among men and decontextualizes him, removing him from other people, from the ground on which he stands, and from any surrounding environment. He is a human Symbol, recalling the imperial eagle at the opening of the scene (and the opening and closing of the film), which is shot from the same angle and stands similarly out of place and time. Thus do Riefenstahl's techniques of constant movement and kaleidoscopic displacement of viewer and object lead, inexorably, to the only solid figure, a figure who must stand outside of the clashing masses and vertiginous effects of the movement-image *in extremis*.

Returning to the question of whether elements of *Triumph of the Will* were reshot or restaged, we can now see that the whole question is something of a false lead. For the film was an integral part of the Party Convention from the beginning, and the formal qualities of the film shape its ideological content. The more significant issue, then, is that of the intertwining of systems of total performance at Nuremberg in 1934. There are at least three such systems – Wagner's music-dramas, Speer's rally, and Riefenstahl's film – and they intertwine, as closed rings in a larger chain of total theatre that was the Nazi state.

The new Meistersingers

Scholars have frequently asserted that Windt's overture to *Triumph of the Will* includes quotations from the Act 3 overture to Wagner's *Die Meistersinger von Nürnberg* (*The Mastersingers of Nuremberg*).[11] In fact Windt's overture contains no such quotations. And yet the confusion is understandable, and not just because of the pseudo-Wagnerian tones of Windt's scoring or the fact that few film critics are Wagner scholars. Like many false rumors, this one captures a larger truth. For the shadow of *Die Meistersinger* hangs over Riefenstahl's film, as it hung over Speer's rally and Hitler's state, and it serves as one marker of the network of *Gesamtkunstwerke* that formed the aestheticization of politics of the Third Reich.

Though *Die Meistersinger* is not to be heard in the film's overture, it may be heard in the fifth chapter of the film (14:04–15:48). In this section, the *"Wach auf"* ("Awake!") theme from *Meistersinger*'s Act 3 plays while day breaks over the quaint houses of Nuremberg. The *"Wach auf"* chorale is a musical setting of Hans Sachs' poetic allegory in praise of Luther, *Die Wittenbergische Nachtigall* (1523). The implication was as clear in 1934 as it was in 1868: Nuremberg, the city of Hans Sachs, must once again reawaken from its long slumber, and embrace a new reformation, a new vision of nation and God. The Party banners that fill the Congress Hall in the last scene of the film all bear the same insignia – *Deutschland Erwache* (*Germany Awake*) – a motto coined by Hitler himself, thus harkening back once more to the *"Wach auf"* chorale. Would German audience members understand such references, and their implications? Many would, at least implicitly, for Hitler and Goebbels had made *Die Meistersinger* a centerpiece in their campaign to reconstruct the German state as a total work of art.

That Hitler was a fanatical Wagnerian is well known, as is the fact that the Nazi state was formed with an eye to Bayreuth.[12] Riefenstahl's own account of the

Führer's musings in the spring of 1932 may stand in as an emblem of the relation of Hitler to his proclaimed Master:

> He spoke about Wagner, about King Ludwig of Bavaria, and about Bayreuth, but after a while he suddenly changed his expression and his voice. With great passion he declared: "More than anything else I am filled with my political mission. I feel that I have been called to save Germany – I cannot and must not refuse this calling."
>
> (*Memoir* 107)

Hitler's movement from Wagner to his own messianic "mission" is entirely typical. Under Hitler, as Joachim Köhler puts it (with poetic hyperbole), "Germany became Wagnerian opera" (242). What Benjamin famously called the aestheticization of politics under fascism could be found on every level of culture. On one level there were the mass rallies, the enormous building projects, the Party broadcasts and propaganda films. On another level there was a thoroughgoing transformation of the structure of everyday life by replacing Christian holidays with National Socialist celebrations, forcing all children to join Party youth corps, replacing labor unions with the Party Labor Corps, establishing the *Sieg Heil* as a universal greeting, distributing *Mein Kampf* to every German household, and so forth. Beneath such transformations lay a deeper conception, explored in detail in several studies, of the *Volk* itself as raw clay to be sculpted into organic unity by the hand of a master artist.[13] "Politics, too, is an art, perhaps the highest and most far-reaching one of all," said Goebbels in echo of his leader, "and we who shape modern German politics feel ourselves to be artistic people, entrusted with the great responsibility of forming out of the raw material of the masses a solid, well-wrought structure of a *Volk*" (quoted in Brenner 178).

More than any other single artwork, Wagner's *Meistersinger* served as a model of this "well-wrought structure." After gaining power, the Nazis made *Meistersinger* their unofficial anthem, a highbrow counterpart to the boozy "*Horst-Wessel-Lied*" popularized by the SA. Witnessing this usurpation, Ernst Bloch urged denial: "The music of the Nazis is not the Prelude to *Die Meistersinger*, but rather the '*Horst-Wessel-Lied*'; they deserve credit for nothing else, and no more can nor should be granted them" ("Über Wurzeln" 320). But whether they deserved credit for it or not, they had taken *Meistersinger* – and not just the Prelude – as their own. The famous "Day of Potsdam" (21 March 1933), an elaborate ritual orchestrated by Hitler and Goebbels, in which President Hindenberg and Chancellor Hitler inaugurated their new government, climaxed in a performance of *Die Meistersinger* at Berlin's Staatsoper. Similarly, the first Bayreuth production under the new regime, with Hitler in attendance, was *Meistersinger*. This 1933 performance was broadcast by radio to the German nation, and Goebbels spoke at the intermission:

> [t]here is certainly no work in the entire music literature of the German people that is so relevant to our time and its spiritual and intellectual tensions as is

Richard Wagner's *Meistersinger* … Of all his music dramas the *Meistersinger* stands out today as the most German. It is simply the incarnation of our national identity.

(quoted in Spotts, *Bayreuth* 173)

Unsurprisingly, the first day of the 1934 Nuremberg Party Convention culminated in a production of *Meistersinger* designed by Benno von Arent, working in collaboration with Hitler himself. The Führer, along with numerous Party officials, was in attendance. This influential production, which was frequently revived and imitated during the Third Reich, featured massed crowd scenes meant to directly reflect the Nuremberg Party Convention (Figures 5.1 and 5.2).[14] This linkage between opera and rally was emphasized yet again in 1935, when Hitler ordered that *Meistersinger* be performed at every Nuremberg Party Convention forever.

The music-drama that "reawakened" German unity would eventually serve as a morale booster for battered German troops. When, in 1943, wounded soldiers and armaments workers made their pilgrimage to Bayreuth (as guests of the Führer himself, who paid for their tickets and transportation out of his personal funds), they came to see *Meistersinger*, the only opera featured at the Festspielhaus that season. On stage, alongside the trained opera singers, performed boys from the Hitler Jugend, girls from the Bund Deutscher Mädel, and men from the SS. Rally and music-drama, Nuremberg and the Third Reich, Nazi Party and Meistersingers, Hitler and Hans Sachs, everyday life and fascist liturgy: all were intertwined from the beginning in the Third Reich, and nowhere more so than with *Meistersinger*.

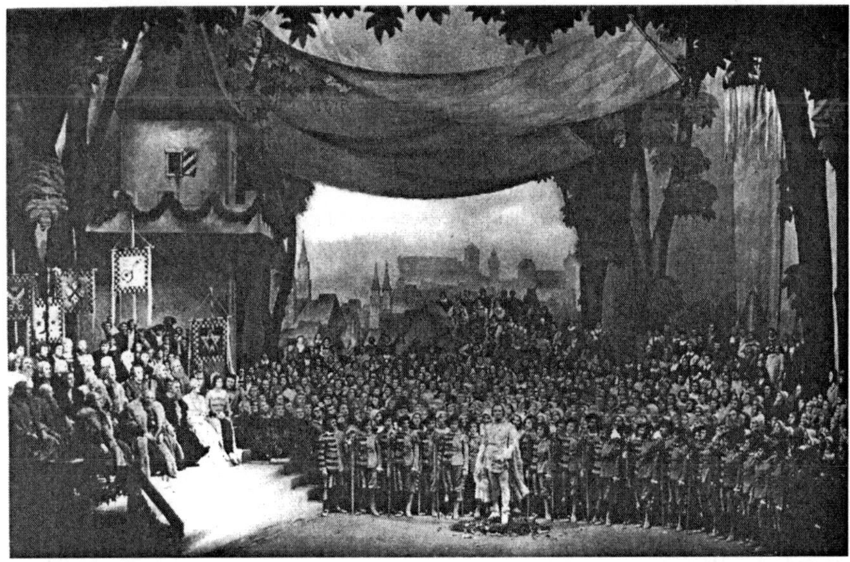

Figure 5.1 Die Meistersinger, Act 3, Benno von Arent production, 1935.

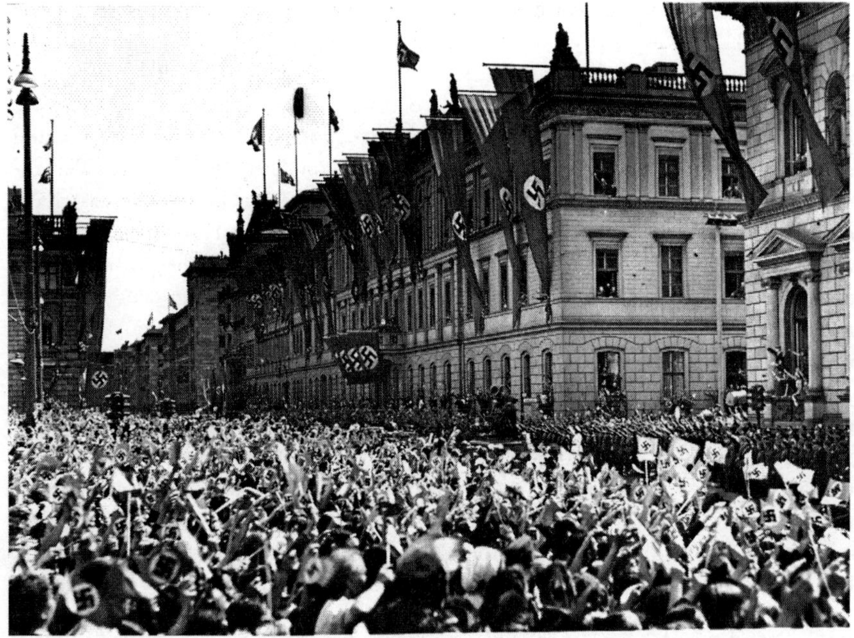

Figure 5.2 *Triumph des Willens*, film still, 1935.

Of all of *Meistersinger*, the "*Wach auf*" chorale in Act 3 was particularly dear to the Nazi heart. In Party mythology, a direct line ran from Hans Sach's "*Wach auf*" to Wagner's "*Wach auf*" to Hitler's "*Wach auf*."

How often in years past has its rousing mass chorus "Awake! Soon will dawn the day," been found by an ardently longing, believing German people to be a palpable symbol for the reawakening of the German nation from the deep political and spiritual narcosis of November 1918,

proclaimed Goebbels in his radio broadcast during the 1933 Bayreuth *Meistersinger*.[15] A custom dating back to 1924 was for Nazi enthusiasts to demonstrate their support by standing (and occasionally singing, shouting, and stamping) during the "*Wach auf*" chorale, a custom that continued to be practiced throughout the Third Reich. The meaning of this call changed with the course of history, however. Whereas Nazi supporters before the war generally connected the call to their seizure of power, the official interpretation changed once the pain and duration of the war had become clear. "When this war is finally over," Hitler announced to munitions workers in 1940, "a great period of reconstruction will set in, a great cry of '*Wach auf*!' will be heard throughout the land and out of all this work that great German

Reich will emerge of which a great poet once dreamed" (*Reden* 2:1633). Thus would German history from Hans Sachs through Wagner find its apotheosis in the conclusion of the Second World War, the wake of which would mark the third and greatest reawakening of the German *Volk*.

So the strains of the *"Wach auf"* chorale that soar over images of reawakening Nuremberg in the third scene of *Triumph of the Will* are far more than rousing accompaniment. The melody marks the utopian aspirations of the Party Convention itself, aspirations rooted, however perversely, in the same Schillerian dreams of an Aesthetic State that originally influenced Wagner's vision of the *Gesamtkunstwerk*. It marks, in other words, the film's connection to the tradition of the *Gesamtkunstwerk*, and its participation in the interlocking systems of total performance of the totalitarian state. Unsurprisingly, this melody is accompanied by distinctly *völkisch* images of the sort that was already associated with Nazi kitsch and the Hitler-approved productions of *Meistersinger*. Steeply gabled rooftops, smoking chimneys, winding streets; a latched window with lace curtains opened to show two potted plants on the windowsill, two miniature Nazi flags, and the half-timbered houses of Nuremberg beyond; a slow boat-ride along the Pegnitz, with the passing scenery reflected in the shimmering water. (And for a few seconds, as the boat passes a stone monument, the shadow of a cameraman – no "organic" artwork, after all, being entirely able to avoid revealing its own mechanical traces.[16])

The centrality of *Meistersinger* to the chain of total performance in Nuremberg raises the issue of Wagner's music-drama itself, and more particularly its relation to the *Gesamtkunstwerk*. Drawing from Žižck's *Sublime Object of Ideology*, David Levin has argued that the *Gesamtkunstwerk* relies on a necessary Other, a figure who must be present in order to be excluded. That figure is, according to Levin, the Jew, and his presence and his exclusion are nowhere so manifest as in *Meistersinger*.[17] "Given Wagner's commitment to the *Gesamtkunstwerk*, to a program of seamless aesthetic totalization," argues Levin,

> the Jew functions as the structural guarantor of that totality by representing, within the work, that which does not belong, which must be exorcised. We might think of Jews, then, as the "I don't" that guarantees a series of polygamous unions: the reconciliation of language and nature in a non-Jewish artwork of the future; the union of the arts in the *Gesamtkunstwerk*; or, more concretely, the union of Walther and Eva, which is, of course, repeatedly (if only temporarily) marred by what must nonetheless be seen as its guarantor . . . That program finds expression in Wagner's music dramas – most notoriously, no doubt, in *The Mastersingers of Nuremberg*.
>
> ("Reading" 131)

Whether or not antisemitism is central to *Meistersinger* – whether, to put the matter differently, Wagner's Beckmesser is a Jew – is a debate that need not concern us here.[18] More important for our present discussion is the point that Levin raises about the nature of the *Gesamtkunstwerk* itself, that the *Gesamtkunstwerk* structurally relies on an Other whose purpose it is to *not belong*, and that this reliance is especially exemplified by *Meistersinger*. Whether one reads him as a Jew or not, Beckmesser is at any rate the necessary exclusion of Wagner's opera, the guarantor of totality who must be exorcised.

If *Triumph of the Will* participates in an interlocking system of total performance, and if that system is marked throughout by *Meistersinger*, then the question arises: who, or what, is the Beckmesser here? *Is* there even such a figure? On at least a surface level, the film seems far more concerned with belonging than exclusion. Take, as one example among many, the boisterous camp scenes that immediately follow the "*Wach auf*" section discussed above. The transition from the daybreak-over-Nuremberg scenes to the camp scenes is accomplished by the technique of superimposing one symbol (the towers of the St Sebaldus Church) over the next (rows of military tents), a technique Riefenstahl frequently employs to give the film a symbolic unity. The effect of this superimposition is to suggest that these camps are sacred sites as well – so many little churches in canvas. In case the implication is missed, the audio track doubles the visual, as the ringing bells of the church become the reverie bells of the encampment (an effect that also, and not incidentally, extends the "*Wach auf*" theme into the next chapter of the film). And certainly the same atmosphere of the camp seems spirited and inclusive, a vision of *Volksgemeinschaft* ("folk's community") in action. The scenes in the military encampments are in fact euphoric celebrations of belonging. Where, then, are we to find the "structural guarantor" of this totality?

Not, or at least not chiefly, in the figure of "the Jew." To be sure, the faces Riefenstahl shows us throughout her film – faces of adoring women and children, but most of all adoring and adored men, distinguished by their "Aryan" features – bear witness to a "racially purified" *Volk*. And there are some statements of explicit antisemitism in the film, such as an opening-ceremony clip of the notorious Jew-baiter Julius Streicher, who proclaims that "a people that does not protect the purity of its race goes to seed!" (0:31:31–0:31:40). By and large, however, the celebration of "Aryan" features only implies a "racial" Other in the film, and the explicitly antisemitic gestures are few, quick, and coded. While Riefenstahl is surely wrong when she claims there are no antisemitic elements in *Triumph of the Will*,[19] it would also be wrong to see "the Jewish problem" as a dominant theme of the film, or "the Jew" as the structural guarantor of its totality.

Where, then, may this structural guarantor be found? In fact – everywhere, or almost. To begin with, we find it in the brown shirt of every SA stormtrooper. The Convention took place in the immediate wake of a crucial event in the formation of the Nazi state. Three months earlier, in June 1934, Hitler had ordered the "Night of the Long Knives," the murder of SA leader Ernst Röhm and roughly 85 others in anticipation of a supposed putsch. Though the putsch attempt was almost certainly a lie concocted to get rid of undesirables, the threat posed by Röhm was real. Most obviously, Röhm's control of the SA posed a real and potent challenge to Hitler's desire for single, total control of the state. Moreover, Röhm had been calling for a "second revolution," one that would replace the army with the SA and establish a radically noncapitalist state. To the army officers, conservative burghers, and traditionalist aristocrats Hitler needed for the consolidation of his power, Röhm was simply unacceptable. Added to this was the fact that Röhm had never made a secret of his homosexuality, making him a lightning-rod for slander both inside and outside the Party. There is a Beckmesser of *Triumph of the Will*, in other words, and he is Ernst Röhm. And though he was executed shortly before the Party Convention, his ghost hangs over the Convention as well as over Riefenstahl's film, both of which are an exercise in exorcism. Both were calculated to reincorporate the SA into the emergent totalitarian state by making Röhm a model of that which does not belong.

The new Beckmesser

The name "Röhm" is never uttered in *Triumph of the Will*, itself a telling detail, marking his sudden collapse from prominent Nazi leader to complete unmentionable. Allusions to him, however, are abundant and centrally placed. The four principal points at which Röhm and the Röhm affair are alluded to are Hitler's opening proclamation (read by Adolf Wagner) at the inaugural ceremonies of the Convention (0:28:37–0:29:26), Victor Lutze's nighttime speech to the SA (0:42:15–0:44:05), Hitler's speech to the SA and SS men before the consecration of the flags (1:11:55–1:14:48), and the end of Hitler's closing speech at the Nuremberg Congress Hall (1:44:30–31:45:10). In her 1965 *Cahiers du Cinéma* interview, Riefenstahl insisted that, when she began filming, the "total structure [*la construction d'ensemble*] imposed itself. It was purely intuitive" (62). The evidence of the film, however, shows that this structure reflects precisely the propagandistic demands of the Party leadership. If indeed such a structure was "intuitively" arrived at by Riefenstahl, then one must conclude that Riefenstahl's intuition reflected the desires of Party ideology almost exactly, for she uses these references to Röhm as the backbone of her production. Table 5.1 demonstrates how these references are well spaced throughout the film so as to give the film shape and coherence. In this respect, the film not only reflected the structure of the Party Convention itself (which pointedly opened and closed with allusions to the Röhm purge) but emphasized that structure through its own pacing over the course of two hours.

In her interview with Ray Müller, Riefenstahl described her process of making *Triumph of the Will* as "like a musical composition" made up of climaxes and anticipations, hills and valleys. Though she has repeatedly painted herself as a political naïf, Riefenstahl constructed a filmic composition that gains much of its musical pacing from allusions to the Röhm purge, allusions that (in her version) open the ceremonies, close them, and are well spaced throughout.

Of these four major allusions, the most extended is the third, Hitler's speech to the SA and SS at the Luitpoldhain Arena on September 9. The section begins with a long shot of Hitler, SS chief Himmler, and the new SA chief Lutze, walking slowly toward a War Memorial. Surrounding them on all sides are countless rows of SA stormtroopers. A parade of flags follows, and then Hitler's speech.

Table 5.1 Structural positioning of allusions to Röhm purge

	1st allusion	2nd allusion	3rd allusion	4th allusion
	(0:28:37–0:29:26)	(0:42:15–0:44:05)	(1:11:55–1:14:48)	(1:44:30–1:45:10)
	Hitler's opening proclamation	Lutze's speech	Hitler's speech to SA and SS	Hitler's closing speech
1–10 min.	10–20	20–30	30–40	40–50	50–60	60–70	70–80	80–90	90–100	110–20

Note

Upper row indicates allusion; lower row indicates minutes on film counter.

SA and SS men! A few months ago a dark shadow cast itself across our Movement. The SA and other institutions of the Party had nothing whatsoever to do with this shadow. They who would believe that a rift has opened in the unity of the Movement deceive themselves. It stands fast as this block here and nothing in Germany will break it. And when anyone does harm to the spirit of my SA then the SA will not be harmed but those who do this harm will injure only themselves! And only a fool or a known liar could think that I would ever disband any organization that took us so many years to build. My comrades, we stand fast together for our Germany and we *must* stand fast together for *this* Germany.

The themes of this address are clear enough. To begin with, Hitler is reassuring the stormtroopers that their purge is over, and that they will be safe from him as long as they are loyal. Secondly, Hitler is exonerating the SA by assigning all blame to a nameless "dark shadow," a shadow that "had nothing whatsoever to do" with the SA. Having purged and purified the organization, he is now reabsorbing it to himself more fully than ever before. Other speeches, by both Hitler and Lutze, reiterate these points. Further, the transition of loyalty from Röhm to Lutze is reemphasized by giving Lutze an especially lengthy address in the film (Scene 10), and by lingering on the adulation of the SA for Lutze before, during, and especially after his address. Tellingly, Lutze is the only Party leader other than Hitler who is shown receiving mass adulation. Given Lutze's notorious lack of charisma, and the very conflicted feelings that the rank and file felt about him as a replacement for Röhm, these choices are yet further indication of Riefenstahl's manipulation of footage to support the propaganda purposes of the Third Reich. In addition to these explicit attempts to use the Röhm affair as a means of reincorporation are numerous subtler gestures. Consider, for instance, Hermann Göring's uniform during the final parade in front of the Nuremberg city hall (Scene 15, 1:19:40). He is dressed in an SA uniform for this parade, despite the fact that he was an air force marshal. Why the costume change? Most likely as further reassurance to the SA, especially as Göring was one of the chief instigators of the Röhm purge.

The real feelings of the SA at the time were not only more conflicted than Riefenstahl would have her audience believe; they were downright dangerous. The American journalist William L. Shirer, an eyewitness to the events, notes that on September 6 "there has been no sign of an attempt [on Hitler's life] yet, though some of the Nazis are slightly worried about Sunday, when he reviews the S.A." (21). Shirer's diary then records the events of Sunday, September 9:

> Hitler faced his S.A. stormtroopers today for the first time since the bloody purge. In a harangue to fifty thousand of them, he "absolved" them from blame for the Röhm revolt. There was considerable tension in the stadium and I noticed that Hitler's own S.S. bodyguard was drawn up in front of him, separating him from the mass of brownshirts. We wondered if just one of those fifty thousand brownshirts wouldn't pull a revolver, but no one did. Viktor Lutze, Röhm's successor as Chief of the S.A., also spoke. He has a shrill, unpleasant voice, and the S.A. boys received him coolly, I thought.
>
> (22)

It was in such an atmosphere of internal fragmentation, with the ever-present threat of political assassination, that the 1934 Party Convention took place. And it was this threat to the state that needed to be exorcised in order that Hitler's *Gesamtkunstwerk* might be ever more total. Beyond the fears of internal instability, the reintegration of the SA into the total state was important, too, because of what the SA represented in Nazi mythology: it was, as Röhm repeatedly asserted but as Hitler also believed, a *Volk's* militia, the grass-roots military expression of the racial Will. So a falling away of the SA posed a profound symbolic as well as a military threat to the myth of the *völkisch* state. For all of these reasons, the murder of Röhm not only eliminated a political inconvenience, but it left Germany, particularly after the success of the 1934 Convention and the increased power of the SS, far more unified in its subordination to a single dictator.[20]

But there is another reason as well that Röhm served as a "structural guarantor of … totality by representing, within the work, that which does not belong." Röhm, after all, was not just a threat because of his socialism; he was also a threat because of what he called his "criminal peculiarity."[21] Röhm's homosexuality was not a prime reason for his murder, and yet it cannot be discounted as a contributing factor. Social Democrats had long considered "The Brown House of Homosexuals" (as the SA headquarters was sarcastically referred to) a key chink in the National Socialist's armor (Hancock 628f). Army conservatives were likewise outraged by the "corruption of morals" at the heart of the NSDAP, as were many in Hitler's inner circle (notably Hess, Buch, Rosenberg, and the rabidly homophobic Himmler). However much such attacks may have helped to isolate and stigmatize Röhm, and thus enable the Röhm purge, one thing is clear: homosexuality was certainly seized upon after the fact as a justification. The official Nazi communiqué, broadcast to Germany the evening before Hitler's decision to kill Röhm, referred to the SA leader's

> unfortunate tastes (which are all too well known) [and] which weighed so
> heavily on the situation that the Führer found himself caught in a grave conflict
> of conscience … The Führer has ordered this diseased abscess pierced and
> drained, mercilessly. He will no longer tolerate the endangering of millions of
> decent people by a few of morbid unhealthy passions.
>
> (quoted in Gallo 247)

Speaking to the Reichstag after Röhm's murder, Hitler justified his action by
referring to "[t]he life which the Chief of Staff and a certain circle around him
began to lead, [which] was intolerable from any National Socialist viewpoint"
(quoted in Hancock 636). While it may not have begun that way, the Röhm purge
ended as an anti-homosexual crusade. Legal prosecution of homosexuals increased
in the wake of the purge, and laws persecuting homosexuals (particularly Paragraph
175 of the German Penal Code) were greatly strengthened in 1935.[22]

More intangible than the scandal that Röhm brought to the NSDAP was a
general unease with the erotics of male bonding that were so central to Nazi
aesthetics. Several scholars have noted the paranoia among Nazi leaders toward
the "epidemic effect" of "homosexual lapses" (as one Nazi directive put it) within
homosocial organizations such as the army, SA, SS, and Hitler Youth. "It is
remarkable that the Nazis should have regarded all German males as susceptible to
homosexual seduction to such a powerful degree," concludes Harry Oosterhuis.

> In fact, the consideration forced itself on them again and again that their own
> movement, which was based on male bonding, might evoke homosexuality,
> and that, as fertile soil for a secret state within a state, [homosexuality] could
> undermine the National Socialist movement from the inside out.
>
> (195–6)

Eve Sedgwick describes this dynamic in Foucauldian terms, as a regime of knowledge that characterizes twentieth-century fascism. "Fascism is distinctive in this
century not for the intensity of its homoerotic charge," writes Sedgwick,

> but rather for the virulence of the homophobic prohibition by which that
> charge, once crystallized as an object of knowledge, is then denied to knowledge
> and hence most manipulably mobilized. In a knowledge regime that pushes
> toward the homosexual heightening of homosocial bonds, it is the twinning
> with that push of an equally powerful homophobia, and most of all the
> enforcement of cognitive impermeability between the two, that will represent
> the access of fascism.
>
> (50–1)

What Sedgwick describes is a peculiar libidinal engine, one that heightens homosocial bonds, charges them erotically, and at the same time denies precisely those
energies it fosters. One result of this denial is that the regime can then redirect the
unacknowledged libidinal energies to its own ends.

Such erotically charged bonds were central to the Party Convention, and were underscored in several ways by Riefenstahl in *Triumph of the Will*. In numerous scenes (especially 9, 11, and 14) long shots of enormous military columns are intercut with shot after shot of handsome Nordic faces, faces the camera caresses. Riefenstahl's fascination with handsome male physiques is well known, and will equally dominate *Olympia* three years later. But the adoring female gaze serves here to heighten the erotic charge of the male bonding that is the main subject and aim of the Party Convention. Riefenstahl was considered by many a peculiar choice to direct *Triumph of the Will*, and several Nazi leaders (Goebbels especially) attempted to have her removed. As a female director, and a woman famously unashamed of her sexuality, Riefenstahl sharply contradicted "home and hearth" notions of German womanhood. And yet Hitler's peculiar genius for mass manipulation shows itself in his controversial choice. For she provided just the sort of erotically charged male images the regime called for, and yet, as a woman, she could never be guilty of the crime of Ernst Röhm. In *Triumph of the Will*, men could see themselves, beautifully bonded, through a woman's eyes. Riefenstahl's direction, one might say, allowed for a *cross-dressed gaze*.

This effect appears particularly strongly when the camera's eye is directed toward its most adored object. We have already seen that Riefenstahl presents Hitler as the still center around which the turning world of the film revolves, a center made all the more necessary because of the pioneering techniques of disorientation she employs. But there is more to Hitler's structural importance than this. For, in addition to being a documentary, in addition to being propaganda, *Triumph of the Will* is also a love story. That story begins with Hitler's arrival by Junker plane. As the plane cuts through the clouds over Nuremberg, Riefenstahl juxtaposes images of the plane with marching columns of men far below; both are moving in the same direction, and in several shots the shadow of the plane actually falls on the marching columns. These two parties are moving, of course, to a mutual rendezvous. But that rendezvous will be held in abeyance for a while. When Hitler steps out of his plane, he is greeted by a cheering throng, made up mostly of women and children. Riefenstahl focuses particularly on the wonder-struck expressions on the faces of his female admirers. Between the landing of the plane and the beginning of the motorcade, all of the close-ups are of Hitler and of ecstatic women. Hitler will not address them, though; for the two hours of the film, with but a single possible exception, he is only shown addressing groups of men.[23] At the airport, we are still in a space of acceptable libidinal energies, but these adoring female fans are not the true romance of the film. The true romance begins 11 minutes later, with the nighttime serenade of Hitler. Playing Hitler's favorite marching songs outside his window, the troops offer themselves to the leader. In Riefenstahl's version of events, Hitler remains coy, not even so much as stepping out on to his balcony to acknowledge the crowds. In Riefenstahl's version of events, too, this is an exclusively male serenade; the massed women of the landing field have been left far behind. Both of these representations – Hitler's coyness and the almost exclusively male serenade – are contradicted by Shirer's eyewitness account, and appear to be directorial conceits.[24]

What follows is a succession of troths pledged to Hitler by a succession of Nazi officials. The first Nazi leader to speak, Rudolf Hess, ceremonially opens the Party Convention in the fifth scene of the film. Turning to Hitler, who still has not spoken and will not speak until the next scene, Hess declares that "[o]ur thanks is the vow to stand with you in good days and bad, come what may!", echoing, with these words, the phrasing of Lutheran marriage vows. Similar oaths are taken by Lutze in Scene 10 ("We SA workers will always be true only to the Führer and fight for the Führer") and Baldur von Schirach in Scene 11 ("Because you embody the concept of fidelity for us, therefore we wish to be faithful"). Each pledge, of course, is made not only on behalf of the official but on behalf of the masses of men he represents: the SA, in the case of Lutze, the Hitler Youth, in the case of Schirach, and the whole Party, in the case of Hess. The group nature of these oaths is made especially clear in Scene 14, when Lutze speaks again, saluting Hitler on behalf of his SA men. "My Führer, just as we have already done our duty to you in the past, so too in the future we await your orders alone," he says to Hitler, and then, turning to the masses of stormtroopers, continues. "And we, comrades, know only to obey the orders of our Führer and to prove that we have remained true to the Führer." Whereupon Lutze leads the assembled masses in a series of *Sieg Heils*, and Hitler at last takes the podium to make a return promise. For the first time in the film, the men's vow of fidelity will be returned. Citing once more the "dark shadow" of Röhm, Hitler now casts that shadow aside, exonerates the SA from any guilt by association, and promises to protect the SA from destruction. "And when anyone does harm to the spirit of *my* SA," Hitler announces, "then the SA will not be harmed but those who do this harm will injure only themselves!" Playing the conventionally feminine role for much of the film, Hitler has allowed himself to be wooed. Playing the masculine now for all he is worth, Hitler offers firmness, protection, and a promise of his own. Throughout the film, as Table 5.2 indicates, vows of fidelity to and from Hitler are doubled by attacks on Röhm. Male bonding and Röhm's exclusion reinforce each other; more than this, they are two sides of the same fascist coin.

The romance of Hitler and his men culminates in the last scene of the film. Here, at the closing rally in the Congress Hall, Hitler finally gives himself entirely over to the throng. In his earlier speeches in the film, Hitler maintains a rather cool self-control, showing only brief flashes of the manic oratorical style for which he became notorious. In his final speech to the Convention, Hitler abandons his composure for Dionysiac rapture, or – to put the matter perhaps more accurately – performs the role of the rapturous visionary with consummate skill. Warming up to his role, Hitler takes about a minute and a half (1:38:43–1:40:15) to transform from collected speaker to unbridled superman. Riefenstahl echoes and reinforces this transformation with her editing technique. In the opening minute and a half of the speech, Riefenstahl intercuts close-ups of Hitler's face with long shots of the Congress Hall and close-ups of Nazi leaders listening diligently. The first close-ups of the crowd only come after Hitler has passed into ecstatic mode, and these affection-images echo Hitler's ecstasy. Thereafter, as Hitler's rapture builds, so too does that of the

Table 5.2 The doubling of fascist male bonding with allusion to Röhm

Hitler's arrival	Nighttime serenade of Hitler	Hess vows fidelity to Hitler [1st allusion to Röhm]	Lutze and Schirach vow fidelity to Hitler [2nd allusion to Röhm]		SA vows fidelity to Hitler and Hitler vows protection of SA [3rd allusion to Röhm]			Consummation [4th allusion to Röhm]		
1–10 min.	10–20	20–30	30–40	40–50	50–60	60–70	70–80	80–90	90–100	110–20

(overwhelmingly male) throng. Two minutes into the speech (1:40:40), Hitler makes the first gesture of the entire film that seems genuinely unrehearsed: his eyebrow quickly raises, in apparent surprise at the overflowing enthusiasm of the crowd. It is a gesture that will be repeated several more times before the end of the speech; Hitler too, it seems, has been caught by surprise, has been swept up in the moment. Now Riefenstahl cuts back and forth between shots of Hitler and shots of the crowd, singling out not only officials but also anonymous individual Party members. In the midst of this collective frenzy, Hitler refers one last time to the Röhm affair. "Once our enemies worried us and persecuted us and from time to time removed the lesser elements from the Movement for us," he declares. "Today we must examine ourselves and remove from our midst the elements that have become bad – *and therefore do not belong to us!*" (1:44:29–1:45–05). Three minutes later, Hitler steps back from the podium, accepting wave after wave of *Sieg Heils* from the maddened crowd. He salutes back, himself in ecstasy. All are swept up in this *Liebestod*. As the whole Hall sings the *"Horst Wessel Song"* one last time, the camera pans to a line of banners reading *Deutschland Erwach*, recalling again the *"Wach auf"* chorale of *Meistersinger*. Thus do the interlocking rings of total performance – Wagner's music-dramas, Speer's rally, Riefenstahl's film – come together one last time in the production of the total state.

They do so, as we have seen, under the shadow and the catalyst of the Röhm affair. The affair was central to the 1934 Party Convention, which doubly relied on Röhm's elimination to achieve its unity and its totality. It relied on Röhm's elimination because several sections of the German state needed to be reassured that no "second revolution" would occur. And it relied on Röhm's elimination because the exorcism of Röhm operated as a structural guarantor of totality by legitimizing the eroticized male bonding of the Nazi state. This second aspect of the reliance is central to the structure of Riefenstahl's film, which underscores the structural dynamic already inherent in the Party Convention of 1934. Riefenstahl's decision to dress up her cameramen in SA uniforms, indeed, may serve as an emblem of her whole enterprise. Riefenstahl's decision, of course, was based on her desire to hide the realities of film production from the viewer, thus furthering the film's aspiration to stand as an autonomous artwork in its own right. But her decision also symbolizes a deeper aspiration to costume the SA as an organically unified body, to cinematize the brownshirts and so to incorporate them into the larger *Gesamtkunstwerk*.

By the time of the next Party Convention, in September of 1935, a new structural guarantor would be found. Röhm's murder had become old news, and the political threat he posed had largely dissolved. His once fearsome SA was stripped of size and power, increasingly marginalized and subordinated to the SS and the army. While the crusade against homosexuality would gain in strength over the coming years, and would continue to be necessary to the regime, neither Röhm, nor "second revolution," nor homosexuality would be the central pariah of the 1935 Convention. Internal threats now largely defused, Hitler would turn elsewhere for his necessary Other. In his opening speech to the Nuremberg Party Convention of 1935, Hitler raised the "Jewish question" for the first time since becoming Reich Chancellor. Addressing the Reichstag, Hitler recommended that "Jewish Laws" be imposed, stripping those considered Jews of their German citizenship, and banning marital and sexual relations between "Jews" and "Aryans." In subsequent speeches during the Convention, Hitler would return to the theme. Hitler's total work of art had found another structural guarantor to place at center stage, and after 1935 the new Beckmesser of the new Nuremberg would be first and foremost, unambiguously, a Jew.

A new awakening

Eight years after *Triumph of the Will*, a sharp satire of Nazi aesthetics was shown on American movie screens. Its producer was Walt Disney. Created on behalf of the war effort, the animated short *Education for Death: The Making of a Nazi* (1943) illustrated and ridiculed Nazi methods of indoctrination.[25] In one section, the film re-tells a Nazi re-telling of the "Sleeping Beauty" story.[26] The tale is told to Nazi children as a modern allegory: the witch represents Democracy, Sleeping Beauty represents Germany, and the Prince represents Hitler. While this allegory is related, images and music ridicule it for the film audience. Prince Hitler enters on a white horse while a drunken rendition of Wagner's "Ride of the Valkyries" plays. The "Beauty" he awakens, naturally, is a blowzy Brünnhilde, an imperial eagle on her great beer-belly ("*Deutschland Erwache!*", her breastplate might read, or perhaps "*Wach auf!*"). Prince Hitler and Brünnhilde Beauty trade a series of maniacal *Heils* before Brünnhilde sings "*Heil Hitler*" to the tune of her "*Ho-jo-to-ho!*" The film concludes with German soldiers goosestepping away in perfectly ordered columns, columns that transform into crosses marking soldiers' graves.

Education for Death is one of the most potent retorts to Riefenstahl ever filmed, but Disney was not always so antipathetic. When Riefenstahl visited Hollywood in 1938 in the hopes of finding a distributor for *Olympia*, the entire industry boycotted her – with the exception of Disney. "My experiences with Walt Disney … were different," Riefenstahl recalls in her memoir,

> Early in the morning he welcomed us at his studios and we spent the whole day with him. Patiently, but also proudly, he demonstrated how his cartoon figures were made. He explained the usual technique and showed us sketches for his new production "The Sorcerer's Apprentice" (in *Fantasia*). I was fascinated. For me Disney was a genius, a magician, whose imagination seemed boundless.
>
> (239)[27]

Given that Disney was one of the few major gentile film producers in Hollywood, and an employer widely perceived as harboring antisemitic, anti-black, and anti-union sympathies, it is perhaps not surprising that he was the only producer to publicly welcome Riefenstahl.[28] Moreover, they had met earlier that year at the Venice Biennale, where Disney's *Snow White and the Seven Dwarfs* had competed against Riefenstahl's *Olympia* for the Coppa Mussolini.

Snow White, in the Disney version (though not in the Grimm Brothers'), ends with the Prince awakening the heroine with a kiss. Snow White, for Disney, becomes Sleeping Beauty. Does this fairytale also become an allegory? Does Snow White's awakening, like Sleeping Beauty's awakening in *Education for Death*, have a political analogue? Disney and Riefenstahl shared little, and yet they shared much. "He has the German feeling – " said Riefenstahl of Disney in 1939, "he goes so often to the German fables and fairy-tales for inspiration" (Jäger 13). But there was more to Disney's "German feeling" than fairytales. If Riefenstahl's *Triumph of the Will* marked a new chapter in the history of the total work of art, a chapter in which several mass-cultural, iconic *Gesamtkunstwerke* are locked together into a chain of total performance, then this strategy found new life in the totalizing creations of Walt Disney.

Chapter 6

Total world

Disney's theme parks

Mr. A. Hitler, the Nazi old thing, says that Mickey's silly. Imagine that! Well, Mickey is going to save Mr. A. Hitler from drowning or something some day. Just wait and see if he doesn't. Then won't Mr. A. Hitler be ashamed!

(Disney, "The Cartoon's Contribution" 138)

Passage to America

By the mid-nineteenth century, a reasonable German might well have concluded that the Romantic dream of an Aesthetic State had ended in failure. The answer to the old query, *why has Goethe not been able to do for the Germans what Homer did for the Greeks?*, seemed no longer that Goethe was a lesser talent but that modern society simply had no place for a new Homer. Where Schelling and the Schlegels had enthusiastically anticipated the rise of a unified Germany, a new mythology, and a modern synthesis of aesthetics and daily life, Germany had proven tenaciously resistant to such attempts. Society from the standpoint of 1850 might well have looked like a realm in which regionalism had triumphed over unity, and cold, hard "realism" over mythopoesis.

What our hypothetical German would never have predicted was the resurgence of the Romantic dream of an aestheticized nation, and the new form that this resurgence would take. Wagner's prescience lay largely in this: that he saw the resurgence and understood its form. However obliquely, Wagner understood that Goethe was not born too late but too early, his failure not of talent nor of will, but of media technology. In the wake of the collapse of the Dresden uprising, Wagner held not only to the dream of re-mythologizing society but, crucially, understood the central importance of mechanized total media in the fulfillment of this project. Though the founding of Bayreuth would change the nature of the question, the full effects of Wagner's innovation would take some time to be realized. By 1933, the old query was fully transformed, and the new question could read, *why has Wagner been able to do for Germany what Homer did for the Greeks?* How has a new mythology taken hold, how have politics been reinvented as sacred ritual, how have the masses become aestheticized? Did the *Geist* of Wagner find its apotheosis in Hitler? And if one turns ahead again a few years, to 1980 perhaps, then the question undergoes yet another permutation. *Why has Disney been able to do for America what Wagner did for Germany?* Did the *Geist* of Disney find its apotheosis in Ronald Reagan? When he envisioned America as "the land of the future, where, in the ages before us, the burden of the World's History shall reveal itself" (86), Hegel may have been more prescient than he knew.

Who ever would have guessed that this burden – which is not, *pace* Hegel, the burden of "the World's History," but rather just the burden of German idealism – would end up revealing itself in American laughter? Laughter was always the enemy of the *Gesamtkunstwerk*, the pin that punctured the over-inflated balloon. "Laughter I have pronounced holy: you higher men, *learn* – to laugh!" (296) pronounces Nietzsche's Zarathustra, the "sooth-laugher" in *Thus Spoke Zarathustra* (1885), and then again in the "Attempt at Self-Criticism" (1886), Nietzsche's anti-Wagnerian preface to *The Birth of Tragedy*. Nietzsche's weapon was well suited to the task. Of all the exclusions of the Wagnerian stage, laughter is perhaps the most completely barred, and would be the most corrosive if it were admitted. It is a prohibition that remains throughout the German tradition. From the *Ring* cycle to the Bauhaus *Totaltheater* to Brecht's *Lindbergh Flight* to Riefenstahl's *Triumph of the Will*: whatever its incarnation, the *Gesamtkunstwerk* has tended to be an earnest matter. Participation may be encouraged; joking generally not.

If laughter is Nietzsche's retort to Wagner, then Disneyland is America's retort to Nietzsche. "Laughter is America's most important export" (*QWD* 175[1]), said Disney, thinking of his own expanding empire of guffaws. A community of laughter, a factory of laughter, a *world* of laughter: Disneyland proves, against Nietzsche, that the total work of art can assume laughter, too, into itself, can totalize the gag. Another "Strength through Joy," perhaps, but Joy this time as light-hearted, devil-may-care chuckles rather than as striving militancy. Or rather, as the two combined, as muscular Mickey-ism, squeaking softly while carrying a big shtick. As such, Disneyland marks the rebirth of the total work of art in the wake of its catastrophic realization in the Third Reich. After the collapse of Hitler's Total State, after the transformation of the Nuremberg rally ground into a racetrack, after the "re-functioning" of the Nazi Party Congress Hall into a municipal storage depot, it would be a long time before German artists would again return to the *Gesamtkunstwerk*.[2] No such memories troubled the world's new superpower in the wake of the war. With the opening of Disneyland on 17 July 1955, the monumental German sublime found new life as the monumental American ridiculous.

A trinity of wafers

At first glance, Disney would appear to share little ground with Wagner. While Wagner gravitated toward Teutonic *Ernst* and *Wille*, Disney tended to associate nature with a sense of childlike glee and simple silliness. On this count, two more disparate sensibilities would be hard to come by. Whereas Wagner's attacks on modern culture entailed strong critiques of the role and form of "high art" in European society, Disney rarely if ever directed attacks against high art per se. The relatively peripheral role of high art in American culture allowed Disney to avoid the confrontation altogether; thus he could set the "Dance of the Hours" to dancing hippos wearing tutus – a move that would have appeared downright dadaist if staged in Europe – with little fear of being branded an iconoclast. Wagner and Disney differed substantially, too, in their understanding of the relationship between modern culture and capitalism. Unlike the early Wagner, Disney linked the evils of "modern culture" not with capitalism, but rather with capitalism's seedy underside, its sad but "avoidable" traces: the urban slums and the fashionable elite, the filthy sidewalks and the phony hucksters, the rat-race competition and the depressing lack of play.

Nor would Disney appear to have much in common with broader genealogies of the total work of art. Unread in philosophy and largely unfamiliar with the European avant-garde, Disney might seem an unlikely candidate for a lineage that includes Schlemmer, Moholy-Nagy, Kandinsky, Gropius, Meyerhold, Eisenstein, Brecht, and Riefenstahl. An unabashed champion of middlebrow aesthetics and a titanic genius of kitsch, Disney shares none of the discomfort with the comfortable bourgeois that characterizes the other figures in this work. Above all, there is no tone of revolution – political, aesthetic, or otherwise – to his work. While its social impact has been almost incalculable, Disney's work has never been a call to arms. Disneyland offers, as a recent exhibition termed it, an "architecture of reassurance."[3] Surely nothing could be further from the radical aspirations of the *Gesamtkunstwerk*.

And yet. Disney's sense of nature, like Wagner's, was of a thing at once mythic, real, essential, timeless, spontaneous, naïve. Disney's sense of modern urban culture, like Wagner's, was of a thing corrupt, fake, overly intellectualized, antagonistic, heartless. Disney, like Wagner, imagined his work to be part of a grand project of re-harmonizing humanity and nature. Disney's work, like Wagner's, was launched against the degraded condition of modern "culture," against the dark side of industrial capitalism. More importantly, Disney's project, particularly in the theme parks, was to create a grand unification of all the arts, welded to commerce and technology. Disney's worlds, in other words, represent the most decisive entrance of the total work of art into mass commodity culture. It is a direction that would be inconceivable without innovations in media technology; but then, the total work of art has always been connected to mass culture and technological innovation.

Like Wagner, Disney embraced a nostalgic vision of the landscape, a vision that ironically underlay his turn to technology. Farmland, wilderness, and rural Americana dominate Disney's work from *Plane Crazy* (the first Mickey Mouse film) through the barnyard humor of *Steamboat Willie* to the nature films, the animated animals, and the theme parks. If there were a single creative font for all of this imagining, it would be a family farm near the small Midwestern town of Marceline, Missouri, where Disney lived between the ages of four and nine. As Disney's daughter Diane Miller recalled many years later,

> Father thinks that one reason Marceline means so much to him is that he
> arrived there at the impressionable age of four and was wildly elated by the

move from a crowded, smoky city to a farm where there were cows and horses and chickens and orchards. He can still draw a mental – or rather a sentimental – map of the whole community as it was then. Grandfather's house is gone now but every plank and nail in it still exists in Father's mind.

(11)

As a matter of fact, Disney's years on the farm were painful ones. His father, an itinerant jack-of-all-trades who took his family across much of the American map in search of work, was a harsh taskmaster who beat his children regularly and denied them playthings. Added to this, poor crops and mortgage payments rendered the family almost pathetically poor, and a collapse in the apple market finally forced them to St Louis. When the Disney family left the farm for St Louis in 1910 (their fourth move in 17 years), Walt would never again return to rural life. But the memory of Marceline stayed with him, and grew into a symbol of an ideal America: safe, rooted, secure, communal, and able to enjoy the fruits of industrial capitalism (trains and movies were particular favorites) without the accompanying ills.

It was also at Marceline, according to his daughter, that Disney first developed his "special feeling" for animals (11). Animals and children: the two were always linked in the Disney imagination. Indeed, Disney claimed that they made better subjects for animation than adults, that they were, so to speak, better aesthetic objects. "Often the entire body [of an animal] comes into play," Disney told his audience in an unusually lengthy address from the 1950s,

> Take the joyful dog. His tail wags, his torso wriggles, his ears flap. He may greet you by jumping on your lap or by making the circuit of the room, not missing a chair or a divan. He keeps barking, and that's a form of physical expression, too; he stretches his big mouth. But how does a human being react to a stimulus? He's lost the sense of play he once had and he inhibits his physical expression. He is the victim of a civilization whose ideal is the unbotherable, poker-faced man and the attractive, unruffled woman. Even the gestures get to be calculated. They call it poise. The spontaneity of the animal – you find it in small children, but it's gradually trained out of them.
>
> (*QWD* 183)

Disney's position here recalls a recurring theme of German Romanticism – from Schiller's essay "On Grace and Dignity" through Kleist's "On the Puppet Theatre" to Wagner's "Art and Revolution" – that the beautifully spontaneous action is an almost vanished trait, a victim of so-called "civilization." For Kleist, it is only in the marionette, the animal, and the youth that such graceful actions can still be found. Disney's search for playfulness and spontaneity is in one sense a diminution of Kleist's anguished yearning for supernatural grace, and yet it is only a small but intriguing elaboration of Kleist's position to suggest, as Disney does, that the most spontaneous (and therefore most aesthetic) of all creatures would be a puppet-like animal, or the animated child.

By the early 1930s, Mickey Mouse had emerged as the central symbol of nature as seen through the Disney lens. Mickey was not only a personification of the ideal natural landscape, he was also a figure, like Wagner's Parsifal, of the *puer aeternus*. "[Mickey is] a clean, happy, little fellow who loves life and folk ... He is Youth, the Great Unlicked and Uncontaminated," writes Disney in 1933 ("Cartoon's" 138). People are drawn to the Mouse, Disney continues, because Mickey represents them at their most essential:

> The Disney audience is made up of parts of people, of that deathless, precious, ageless, absolutely primitive remnant of something in every world-wracked human being which makes us play with children's toys and laugh without self-consciousness at silly things, and sing in bathtubs, and dream and believe that our babies are uniquely beautiful. You know ... the Mickey in us.
>
> (138)

Mickey's appeal is so universal, Disney believed, that the Mouse effectively brought the whole world together. Disney took delight in the fact that:

> Mr. Mussolini takes his family to see every Mickey picture; Mr. King George and Mrs. Queen Mary give him a right royal welcome; while Mr. President F. Roosevelt and family have lots of Mickey in them, too. Doug Fairbanks took Mickey with him to savage South Sea Islands and won the natives over to his project. Mickey is the one matter upon which the Chinese and the Japanese agree.
>
> (138)

Disney was never alone in viewing his creation as a global icon. Ub Iwerks, one of Mickey's original animators, noted that Mickey's shape recalls Jung's archetypal symbols of wholeness, and audaciously described Mickey's neotenized head as "a trinity of wafers" (quoted in Croce 97). John Hench, one of Disney's closest associates and a chief designer of Disneyland, admired Mickey's "series of round shapes" that "relate to each other as they do in the musculature of a human being," and saw the Mouse as "a symbol of life" (*Designing* 85).

Mickey Mouse exemplified, for Disney, all that culture *could* be. Unlike some of his associates, who hated the term "culture,"[4] Disney distinguished between two types of culture, a good one and a bad one. "At times," Disney admits,

> I've even caught myself viewing the word "culture" with suspicion – it seems to have an un-American look to me – sort of snobbish and affected. Actually, as I understand it, culture isn't that kind of snooty word at all. As I see it, a person's culture represents his appraisal of the things that make up life. And a fellow becomes cultured, I believe, by selecting that which is fine and beautiful in life, and throwing aside that which is mediocre or phoney ...
>
> Well, how are we to recognize the good and beautiful? I believe that man recognizes it instinctively ...

> I believe that you will find this spontaneous reaching out for the fine and beautiful in all mankind; it is man's indestructible and godlike quality, and the guarantee of his future.
>
> (quoted in Feild 283–4)

Like Wagner, Disney balanced his suspicion of "culture" with an appeal to another definition of the term, one rooted in instinct and spontaneity, and realized by the masses.

Disney's search for "good culture" often led him, like Wagner, to folk sources. *Snow White and the Seven Dwarfs, Pinocchio, Fantasia, Cinderella, Sleeping Beauty*: many of the most successful of Disney's films draw from European (frequently Germanic) folklore.[5] As with Wagner, but also as with such later practitioners of the total work of art as Leni Riefenstahl, Disney's vision of progress is linked to a longing for European antiquity. "I think we have made the fairy tale fashionable again," Disney commented. "The fairy tale of film – created with the magic of animation – is the modern equivalent of the great parables of the Middle Ages" (*QWD* 139). Acknowledged or not, there is an inescapably Romantic desire behind this kind of reinvention and return. Indeed, many of the keywords of German Romanticism – words like "fairytale," "fantasy," "imagination," and especially "magic" and "dream" – are incessantly repeated in Disney corporate discourse. Disney, one reads time and again in company literature, is "the Dreamer," his creation "the Dream," his mission to "create Magic," to return "children of all ages" to a world of "fantasy." "We really *do* make dreams come true," write the Imagineers (Disney's term for his technical staff), repeating a theme heard continuously in the organization (*Imagineering* 12). It would overstate the case to grant such clichés the status of a philosophy, but there is certainly throughout the Disney organization a vaguely Romantic-idealist *Weltanschauung*. The wellspring of the Walt Disney Company, by its own account, lies in unbounded creativity, in limitless imagination – in short, in the Dream. Like Schiller's *Spieltrieb* ("play-drive"), the creative state of "Imagineering" is a source of infinite possibility and infinite realization: dream it and it shall be.

Disney first began to experiment with total performance with the creation of *Fantasia* (1940). He conceived of the film as a feature-length experiment in "visualized music," which would make use of technical innovations in sound and animation technology in order to provide visual expressions of works by classical composers. It was to be something unlike anything ever done by another studio, a groundbreaking fusion of arts and an all-consuming sensory experience. To achieve these immersive effects, Disney Studios invented a stereo sound system, Fantasound, with which theatres had to be equipped in order to show the film. Initially at least, this innovative sound system was only one aspect of a larger vision. Disney had originally envisioned projecting *Fantasia* on extraordinarily wide screens; positioning speakers all around the audience (what today would be called "surround sound"); projecting shadows and other effects on the interior theatre walls, outside the frame of the screen; showing parts of the film in 3-D; and spraying the audience with perfume during the flower ballet of *The Nutcracker Suite*. Theatre managers balked at such effects and, like Wagner, Disney had to settle for his work to be shown in theatres that were not built to fully realize his immersive vision. But Disney continued to work on *Fantasia*, adding and subtracting material, in anticipation of future productions. Intriguingly, one of the pieces worked on in the early 1940s was Wagner's "Ride of the Valkyries."[6] Although increasing American involvement in the Second World War ultimately made such an explicitly Wagnerian sequence too controversial, the triumphant American spirit of the postwar period would prove fertile ground for Disney's grandest experiment in theatrical totality: his theme parks.

A joyous kingdom of play and semblance

While all cultures develop collective representations, Warren Susman has argued that "few have done it so self-consciously" as America in the late 1940s and 50s (26). More precisely – and in many ways similar to the experience of Bismarck's Germany – postwar America struggled with the cultural contradictions of a rapid establishment of a modern welfare state and newfound international dominance. This period, in short, marks the intensification of what George L. Mosse has described (writing of a German context) as the "nationalization of the masses."

To a significant degree, America of the postwar period adopted the national model that welfare-state advocates had been fighting for since the late nineteenth century. The Full Employment Act and the Atomic Energy Act (both of which passed in 1946), and the Housing Act (1954), helped to establish a welfare-state, broadly Keynesian model as the foundation for postwar America. In international relations, America quickly embraced its newfound superpower status after the war, founding the National Security Council and the Central Intelligence Agency and launching "a series of unprecedented international initiatives" between 1946 and 1949 (Susman 20).

The urgent demand for domestic and international security, however, was part and parcel of the talk – prevalent even at the time – of the postwar period as an "age of anxiety." Of all of these anxieties, Susman argues, mass culture was one of the most pressing.

> In the nineteenth century, of course, American dreamers had argued that the mass involvement of the citizenry realized the American dream. Now, questions arose about the possibility that such mass participation would encourage dogmatic ideology and lead to a totalitarian state ... Mass culture: fearful writers now produced a series of major tracts about it. Interestingly enough, if one had bothered to look, one would have discovered that many of the same critics who attacked mass culture in the 1940s and 1950s were, in the teens and twenties, its greatest proponents.

> (24)

American mass culture in the 1940s and 50s (aided by welfare-state initiatives, mass-communications technologies, and Cold War propaganda) was becoming increasingly nationalized and centralized. And yet many Americans who had previously embraced this process of mass nationalization began, in the wake of WWII, to worry intently about its potentially totalitarian effects.[7]

What Disneyland offered was a way of nationalizing the American masses while simultaneously assuaging postwar anxieties about the perils of mass culture. It was a land that celebrated an idealized version of American-ness for a mass American audience, and yet did so in a manner that looked nothing like Cold War visions of totalitarian states. At Disneyland (unlike, as American movies constantly reiterated, in cold, gray Moscow) the sun was warm and the people *had fun*. Disneyland presented itself as an antidote to so many Cold War depictions of mass totality, from Hitler's Germany to Stalin's Russia to Orwell's Oceania.

While Disneyland avoided the trap of totalitarian bleakness on one side, it avoided the anarchy of urban culture on the other. In the late 1940s, Disney conceived of his "land" as an answer to Coney Island, the Brooklyn amusement park that typified, for many middle-class Americans, the corruption of modern urban life. Spatial disorganization, litter, traffic, poor crowd control, "carny" atmospherics: the hardboiled grit of Coney Island was, for Disney, a particularly virulent form of a national disease. "When I started on Disneyland," Disney told one reporter, "my wife used to say, 'But why do you want to build an amusement park? They're so dirty.' I told her that was just the point – mine wouldn't be" (*QWD* 47).[8] According to Hench, one of the chief designers of Disneyland,

> [i]n modern cities you have to defend yourself constantly and you go counter to everything that we've learned from the past. You tend to isolate yourself from other people … You tend to be less aware. You tend to be more withdrawn. This is counter-life … you really die a little … I think we need something to counteract what modern society – cities have done to us.
>
> ("Interview")

Like Wagner's Festspielhaus, Disneyland was intended as a counter-space to the modern city, and as such was counter-cultural, so to speak, from its origin. Again like Bayreuth, it aimed to return the folk to their true way of being. "Americans are a sociable folk," writes Disney; "we like to enjoy ourselves in crowds, at sports arenas, fairs, and carnivals, at concerts, and at the theatre" (*QWD* 12). Disneyland would allow the folk to express their inherent sociability, but free of the contamination of modern cities.

In Chapter 3, we saw that the Bauhaus "Theatre of Totality" was constantly in danger of being overwhelmed by the rapidly growing spectacle of Weimar-era urban culture. Disney faced much the same problem when constructing his own total theatre, and his solution, in short, was to isolate his total theatre as much as possible from the voracious mouth of commercial culture. Though his strategy was structurally similar to Wagner's, Disney's practice had to be technologically more sophisticated in order to maintain its autonomy amidst a more ubiquitous and insidious commodity spectacle. Mere geographic isolation and immersive theatrical techniques would no longer suffice: more radical strategies would have to be invented. If Disney's utopian vision – "*To create happiness for people of all ages everywhere,*" in the words of one Disney publication (Disney Institute 30) – was to make use of the increasingly ravenous energies of the market without being subsumed by them, then higher walls must obviously be built. The maintenance of brand aura in an increasingly symbolic system of capital required strategies of separation and occlusion that went far beyond anything imagined at Bayreuth.

In 1952 Disney hired the Stanford Research Institute to locate a suitable place for his park. The Institute eventually settled on Orange County as the best site, since land (most of it orange groves) was cheap, the terrain was flat, and a new freeway would make the area easily accessible from Los Angeles. After two years of negotiations with the 20 families who owned the site, the newly founded Walter Elias Disney (WED) Enterprises had quietly bought up 160 acres of property. WED Enterprises bulldozed the land, burning orange, walnut, and eucalyptus trees, in order to create a stage upon which to manufacture an entirely new landscape of hills, valleys, and lakes. Once the stage was set, any incursions by the outside world were to be repelled. Disney erected a 15-foot-tall earthen bank around Disneyland so that nothing of the surrounding environment could be seen from within, negotiated with the Town Council to prevent tall buildings from being erected within sight of the park, and even tried to prevent airplanes from flying overhead. Disney was horrified, for example, by the sight of telephone poles in and around his park, and soon paid the electric company to bury them. The land would be, truly, a world apart, in this sense more reminiscent of American utopian communities than amusement parks. "I don't want the public to see the world they live in while they're in [Disneyland]," Disney said. "I want them to feel they're in another world" (*QWD* 59) (Figure 6.1).

Disney's closed and tightly controlled world was linked, however, to a larger network of total performance. In addition to the films that provided the characters, settings, music, songs, and general ideology of the theme park, Disney also connected his land to the emergent medium of television. The television show *Disneyland* aired between 1954 and 1958, and was the first ABC series to top the Nielson ratings. The pilot, entitled "The Disneyland Story," was essentially an extended advertisement for the theme park, featuring "behind the scenes" pieces about the park's construction and come-ons about the park's attractions. Later episodes of the show combined features on Disneyland with previously released theatrical features and original productions. Even after the name of the show was changed, in 1958, from *Disneyland* to *Walt Disney Presents*, Disneyland continued to be exhibited on the show, and the Walt Disney Company produced separate specials to further market the park. The point is not merely that Disney was a canny marketer or a pioneer of cross-media "synergy." More than this, Disney's use of television, film, and theme park as collaborative media in the creation of a

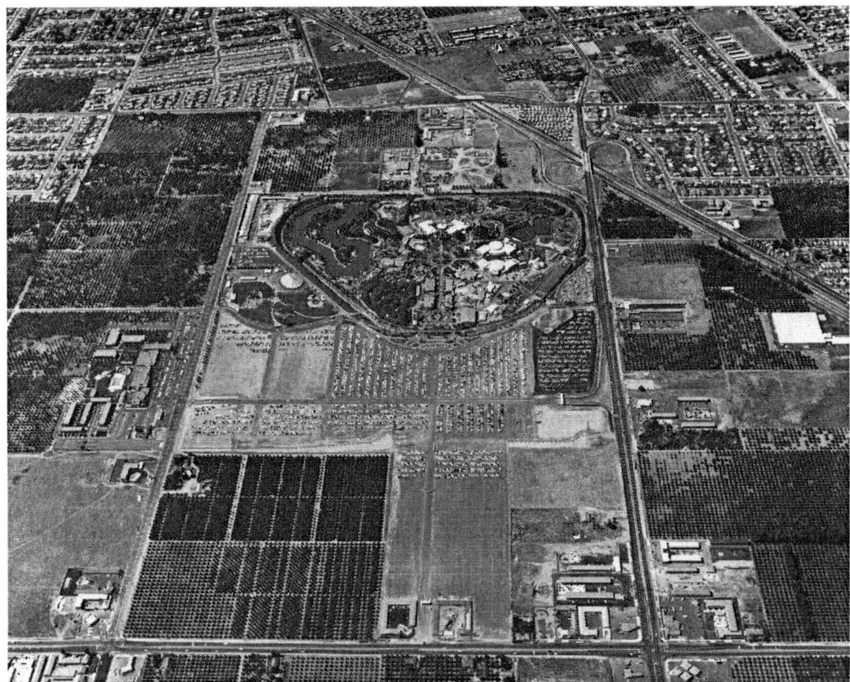

Figure 6.1   Aerial view of Anaheim, including Disneyland, *c.* 1955.

single mythic world echoes the interlocking chain of total performance examined in the previous chapter. Here, as at Nuremberg, an electronic mass medium and a live mass event are designed to reinforce each other, such that each becomes a *Gesamtkunstwerk* in its own right while simultaneously connecting to another link on a larger chain of total performance.

Needless to say, Disneyland occupies a central place in this chain. It is the home of Mickey Mouse, but also of Sleeping Beauty's Castle, a neo-Romantic confection modeled on Ludwig II's Neuschwanstein.[9] Sleeping Beauty's Castle is "the center of Disneyland" and "the focal point around which the park was built," according to Imagineer John Hench (*Designing* 53). It had much the same symbolic resonance in Disney's day that Neuschwanstein had for Wagner's Dream King, emphatically evoking a fairytale world of fantasy over against the disenchanted workaday world of modern life. With time, as several anthropologists have pointed out, a visit to the Mouse and the dream Castle assumed the character of a pilgrimage.[10] Some of the best analyses of Disneyland's ceremonial function are provided by the Imagineers themselves. John Hench, for instance, writes that:

> [i]t still amazes me that such simple features of landscape and architecture work so well to transport guests from their everyday lives to the specially

sanctioned playtime that the park alone offers. As guests traverse the tunnel, they leave behind the everyday routine of working, maintaining shelter, obeying rules; they enter a space where they can play voluntarily, and where we know they will have the opportunity to feel more alive.

Once inside, guests find themselves in a place full of heightened color, bright flowers, soft music, pleasant smells, and activity all around. The circle of green that surrounds the hub is a ceremonial symbol, the center; guests gather here first to plan their playtime. By day, every scene around them gleams in the sunlight; after sundown, colored lights glow and sparkle in the night. Here, things are as they might once have been, or yet could be.

(Designing 65)

The landscape and architecture that encompass Disneyland work in much the same fashion as at Bayreuth, creating a vast, complex, and multi-sensory limen to mark the transition from the ostensibly real world of the exterior to the fantasy world of the performance space.

The pilgrimage to Disneyland has a particularly nationalistic cast. "Disneyland will be the essence of America as we know it," commented Disney (*QWD* 56). While proposing to represent something essential in all humanity, Disneyland, like Bayreuth, links this natural, universal state of being to a particular cultural identity. This linkage is particularly evident in a site like Main Street USA, which Disney referred to as "everyone's hometown – the heart line of America" (65). The nationalistic, and at the same time the quite personally nostalgic, rhetoric of this design is clear enough, and is further reinforced by a large plaque in the Town Square at the end of Main Street, which reads:

> TO ALL WHO COME TO THIS HAPPY PLACE:
> WELCOME.
> DISNEYLAND IS YOUR LAND. HERE AGE
> RELIVES FOND MEMORIES OF THE PAST …
> AND HERE YOUTH MAY SAVOR THE CHALLENGE
> AND PROMISE OF THE FUTURE.
> DISNEYLAND IS DEDICATED
> TO THE IDEALS, THE DREAMS, AND THE HARD
> FACTS THAT HAVE CREATED AMERICA …
> WITH THE HOPE THAT IT WILL BE A SOURCE OF
> JOY AND INSPIRATION TO ALL THE WORLD.

The connection made here between Disneyland and America is so close that the former becomes virtually metonymic for the latter. "Disneyland is your land," the sign proclaims, echoing the words of Woody Guthrie about America (absent, of course, Woody's sly irony). By the end of the inscription, the reader is left somewhat confused: does the pronoun "it" in the final phrase signify Disneyland or America? The answer would seem to be either, or both.

The fantasy that Disneyland offers depends, as do all *Gesamtkunstwerke*, on strategies of exclusion. Even a very partial list of such exclusions would be a long one. The theme park largely omits references to, for instance, slavery, depressions, strikes, ghettos, lynchings, Jim Crow, industrial workers, protest movements, class struggles, and Native Americans in any context other than that of "Frontierland" myth. Racist stereotypes such as bone-through-nose headhunters and terrified black porters in the Jungle Cruise, and *Song of the South*-style banjo-playing blacks in the American Adventure, were always part of the attraction of Disneyland (Jungle Cruise, perhaps the most explicitly racist of the rides, was also Disney's favorite). When resistance leaders appear at Disneyland (e.g. robotic versions of Chief Joseph, Frederick Douglass, Susan B. Anthony, Martin Luther King), they are generally introduced in order to be incorporated into the overarching Disney myth of an ultimately inclusive and triumphant America. Moreover, travel costs and ticket prices (significantly higher than other leisure parks) helped keep the poor at bay, as they still do (Bryman 94; Wallace 53). Disney's rejection of Coney Island, in other words, was not simply a rejection of urban grit, but a rejection of everything that suburban 1950s America associated with "bad" modernity. Racial strife, gender strife, class warfare, recent immigrants, industrial labor, and "un-American activities" were all necessary exclusions of what Herbert Schiller has called the "transcendent Disney message": "behold a world in which there is no social conflict" (99).

Along with this utopian message comes an ontological claim that Disneyland is more real than "the outside world." Disney often corrected doubters who dismissed Disneyland as a fantasy world. "You have it all wrong," the *Los Angeles Times* quotes him as saying; "[t]he park is reality. The people are natural here; they're having a good time; they're communicating. It's the outside that's the fantasy" (Wong C1).[11] As at Bayreuth, the "reality" of Disneyland is located in a mythic time which encourages nostalgia, hope, and fantasy while discouraging present consciousness. "Here you leave today –" according to Disney, "and visit the worlds of yesterday, tomorrow, and fantasy" (*QWD* 62). Or, as one of his publicists put it: "[i]n Disneyland, clocks and watches lose all meaning, for there is no present. There is only yesterday, tomorrow and the timeless world of fantasy" ("Disneyland Offers" 86). At Disneyland, as at Monsalvat, time becomes space.

And yet a critical difference exists between this "timeless world" and Wagner's: in Disneyland the spectator can actually move *within* the idealized landscape of the theatre. The spectator at Disneyland originally had a choice of four mythic "lands," each one announcing itself as a distinct landscape within an overall mythic world – Frontierland, Fantasyland, Adventureland, and Tomorrowland – all of which are connected by a central thoroughfare, Main Street, USA. A *Buck Rogers*-like notion of techno-wizardry can be seen most clearly in the zone of the park called Tomorrowland, which features various corporate-sponsored attractions intended to convince visitors, in Disney's words, that "tomorrow can be a wonderful age" ("Tomorrowland"). While most of the park is iconic, the technopianism of Tomorrowland is enthusiastically crystalline, reveling in at least the myth of technology. Moreover, the existence of these different fantasy zones, each of which is marked by its own miniature journey and itinerary, recalls once again the medieval understanding of the landscape, and the Bayreuth strategy of retro-cartography. But a significant development has been made from Bayreuth, for at Disneyland the active involvement of the audience in the interior of the theatre is greatly increased. Not only the journey to Disneyland, but the journeys between the lands *within* Disneyland became active spatial stories, and the spectators essentially actors in the spectacle itself.

The existence of different magic lands, however, creates at least one problem for Disneyland that Bayreuth avoids. Unlike Bayreuth, Disneyland must prevent the increased audience agency within the theatre from subverting the totality of the *Gesamtkunstwerk*. The solutions developed at Disneyland are various and complex. To begin with, the zones themselves are of a piece with a single, overarching myth, one tightly modeled on Disney's brand of American neo-Romanticism. The choice of mythic zones is really a selection between permutations of a single zone, a master-zone fixed with the imprint of its creator and conceived of as a vast participatory movie. "In designing Disneyland," writes John Hench, "we thought of the park as if it were a three-dimensional film" (*Designing* 23). In Disney parlance, the space between the entrance turnstiles and Main Street USA is the "lobby" of the theatre, featuring posters announcing the rides as "coming attractions." Main Street itself is Disneyland's "center stage," the route through which one must travel to enter the various mythic zones that spiral off in all directions. "When you talk to Disney cast members about the parks," reads a Disney handbook, "you will hear them described as 'living movies,' movies in which the guests themselves participate" (Disney Institute 24). Similarly, transitional spaces between one "zone" and another (say, Main Street and Adventureland) are called "cross-dissolves," the liminal spaces treated like a movie made concrete. In other words, like Brecht's *Lindbergh Flight*, Disneyland takes a unidirectional mass medium and stages it as participatory. Where Brecht had attempted to at once allegorize radio and reconfigure it as a dialogic medium, Disney attempts to do much the same with film at Disneyland. Indeed, despite their great differences, Brecht and Disney both attempt to incorporate audience agency into their mass-cultural performances in ways that are ultimately illusory. With Disneyland as with *The Lindbergh Flight*, the barrier between spectator and spectacle is eliminated more in appearance than in reality, and the actual function of the spectator continues to be heavily scripted so as not to conflict with the totality of the work as a whole.

Sweeping consumers from lobby to center stage was one thing; encouraging them to play their parts correctly once there quite another. In order to properly script the performance of the audience, the interactive landscape of Disneyland had to be carefully planned. Main Street USA was central to this strategy of crowd control. Main Street leads the visitor-actor to the Plaza, which functions as a large hub from which the other "lands" radiate outwards. A major landmark distinguishes each theme area and acts as a beacon to draw spectators into the area. Within the theme areas, smaller patterns of circulation were created, each of them leading back again to Main Street USA. In order to minimize the sense of social control on the visitor-actors, these lesser pathways were carefully planned to seem natural: the Imagineers made no walkways for the opening days of the park, in order to see where people would naturally walk, and then laid down permanent paths along those routes.[12] Literary critic Susan Willis refers to this "erasure of spontaneity" (123) as a central feature of Disneyland, but it is an erasure of spontaneity, oddly enough, in the interest of a return to spontaneity.

"Interestingly enough for all of its success," writes one Imagineer, "the Disney theme show is quite a fragile thing. It just takes one contradiction, one out-of-place stimulus to negate a particular moment's experience" (Disney Institute 109). The "fragility" of the Disneyland experience gives rise to the rigorous process of "theming," which may be defined as the almost obsessive incorporation of a uniformity of style throughout the Disney landscape so as to ensure a unified audience experience. The process of theming often involves a translation of signs of labor into elements of landscape, such that electric outlets at Disneyland are themed to resemble the bark of living trees, speakers themed to look like rocks, and so forth, right down to "the utensils in the restaurants, the trees and flowers on the property, and of course, the attractions in the parks," as the Imagineers put it (108–9). This rigorous process suggests that the total work of art itself might be understood as one vast project of theming, music to drama to stage design to costume to text. And at Disneyland not even workers are left out of the total experience. As Disney executive Dick Nunis explained to *Parade* magazine, "when we hire a girl [as a worker at Disneyland], we point out that we're not hiring her for a job, but casting her for a role in our show. And we give her a costume and a philosophy to go with it" ("How Disney" 4).

For the aspiring worker, Disney University (founded in 1955) functions as something of a dramatic conservatory. As part of their course-load there, new employees are trained in the Disney language, much of which involves replacing managerial terms with theatrical ones; thus an employee becomes a "cast member," a public area "onstage," a restricted area "backstage," hiring for a job is referred to as "casting," a job interview an "audition," and a uniform a "costume." This theatrical language applies to *all* Disney employees, not just actors, leading to the peculiar experience of addressing electricians and executives equally as "cast members." The show, such appellations make clear, is not just what happens "on-stage," it is what happens *everywhere*. The aim of such rhetoric is to replace the simple worker with a new composite: the worker-actor. This worker-actor belongs to an ostensibly egalitarian social order in which the all-consuming importance of the "show" and the team-work that it demands supposedly relaxes distinctions of rank. Ever since the founding of the Walt Disney Company, everyone was expected to be on a first-name basis, and employees were expected to call Walt "Walt." "If we didn't," one employee told *Time* in 1954, "we'd get fired" ("Father Goose" 44). A Disney University training manual refers to labor as the "total work experience," suggesting that work is just one more "total experience" the park has to offer (*Disney Way* IV-14). Indeed, the notion of labor itself is meant to be more or less alien to Disney employees, since "creating fun is our work, and our work creates fun – for us and for our guests" (quoted in Findlay 75). According to the Imagineers (at least on the record), their job is not so much work as "a state of mind. It's a freedom to dream, to create, and mostly, to do" (*Imagineering* 12). Off the record, of course, their remarks can be more pointed. "They would just literally take all your creative energy and ideas and it was all under the disguise of auditioning or just being a cast member," remarks one former employee. "So people just gave and gave and gave of themselves, of their creative energy, but you didn't really ever get credit, you didn't really ever get compensated; you were making your salary."[13] Another former employee speaks of being "themed to death" even outside the parks, such that even the pens on her desk were expected to bear the Disney logo. Not that the belief in Disney "magic" and the greatness of Disney "Traditions" is always an act. Indeed, a 1987 study gives evidence that the initiatory system of Disney training is so successful that many Disney University graduates react very negatively to perceived deviations from the "Disney way" (Smith and Eisenberg). As a result, the labor pool becomes highly self-regulating. Anecdotal evidence of this was provided by my guide at Walt Disney World: when speaking of the "magic" of her job, she began to cry unfeigned tears.

By means of their theatrical training, the Disney Company attempts to alienate its employees not so much from the product of their labor as from the fact that they labor at all. Such alienation further conceals the realities of production, as the labor process itself becomes aestheticized. The strategy is a natural extension of the *Gesamtkunstwerk*, which has always aimed to break down walls between spectator and spectacle, art and everyday life. It is with such strategies that Disney outplays the hand of the avant-garde, realizing in practice what so many garreted artists could only dream about. Still, training several thousand employees to whistle while they work is a difficult task, one which can be largely avoided if the employees are simply replaced with robots. Enter the "Audio-animatronics": lifelike robot actors. Whole attractions – Pirates of the Caribbean or Jungle Cruise, for example – are nothing more nor less than journeys through elaborately staged Audio-animatronic worlds. The appeal of the Audio-animatronics is twofold. On one hand, their reliability pleased Disney himself and continues to please Disney management, as evidenced by their remarks on the superiority of robot to human actors: robots never forget their lines, form unions, ask for salaries, or go on strike.[14] On the other hand, the robots also entertain Disney audiences because of their very status as automata. The robotic birds of the Enchanted Tiki Room, for example, would never be such crowd favorites if they were the real thing; it is their ingenious mechanization that captivates. This latter appeal of the Audio-animatronics finds no counterpart in Wagner's aesthetics, which were always concerned with the simple concealment of mechanization, but it does recall the magical bibelots of the German baroque *Wunderkammern:* the mechanical crèches, the silver singing birds, the clocks with soldiers who paraded on the hour. As with the magical-mechanical automata of those antique private museums, the Disney robots fascinate by their supernatural aura, and their playful resemblance to divinity and childhood.

Finally, and most importantly, the Audio-animatronics are considered actors par excellence at Disneyland because each is a *Gesamtkunstwerk* in miniature. "Walt has often described the 'Audio-Animatronics' as the grand combination of all the arts," reads a Disney press release. "This technique includes the three-dimensional realism of fine sculpture, the vitality of a great painting, the drama and personal rapport of the theatre, and the artistic versatility and consistency of the motion picture" (quoted in Schickel 335). Left out of this description is the additional art of music, which almost unfailingly accompanies an Audio-animatronic exhibit, as well as the art of industrial design that animates each creation. Each Audio-animatronic is therefore a microcosm of the great artistic unity that is Disneyland itself; the robots are not only the ideal actors, but also the ideal inhabitants of this mechanized utopia.

Tomorrow the world

A generational leap in Disney's total work of art came with Walt Disney World and the later parks.[15] By the mid-1960s, Disney had become dissatisfied with the way in which the environment around his Anaheim theme park had become contaminated by the signs of modern urban life; despite his best attempts to keep them at bay, restaurants, hotels, and other attractions rapidly surrounded the perimeter of his land. The problem was that Disney owned less than 200 acres, beyond which he exercised little control. For the new park in Florida, Disney was determined to do things differently. "The one thing I learned from Disneyland," he said, "was to control the environment" (*QWD* 73). And control it he did. Operating in great secrecy so as not to drive up land prices, WED proceeded to buy up territory in central Florida. Disney wanted enough land, he said, "to hold all the ideas and plans we can possibly imagine" (*QWD* 74), and also to provide a sufficient buffer zone between his new park and the surrounding world. Eventually 27,443 acres (about twice the size of Manhattan) were purchased for Disney's "total destination vacation resort," and WED began to exercise its considerable new power within local politics. Its primary desire was an enormous and utterly unprecedented one: WED wanted more or less complete autonomy within the state of Florida. After considerable debate, the Florida State Legislature granted extra-territorial status to the "Reedy Creek Improvement District" (the somewhat deceptively titled Disney land-acquisition organization) in 1967, and today the zone operates as a virtually independent state.

Walt Disney World's Magic Kingdom (the heart of Disney World) is essentially a replication of Disneyland, consisting of an almost identical landscape of mythic lands linked together by Main Street, USA. As such, Disney World was the first in what would become a series of mechanically reproduced worlds modeled on the original Magic Kingdom of Disneyland. Here, too, Disney blazed new ground in the mechanized production of total worlds. Treating his idyllic world as an industrial design prototype, Disney severed the link between utopian landscape and geographic place; henceforth the Magic Kingdom could appear, in remarkably similar form, almost anywhere: Orlando, Tokyo, France. Within one of these Kingdoms, the problem is not so much that "there's no there there"; there is emphatically a "there there," but one that has little or nothing to do with the actual place one happens to be. It is only a step beyond this plan to design, as Disney did, an urban utopia the form of which could be replicated across the globe. Such was his "Experimental Prototype City of Tomorrow," or EPCOT. EPCOT was originally a vision of a vast, reproducible city of the future that would be sponsored by Disney and run as a perfectly "planned, controlled community," in Disney's words (quoted in Fjellman 116). It was meant to be the centerpiece of Walt Disney World, "the most exciting and by far the most important part of our Florida project … in fact, the heart of everything we'll be doing in Disney World," according to Disney (*QWD* 70). Disney's ultimate answer to "the problems of our cities," it would draw from "the ingenuity and imagination of American free enterprise" in order to design an urban space that would "be dedicated to the happiness of the people who will live, work, and play here" (*QWD* 71). In scope and ambition, EPCOT was a vision far surpassing his theme parks, an avant-garde attempt to eliminate divisions between theatre and life. It was a dream at least partially realized by the Disney corporate town of Celebration, Florida, founded in 1996.[16]

Even setting such projects as EPCOT and Celebration aside, Walt Disney World represents another advance in the reliance upon hidden production seen earlier at Bayreuth. The literally unique political, legal, and territorial freedom that WED Enterprises enjoyed in its construction of Disney World was married from the outset to its new science of "depth-computerization." Everything in this new World would be planned from the very beginning around a nexus of integrated electronic monitoring systems, a process that is referred to by Disney management as a "Total Systems Approach." One of the main aspects of the Total Systems Approach was the Automatic Monitoring and Control System, which, according to a WED vice-president interviewed by Anthony Haden-Guest in the early 1970s, "gives Disney at one center and many other places the ability to monitor, and be aware of, really … the total status, everything that goes on within the confines of the park, in so far as it is measurable" (278). Based on a system originally developed to monitor nuclear missiles, the AMCS allows Disney World to operate as a total theatre by constantly testing the site for disturbances. "These are quite small computers that are hooked up literally to thousands and thousands of individual sensors in the park," continued the executive.

Another aspect of the Total Systems Approach at Disney World is a vast network of tunnels beneath the "show." The tunnels were in fact the first sites constructed at Disney World, and were located at ground level; they were then covered over with the soil dredged from an artificial lake, and Disney World was placed atop them. Dubbed "utilidors," the miles of tunnels house storage facilities, staff cafeterias, laundries, dressing rooms, and vast pneumatic tubes designed to "whisk refuse away like magic" (quoted in Wilson 176). In addition to housing such backstage functions, the utilidors also provide a means for characters to leave one mythic zone without passing through another. Thus a space-suited actor from Tomorrowland can make his way to the parking lot while still in costume without having to cross through the cowboy country of Frontierland. In this way the utilidors serve not only as a means of sweeping away the refuse of the "outside" world, but also of preventing contamination of one mythic zone by another. Finally, the utilidors function, spatially and temporally, as an inverse of the mythic zones above. While the cartography of Disney World is pseudo-medieval, that of the utilidors is decidedly modern in the Disney sense of the word: that is, geometric and utilitarian, devoted to time and decay. Unlike the land above, the utilidors are organized in straight lines between points. Here space reverts to units of feet and yards and miles, and time to the motions of a clock. Whereas time becomes space in Disney World, in the utilidors time and space become unbuckled again; in the utilidors lie the chronology, the distance, and the production that appear in the upper world as spacialized myth.

While the utilidors of Disney World are a latter-day evolution of the sunken orchestra pit of Bayreuth, their far greater size and range of function is mirrored in a greater concern for their concealment. Though Disney promotional material is rich in depictions of all aspects of the parks, one searches in vain for a map, photograph, or design sketch of the utilidors. While Disney now runs a (not inexpensive) tour of part of the tunnels, photographs of them are strictly forbidden. If a tourist should take such a picture, policy is strict: the company confiscates the camera, develops the film, and returns only the unrestricted photographs. To expose the utilidors is to shatter the "magic" of the park; Walhall still needs its Nibelheim.

While Disneyland and Disney World share much in common with the strategies of Wagner's Festspielhaus, they also owe much to the Great Exhibitions, with their celebration of commerce, industry, invention, and the buffet of nations.[17] At times the convergence of these two totalizing traditions can be disconcerting. Take, for example, the buffet restaurant in Disney World called "The Crystal Palace," the arched arcade ceilings and glass-and-steel structure of which are a copy of the original Crystal Palace in miniature form. This remarkable structure sits at the central hub of the Magic Kingdom, right across from Cinderella Castle. Sitting within the glass walls of Disney's version of Crystal Palace, gazing across at Disney's second version of Neuschwanstein, one finds the whole history of the total work of art, arrayed now not as dialectic but as comic resolution.

From Brunelde to Oklahoma

> The Great Theatre of Oklahoma calls you! Today only and never again! If you miss your chance now you miss it forever! If you think of your future you are one of us! Everyone is welcome! If you want to be an artist, join our company! Our Theatre can find employment for everyone, a place for everyone!
>
> (Kafka 252)

Near the end of Kafka's early, unfinished novel *Amerika*, the young hero Karl is kidnapped and forced into servitude to a gargantuan, slothful ex-diva named

Brunelde. The event represents the nadir of Karl's luckless American adventures. Made to sleep on a heap of velvet curtains in a corner of her crumbling apartment, Karl must listen to Brunelde make love upon a couch she rarely leaves, and he is soon kicked out on to the terrace like a dog. Karl attempts to escape, is thwarted and beaten unconscious, and soon thereafter the chapter abruptly ends. We never learn how Karl makes his way out of his particular Wagnerian nightmare – all we know is that the next time we see him he is on a street corner, viewing an advertisement for "The Nature Theatre of Oklahoma." Swept up by its promise that "everyone is welcome," Karl is off to find a place in the new Theatre. He soon discovers that it is "on a much larger scale than he could have conceived possible" (274), as all around him stand hundreds of actors, perched on separate pedestals, dressed as angels in white robes with great wings on their shoulders, blowing through gold-glittered trumpets. The placard did not lie: the Nature Theatre does indeed offer employment for all. Though he considers himself unsuited to be an actor, Karl eagerly takes a job behind the scenes as a technical worker. A new job, a new community, a new place in the "limitless" spectacle of the New World: for the first time in the novel, Karl seems to have found a home. Nor does he need to worry about the future: "it's an old theatre," an angel tells him, "but it's always being enlarged" (280).

The concluding chapters of Kafka's novel come close to an illustration of the mass-cultural development of the total work of art, from the velvet draperies of Brunelde to the Nature Theatre of Oklahoma, "the biggest theatre in the world" (279). Our analysis suggests something of the character of this theatre as well as its enlargement. Whatever their differences, the theatres of Wagner and Disney both have the reunification of nature and humanity as one of their central aims. The form of total work of art that they share attempts to forge this reunification by its performance in the exterior as well as the interior landscape. Its performance in the exterior landscape is primarily one of retrocartography by means of pilgrimage, while its performance of the interior landscape is primarily one of absorbing the audience into a spectacle of the desired natural state, a theatricalized form of nature more natural than the non-theatricalized world. To affect this absorption in nature, both Bayreuth and Disneyland must turn to the machine, a reliance that must be concealed from the spectator. As the size and scope of the reliance grow, so too do the strategies of occlusion. As fears of absorption into an increasingly ubiquitous society of spectacle grow, so too must strategies of autonomous separation. Moreover, as the spectator becomes capable of exercising a degree of choice within the theatre, more pervasive yet subtle controls must be brought to bear over spectatorship. Finally, through all of the above means, Bayreuth and Disneyland have become significant tools in the formation of modern conceptions of nationhood.

The mass-cultural evolution of the total work of art may now be found across the American, and increasingly the global, landscape. One indication of this trend is the recent spate of books by business advisors and economists arguing that providing goods and services is no longer enough for today's corporations to compete; today's corporations, the current thinking goes, must create carefully staged, unified aesthetic experiences in order to attract consumers.[18] The unification of media in the theatricalization of capital is a proliferating phenomenon, spreading far beyond amusement parks to resorts, malls, shops, hotels, restaurants, and urban design. Certain movies, too, are inseparable from this trend, especially if they can be linked to cultic sites: consider the group of *Star Wars* fans who camped out for six weeks in front of Mann's Chinese Theatre ("the ground-zero of movie fandom") to see the next installment of a saga that one fan described as "a life-defining moment," another as "a cultural icon," and a third as a "modern American mythology that transcends every race, religion, generation, class" (Purdum). Once they had viewed *The Phantom Menace* together – and together, in effect, with much of America at the time – the group was to take a celebratory trip to Disneyland, after which they would attend the premieres of the film in Sydney, London, and Paris. The story may give a clue to the next frontier of the mass-cultural *Gesamtkunstwerk:* namely, the interfacing of multiple total theatres within a single global nexus, a neo-medieval landscape under the sign this time not of Christ, nor of Reich, but of a mechanized Bacchus.

Chapter 7

Total vacuum

Warhol's performances

> HIGH TIMES: Who was the first artist to influence you?
> WARHOL: It must have been Walt Disney. I cut out Walt Disney dolls. It was actually Snow White that influenced me.
>
> (O'Brien 236)

> Some company recently was interested in buying my "aura." They didn't want my product. They kept saying, "We want your aura." I never figured out what they wanted. But they were willing to pay a lot for it. So I thought that if somebody was willing to pay that much for it, I should try to figure out what it is.
>
> (Warhol, *Philosophy* 77)

Mickey, Leni, Ludwig

Aesthetic aura persists not *despite* but precisely *because of* instruments of mechanical reproduction; this, at least, has become retrospectively clear at the moment of mechanical reproduction's eclipse by digital media. Though mechanical reproduction, as Walter Benjamin argued, may strip an artwork of its aura in the sense of its originality or uniqueness, not even this now seems assured. Consider the prices that mass-produced Bauhaus "originals" now fetch on the contemporary art-market. Consider, too, the way in which mass reproductions of an artwork often serve only to add to the luster of the original, such that the production of a million ten-dollar *Mona Lisa* posters is inseparable from the ongoing worship of the *Mona Lisa* and even – more intriguingly – of Warhol's *Mona Lisa (Colored)*. Moreover, even when mechanical reproduction strips the uniqueness of an artwork, it may create a wholly new ritual function for it. As we saw in the last chapter, the mass reproduction of Disney products, across the full scope of available media, is inseparable from the mythological role they play in American society; each Disney character functions simultaneously as logo, franchise, artwork, and archetype, linked symbolically and commercially to the pilgrimage site that is Disneyland.

The Walt Disney Company, however, produces iconic *Gesamtkunstwerke* that obscure the mechanical and mass-reproduced aspects of its Kingdom, and therefore provides an ambiguous antithesis to Benjamin's claim. A more direct antithesis, and a fuller understanding of the auratic qualities of mass reproduction in a capitalist economy, may be found in the crystalline works of the Bauhaus and the subsequent creations of Andy Warhol. These phenomena suggest (as Benjamin himself would suggest in sections of the Arcades Project) that the shape of mass culture in capitalist societies tends to follow a network of mechanical reproduction, commodity fetish, and totalizing aesthetics that first took form in the Crystal Palace and Bayreuth. The form that artistic aura takes under such a network is not the same as under the ideology of *l'art pour l'art*, but it is profoundly present nonetheless. While mechanically reproduced artworks might be developed in opposition to this network, their oppositional force derives not from their mechanical-reproductive form itself but from the manner in which this form is employed.

Some of Warhol's work in the 1980s forms a virtual reproduction, in reverse, of the argument of this book. In 1981, Warhol composed a series of ten silkscreens entitled *Myths*, including a reproduction of Mickey Mouse. Mickey is rendered there as an icon and an archetype, one of a pantheon of American gods that include Uncle Sam, Dracula, Santa Claus, Liz Taylor, the Wicked Witch, a black "Mammy," Superman, Howdy Doody, and Warhol himself (together with his own shadow). The next year, Warhol would turn his attention to Albert Speer's "Cathedral of Light" design for the Nuremberg rallies for a series entitled *Zeitgeist*. The silkscreen, which Warhol dubbed simply "Stadium," doubles a highly abstracted, black-and-white image of the coordinated searchlights over Luitpold-hain Arena, forming a picture of almost Bauhaus-like simplicity. Though Warhol, a friend of Riefenstahl's and admirer of her films,[1] certainly knew the origin of these images, there is no trace of historical context here: Nazi spectacle, like Mickey Mouse, is at once reduced to mere stylish prettiness and raised to the status of "myth." Finally, Warhol's return to the German roots of his own *Geist* would emerge again in 1987, when he silkscreened an image of Ludwig II's Neuschwanstein, marking yet one further reproduction in the history of reproduction of which Neuschwanstein was an already simulacral point of origin. Neuschwanstein, a copy of Romantic copies of medieval castles that never existed, copied again in countless objects of German neo-Romantic kitsch and once again as the centerpiece of Disneyland's Magic Kingdom, which is itself reproduced with slight variations at Walt Disney World, Disneyland Paris and Tokyo Disney, is the ideal architectural object for the Warhol treatment. If ever a structure were a mass-media celebrity, it would be Neuschwanstein; Neuschwanstein is the Mickey Mouse to the Wicked Witch of Speer's "Cathedral of Light." One wonders whether, having reproduced this perfect object of reproduction, this tower at the very heart of the *Gesamtkunstwerk*, Warhol simply had no further to go. A few days later he would be found dead in a New York hospital.

Warhol's work recalls and extends many of the themes we have examined thus far. The strategy of interlocking rings of total performance, pioneered at Nuremberg and transformed at Anaheim, finds its next chapter in Warhol's creations, which mimic the synergistic strategies of corporate empires. Likewise, Paxton's Crystal Palace and the Bauhaus theatre also find their latter-day extension in his crystalline creations. Warhol's multiple projects at the Factory attempted to unify a wide range of media, including painting, film, theatre, music, and fashion, into a single system of performance that openly celebrated not only mechanical reproduction but commercial culture. The unification of all media within a single system (which might be called *the Factory* or simply *Warhol*) represented a leveling of values that was at once utopian and vacant. In Warhol's Factory, the mechanical Third Kingdom first proclaimed in the Crystal Palace rises again, omnipresent and vacuous, living and spectral.

Exploding Plastic Inevitable

While Schlemmer and Moholy-Nagy's work would lead, in part, to innovations in shop-window design, Warhol would begin there, designing displays at the age of 19 for a Pittsburgh department store. At the Carnegie Institute of Technology, where Warhol studied art, many of his professors were industrial and commercial designers deeply influenced by the theories and practices of Gropius *et al.* It was an influence they passed on directly to the students, primarily through Laszlo Moholy-Nagy's *Vision and Design* and Paul Klee's *Pedagogical Sketchbook*, two Bauhaus texts that formed the backbone of the Carnegie Institute education (Bockris 66). Out of this early exposure to Bauhaus theory grew Warhol's early experiments, while still at Carnegie, with reproduction and the use of mass-media images, including his use of blotted line techniques and tracing of photographs taken from *Life* magazine. When Warhol moved to New York and began to work as a commercial artist for fashion magazines, he entered a world dominated by a small set of directors and designers, mostly of European birth, who had developed a sophisticated style of commercial art heavily influenced by the Bauhaus. Though Warhol tended, like many artists, to talk about his work as largely naïve, his debt to the Bauhaus from his earliest years of artistic training was significant, and would be most plainly visible in his choice of a name for his studio: the Factory.[2]

But such explicit connections are often less revealing than underlying structural ones. In 1971, 22 years after graduating from Carnegie, Warhol would write that:

> [b]usiness art is the step that comes after Art. I started as a commercial artist, and I want to finish as a business artist. After I did a thing called "art" or whatever it's called, I went into business art. I wanted to be an Art Businessman or a Business Artist. Being good in business is the most fascinating kind of art … [M]aking money is art and working is art and good business is the best art.
>
> (*Philosophy* 92)

What Warhol suggests here is not merely the collapse of a division between art and commerce, but also a quasi-teleological system where "business art is the step that comes after Art" and is Art's perfection. The ultimate synthesis of art and commerce he calls "Business art. Art business. The Business Art Business" (92). Warhol's writings recall Schlemmer's quasi-Hegelian point that art is annihilated and transfigured by capital ("speed and supertension of commercialism make expediency and utility the measure of all effectiveness, and calculation seizes the transcendent world"); and yet, of course, Warhol holds out no corresponding hope for a "cathedral of socialism." The profound tension expressed in the manifesto "The State Bauhaus in Weimar" – a tension between a desire for a socialist society and a mystification of capital and mechanical production – is far more deeply buried in Warhol, whose embrace of capital and mechanical reproduction appears, at least at first glance, to approach the absolute.

Warhol's earliest experimentation with the aesthetics of total art came with *Andy Warhol, Up-Tight*. Opening in 1965 at the Film-Makers' Cinematheque in New York, *Up-Tight* combined film (Warhol), slides and film projection (Warhol and Paul Morrissey), music (the Velvet Underground and Nico), dancing (Gerard Melanga and Edie Sedgwick), photography (Billy Linich and Nat Finkelstein), movie cameras (Barbara Rubin), and, of course, drugs (principally amphetamines and LSD).[3] The next year *Up-Tight* developed into an even more lavish spectacle dubbed (possibly by Paul Morrissey) *Exploding Plastic Inevitable*.[4] The number of performers, the size of the audience, the publicity, and the technical sophistication of the show had all increased. Warhol's description:

> [i]nside, the Velvets played so loud and crazy I couldn't even begin to guess the decibels, and there were images projected everywhere, one on top of the other ... Stephen Shore and Little Joey and a Harvard kid named Danny Williams would take turns operating the spotlights while Gerard and Ronnie and Ingrid and Mary Might (Woronov) danced sadomasochistic style with the whips and flashlights and the Velvets played and the different-colored hypnotic dot patterns swirled and bounced off the walls and the strobes flashed and you could close your eyes and hear cymbals and boots stomping and whips cracking and tambourines sounding like chains rattling.
>
> (Warhol and Hackett 163)

Stephen Koch, who was also present at the shows, describes them thus:

> [h]igh on the walls, high above the immense floor-throbbing woofers and merciless tweeters, the films and light shows poured like an endless, drenching visual rain. But as the music alternated between cacophony and the ... "acid" maundering of the Velvet Underground's ... guitars, the effort to create an exploding (more accurately, imploding) environment capable of shattering any conceivable focus on the senses was all too successful.
>
> (71)

Regardless of whether one responded positively to the "merciless," "maundering" effects of Warhol and company, most critics (as well as, more predictably, the performers themselves) agreed with Koch's estimation that the shows were "all too successful" at transforming the cultural environment of the period. According to

Lou Reed, the show "created multi-media in New York. Everything was affected by it. The whole complexion of the city changed, probably of the country. Nothing remained the same after that" (quoted in Bockris 248). "We all knew something revolutionary was happening," remarks Warhol.

> Things couldn't look this strange and new without some barrier being broken. "It's like the Red Seeeea," Nico said, standing next to me one night on the Dom balcony that looked out over all the action, "paaaaarting."
>
> (Warhol and Hackett 162)

If it did not quite part the sea, then the *Exploding Plastic Inevitable* (or *EPI*) at least invented the multimedia rock performance, and (particularly after becoming a road show) popularized the 1960s Happening.

Marshall McLuhan, as might be expected, includes a photograph of *Exploding Plastic Inevitable* in his book *The Medium Is the Massage* (sic), accompanied by the quotation, "'History as she is harped. Rite words in rote order'" (108–9). The quotation is a reference to the "Bardic songs" of "pre-literate Greece" (113), which, suggests McLuhan, arise again in the guise of electronic Happenings such as *Exploding Plastic Inevitable.* "Electronic circuitry confers a mythic dimension on our ordinary individual and group actions. Our technology forces us to live mythically," writes McLuhan (114), and elsewhere argues that "'time' has ceased, 'space' has vanished. We now live in a *global* village … a simultaneous happening" (63). Such points recall once more the by-now-familiar Romantic narrative of technology, extended to its furthest point, recovering long-lost community. In McLuhan's formulation, *EPI* is but a microcosm of a far larger "simultaneous happening," a return to lost community and "mythical" life by means of electronic circuitry. "We have now become aware," McLuhan concludes, "of the possibility of arranging the entire human environment as a work of art" (68). Just how influenced Warhol and company were by such musings is unclear, though certainly Warhol read and admired McLuhan, and many of the Factory participants were similarly influenced by the media theorist.[5] Regardless of the influence of such interpretations on Warhol's work, however, they are representative of the reception of many such multimedia Happenings in the late 1960s. Indeed, even the term "Happening" itself – with its suggestion of spontaneous arising rather than planned and therefore artificial theatricality – expresses an indebtedness to organicist notions of art, and a longing for an organic community from which such art might naturally spring.[6]

Thus is the crystalline *Gesamtkunstwerk* reinvented on the American stage. In a 1966 television interview with Lane Slate, Warhol mentioned that "since I don't believe in painting any more I thought [*EPI*] would be a nice way of combining, uh … and we have this chance to combine music and art and films all together" (Goldsmith 84). Similarly, speaking of the original home of *Up-Tight*, Warhol noted that "the Cinematique was really combining all the arts together" (quoted in Bockris and Melanga 25). The combination of the arts, then, was a stated aspect of the Warhol's multimedia project, a project that bears a particularly strong connection to the total-theatrical experiments of the Bauhaus. In "Man and Art Figure," as we have seen, Schlemmer imagines a mechanical-organic spectacle controlled by a "'perfect engineer' at the central switchboard, from where he would direct a feast for the eyes" (22). The description might have been applied to Warhol himself during an *EPI* production. Not only was Warhol the Velvet Underground's producer (and the sole reason they were forced to perform with Nico), but the films, the slides, and the Superstars used in *EPI* were all marked with his brand. More than this: he watched from behind the scenes, shaping the whole production while it was unfolding with such apparent randomness. "I'd usually watch from the balcony or take my turn at the projectors, slipping different-colored gelatin slides over the lenses and turning movies like *Harlot, The Shoplifter, Couch, Banana, Blow Job, Sleep, Empire, Kiss, Whips, Face, Camp, Eat* into all different colors," Warhol recalls in *POPism* (163). "People were coming because of Andy," writes Bockris, "who from his nightly perch on the left side of the balcony next to the projector, high above the deafening din, ran the film and slide projectors and changed the light filter, directing the people on stage with light" (247).

The whole effect recalls not only the *Organismus der Mechanik* of Schlemmer, but also Moholy-Nagy's "*GESAMTBÜHNENAKTION*" with its "masses or accumulations of media," especially "motion pictures, phonographs, [and] loud-speakers," and its replacement of meaningful connections by "multifarious complexities of light, space, plane, form, sound, man." Where Schlemmer and Moholy-Nagy's experiments in total theatre ended up, despite intentions, mirroring the vertiginous effects of the commodity spectacle, *EPI* did much the same in a period of far more rapid commodity exchange. With Warhol, however, the tension felt by the *Bauhäusler* had largely disappeared. No longer expressing an unambiguous longing for a society outside of commodity relations (though often expressing a longing for full inclusion in such relations), Warhol proudly polished the mirror his multimedia extravaganza held up to the mass market. *EPI*, after all, was not only a participatory multimedia event, but also a kaleidoscopic showcase of the many wheels of the Warhol empire. Warhol's art, Warhol's films, Warhol's band, Warhol's Superstars – all of these elements were brought together as separate entities unified within the larger system of Warhol's Factory. The unifying principle, meanwhile, was kept largely out of sight, "manoeuver[ing] it all into sound, image, and light symphonies,"[7] or else, when present, hidden behind a mask of indifference and a metallic-silver wig.

One might say that there were two Warhols behind the multimedia shows, just as there were two Warhols at the Factory: one a controlling impresario/artist and the other a shy spectator/collaborator. Much like Brecht's Berliner Ensemble in the 1950s (and Warhol's conflicted feelings about domination and collaboration are reminiscent of Brecht's), a Warhol production in the 1960s could vacillate oddly between being a Warhol showcase and a communal artwork overseen by Warhol. "Anyone in the audience could come up and work the lights," recalls Sterling Morrison (the Velvet Underground's guitarist) of performing for *EPI* in 1966.

> We never had things like "When we do this ten second break, then hit me with
> the blue spot." That's what I hate about modern rock and roll shows. They're
> so regimented. We just played while everything raged around us without any
> control on our part.
>
> (quoted in Bockris and Melanga 36)

Morrison's "without any control on our part" is strictly accurate, for, while there
was a certain amount of leeway for improvisation and audience participation,
control was still being exerted from outside the band. If "anyone" could come up
and work the lights, Warhol nevertheless had control over the master switch.

The tension between these two modes of performance, collaboration and
control, occasionally produced real fault lines in the project. Take, for example,
Gerard Melanga's letter to Warhol (recorded in Melanga's *Secret Diary*) from 4
September 1966. The occasion is that Melanga, whose "whip-dance" was an
integral part of the *EPI*, felt upstaged by another dancer. "I want to make it clear to
you," Melanga writes to Warhol,

> that (1) I was dancing with The Velvets long before you signed them into a
> corporation empire, and even before you knew them; (2) that my dancing is an
> integral part of the music and the show as is your movies; (3) I do not represent
> a "go go" dancer in the show but an interpretive-visual happening. You are
> slowly taking this away from me by allowing outside elements to interfere with
> my dance routines. Also Larry was supposed to have the spotlight on me when
> not projected on The Velvets. Instead, that spotlight wandered away from
> what was supposed to be seen happening on stage.
>
> (53)

Melanga's frustration reveals the limits of the sort of "anything goes" Happening
Morrison fondly recalls. Predictably, Melanga's appeal to Warhol for more of the
spotlight participates in both the rhetoric of open collaboration ("my dancing is an
integral part of the music and the show as is your movies") *and* of control by a
master artist ("you are slowly taking this away from me"), both the rhetoric of the
avant-gardist ("you signed them into a corporation empire") *and* of the artiste ("I do
not represent a 'go go' dancer"), both the rhetoric of collaborative improvisation
("interpretive-visual happening") *and* of orchestrated performance ("what was
supposed to be seen happening on stage"). Above all, the letter acknowledges one
unavoidable fact: Warhol, if not quite the wizard behind the curtain, was the
governing spirit of *EPI*, and its ultimate source of redress.

Total Warhol

As much as the *Exploding Plastic Inevitable* was a Warholian *Gesamtkunstwerk*, Warhol's
real total theatre may not have been *EPI* at all. Warhol's ultimate *Gesamtkunstwerk*
may have simply been Warhol himself.[8] Warhol was, or at least aimed to be, his

own multimedia spectacular, an all-consuming vortex that aimed to synthesize all modes of performance. In 1966, Warhol placed an advertisement in *The Village Voice* that read, "I'll endorse with my name any of the following: clothing, AC-DC, cigarettes, small tapes, sound equipment, Rock 'N Roll records, anything, film and film equipment, Food, Helium, WHIPS, Money; love and kisses Andy Warhol" (Warhol and Hackett 152). In time, he not only met but exceeded the list, synthesizing visual arts, music, dance, film, theatre, fiction, Happening, memoir, magazine publishing, television show, his own modeling career – the list goes on – into a single, highly marketable product that went by the name of Warhol. By the end of his life, he was fantasizing about Warhol perfumes, hotels, and restaurants, as well as actually having himself robotically cloned by an entertainment firm. At a price of $400,000, the entertainment company AVG Productions was building a computerized automaton that could make 54 of Andy's trademark gestures and quips, for use in a planned theatrical production (Bockris 458–9). As a master of multimedia, Warhol was also ahead of his time in his understanding of the commercial possibilities of synergy. While *EPI* was used as a showcase for Warhol's multimedia empire in the late 1960s, in the 70s Warhol encouraged celebrities to commission portraits by publishing stories on them in *Interview*. In the 80s, Warhol's television shows (including *Fashion*, *Andy Warhol's T.V.*, and, for MTV, *Andy Warhol's Fifteen Minutes*) provided a platform for the models, actors, designers, and products connected to the Warhol universe. Here the Superstars, the TV shows, the gallery exhibitions, the multimedia Happenings, and the dandiacal body of Warhol himself were interwoven into a camp-commercial utopia that obliterated distinctions not only between art and commerce but between art and everyday life.

Like one of Schlemmer's "art-figures" made flesh, Warhol frequently expressed a desire to be a kind of mechanical organism himself. "I think everybody should be a machine," he told Gene Swenson (writing for *ARTNews*) in 1963 (16). And: "[t]he reason I'm painting this way is I want to be a machine. Whatever I do, and do machine-like, is because it is what I want to do" (18). Or, similarly, to Letitia Kent of *Vogue* in 1970: "[i]f we could become more mechanical, we would hurt less – if we could be programmed to do our jobs happily and efficiently" (190). Warhol also described machines as his closest relations. "When I got my first TV set, I stopped caring so much about having close relationships with other people," he writes in his *Philosophy*.

> So in the late 50s I started an affair with my television set which has continued to the present, when I play around in my bedroom with as many as four at a time. But I didn't get married until 1964 when I got my first tape recorder. My wife.
>
> (26)

As a machine among machines, Warhol on one hand embodied a Taylorite fantasy who, according to one colleague, "did everything for money. His main goal was to learn how to do everything faster" (quoted in Bockris 95).

But Warhol's machine-man performance was not simply an echo of mass reproduction. It also attempted to recapture a less-alienated position for labor within the commodity spectacle.[9] David Harvey, describing the condition of labor and the body in capitalist society, notes that "[c]apital circulates, as it were, through the body of the laborer as variable capital and thereby turns the laborer into a mere appendage of the circulation of capital itself" (*Limits* 157). Through his artistic labor, Warhol attempted to make himself into a machine through which capital could circulate with utmost efficiency, but he attempted to resist the marginal status to which that circulation relegated him. The totalizing spectacle that Warhol created around himself was in a certain sense a mirror of commodity relations, but it was a mirror with the significant difference that a single laborer at least (Warhol) might become a central source of signification rather than a "mere appendage." This was ultimately a difference that could only be expressed as desire, for, as Warhol repeatedly demonstrated through his own work, the line between the circulation of capital and the circulation of art was already next to nonexistent.

Where Paxton's Palace mystified and naturalized the commodity, and the Bauhaus artists regularly saw mechanical reproduction as a route back to organic society, Warhol had a recurring, peculiarly American, postmillennial vision: that the mechanized Kingdom of Capital has already arisen, and the egalitarian ideal has already been achieved. "What's great about this country," writes Warhol,

> is that America started the tradition where the richest consumers buy essentially the same things as the poorest. You can be watching TV and see Coca-Cola, and you can know that the President drinks Coke, Liz Taylor drinks Coke, and just think, you can drink Coke, too. A Coke is a Coke and no amount of money can get you a better Coke than the one the bum on the corner is drinking. All the Cokes are the same and all the Cokes are good.
>
> (*Philosophy* 101)

Warhol's utopian vision of equality and goodness was a peculiarly American sort of communal dream.

> Someone said that Brecht wanted everybody to think alike. I want everybody to think alike. But Brecht wanted to do it through Communism, in a way. Russia is doing it under government. It's happening here all by itself without being under a strict government; so if it's working without trying, why can't it work without being Communist?
>
> (Swenson 16)

Today America, tomorrow the world. "The most beautiful thing in Tokyo is McDonald's," deadpans Warhol. "The most beautiful thing in Stockholm is McDonald's. The most beautiful thing in Florence is McDonald's. Peking and Moscow don't have anything beautiful yet" (*Philosophy* 71).[10] Such statements only heighten the impression that Warhol's celebration of American mass commercialization is a celebration of the simulacrum, a mirror of consumer society that becomes, in the end, merely another reflective shard in an all-encompassing hall of mirrors. Perhaps Benjamin, who once called the fascist commodification of politics "the *flâneur*'s last practical joke" ("Paris" 156), simply died too early to hear the true punch line.

This joke is more clever, however, than many critics have realized. Baudrillard, for one, misses it in his influential reading of Warhol in *The Consumer Society*.[11] Baudrillard summarizes the relationship between the consumer society and Pop art as follows:

> the logic of consumption eliminates the traditional sublime status of artistic representation. There is, strictly, no longer any privileging of the essence or signification of the object over the image. The one is no longer the truth of the other: they coexist in the same physical and logical space, where they also "operate" as signs (in their differential, reversible, combinatorial relation). Whereas all art up to pop was based on a "depth" vision of the world, pop regards itself as homogenous with this *immanent order of signs*: homogenous with their industrial, mass production and henceforth with the artificial, manufactured character of the whole environment, homogenous with the spatial saturation and simultaneous culturalized abstraction of this new order of things.
>
> (115)

In Baudrillard's reading, Pop art is a pure simulacral product of the homogenous order that gave it birth, and celebrates that order as the "ideal society" (118). True of Pop generally, it is more so of Warhol in particular, whom Baudrillard considers "the most radical [Pop artist] in his approach" and the artist who "best sums up the theoretical contradiction" of Pop (118). Baudrillard is hardly alone in this reading; in its general features, it recurs frequently. Roland Barthes, for instance, argues that:

> Pop cleanses the image of everything in it that is not rhetoric ... The philosophical meaning of these labors is that things have no essence other than the social code which manifests them, so that ultimately, they are no longer ever produced (by Nature), but immediately "reproduced."
>
> (239)

And Deleuze writes in *Difference and Repetition* that "Pop art pushed the copy, copy of the copy, etc., to that extreme point at which it reverses and becomes a simulacrum (such as Warhol's remarkable 'serial' series, in which all the repetitions of habit, memory, and death are conjugated)" (293–4). If the overwhelming spectacle of commodity culture threatened to render the Bauhaus theatre a mere reproduction of an omnipresent original, then the answer of Pop seems to have been ecstatic absorption into the commodity culture from which it springs.

A potential problem with any line of interpretation that reads Warhol's work as pure simulacrum is that it does not quite take seriously the slyness of Warhol's celebration of mass reproduction and mass consumption. Not that Baudrillard is unaware of this slyness; he attempts to account for (and simultaneously *discount*) it by reminding us that:

> a *certain smile* is one of the *obligatory signs* of consumption: it no longer represents a humour, a critical distance, but is merely a reminder of that transcendent critical value which today is given material embodiment in the knowing wink. This false distance is present everywhere: in spy films, in Godard, in modern advertising, which uses it continually as a cultural allusion. It is not really clear in the end whether this "cool" smile is the smile of humour or that of commercial complicity. This is also the case of pop, and its smile ultimately encapsulates all its ambiguity: it is not the smile of critical distance, but the smile of *collusion*.
>
> (121)

Baudrillard is certainly correct to point out that the "knowing wink," by Warhol's time, no longer necessarily suggests critical distance, but has become inextricably linked to the cycle of consumption itself. Hence the foreclosure, in a postmodern American context, of the genuinely satiric possibilities of a work such as Schlemmer's *Figural Cabinet*. But the profoundly nihilistic statements of Warhol's suggest not a "certain smile" but something else, something that is not quite, as Baudrillard would have it, "*collusion*." They suggest, in short, a black-humor awareness of the essential deathliness of consumer society. This is so even if one puts to the side such frequently cited silkscreens as Warhol's "Death and Disaster" series (of dead celebrities, car crashes, electric chairs, mushroom clouds, etc.).[12] Indeed, such supposedly critical works add little to the debate over Warhol's oppositional stance (or lack thereof), as they are no more necessarily critical than are his silkscreens of Brillo boxes, soup cans, and celebrities. Which is to say that, regardless of subject-matter, Warhol's silkscreens leave radically ambiguous the question of reception. Are his incessantly repeated images of lynchings, for instance, social commentary or mere tabloid voyeurism? Are his images of dollar bills critique or reification? We might well reply, quoting Peter Bürger, that "the painting of 100 Campbell soup cans contains resistance to the commodity society only for the person who wants to see it there" (61). In Warhol's expressionlessness (which includes not only his silkscreens and films but also his self-performance, his notorious "blank stare" and his I'll-be-your-mirror interview style) there lies, if not a critique, then at least an unsettling expression of profoundly reified subjectivity. If this nullity has ceased to be unsettling (or if it never was), then it is the postmodern potential for critical art generally, rather than Warhol's work in particular, that begs examination.[13]

And yet there is also more to Warhol's relation to commodity culture than potentially discomforting mimesis. The slyness of Warhol's irony, the slipperiness of his critique is too often downplayed, but it is central to his transformation of the total work of art. In order to appreciate Warhol's distinctly postmodern estrangement effects, we must first recall the fundamental differences between the American art scene in the 1960s and the European art scene in the early decades of the twentieth century. As Huyssen writes:

> the postmodernist revolt against the institution art in the United States was up against bigger odds than futurism, Dada, or surrealism were in their time. The earlier avant-garde was confronted with the culture industry in its stage of inception while postmodernism had to face a technologically and economically fully developed media culture which had mastered the high art of integrating, diffusing, and marketing even the most serious challenges. This factor, combined with the altered constitution of audiences, accounts for the fact that, compared with the earlier 20th century, the shock of the new was much harder, if not impossible, to sustain.
>
> (*After* 168)

For Bürger (as for Baudrillard), the complex of factors Huyssen describes makes Warhol's "Neo-avant-garde" work a lifeless echo of the European avant-garde. No longer capable of posing a genuine challenge to commodity culture and artistic institutionalization, Warhol's work "stages for the second time the avant-gardiste break with tradition, becomes a manifestation that is void of sense and that permits the positing of any meaning whatever" (Bürger 61). But, again, in order to appreciate (and at the same time not overstate) Warhol's critical force, we must appreciate its elusiveness. Brecht's car has lost its traction on new American roads; to regain control, Warhol must turn violently into the swerve.

Take, for example, Warhol's well-known process of silkscreening. Despite his Bauhaus-influenced embrace of industrial terminology and techniques for his artistic practice, Warhol's usual method of artistic reproduction at the Factory was not one of fully mechanical reproduction. While critics have almost uniformly taken Warhol at his word (either to praise or condemn him) when he speaks of his works as mechanically reproduced products, silkscreening (Warhol's preferred technique) is in fact a more complex case. As a method of artistic reproduction, silkscreening does not fall neatly on either side of the divide separating industry from art. While it began as an industrial technology in the early twentieth century and gained currency as a mode of factory production during the First World War, silkscreening had largely faded from factory production by the 1960s. American artists, meanwhile, had begun using the technique during the early 1930s, taking advantage of both its industrial *and* its handicraft aspects. For, while lending itself to the reproduction of images, the silkscreening process itself also involves numerous creative decisions (including what colors of paint to apply, how much of each color to use, where each color should be placed, how hard to press the paint through the screen, etc.). As a result – and to a degree that cannot be said of, say, a photocopy machine – no silkscreen is a mere reproduction of any other. By the 1960s, then, the status of silkscreening vis-à-vis mechanical reproduction was by no means clear. Neither quite industry, nor quite craft, nor quite art, silkscreening at once reproduced and questioned the distinctions introduced by mechanical reproduction. Warhol's silkscreens, which were executed (either by Warhol himself or by his assistants) in innumerable different ways, featuring changes in color and emphasis, as well as streaks, blotches, dribbled paint, and blurring, were less products of mass reproduction than works hovering somewhere between reproduction, handicraft, and art. While repetition is central to Warhol's work, Warhol always repeats with a difference. To put the matter another way, Warhol's silkscreens act somewhere between repetition and representation, in Jacques Attali's sense of those terms.[14]

Another aspect of Warhol's slyness that Baudrillard, Barthes, Bürger, and Deleuze miss is the ambiguously oppositional effect of Warhol's aesthetics of camp. Though definitions of the term are notoriously elusive,[15] recent accounts of camp have tended to concentrate on its function as a marker of gay identity vis-à-vis the capitalist entertainment industry. Moe Meyer calls camp "a suppressed and denied oppositional critique embodied in the signifying practices that processually constitute queer identities" (1), and Matthew Tinkcom defines it as "the alibi for gay-inflected labor to be caught in the chain of value-coding within capitalist political economies" (108). Neither definition is particularly mellifluous (we are a long way from the wry wit of Susan Sontag), but both are helpful in that they stress the inseparability of "camp" from larger systems of symbolic and economic production. To be sure, they have different emphases. Where Meyer's reading, supported by the essays he selects for his anthology *The Politics and Poetics of Camp* (1994), stresses the role of camp in gay identity-formation, Tinkcom's stresses its role in a capitalist system of labor. Both aspects of camp are important, however, and the two cannot be unbuckled. In the case of Warhol and his Superstars, camp was a signifying practice of gay male identity, sometimes subtly (silkscreens of Elizabeth Taylor, a film of a man sleeping, an unmoving shot of the Empire State building), sometimes not so subtly (films about hustlers, films about drag queens), sometimes unmistakably (a film featuring cowboy strip poker). At the same time camp was a way for Warhol and his Factory to both *be* and *not be* a Hollywood studio, to *be* and *not be* a "factory" of industrialized commodities.

One way Warhol simultaneously mimicked and mocked and worshipped Hollywood was by camping on B-movie production techniques. Rather than making a very few, finely crafted films in the manner of the anti-Hollywood auteur, Warhol and his Superstars made a stupefying number (no one has made a precise count, and countless reels have been lost, but they easily number in the hundreds) in the years between 1963 and 1968. As Sontag has written, such extravagance is one of the hallmarks of camp (283). But, more precisely, Warhol's mass-production technique camps on the odd combination of assembly-line efficiency (the penny-pinching producers, the strict budget accountability) and bloated superfluity (the infinite sequels, the remakes and knock-offs) that characterizes mass movie production. Cheap, disposable, and gluttonously overstuffed, Warhol's Factory was a funhouse mirror held up to Hollywood. Warhol further twisted the reflection by putting the fringes of society at the center of his productions. Particularly before Valerie Solanis' attempted murder of Warhol in 1968, the Factory was famously open to anyone willing to take the elevator up to the right floor, and Warhol drew his Superstars from the ranks of the socially and politically marginalized: drag queens, flamboyant performers, drug addicts, beautiful lost things, and queers of all stripes. "We were all odds-and-ends misfits," recalls Warhol in *POPism*, "somehow misfitting together" (219). Above all, however, the community of the Factory was one of young gay men, and the images and subject-matter of films such as *My Hustler* (1965), *Bike Boy* (1967), and *Lonesome Cowboy* (1967) were unambiguously homoerotic.[16]

If a sign of the Factory's difference was its queerness, then a related sign was its interest in what Warhol called "leftovers." "I always like to work on leftovers, doing the leftover things," writes Warhol in his *Philosophy*. "Things that were discarded, that everybody knew were no good, I always thought had a great potential to be funny. It was like recycling work" (93). Such passages exemplify the double-edged nature of Warhol's camp. On one hand there is the interest in the "discarded," the "no good," the "leftovers," which shaped Warhol's production aesthetic in the 1960s, allowing the Factory to become a Hollywood studio for those on the outside looking in. As Tally Brown, a regular participant during its heyday, puts it, the Factory was about

> creating Hollywood outside Hollywood, where you don't have to bother with learning to act, making the rounds, going to agents, getting your 8×10 glossy, doing small parts, being an extra, and gradually working up to become a star. You just got on camera and were a Superstar!
>
> (243)

Or, in the words of Superstar Holly Woodlawn, "it was like the Hollywood star system … At that point, we were on the same level as Hollywood, if not higher" (528). This camp version of the American mass culture, especially in the five years before the attempt on his life, was not simply reducible to signs of consumption. It was an attempt, like Warhol's self-performance, to recapture a less-alienated position for labor within the commodity spectacle, and to incorporate gay-inflected labor within the system of a capitalist political economy. And yet, again like Warhol's self-performance, there is also something more troubling here. For, in recreating Hollywood at the Factory, Warhol and his Superstars also recreated the restless need to make the cycle of "art business" production ever more efficient, to eat up its leftovers, to reuse its outtakes, and recycle its work. In the course of its masquerade, the Factory risked becoming too much the thing it mimicked.

Vacuum salesman

"I think we're a vacuum here at the Factory," Warhol told Gretchen Berg, in a 1966 interview for *The East Village Other* (91). It was a metaphor he used often, occasionally followed by the ejaculation, "It's great!" The vacuum is, indeed, the endpoint not only of Warhol's total theatre but also of any closed cycle. "The ideal underlying the total market," writes Christian Enzensberger, "aims not only at exterminating the living, but ultimately the commodity too; the ideal would be the noiseless odorless painless absolute and antiseptic annihilation of all things, including itself" (*Smut* 98). When, a century earlier, Semper referred to the Crystal Palace as a "glass-covered vacuum" (*glasbedeckte Vakuum*) (68), he meant the phrase as an enthusiastic description of the enchanting technology of the space. But the negative connotations cannot be avoided: hand in hand with the enchantments of the Crystal Palace went a certain vacuousness, a leveling of all objects and their associations to the same universal equivalence of monetary exchange. The exhibitions and arcades of the late nineteenth century, as Benjamin understood, were at once enchanting, overstuffed, and empty, precursors of the twenty-first-century phenomenon of 1001 television channels and nothing on. "I've always believed in television," Warhol told Letitia Kent for *Vogue* in 1970.

> A television day is like a twenty-four hour movie. The commercials don't really break up the continuity. The programs change yet somehow remain the same … or something. Critics complain that our movies are slow. Well, each segment of the Peyton Place series runs for half an hour and nothing really happens.
>
> (187)

The "nothing" that "really happens" in Warhol films such as *Sleep* and *Eat* is but a mirror image of the "nothing" that "really happens" already on television. Or the nothing that really happens in Warhol himself. "Everything is nothing. I'm still obsessed with the idea of looking into the mirror and seeing no one, nothing" (*Philosophy* 7).

Warhol attempted to act out in his own life the empty script he saw surrounding him ("It's much harder, you know, to *be* your own script than to memorize someone else's" [Kent 187]), and there is something undeniably Brechtian about this estranging sort of performance. "I strongly wish that after their invention of the radio the bourgeoisie would make a further invention that enables us to fix for all time what the radio communicates," wrote Brecht in 1927. "Later generations would then have the opportunity to marvel how a caste was able to tell the whole planet what it had to say and at the same time how it enabled the planet to see that it had nothing to say" (*BOF* 37). Warhol might well have agreed, though he might have added that nothing was better than nothing. When asked why he chose to paint Campbell soup cans, Warhol characteristically replied, "I wanted to paint nothing. I was looking for something that was the essence of nothing, and that was it" (quoted in Bockris 154). Warhol's everything-is-nothing philosophy, like his famous "Warhol stare," was the face of the urban spectator in a society too rapidfire for flâneurship, an exaggerated version of the stupefaction created by the sensory overload of the commodity spectacle. By the late twentieth century, writes Harvey, "[t]he bombardment of stimuli, simply on the commodity front, creates problems of sensory overload that make Simmel's dissection of the problems of modern urban living at the turn of the century seem to pale into insignificance by comparison" (*Postmodernity* 286). By such sensory overload, commodity culture creates "either a stupefied nirvana or a totally blasé attitude" (Harvey, *Spaces* 168), and Warhol's totalizing self-performance gives abundant evidence of both responses. His comments about commodified culture are simultaneously adoring and supremely indifferent. "I love Hollywood," said Warhol. "They're beautiful. Everybody's plastic, but I love plastic. I want to be plastic" (quoted in Koch 62). Or: "Vacant, vacuous Hollywood was everything I ever wanted to mold my life into. Plastic, white on white" (Warhol and Hackett 46). In a 1963 radio interview with Ruth Hirschman, he described his art as "really nothing, so it really has nothing to say" (36). Like the film he made of the Empire State Building shot from a single angle, unmoving, for eight hours, Warhol's view of the commodity spectacle is so abjectly awestruck as to seem virtually catatonic. According to Koch, the theme "from which all [Warhol's] work grows" is simply the theme of death (133), and Warhol frequently concurred, telling Swenson, for instance, that "I realized that everything I was doing must have been Death" (19). If Warhol's grand theme is death, then it is not simply personal but societal deterioration that is at issue here.

Warhol may have loved working with leftovers, and converting them into productive work, but he was terrified of becoming a leftover himself. In the spirit of Schlemmer's *absolute Schaubühne*, which aimed to eliminate the human from the stage, Warhol longed for a machine that would eliminate every trace of bodily "leftover," that would whisk away even the last remnants of organic matter that continue after death. "At the end of my time, when I die," writes Warhol,

> I don't want to leave any leftovers. And I don't want to be a leftover. I was watching TV this week and I saw a lady go into a ray machine and disappear. That was wonderful, because matter is energy and she just dispersed. That could be a really American invention, the best American invention – to be able to disappear.
>
> (*Philosophy* 112–13)

Thinking over the matter further, however, Warhol sees a potential problem with this desire: if some machine could truly make all "leftovers" disappear, then that machine would obliterate the mechanical nature that lies even in "leftovers." Warhol's desire to spirit away any remaining trace of organic material runs up against the need to be constantly productive. "I guess disappearing," concludes Warhol upon further reflection, "would be shirking work that your machinery still had left to do" (113). Warhol's contradictory desires reflect a conflict between two separate capitalist injunctions: to eliminate anything that is no longer productive, and always to be productive. The question of "leftovers," then, becomes fraught. If the body that has ceased to labor should simply disappear, would such a disappearance constitute an avoidance of future labor?

Over and again, Warhol's vacuum metaphor returns to the body, which must be rendered a total work of art, a perfectly seamless organism, a flesh-and-blood realization of Schlemmer's art-figures. The signs of production that must be buried now are the signs of the labor of living itself. *The Philosophy of Andy Warhol* opens and closes with long conversations, and their leitmotif is purification: purification of the body, of the living space, of the mind. It begins with drying up zits:

> I dunk a Johnson and Johnson cotton all into Johnson and Johnson rubbing alcohol and rub the cotton ball against the pimple. It smells so good. So clean. So cold. And while the alcohol is drying I think about nothing. How it's always in style. Always in good taste.
>
> (8)

As in the Festspielhaus, material signs that are rebutted on all fronts can well up again from beneath. Attempting to remove all signs of a body beneath the skin with Johnson and Johnson rubbing alcohol exactly parallels, in such passages, the attempt to remove all thoughts from the mind. The skin becomes the protective sheath of the total system, from which all signs of imperfection must be removed. Thus does *The Philosophy of Andy Warhol* begin; it ends with vacuuming up dust:

> I still have to do the top drawer of my bureau. And then I have to start vacuuming because if I'd done the vacuuming first I'd have all the dust back again. So anyway, I do the top drawer. I pull it out. No matter how many times I clean it, it's still a mess. I can keep it clean for exactly one hour after I've cleaned it. I have to accept in my mind that this is a never-ending thing.
>
> (208)

To accept that this process of purification is "a never-ending thing" is part of the trouble of erasure of signs of production in any total system. Clean is always the not-yet-unclean, nothing is always the not-yet-something, and closed totality is always threatened by violation. Another trouble arises as well: vacuums clean houses, but they cannot clean minds. For this kind of cleaning, recording devices are needed.

> I have no memory. Every day is a new day because I don't remember the day before. Every minute is like the first minute of my life. I try to remember but I can't. That's why I got married – to my tape recorder. That's why I seek out people with minds like tape recorders to be with. My mind is like a tape recorder with one button – Erase.
>
> If I wake up too early to check in with anyone, I kill time by watching TV and washing my underwear.
>
> (199)

Watching TV while washing your underwear: never has the assonance between "watching" and "washing" been so loaded. Or so unloaded, rather, so empty.

"I like being a vacuum," Warhol told Gretchen Berg in 1966; "it leaves me alone to work" (91). Or, as the Talking Heads sing on *Fear of Music* (1979): "Heaven is a place / Where nothing ever happens." Which could be read two ways: either that nothing happens, or that everything that happens is nothing, forever.

Comfort in the void; but as the saying goes, nature abhors a vacuum. Not only does air constantly seek a fault line through which to enter, but the air, too, is suddenly rendered dangerous to any organic material within. When a vacuum seals off organic material from the outer atmosphere, the vacuum both preserves the material from decay and at the same time renders it acutely susceptible of becoming poisonous should a leak occur. It should come as no surprise, then, that Warhol, like any *Gesamtkunstwerk*, was under a constant threat of leakage and thus of contamination. This fear of contamination is one that has hounded the total work of art since its inception. We saw it first at the Bayreuth Festspielhaus, with its multiplication of blinders that hide all signs of labor beneath a veneer of perfect organicism. With Warhol, however, whose ultimate *Gesamtkunstwerk* was simply his own self-performance, the fear of contamination comes to press most closely on the artist's body. With Warhol, the artist's body becomes a mimicry of American mass culture, with its overstuffed and vacuous energies, its sublime and banal desires, its power and fragility.

The fragility in particular is visible in three early Warhol silkscreens. The first is a 1962 image entitled "Handle with Care – Glass – Thank You" (Figure 7.1). The insistent repetitions of these factory-produced labels recall the crystalline fragilities of the Factory and of Warhol himself, whose glass was his nowhere-man transparency as well as his "I'll-be-your-mirror" gaze as well as his ubiquitous camera lens. The image is echoed again in several other silkscreens of the same period, including "Fragile" and "Fragile – Handle with Care," which repeat with variations the same theme of shattered glass. This fragility may be found again in "Where Is Your Rupture?" (Figure 7.2), another silkscreen from the early 1960s.[17] This silkscreen forms an interesting comparison to Schlemmer's illustrations of the perfectly geometric figure. As with Schlemmer's figures, a curiously asexual body is overlaid with seemingly rational diagrams. But here, as opposed to Schlemmer's drawings, the diagrams do not show the perfect geometric boundaries of the human figure; rather, numbers are joined to arrows that pierce and fragment the body, rendering it more rather than less exposed. "Where Is Your Rupture?" reads the text, itself rendered only partially legible due to the inherently imperfect printing of the silkscreen process. Finally, a Warhol silkscreen from a year later continues the theme of ruptured seals (Figure 7.3). Entitled "Tunafish Disaster," it excerpts a newspaper article on a case of salmonella poisoning that evidently killed two women. Under repeated images of the fatal can of contaminated tuna fish, a newspaper heading reads, "Did a leak kill … Mrs. McCarthy and Mrs. Brown?" The choice of the tin can is important here, and not only because of Warhol's comments about the Factory being a vacuum. The tin can and its dangers also recall the Campbell soup can, which had made Warhol famous just a year earlier. "Tunafish Disaster" is the shadow side of the simulacral perfection of the Campbell soup can paintings just as much as "Where Is Your Rupture?" is the shadow side of Schlemmer's figural geometries. With both prints, Warhol draws our attention to the fear of leakage upon which every total system rests, from Wagner's Festspielhaus to the Bauhaus *Totaltheater* to Warhol's Factory. It is a fear that must be regularly and repeatedly assuaged by means of a mechanical process, a vacuum-seal forced between the remnants of organism and the surrounding, contaminating, air.[18]

At once echoing, sanctifying, and camping on commodity culture, Warhol gives us America as a realized utopia in the literal sense of the word. America, in other words, as a heavenly Nowheresville. If Disney's Audio-animatronics are the perfect inhabitants of the mechanized utopia of Disneyland, then Warhol performs the perfect citizen of late twentieth-century commodity spectacle, a "grand combination

Figure 7.1 Andy Warhol, *Handle with Care – Glass – Thank You*, 1962.

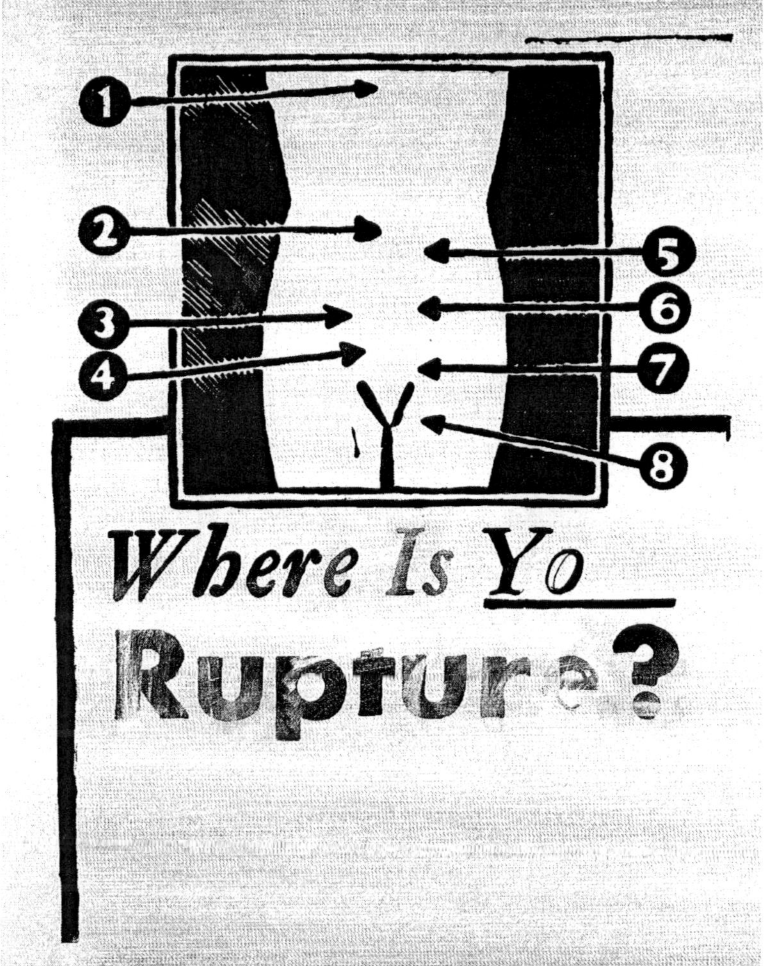

Figure 7.2 Andy Warhol, *Where Is Your Rupture?*, 1960.

of all the arts" that reflects the larger totalizing system of which it is a part. With Warhol, however, unlike with Disney's robots, that reflection was generally a repetition with a difference, a camp version of mass culture. Especially before Solanis' attempt on his life in 1968 – and the far greater conservatism of the post-68 reorganized Factory – Warhol's relation to mass-cultural totalities such as Disneyland was a camp imitation that carried with it both rapt admiration and subtle critique. If Brecht's direct attacks on the Wagnerian *Gesamtkunstwerk* reflected a historical moment when dialectical opposition to the cultural marketplace was more readily at hand, then Warhol's camp reflects a rather different moment, one

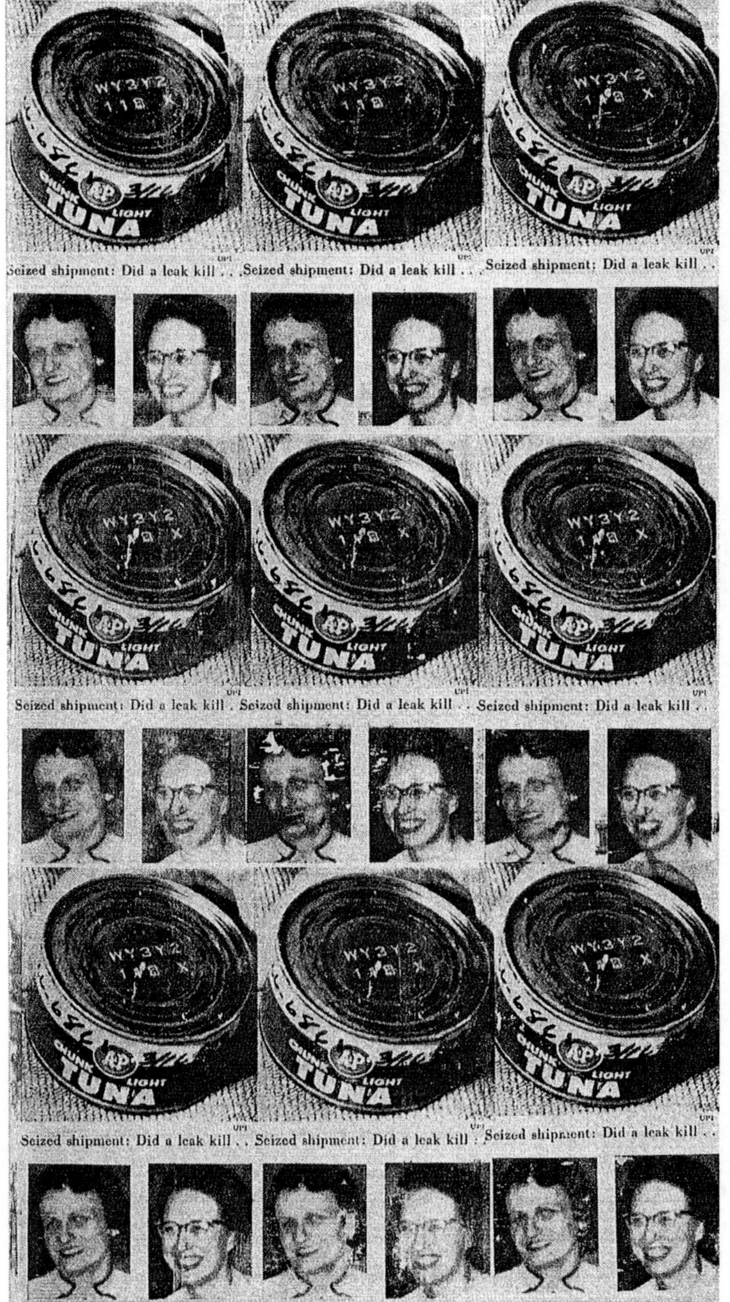

Figure 7.3 Andy Warhol, *Tunafish Disaster*, 1961.

in which the market's effect on daily life had become so total that difference is generally marked through ironic appropriation rather than opposition. If Warhol's camp marks a recuperation of laughter as an oppositional element in the history of the total work of art, then it does so by utilizing a very different sort of laughter than Disney's. Warhol's laughter is the laughter not of pretended innocence but of knowing estrangement, not of reassurance but of mimicry.

A final significant contribution of Warhol to the history of the relation between mass culture and the total work of art was that he was able to resolve the fundamental tension of the crystalline *Gesamtkunstwerk* that we first witnessed in Weimar and Dessau. Where the Bauhaus theatre was caught between utopia and consumer culture, Warhol declared both to be realized in an inseparable unity. Where the Bauhaus theatre was caught between closed totality and engagement with the surrounding culture, Warhol simultaneously embraced hermeticism and mimesis, explicitly modeling his work on a far more ubiquitous and powerful consumer society than the Weimar/Dessau Bauhaus ever knew. In multimedia Happenings and in the development of the all-consuming Warhol "brand," Warhol synthesized the conflicting strands that Schlemmer and Moholy-Nagy maintained in tension. The most unnerving element of critique in Warhol's work essentially presumes this synthesis, for his darkly comic edge emerges only when one realizes that Warhol simultaneously means and does not mean what he says about mass culture and utopia, that Coke really is "it," and that "it" is nothing, and that that's great.

Describing the stage of his "electro-mechanical theatre," the Russian Constructivist El Lissitzky once wrote that "[a]ll energies must be organized into a unity, crystallized, and put on show" (347). This trinity of features – unity, crystallization, and being-put-on-show – may serve as a hallmark of a lineage of total art with its structural roots in Paxton's Crystal Palace. It is a lineage as much commercial as avant-garde; indeed, a close examination of the history of the total work of art ought to help to dismantle precisely that distinction. As the site of the collapse of art into commodity spectacle, and therefore as the swan song of what Huyssen refers to as "the classical avantgarde" (*After* 168), the Factory extended to the null point a project already significantly developed in Weimar and Dessau. Working half a century after the *Totaltheater*, Warhol was able to see what Schlemmer and Moholy-Nagy could only dimly glimpse: that any total artwork in a consumer society would largely be a reflection of the totalizing system from which it emerges. The reflection, however, is never simple, never exact – this is where the "art" enters in – but a fantasia of lights and colors playing on a crystalline face, on the exquisite angles of a jagged living stone.

Warhol's final friend

In the last couple years of his life, Warhol became fascinated by working with computers. One of his final works is a self-portrait with his Amiga, one of the first generation of personal computers capable of supporting full-color digital art (Figure 7.4). The work was created for the cover of *Amiga World* magazine, published by

Amiga's parent company, Commodore. The portrait is a classic Warholian closed circle: we see Warhol caught in the computer screen, captured by Warhol, caught in the computer screen, captured by Warhol, and so on ad infinitum. Warhol, in other words, has moved his mirror into the world of digital space. The issue included an interview with Warhol, conducted while he changed the colors on an image of Dolly Parton on his Amiga. "It's really great not to get your hands in paint," comments Warhol, turning his attention away from Dolly Parton and towards the composition of the self-portrait that will eventually provide the cover of the magazine. "Is this the greatest thing since sliced bread?" ask Guy Wright and Glenn Suokko for *Amiga World* (336). "Oh yeah, it is," answers Warhol, his hands spotless as he paints in cyberspace. Had he lived, this might have been his next frontier: the Exploding *Digital* Inevitable.

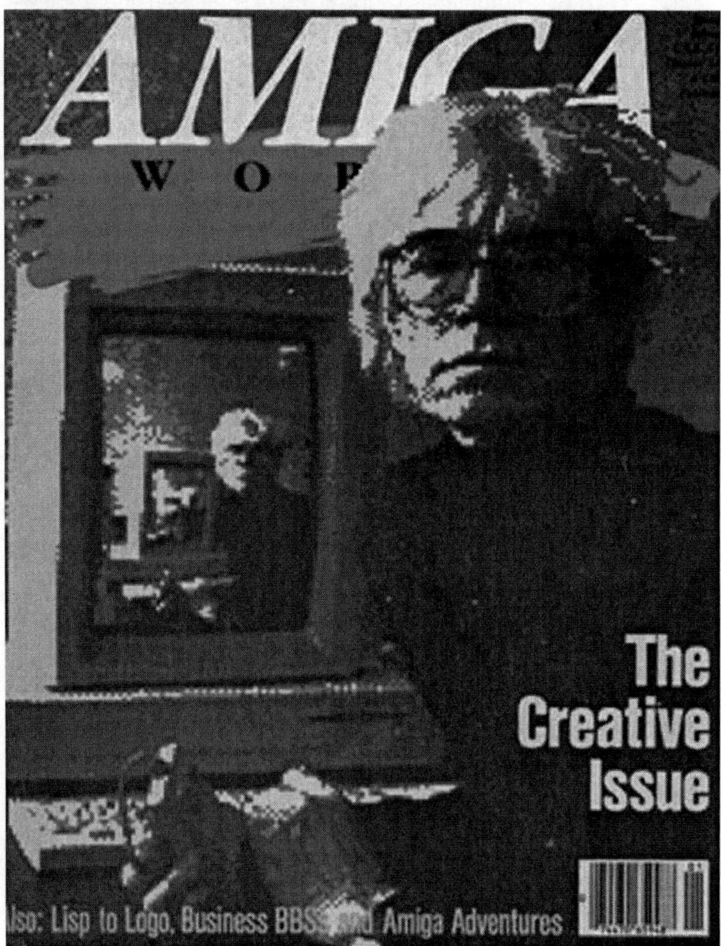

Figure 7.4 *Amiga World*, cover, 1986.

Total immersion
Cyberspace and the total work of art

Forget about Andy Warhol's petty promise of fame for fifteen minutes. We will all become angels, and for eternity! Highly unstable, hermaphrodite angels, unforgettable in terms of computer memory. In this cold cubic fortress of pixels that is cyberspace, we will be, as in dreams, everything: the Dragon, the Princess, and the Sword.

(Stenger 52)

Fortress of pixels

Housed within an 18-story geodesic sphere, Disney's *Spaceship Earth* "explores the history of human communications" by giving customers the opportunity to "Ride the Time Machine from the Dawn of Civilization to the Beginning of Our Tomorrow" (Walt Disney Co., "Spaceship Earth," "Intercot"). A press release issued by the ride's sponsor, AT&T, describes the ride's function more baldly, asserting that "the new ride and an interactive communications exhibit area entertains [*sic*] visitors of all ages with the wonders of AT&T's leading-edge technology." The ride lasts just under 13 minutes. Beginning with a shamanic ritual in a Lascaux-like cave, we proceed through the invention of writing by the Egyptians (featuring "authentic recreations of actual graphics" [Walt Disney Co., "SE Fact Sheet"]), the invention of the alphabet by the Phoenicians, a Greek amphitheatre, and so on through communications history, eventually arriving at the "revolution" of the present. A teacher conducts classes by computer-screen; a mother puts her daughter to bed by video-phone; a scientist conducts a test by remote hologram. "Physical distance is no longer a barrier to communication," intones the voice of Jeremy Irons. "We live in a truly Global Neighborhood." Now a vast network of fiber-optic cables surrounds us, shooting beams of light back and forth along its strands. In a moment the network twists together above our heads and twines around a model of the geodesic sphere of *Spaceship Earth*, a *mise en abyme* of the ride itself, placed next to a sign bearing the AT&T logo and reading "Bringing people together anytime, anywhere."

It would be hard to find a better dramatization of cyberspace, in all its utopian sublimity and corporatized banality, than this centerpiece and symbol of EPCOT

Center. Starting with the Buckminster-Fuller-inspired geodesic sphere (indeed, starting with the name of the ride, which is borrowed from Fuller's writings) the ride places front-and-center the utopia-or-oblivion sentiments of the American architect. Meanwhile, its repeated references to the "New Global Neighborhood" are a direct echo of the "global village" enthusiasms of Marshall McLuhan. McLuhan's famous comments to *Playboy* in 1969 that computer networks would create "a technologically engendered state of universal understanding and unity" (72), would not have sounded out of place had they been read by Jeremy Irons at the conclusion of the ride. But both Fuller and McLuhan would likely have found a snake in this garden. For, as the ride repeatedly emphasizes, the alpha and omega of this new global order is the corporation that makes it so. Fired off in a time machine from the dawn of civilization to the dawn of tomorrow, we find that we have been led everywhere and nowhere, our dreams still produced by the system that is their endpoint. Like Warhol's Amiga image, we travel through a closed cycle. And we exit *Spaceship Earth*, tellingly, only steps away from the point at which we entered.

The simplest and most illuminating definition for *cyberspace* exists, appropriately enough, in cyberspace, in the Microsoft-owned dictionary *Encarta*. The definition reads:

1   imagined place where electronic data goes: the notional realm in which electronic information exists or is exchanged; *an e-mail message lost in cyberspace*
2   virtual reality: the imagined world of virtual reality

Encarta, then, offers two basic definitions of the term. The first, which we may call "networked cyberspace," is the environment of electronic communication, represented in the Disney ride by images of wired computers, video-phones, remote holograms, and fiber-optic cables. It is this aspect of cyberspace that William Gibson (the word's originator) has particularly stressed.[1] The second, which we may call "VR cyberspace," is that of a virtual space generated by a computer system. This space typically relies on multimedia techniques to produce an immersive, simulacral experience that attempts to produce an organically unified world. This form of cyberspace is particularly exemplified by the "Ride the AT&T Network" exhibit, which attempts to fully absorb the spectator in a computer-generated "experience."

Capturing cyberspace, either in its VR or network form, is like painting the light at dawn; we apply the brush, and already the scene has shifted. One thing that emerges clearly, however, is that a number of works in cyberspace, and perhaps even cyberspace itself, bear significant relations to the *Gesamtkunstwerk*. This chapter will explore these relations by looking at two art installations (Char Davies' installation *Osmose* and Roy Ascott's installation *Aspects of Gaia*), two worlds of "total entertainment" (Bill Gates' mansion and Blizzard Entertainment's *World of Warcraft*), and, lastly, a VR installation entitled *Beyond Manzanar*. The first four of these works suggest ways that Wagnerian aspirations continue to shape the worlds of cyberspace, and ways in which cyberspace, conversely, may realize Wagnerian aspirations. The last work provides something quite different: a Brechtian critique of the digital *Gesamtkunstwerk*.

Cyber-arts and the *Gesamtkunstwerk*: Aspects of *Gaia* and *Osmose*

Char Davies and Roy Ascott are two artists who have been at the forefront of the development of cyber-arts. Previously director of visual research at Softimage (which animated the dinosaurs in *Jurassic Park*, among other projects), Davies became an artistic director for Microsoft when Softimage was acquired by the Gates behemoth. In 1998, she founded her own firm, Immersence, which principally develops and publicizes her VR installations.[2] She has also worked with Roy Ascott at the Center for Advanced Inquiry in the Interactive Arts (CAiiA) at the University of Wales College, Newport. Her work reflects many of the same desires as Ascott's, desires that have been central to the history of the *Gesamtkunstwerk* as a whole.

For Davies, as for the Wagner of the Zurich period, humanity's alienation from nature is principally a historical phenomenon. The culture of the modern West, with its "privileging of mind over matter," its "devaluation of the body," its "plundering of non-human beings and their habitats as objects for human use," has severed primal relations between humanity and nature, humanity and itself. "[T]he increasing loss of access to Nature – as a source of our human spirituality – may prove to be at the root of our collective psyche's deepest wounds," Davies concludes ("OSMOSE: Notes" 72). Following Henri Lefebvre and other critical theorists, Davies connects the rise of technology to a

> Cartesian philosophic tradition, a tradition whose dualistic privileging of mind over body, male over female, and human over "nature", has arguably contributed to an historic devaluation and objectification of the body, women, and animals, and to the ongoing plunder of the natural environment as a resource for profit and human consumption.
>
> ("Rethinking VR")

The problem, as Davies sees it, is much more serious than a mere misuse of technology: *techne* itself is held up to suspicion, and "King Logos" made the demiurge of a fallen Western world.

Given the sharpness of her critique of Cartesian reason and Western technology, it may seem odd that Davies ever became a cyber-artist. And not just any cyber-artist, either: Davies is a particular champion of the sort of "strong VR" that relies upon expensive, cutting-edge equipment such as head-mounted displays and motion-sensitive bodysuits, which she uses in order to produce her profoundly immersive virtual worlds. What makes this conflict even more extreme is that Davies sees VR as both an extension and an exacerbation of the very ills she finds in modern culture. "The origins of 3-D digital technology lie deep within the Cartesian philosophic tradition," she writes, adding that "[a]s progeny of the western-military-industrial paradigm, the technology associated with so-called virtual reality is anything but neutral" ("Rethinking VR"). Quoting from Ziauddin Sardar's *Cyberspace and the Darker Side of the West,* Davies writes that VR is "'the product of the collective consciousness of Western culture' issuing from a techno-Utopian ideology ripe with subconscious perceptions and prejudices" ("Rethinking VR"). With its lines of code and its Cartesian grids, its emphasis on constant focused vision, and its recurring motifs of warfare, domination, and joysticks, VR is the epitome of the modern alienation that Davies laments. VR "not only reaffirms our separateness but also our stance as Master of all we survey"; it is a "literal enactment of Cartesian ontology" ("Rethinking VR").

Why, then, Davies' embrace of VR? At this point in our study, it should come as no surprise that Davies' rationale draws from the familiar motif of technology as poison and cure. Thus Davies, like Wagner, raises "the challenge of using the technology alternatively, as an *antidote,* in terms of reaffirming our embodied participation within the natural world rather than our instrumentally objectifying conquest of it" ("Rethinking VR"). What Davies proposes is that VR be turned against itself, and against the larger cultural matrix from which it springs. "My research is founded on the premise that VR technology and the medium of immersive virtual space can, *if its conventions are effectively subverted,* serve as a means of facilitating a renewed, refreshed, perception of our place in the world" ("Rethinking VR"). Instead of VR environments being hypostatic versions of Cartesian consciousness, they might be immersive experiences of a return to nature, experiences that would be "*unlike* the space of our usual perceptions," and which therefore might have "transformative potential" ("Rethinking VR"). The challenge is "to rethink the technology, not as a means of escape but of *return*" ("Rethinking VR").[3]

Davies' VR project *Osmose* puts much of this theory into practice. The equipment for *Osmose* is a stereoscopic 3-D head-mounted display and a motion-sensitive bodysuit with a breathing and balance sensor, all of which is worn by the "immersant." When the installation is displayed publicly, the larger audience is placed in a public room facing two screens. On one of the screens is projected the shadow of the immersant, while the other screen shows a two-dimensional rendering of the immersant's journey through the world of *Osmose.* The sounds the immersant hears in the virtual world are also broadcast for the larger audience. For the immersant herself, however, the experience is solitary and all-consuming: once the head-mounted display and the bodysuit are on, the immersant has very little sensory access to the exterior world. She is free to experience, almost as though without mediation, the "archetypal aspects of Nature" ("OSMOSE: Notes" 67).

Upon first entering *Osmose,* the immersant discovers a three-dimensional grid extending into black space. According to Davies, the grid is at once "an orientation site" and "a reference to the Cartesian xyz coordinate system." This initial "orientation" is therefore double-edged. On one hand, the simplicity and order of the Cartesian grid allows the immersant to become familiar with "the breath and balance interface" which she will use to navigate their virtual journey; but, on the other hand, the grid suggests the modern world of Western *techne* which *Osmose* is designed to unravel. The immersant begins, in other words, in exile from the Garden. But she soon discovers, after some trial and error, that she is not so much standing on the Cartesian grid as floating above it, like a ghost perhaps, or an angel, or a fetus.

Soon thereafter, the immersant finds herself in a forest clearing dominated by an oak tree near a pond (Figure 8.1). Lights flicker around her like fireflies, and faint, fairy-like sounds play. Though often mistaken for instrumental music, these sounds are actually two voices, digitally altered, uttering phonetics. (It is perhaps no stretch to hear in this intermingling of primary sounds the opening of *Rheingold*, with the mechanically operated Rhinemaidens singing phonemes to one another – technology, in both cases, aiding the recovery of an ur-tongue.) In the fashion of the iconic *Gesamtkunstwerk*, no traces of the underlying mechanics can be seen. Night descends on the space and dawn emerges; subtle changes in light and color mark the passage of time and the cycles of days. The great oak itself suggests an ur-tree, a vision of Yggdrasil rooted in a primeval marsh. Davies calls this zone the "Lifeworld" ("Osmose: Towards"), and here, as at Montsalvat, time becomes space. The journey from the orientation grid to the Lifeworld is much more than a mere transformation of perspective: it is a trip backwards through Western history, from the modern to ancient. According to Davies, the immersant "will realize she has entered a non-Cartesian place" when she passes from the grid to the Lifeworld ("Osmose: Towards"), thus sweeping back into bygone, pre-Enlightenment days. Like the spectators at Bayreuth, the immersant reunifies herself with a premodern age of myth and symbol. Like both Bayreuth and Disneyland, *Osmose* is a project of retrocartography, of returning the spectator to an earlier (and supposedly superior) form of mapping the land.

The map of *Osmose* is vertical more than horizontal, and navigation is primarily controlled by the immersant's breath. By breathing sharply in, the immersant can rise up to the branches of the tree and above, into the sky, where she finds excerpts from writings that inspired the project (including passages of Rilke, Merleau-Ponty, and Gaston Bachelard). Breathing more softly allows the immersant to float gently, fetus-like, in place.[4] *Osmose* marks a return not only to nature but to the womb – a return, in short, to Mother Earth. Exhaling sharply, the immersant can descend through the marshy earth, down through semi-transparent roots and rocks and rivulets of light. If she continues this descent, she will eventually break through the earth itself into a sort of cavern. In this subterranean Niebelheim, great luminescent columns stream forth lines of code, the actual 20,000 lines that programmer John Harrison used to construct the site. "The code realm," writes Davies, "was intended to function as the conceptual substrate of *Osmose*, drawing attention to the computer-generated artificiality of the experience" ("Osmose: Towards"). Here the mechanical substructure that underlies the simulacrum is exposed, apparently in contradiction to the organic aspirations of the total work of art. And yet, in the fashion of the crystalline *Gesamtkunstwerk*, the mechanical is exposed here only in

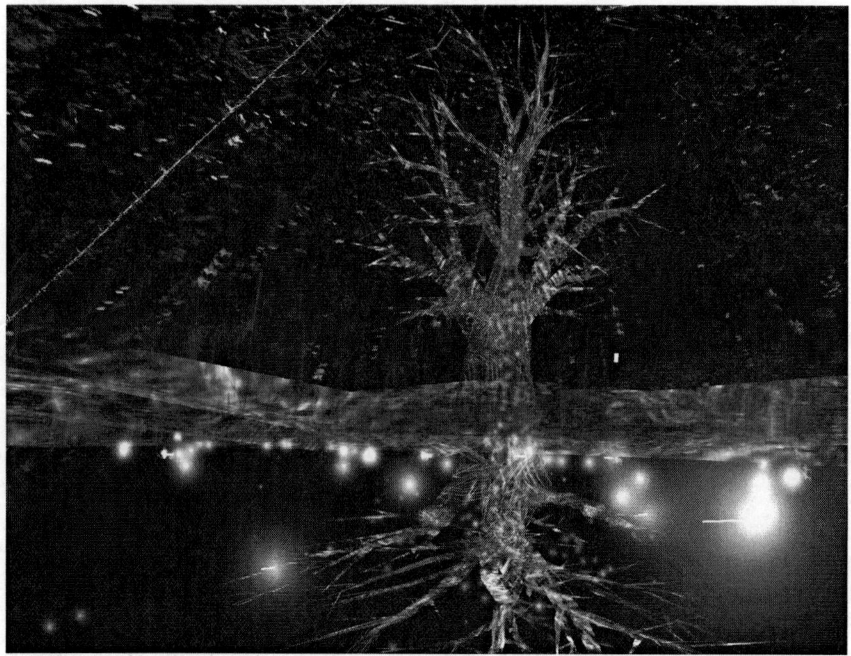

Figure 8.1 Char Davies, *Osmose*, "Tree Pond," digital frame captured through head-mounted display during live performance, 1995.

order to be reincorporated into the larger organic whole. The lines of code are themselves simulacra of the natural, glowing with light and flowing very much like the stream that feeds the pond of the Lifeworld. And the immersant interacts with these lines of code, floating between them in very much the same way that she floated among the branches of the ur-tree above. The exposure of the underlying code of *Osmose* creates not so much estrangement as greater unity, a unity that incorporates a rhetoric of the mechanical, much like the so-called "mechanical organisms" of the Bauhaus theatre. Without any dialectical tension between the base "code" and the superstructural "Lifeworld" it produces, the code appears merely another aspect of the larger totality, and it is Moholy-Nagy, more than Brecht, who comes to mind.

As at the Bauhaus – as, indeed, at Bayreuth – highly mechanized performance stems from and heightens a yearning for the "organic." Paradoxically, what Matthew Causey calls the "postorganic performance" of virtual space (185) simultaneously evolves from, exacerbates, and aims to resolve such neo-Romantic longings. "The desire to reaffirm our essential physical and spiritual inter-connectedness, to heal the estrangement between ourselves and Nature, between ourselves and 'being,' is a germinal force behind *Osmose*," writes Davies ("OSMOSE" 73). The strategy recalls that of the Festspielhaus, with its darkened house-lights, its "mystic gulf," its unified music and spectacle, and its elaborate system of blinders: all to the end of recapturing a lost, "natural" state. And yet the sense of community is gone. The return offered by *Osmose* is an individual rather than a collective return, as though utopian hopes can only survive when reduced to the size of the self. Moreover, while strong boundaries are established between the alternate world of the VR experience and the "real world" of workaday experience, boundaries *within* the alternate world are dismantled. The result is "an osmotic *intermingling* of spatialities – interior and exterior, mental, physical and social," a synthesis of all contraries in original unity. Predictably, audience response is similar to that often found at Bayreuth, with immersants describing "contemplative, meditative peace," "awe-inspiring depth," "transcendence of time and space," "feelings of undifferentiated unity or merging," "ineffability or verbal indescribability," "a profound sense of joy or euphoria," "an almost religious experience," and "a reconciliation with nature through technology" (Grau 199; Davies, "Changing Space" 296–7).

But the multi-sensory, multimedia effects of *Osmose* are not simply a return to Wagner. The effects of *Osmose* are, in a manner unimaginable before digital technology, a direct reflection of the technology itself. Digital media are fundamentally different from both live performance and analogue recording in that digital media involve the translation of all data into digits, or "bits," which are universally exchangeable with other bits. All digital media are therefore identical in structure; like Campbell's soup cans, a bit is a bit is a bit. Where Wagner had sought to restore the "sister arts" to their original unity, where Schlemmer and Moholy-Nagy had dreamt of a grand synthesis of clashing media, where Disney had aspired to a "grand combination of all the arts" at his theme parks, Char Davies is able to go much further: she is able to work in an *essentially multimedia medium*. This almost paradoxical essence of digital technology represents the *Liebestod* of the "sister arts," at once its death-knell and its realization. The paradox emerges because digital technology exchanges the old discourse of distinct yet intertwined arts for the new discourse of exchangeable bits, a discourse that obliterates inherited aesthetic distinctions. The exchangeability of digital data has a function, in other words, roughly analogous to that of currency after the collapse of Bretton Woods, and carries with it a range of effects almost as radical. Within the digital landscape of virtual reality, the old sisters become new clones: parentless, replicable, universally exchangeable, free-floating.

While Davies has pioneered the use of immersive digital technologies for installation art, Ascott's contributions have centered around the aesthetics of networked cyberspace. In an early essay entitled "Behaviourist Art and the Cybernetic Vision," Ascott looked forward to the day when "instant communication" (2:25) by electronic means would "unify art with a cybernated society" (2:27). This collective, total artwork would be "a self-organizing system; an organism, as it were, which derives its initial programme or code from the artist's creative activity, and then evolves its specific artistic identity and function in response to the environments which it encounters" (2:27). The essay was published in 1966, three years before the creation of the Internet, a medium it anticipates with disarming accuracy.[5]

Similarly, Ascott's 1980 work *Terminal Art* was one of the first attempts at creating a collaborative digital artwork, using an early conference platform called the "Informedia Notepad System."[6]

Ascott more fully realized his vision of digitally networked art with the installation *Aspects of Gaia: Digital Pathways across the Whole Earth*, which first appeared as part of the Ars Electronica Festival of Art and Technology in Linz, Austria, in 1989. The multimedia installation consists of two levels, the top level of which is a series of tents covering large horizontal monitors that the spectators can view from above. On these monitors are projected graphic images contributed by network artists from around the world. These images can then be manipulated by audience interaction. Ascott describes the upper-level performance as follows:

> [g]iving the public a bird's-eye view of images networked in from all over the planet, the large horizontal screens were set into "information bars" around which viewers could sit – on high stools, as if at a cocktail bar – gazing not into an alcoholic haze but into pure dataspace. The networked images that appeared were then changed by means of acoustic sensors fed to appropriate software (in the form of small microphones set on the counter top of the bar) or were modified with line and color by means of a mouse manipulated by the viewer across the counter top. Thus, interaction by voice and gesture led to the creation of new images that could then be retrieved by the computer and stored pending their eventual insertion back into the planetary network.
>
> ("Is" 245)

While the upper level emphasizes interaction, a lower level of the installation emphasizes immersion and a return to the primal Matrix. The lower level consists of a narrow passageway leading underneath the tents above (Figure 8.2). According to Ascott,

> [t]he interface on the lower level involved a railway track curving through a long, low tunnel that flanked the building, carrying a flatbed trolley (upholstered not unlike an analyst's couch), which enabled each participant to glide effortlessly through a darkened acoustical space, looking up at a sea of flickering LED signs scrolling texts drawn from the network of inputs all over the world.
>
> (245)

The track along which the viewer runs is reminiscent of a birth canal, with the viewer (riding through the tunnel on her back) a kind of newborn. The resemblance is not accidental: "[t]his was Gaia's womb," Ascott writes of the lower level, "a kind of telematic, neolithic passageway" (245). Indeed, Ascott's primal womb recalls Wagner's "mystic gulf," which Wagner himself compared to the "holy womb of Gaia" (5:335/9:338). *Aspects of Gaia*, like *Osmose*, is a space that unifies machine and mother, ur- and hyper-, at once techno-Erda and "telematic, neolithic" womb.[7]

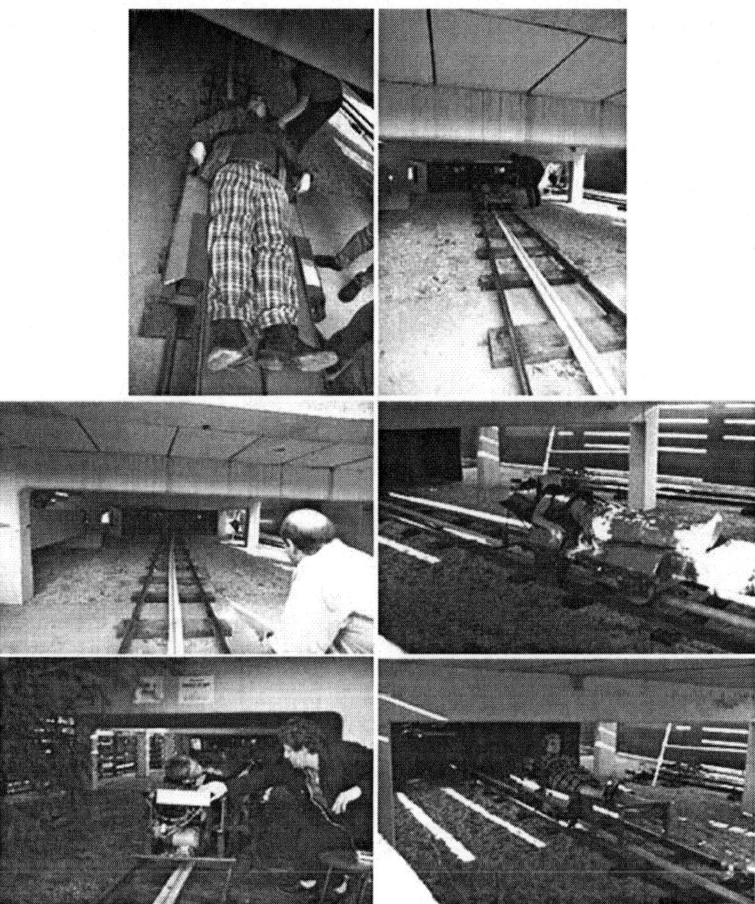

Figure 8.2 Roy Ascott, *Aspects of Gaia*, 1989.

Aspects of Gaia combines the interactivity of networked communication with the immersive effects of VR. For Ascott, this fusion heralds a new age in aesthetic history, one that produces an interactive global synthesis of art and artists. "The emerging new order of art," he writes,

> is that of interactivity, of "dispersed authorship"; the canon is one of contingency and uncertainty. Telematic art encompasses a wide array of media: hypermedia, videotext, telefacsimile, interactive video, computer animation and simulation, teleconferencing, text exchange, image transfer, sound synthesis, telemetry and remote sensing, virtual space, cybernetic structures, and intelligent architecture.
>
> ("Is" 243)

The result of this relentless technological development is an unprecedented phase of art in which true aesthetic and social synthesis can finally be achieved. The Wagnerian strains are unmistakable to those familiar with the tradition, yet Ascott goes out of his way to make them explicit.

> Out of this technological complexity we can sense the emergence of a synthesis of the arts. The question of content must therefore be addressed to what might be called the *Gesamtdatenwerk* – the integrated data work – and to its capacity to engage the intellect, emotions, and sensibility of the observer.
>
> (241)

Ascott often uses this term *Gesamtdatenwerk* ("total data work") to describe his project, going so far as to make it the title of his article in the art journal *Kunstform International* ("Gesamtdatenwerk: Konnektivität, Transformation und Transzendenz"). Other multimedia artists, many of them influenced by Ascott, have followed suit with Wagnerian references of their own. Multimedia artist and theorist Randall Packer, for example, has coined the term *Gesamtelewerk* ("total tele-work") to describe roughly the same phenomenon as Ascott's *Gesamtdatenwerk*, and has recently contributed to a decidedly Wagnerian manifesto on virtual reality. This collaboratively generated "Telematic Manifesto" (contributors include Packer, Marc Lafia, Joel Slayton, and several others) quotes from Wagner, Moholy-Nagy, and Ascott on its title page, and opens with the following declaration:

> The Gesamtelewerk proposes a resurgence of the optimism of previous efforts to formalize the *Gesamtkunstwerk* (Total Art Work), to devise an integrated medium which blends all the arts and engages all the senses. Introducing telematics into the equation suggests an art that in addition seeks a global embrace, a collective vision to which the artwork, artist, and viewer aspire.

Most recently, Packer and Ken Jordan (a pioneer in Web design) have edited an anthology of documents on the development of multimedia technology, opening with an excerpt from Wagner's *The Artwork of the Future* and featuring essays by Ascott and Davies.

Ascott is even more of a technopian than Davies, and brings to his work a decidedly millennial enthusiasm. He laments the "decline of the modern world, with its relentless fixation upon materialism," but feels that there is "a renewed interest in the spirit" among dissatisfied moderns ("Technoetic" 31). Like many of the artists examined in this book, Ascott argues that modernity, carried to its furthest extreme, can restore the organic community of premodern times. We are at "one of those points in the evolutionary path where a quantum leap can be detected, where the singular, isolated and often alienated human brain becomes part of a hypercortex, sharing in the collective intelligence of a world mind" ("Technoetic" 30). The marriage of technology, art, and ritual that characterizes *Aspects of Gaia* heralds a great recovery of tribal unity in the modern age. If the "holistic potentiality of telematic art" suggests a latter-day *Gesamtkunstwerk* – this time for the "harmonization and creative development of the whole planet" – then the Ars Electronica Centre, where *Aspects of Gaia* was first shown, is Ascott's Bayreuth ("Is" 247). For Ascott, Ars Electronica at once exhibits and helps to forge the new tribalism that lies just beyond the horizon of the modern age.

> To understand the significance of the Ars Electronica Centre in the new world of interactive art and intelligent systems, it is instructive to hyperlink to the old world; to tune into the Creation Chant of the Navajo in the South West United States which sings of "the emergence place in blue water", and then to zap right back to this new place of emergence beside the Blue Danube. There is a kinship here also with the Hopi who have, in the ground of each of their *kivas*, a ritual hole called the *sipapuni*, which represents the place of emergence from the previous world into this fourth world ...
>
> The Ars Electronica Centre is a *sipapuni* for art of the 21st century, designed to bring us into the fifth world, the post-biological future.
>
> ("Technoetic" 30)

Substitute *Greeks* for *Native Americans*, and the debt to Schiller's *Letters* as well as Wagner's *Artwork of the Future* becomes unmistakable.

Significantly (and again recalling Wagner), the restored modern communalism may actually *surpass* the original state. For Wagner, the union of Beethoven, Shakespeare, and Germanic myth will not only recover but exceed the tragedies of Athens (in part, at least in "Art and Revolution," due to the replacement of slave by mechanical labor). Similarly, Ascott suggests that contemporary telematic art surpasses the ritual art of Native American tribes. While the *sipapuni* of the ancient Hopi was an entrance into a "fourth world," Ascott writes that the *sipapuni* of the modern age brings us into a "fifth world," which heralds not a mere return to the past but an entrance into a "post-biological future." In a remarkably Hegelian fantasy, Ascott imagines the whole world becoming an apotheosis of mind, with "the spread of intelligence to every part of the built environment coupled with recognition of the intelligence that lies within every part of the living planet" ("Beyond" 2). Thus the post-millennial Kingdom not only restores but perfects paradise lost.

In the face of such utopian dreams, it is easy to lose sight of the fact that most of the world's population today lacks access even to telephones, not to mention the Internet.[8] Media analyst Frank Beacham (at first a strong Internet enthusiast) was already aware of the complexities of Internet corporatization in 1996, when he lamented that the Internet was moving "from being a participatory medium that serves the interests of the public to being a broadcast medium where corporations deliver consumer-oriented information. Interactivity would be reduced to little more than sales transactions and email" (16). Beacham's concern is shared by a number of media analysts,[9] who worry that crucial laws such as the Telecommunications Act of 1996 (which eliminated most of the restrictions prohibiting one kind of bandwidth company from buying or merging with another) could, over time, consign the Internet to the fate of radio and television before it – that is, to transformation into an essentially broadcast medium and control by a small handful of corporations. Lawrence Lessing, for instance, argues that corporations could layer software applications on top of Internet protocols, allowing them to identify private information. If this layering were to occur, it would be but a small step for corporations or governments to subject networked users to a wide range of controls and surveillance techniques. By such means the connective potential of cyberspace might well flip into the "*bad coherence*" of total "absorption into the Machine" that Wagner saw as the dystopia of modern culture (1:81/3:54; 1:85/5:58). The worst, though by no means necessary, outcome is precisely the vision that first inspired Gibson's *Neuromancer* – the book that first popularized the word "cyberspace" – where the flow of information is transformed into an "electronic consensus-hallucination," a xanadu ruled by corporate kahns (170).

Ascott's technopianism is questionable for another reason as well: networked cyberspace tends not toward totality (as his un-ironic use of the term *Gesamtdatenwerk* would imply) but toward universality. Pierre Lévy in particular relishes the irony that "[a]s cyberspace grows it becomes more 'universal' and the world of information less totalizable" (74).[10] Cyberspace, which Lévy defines as "the new medium of communications that arose through the global interconnections of computers," tends toward universality in a manner unprecedented in the history of technology (xvi).[11] There are two reasons for this. The first is that cyberspace "serves as the communications infrastructure and basis of coordination for other large technological systems," while at the same time "mak[ing] possible the evolution toward universalization and the functional, organizational, and operational consistency of other systems" (93). The second is that "the ultimate signification of the network, the value embodied in cyberculture, is precisely its universality." Networked cyberspace – and its subsets the Internet and the World Wide Web – tends toward universality because the "medium tends toward the generalized interconnection of people, machines, and information" in a way that previous mass media could not (94).[12]

Cyberspace is thus fundamentally different from earlier media such as radio, film, and television, and the audience/participants of networked cyberspace are fundamentally different from the mass "public" that was the target of the pre-digital culture industry (97).[13] It is in networked cyberspace, then, that Brecht's dream of an active mass subject might seem to be achievable. And yet the radically localized, dispersed, and fluid subjects (not to mention the more highly centralized corporations) that shape cyberspace are almost as far from a revolutionary proletariat as they are from Wagner's conception of a *Volk*. The participants and co-creators of networked cyberspace are not, in fact, essentially anything. "The universality of cyberspace lacks any center or guidelines," remarks Lévy. "It is empty, without any particular content" (91). Unless and until corporate control of cyberspace becomes stronger than is currently the case, Lévy's observations remain largely correct.[14] If networked cyberspace is the realization of the neo-Romantic dream of a massively communal artwork, then the dream's realization is profoundly ironic, for the realization occurs within and by means of a center-less space devoid of essential content.

What cyberspace offers is no Desert of the Real, and no Third Kingdom either. What it offers, instead, is an ironic realization of many aspects of the history of the *Gesamtkunstwerk*. There are at least three ways in which this ironic realization occurs. Briefly stated, they are as follows.

1   As an entirely digital landscape, cyberspace ironically realizes Wagner's dream of the ultimate unification of all the arts. Here all the arts – indeed, all things – are rendered equivalent and interchangeable compounds of digital information, made up of bits that can be blended together as easily as two handfuls of sand. The "sister-arts" become infinitely replicable clones.

2   As an increasingly immersive artificial world, cyberspace ironically realizes Wagner's dream of an organic totality produced by cutting-edge technology. On one hand, cyberspace allows for unprecedented technologies of audience immersion. On the other hand, where Wagner had hoped to return his audiences, via immersion, to cultural and racial roots, cyberspace immerses the spectator in a landscape without essential content, with no predetermined location or end, and within which "real" race and gender are indeterminate.

3   As a "universality without totality," networked cyberspace ironically realizes Wagner's dream of the communal nature of the *Gesamtkunstwerk*. The dream of an artwork that arises from, reflects, and at the same time transforms the modern masses is attained to an unprecedented degree, but its shape is not totality but ever-increasing universality, not unity but decentered and unpredictable growth.

The fact that these features (universal exchangeability of component parts, unprecedented technologies of immersion within a space without essential content, collective creation leading to universality) are essential to cyberspace does not mean that they determine the form of specific digital creations. Indeed – and here another irony emerges – specific digital works may attempt to compensate for such fundamental placelessness and lack of totality by repeatedly performing precisely those things cyberspace militates against. As we shall see throughout this chapter, narratives of return to Mother Nature and community, the deep longing for belonging, the attempts to create an axis mundi of the virtual world – these are the compensatory reactions of the digital age, as indeed they were of the industrial. In this sense at least, the transition from factory floor to cyberspace is no revolution at all.

Total entertainment: the Gates house and *World of Warcraft*

Many of the most audacious experiments in cyberspace performance, such as *Osmose* and *Aspects of Gaia*, have been restricted to gallery spaces, if only because they have needed to be sheltered from the immediate demands of the marketplace. In general, cyber-art such as that explored by Ascott and Davies is costly to produce and exhibit, not only because of the expense of the equipment involved (much of which is uniquely engineered and constructed for the project), but also due to difficulties in maintenance (which requires technological savvy on the part of the curators – or at least ready access to knowledgeable programmers). For better or worse, such installations are therefore restricted to institutional art spheres. And yet cyberspace has had, and will increasingly have, its greatest impact on the far more quotidian spheres of bourgeois work and leisure. In order to explore the peculiar concatenation of cyberspace, *Gesamtkunstwerk*, and everyday spectacle, I would like to explore two sites. The first is a virtual "home of the future," designed by Bill Gates as his own mansion and as a prototype for tomorrow's bourgeois domesticity. The second is a massively multiplayer online role-playing game entitled *World of Warcraft*, which attempts to immerse the player in a digital fantasy world. Between Gates' wired home and *World of Warcraft*'s alternate reality, we can find clues about an attempted combination of leisure and the *Gesamtkunstwerk*, a combination we have already seen in Disney's "Total Systems Approach." It is a synthesis we may call "total entertainment."

In 1990, Gates commissioned the Washington State architect Jim Cutler to design the house on the shore of Lake Washington, close to Microsoft headquarters. The house came to public attention after the publication of Gates' bestselling *The Road Ahead*, which devoted an entire chapter to a discussion of the house as a model "home of the future." From the driveway, the structure appears remarkably unassuming, as the building's entrance is located on its top floor, with the rest descending down the other side of a hill. Within, however, it houses a virtual environment that wholly encompasses the spectator as soon as he walks through the front door. As such, it represents a condition to which middle-class home-life is rapidly approaching, a condition of ubiquitous immersion in VR and networked cyberspace. Exotically experimental, it is also prototypical.

Upon entering Gates' house, the guest is given an electronic pin programmed with his likes and dislikes. The pin then serves to monitor the spectator's location in the house and to "tell" the house how to "meet and even anticipate your needs" (251). Gates continues:

> [w]hen it's dark outside, the pin will cause a zone of light to move with you through the house. Unoccupied rooms will be unlit. As you walk down a hallway, you might not notice the lights ahead of you gradually coming up to full brightness and the lights behind you fading. Music will move with you too. It will seem to be everywhere, although in fact people in other parts of the house will be hearing entirely different music or nothing at all. A movie or the news will be able to follow you around the house too. If you get a phone call, only the handset nearest you will ring.

The fluid ubiquity of digital technology, as well as the essentially multimedia nature of digital technology, is especially clear in this "home of the future." The electronic pin activates a media universe – lights, music, film, television – always on call, and precisely designed to the spectator's personal preferences. The guest becomes, in other words, the designer and conductor of his own digital *Gesamtkunstwerk*, which plays only for him. The house echoes this transformation, becoming a festival theatre for an audience of one, with appropriate virtual worlds of sight and sound following the spectator from one room to the next. The palate from which the spectator can select is extremely broad: "[y]ou'll be able to choose from among thousands of pictures, recordings, movies, and television programs, and you'll have all sorts of options available for selecting information" (251). Eventually, even the pin will be an unnecessary intrusion of gadgetry into the theatre of the house. "Someday," writes Gates hopefully, "instead of your needing the pin, we might have a camera system with visual-recognition capabilities" (251). As at Disneyland, greater demands for totality produce greater demands for occlusion and surveillance: the electronic pin gives way to the electronic eye.

The millions of images, films, and sound recordings that lie at the spectator's fingertips in the Gates house certainly create a sense of a temporal implosion. And yet here time does *not* become space, for both time and space are so radically imploded that neither functions any longer as a meaningful category of difference. It would be more accurate to say that, at the Gates house, time and space become transparent and ubiquitous, so fluid as to be emptied of meaning. When Wagner represented Parsifal entering Monsalvat, the space Parsifal crossed was in a broad sense virtual (represented by moving panoramas), but Wagner still felt a need to represent it. At Disneyland, to go from the Mississippi Riverboat to Pirates of the Caribbean is a short walk, but it *is* a walk after all (and often a long wait in line). In Gates' house, on the other hand,

> [i]f you were planning to visit Hong Kong soon, you might ask the screen in your room to show you pictures of the city. It will seem to you as if the photographs are displayed everywhere in the house, although the images will actually materialize on the walls of the rooms just before you walk in and vanish after you leave.
>
> (253)

The total theatre that surrounds each spectator, and is keyed to his electronic pin, is a solipsist's dreamworld, a literal projection in sound and image of the desires of the occupant.

But what happens when two occupants cross paths and their dreamworlds collide? Not surprisingly, Cutler and Gates have had to develop strategies to deal with multiple such occurrences, although Gates gives the question only the most cursory attention in his description. "If you and I are watching different things and one of us walks into a room where the other is sitting," he writes, "the house will follow mediating guidelines. The house might continue the audio and visual imagery for the person who was in the room first, or it might change programming to something it knows we both like" (253). The rather vague description of what "might" happen in the case of such an occurrence, compared with the elaborate descriptions of the nature and function of the personal electronic pin, suggests that the question is of a rather low priority: how often do two people really enter a room together anyway? how often, in such a house, would they even want to?

More than this, the vagueness of Gates' description suggests something even more troubling: that *any* solution to the problem of two people inhabiting the same room would be unsatisfactory. Indeed, both of the "mediating guidelines" that Gates suggests are predictably disappointing. If the virtual world of the "person who was in the room first" overrides that of the person who comes into the room next, does this not interrupt the flow of the second person's virtual experience? Rather than "mediating" between people, this solution would seem to make everyone in a room subordinate to the person who happened to enter first: the early bird gets the room. One can already imagine the rush to enter a room before others, to be the first one to stake out the space for free jazz and Caravaggio, say, rather than having to subordinate one's preferences to those of another. And yet the second solution Gates offers, to "change programming to something it knows we both like," seems even more troublesome than the first. Picture the situation: a guest is sitting in a room listening to the Sex Pistols while enjoying a view of Mount Fuji, when another guest enters, and the house decides that they both enjoy Bach and mandalas. The house switches in an instant from "Anarchy in the UK" to *The Well-Tempered Clavier,* Japan to Tibet, until a third guest enters, and a switch is made again based on a quickly calculated common denominator of mutual preferences. One can easily imagine the result: aleatory cacophony. Starting with Wagnerian aspirations, Gates ends up with John Cage.

The point here is not that a solution to the problem of multiple spectators has yet to be found, but rather that no satisfactory solution could possibly exist. For what Gates struggles with is an exaggerated manifestation of a problem that has hounded the *Gesamtkunstwerk* since its inception: the problem of infection. From Wagner's strategy of darkened houselights and hidden orchestra to Disney's walls and zoning regulations to Warhol's Factory-sealed vacuums, practitioners of total theatre have always had to search for ways to keep the boundaries secure. What makes the Gates house so different, however, is that it offers no overriding total theatre, no "master narrative" to which all the spectators must subordinate themselves. Instead, each spectator creates his own total theatre, his own synchronized, multi-media world, which envelops him like a blanket. The decision to make as many total theatres in the house as there are occupants (which might seem at first blush to be democratic, even egalitarian) in fact multiplies the trouble of totality manifold. In a world of walking totalities, satisfactory "mediating guidelines" will never be found, are simply unimaginable.

As we have seen throughout this study, many total theatres have steadily increased their reliance upon technology in order effectively to simulate the organic, and then must hide the machinery of production under ever more sophisticated blinders. Strategies of simulation, in other words, develop alongside strategies of occultation. In the Gates house, too, we find that the real wonder of the house, its cutting-edge technology, is hidden beneath a veneer of "naturalness." Oddly enough, most of Cutler and Gates' rhetoric about the house is not, as one might expect, crystalline. Instead, both Gates and Cutler favor the language of back-to-nature Romanticism, of organic wholeness and nostalgic longing for the primal earth. But in fact the two forms of utopian rhetoric are not opposed: as we have seen in the lineage from Wagner through Ascott, the advancement of mechanics aims to heal the very estrangement it created.

In their remarks on the house, both Cutler and Gates (like Davies and Ascott) voice concerns about the loss of social interaction in contemporary society. Gates notes that "[o]ne concern often mentioned in talk about the coming communications revolution is that people won't socialize anymore. Commentators worry that our homes will become such cozy entertainment providers that we'll never leave them, and that safe in our private sanctuaries we'll become isolated" (236). Far from exacerbating this concern, Gates sees his house as an answer to it: "I don't think that's going to happen, and later in this chapter, when I describe the house I'm building, I think I make my case." Cutler sees his project in similar terms, viewing it as an answer to social alienation. "People don't even make eye contact anymore. We're just floating," he laments in an interview, but then goes on to argue that homes such as the Gates house will help "to reconnect us to a place" (quoted in Betsky 90). Cutler, whom the architectural journal *Metropolitan Home* has described as a "semi-mystical guru," works largely in unfinished wood. He says he wants to "express the wood, honor its spirit" and hopes that "a hundred years from now there will be no trace that we changed anything on the site" (86). Cutler's sentiments reflect those of his client: "I want my [house] to be in harmony with the land it sits on and with the needs of the people who will live in it," writes Gates (247).

Gates asks us to imagine the house in one of two ways: "You can think of the house as an intimate companion, or you can look at the idea of a house through the eyes of the great twentieth-century architect Le Corbusier, who said that a house is 'a machine for living in'" (247). The first of these two options is unsurprising: the house as "intimate companion" is Gates' answer to a world where "people won't socialize anymore." But the second of these options is peculiar, for Gates and Cutler's vision is in fact antithetical to the "machine for living" ideal of Le Corbusier. To be sure, Le Corbusier was occasionally influenced by the genre of the total work of art, but his vision was far closer to the Bauhaus *Totalarchitektur* than the quasi-Nature-mysticism of Cutler and Gates. The hidden mechanics and organic façades of the Gates house recall not Le Corbusier's "machines for living" but Wagner's mystic gulf and Disney's utiladors. The attempt is to bury not only labor itself but also the tools of labor, to render the machine at once ubiquitous and invisible. Fittingly, the design feature of the house that excites Gates at least as much as the virtual technology is the enormous exposed beams of old-growth Douglas fir that form the house's skeletal core. "The house has lots of exposed horizontal beams and vertical supports," writes Gates. "You'll have a great view of the lake as you go down to the first level, and I hope that the view and the Douglas fir, rather than the novelty of the electric pin, will be what interest you most as you descend" (250–1). The exposure of the main elements of the house would seem to suggest a Modernist desire to reveal the structure of the building, invoking once more the spirit of Le Corbusier. But once more the spirit is out of place. Here the structural elements are vastly in excess of the requirements of building support, and have nothing to do with the house's true foundation, its massive technological substructure. Their actual purpose would seem to be not so much functional as aesthetic, which is to say that they serve less as girders than as symbols. On one hand, they are the architectural markers of Gates' and Cutler's desire to "reconnect us" to one another and to a place. On the other hand, they distract our attention from "the novelty of the electronic pin," and the instruments that disappear into the woodwork.

"Disappear into the woodwork" is no mere metaphor, as Gates' continuing tour of the house makes clear.

> Recessed into the east wall [of the reception hall] will be twenty-four video monitors stacked four high and six across, each with a 40-inch picture tube. These monitors will work cooperatively to display large images for art, entertainment, or business. I had hoped that when we weren't using the monitors *they could literally disappear into the woodwork.* I wanted the screens to display wood-grain patterns that matched the rest of the wall. Unfortunately, we could never achieve anything convincing with current technology because a monitor emits light while real wood reflects it. *We settled for having the monitors disappear behind wood panels when we're not using them.*
>
> (251; italics added)

Gates' efforts to hide this enormous bank of monitors behind a veneer of wood seem to have produced peculiar problems. His initial solution to the question of hiding his monitors was simply to have the monitors generate their own camouflage; "current technology," however, precludes this solution as insufficiently convincing. For the time being, "real wood" must be used to panel over the wall of electronic screens. Gates considers art the next form of camouflage: someday, he writes, "[m]aybe I'll decide to conceal the monitors behind conventional wall art" (258). The shift in camouflage from "woodwork" to "wall art" is significant. In a landscape of countless interchangeable images, any one of which can be called up instantaneously and displayed throughout the house, art becomes so emptied of cultural reference and so unmoored from time and place that it is no longer even thought of as an object that was once created and now mimics organic form. Art becomes just another building material, essentially interchangeable with wood (or with a projected image of wood). "Conventional wall art" might well serve as an appropriate cover for the bank of screens, at least until improved technology enables the screens to hide themselves beneath their own self-generated bark.

The matrix of screens in Gates' house evokes the global network of screens that are the business of Microsoft. Gates describes his plans to further coordinate interactive home-theatre screens and commodity markets in another chapter of *The Road Ahead*. "In the future," writes Gates,

> companies may pay not only to have their products on-screen but also to make them available for you to buy. In an unobtrusive way, the Internet will offer you the option to inquire about images you see. If you're watching a video of *Top Gun* and you think Tom Cruise's aviator sunglasses look really cool, you'll be able to pause the movie and learn about the glasses or even buy them on the spot – if the film has been tagged with commercial information.
>
> (188)

This "tagging" of recordings and images to the Internet suggests a world of instantaneous commodity exchange and nearly ubiquitous commodification. As you pass through the halls of infinite images of the Gates' house, not only can you buy any actor's sunglasses (or the *Girl with a Pearl Earring*'s pearl earring? or Mona Lisa's smile?), you can buy them anywhere, anytime. The result, for Gates, is a nearly utopian state that he dubs "Friction-Free Capitalism" (180). It is the realization of a dream first imagined in *Wealth of Nations*:

> When Adam Smith described the concept of markets in *Wealth of Nations* in 1776, he theorized that if every buyer knew every seller's price and every seller knew what every buyer was willing to pay, everyone in the "market" would be able to make fully informed decisions and society's resources would be distributed efficiently.
>
> (180)

Now such a world is on the verge of shifting from dream to reality, via Microsoft and cyberspace. The end result, for Gates, is a world in which "[o]nce you know exactly what you want, you'll be able to get it just the way you want it" (188). Absorbed in their private dreamworld of images and sounds, guests in Gates' house are simultaneously plugged into a seamless network of exchange, with fiber-optic cables as their umbilical cords. Like so many engineers of totality, Gates offers his "plugged-in" home as a cure for the very crisis it embodies.

The Gates house is an attempt to merge cyberspace (in both VR and networked senses) and the domestic sphere. It aims to transform the bourgeois home into a dreamworld where all art-forms are equally accessible and may be freely combined to suit the tastes of the resident/guest/actor/spectator/conductor/shopper, who is likewise empowered to instantaneously purchase much of what he experiences. A combination of Lévy's vision of universalizing-but-not-totalizing cyberspace with Fordist strategies for hierarchical corporate control, Gates' fantasy of friction-free, on-demand capitalism exemplifies the division within the so-called New Economy. Moreover, the total-entertainment strategies of the Gates house reflect a desire for capitalist utopia that is linked, as in so many virtual *Gesamtkunstwerke*, with

back-to-nature yearnings for earth and organic community. Both of these motifs –
the desire for capitalist utopia and the desire for a return to a state of organic
belonging – return again in another total-entertainment project, the online game
World of Warcraft.

As of 2003, anywhere from 10 to 30 million people globally were living in so-
called "massively multiplayer online role-playing games" (or MMORPGs), in
which players take the roles of imaginary characters to play and socialize in virtual
space (Castronova, *Synthetic* 55). Several such worlds have population sizes that
rival cities. As of December 2004, *Legend of Mir II* and *III* hosted a combined three
million players, while *Lineage* and *Lineage II* hosted roughly four million, mostly in
South Korea (*Synthetic* 53). Such cyber-theatres allow players to take the form of
virtual characters, or "avatars," in a wholly constructed yet organically unified
world.[15] In such massive multiplayer games, Schiller's kingdom of aesthetic play
once more takes mass-cultural form, and does so in a manner undreamed of even
by the Imagineers of Disneyland. In these games, unlike in Disneyland or Gates'
"wired home," one's own character is built of precisely the same "stuff" as the
world at large. Like everything else in the virtual world, one's character is at base a
string digital code, and on the surface a set of pixels. While at Disneyland it is easy
to tell the difference between "characters" and "guests," in these virtual worlds it is
far harder to know which characters are being played by real people and which by
the game's software. Indeed, an extra visual element must be generally added to
the game to make the difference noticeable: characters being played by real people
in these worlds often have their names written above them in special colors, to
distinguish them from computer-run characters.

Owned and developed by Blizzard Entertainment, *World of Warcraft* is one of the
most popular MMORPGs, signing up five million subscribers in its first year of
operation (2005), and increasing in population quickly thereafter (Castronova,
Synthetic 53).[16] *Warcraft* offers a virtual world that is in many ways typical of the
MMORPG, taking place in a Tolkien-inspired fantasy world with *Dungeons-and-
Dragons*-inspired rules (similar fantasy games include *Lineage, Legend of Mir*, and
Everquest, though MMORPGs take place in a wide range of universes).[17] As with the
Disney theme parks, the sheer enormity of *Warcraft* necessitates a series of
boundaries in order to give each player's experience unity and coherence.

A player's first entrance into *Warcraft* is marked by two liminal performances,
the first legal, the second cinematic. The legal one takes precedence. After down-
loading the software, one is confronted several times with "End User Agreement"
policies running more than a dozen clauses long. The Agreements, which one must
repeatedly sign, attempt to establish clear legal control over the "titles, computer
code, themes, objects, characters, character names, stories," and so forth within
the game. As Brecht would have been the first to appreciate, legal boundaries need
to be particularly aggressively marked in the still-ambiguous legal terrain of
cyberspace, and entrance into *Warcraft* is contingent upon contractual assent by all
parties. After creating a character for the game, the player is then shown a short
film that explains the history of the "race" to which the character belongs. The film

quickly initiates the new character into her community, and, once the film is over, the player takes control of the character. Through legal and cinematic means, then, one is transformed into both a "user," with certain legal rights and obligations relative to Blizzard Entertainment, and a "player," in control of a character with a particular homeland and history.

The repeated acquiescence to corporate ownership at the opening of the game reminds us of just how "friction-free capitalism" functions; the game does indeed run relatively "friction-free" (assuming a good Internet connection – no inexpensive ticket) so long as it remains under the total control of Blizzard Entertainment. This total control also allows *Warcraft* to avoid many of the mediating troubles of the Gates house; mediation is made fluid here by subordinating one's own preferences to those of the total world. Like Gates' wired home, however, *Warcraft* is a unified dreamworld that rests on formal divisions. Beneath the smooth interface of *Warcraft* are at least two crucial contradictions that the virtual world both performs and attempts to reconcile.

The first is between bourgeois and aristocratic worldviews, both of which shape the world of the game. On one hand, *Warcraft* offers itself as an idealized meritocracy of a Horatio-Alger sort. All players start at level 1, with roughly equivalent sets of abilities, and work their way up gradually from there. To a degree impossible in the offline world, the status of a character in *Warcraft* depends upon the expenditure of labor time. A new character advances to level two after about 20 minutes of online play, advances to level three roughly a half hour later, and so forth, with levels taking progressively longer to achieve. Technically, advancement comes with the accomplishment of tasks (chiefly killing monsters, completing quests, and discovering new zones), but the rate of accomplishment is predictable enough to make a character's level correlate significantly with the labor-hours a player has actually committed to the game.[18] As with the total-entertainment worlds of theme parks and wired homes, it is difficult to say whether "playing" *Warcraft* is an activity of work or leisure, a difficulty that points to the collapse of distinctions between the two in so-called late capitalism.[19]

This collapse is evident in a very material way. To facilitate exchange, *Warcraft*, like all MMORPGs, uses an economy based on virtual currency. Virtual game currencies, along with virtual characters and game items, can be bought and sold for real-world currencies at various online websites (often against the wishes of the game companies themselves, though occasionally with the companies' cooperation). Using these online exchanges of virtual currencies, characters, and goods for real-world currencies as a guide, economist Edward Castronova has calculated the US dollar value of the virtual economies of online games. He concludes that:

> [t]he nominal hourly wage [in the *EverQuest* virtual world of Norrath] is about USD 3.42 per hour, and the labors of the people produce a GNP per capita somewhere between Russia and Bulgaria. A unit of Norrath's currency is traded on exchange markets at USD 0.0107, higher than the Yen or the Lira.
>
> ("Virtual Worlds")

Inevitably, the fact that these virtual economies have significant real-world values has already created concomitant systems of economic exploitation. According to the *Washington Post*, one group has already "organized what amounted to a sweat shop in Mexico to churn out characters" for the online game *The Dark Age of Camelot*. "They got people to work for little or no money to build up the characters," says Mark Jacobs, the president of the company that runs *The Dark Age of Camelot*, which has tried to fight the practice (Morin B05). In China, meanwhile, "many online gaming factories have come to resemble the thousands of textile mills and toy factories that have moved [there] from Taiwan, Hong Kong and other parts of the world," according to the *New York Times* (Barboza). As of December 2005, these "virtual sweatshops" were paying 25 cents an hour plus room and board. "[I]n some of these popular games," says one game-factory owner, "40 or 50 percent of the players are actually Chinese farmers."

Against *Warcraft*'s meritocratic labor structure is pitched a radically different one that looks back nostalgically to a medieval order. Like the genre of fantasy to which it belongs, *Warcraft* is a pseudo-medieval realm of knights, dragons, wizards, and so forth, and one that borrows liberally from romance tropes such as the quest. While "class" is an important keyword in the game, it has a meaning far from the one it has in modern capitalism. In the game, "class" denotes a social grouping that combines qualities of profession, vocation, essential identity, and caste. Classes ("warrior," "rogue," "druid," and so forth) determine not only what a character does but, in an important sense, who a character is, from their appearance to their attributes to their real and potential abilities. When creating a character, class is one of the two most important features (the other being "race"). *Warcraft*, then, hovers between a humanist meritocracy on one hand and a fixed caste order on the other. Through a separate-but-equal system of castes, each of which is internally meritocratic, the game attempts to bridge this divide. Predictably, the game evokes one of capitalism's recurring fantasies: the myth of halcyon days when powerful aristocrats and a nascent bourgeoisie coexisted in harmony. Like nineteenth-century American Freemasons, who similarly attempted to bridge contradictions between bourgeois and aristocratic orders by appealing to this mythical past, *Warcraft* players socialize in groups identified as "guilds."[20]

The second contradiction the virtual world both performs and attempts to solve is that between the production on which the work relies and the organic order it evokes. As we have seen throughout this study, this contradiction has been one of the driving dialectics of the *Gesamtkunstwerk* from Bayreuth all the way to Gates' house, Davies' *Osmose*, and Ascott's *Aspects of Gaia*. What makes *Warcraft* different is not the dialectic itself, but rather the extremity to which it has been pushed. On one hand, *Warcraft* exists in a metamedium that, as Lévy argues, is literally unprecedented in its possibilities for global subjectivity, the assumption of multiple identities, and the unification of humans and machines into a larger "collective intelligence." Not only does it exist in and through this metamedium, but it would seem to be a significant exemplar of precisely the sort of "multiple, dispersed, and virtual" mass subjects of networked cyberspace. Role-playing, after all, is at the game's core.

And yet nature and territoriality are precisely the things *Warcraft* most forcefully romanticizes. Both come together particularly strongly in the category of "race," along with "class" one of the two most essential aspects of a character (gender, though significant for the character's appearance, does not effect the character's attributes or abilities). In familiar fantasy-genre manner, the races of *Warcraft* include creatures such as elves, dwarves, orcs, and, of course, humans. Selection of a character's race (along with class) determines the character's intelligence, strength, and so forth, as well as the character's appearance, special racial traits, racial attraction and antipathies, racial language (which can be understood only to other members of the race) and inalterable racial alliances. Race is also fundamentally linked to territoriality. Each race has a natural environment with which they are associated, and a history that is linked to that environment. Further, each has a racial homeland and "home city" that are invariably under threat from some other race or alliance of races, and invariably contaminated from within. The history and nature of the race is given to the player at many points throughout the game, and usually serves to bolster racial pride and clarify racial objectives.

Warcraft is, in effect, a game largely based around the defense of homelands against racial others, and together with racial allies. In the cinematic opening to the "human" world, for example, the new player is introduced to this "proud, tenacious race." "You must defend the kingdom against those who encroach upon it, and hunt down the subversive traitors who seek to destroy it from within," a voiceover announces as the player's viewpoint flies over medieval strongholds. "Now is the time for heroes. Now humanity's greatest chapter can be told." When my human character asked for his first quest, the answer was straightforward. "Your first task must be one of cleansing," replied the quest-giver, before enjoining my character to go forth and slaughter a race of "vermin" that has "infested the woods."[21] The point is not that theorists such as Ascott are wrong to hope for a deterritorialized collective intelligence that might emerge out of networked cyberspace. The point is that a very different possibility lies alongside this one, an insistence upon those very aspects (nature, essence, organicism, territoriality, purity, cleansing, totality, exclusion, hierarchy) that so much of cyberspace militates against.

While fantasies of territoriality and nature are central to *Warcraft*, it would oversimplify to say that the game does little more than stage such fantasies. Like any complex performative system, *Warcraft* has myriad possible uses and can be played many ways, with different styles of performance often encouraged by different guilds.[22] In addition, *Warcraft* shares with the larger genre of fantasy a fascination with magic, one of the most promising aspects not only of the game but of the genre as a whole. Modern fantasy is largely a nostalgic form, but the central place it grants to magic should not be seen merely as a desire to recover pre-Enlightenment thought. For magic also expresses a Promethean desire for unboundedness, a desire crucial to productive utopian imagination. It is noteworthy that even Fredric Jameson – hardly a critic drawn to fantasy – writes with some appreciation on this aspect of the genre, calling magic "a figure for the enlargement of human powers and their passage to the limit, the actualization of everything latent and virtual in the stunted human organism of the present" (*Archeologies* 66). While fantasy (unlike, in Jameson's account, science fiction[23]) buries "material and historical constraints," and thus performs the function of ideology, its magical worldview is nevertheless "a celebration of human creative power and freedom" (66). This celebration is ubiquitous in *Warcraft*, a world in which one's character can fly, change shape, cure by touch, and so forth in a manner impossible, as yet, on earth. Like heaven, *Warcraft* is a land where even death is conquered.[24] There might be utopian hope here, except that this utopia is set not in a possible future but in a world of lost enchantment, a magic kingdom that sprinkles fairy-dust on our own unrecoverable past.

Total-entertainment realms such as Gates' "home of the future" and Blizzard's *Warcraft* suggest that the continuation of the digital *Gesamtkunstwerk* of the twenty-first century will not be limited to the world of galleries and museums. Like theme parks, wired homes and online worlds are becoming mass-cultural elements in a single global nexus, a neo-medieval landscape of multiple total theatres linked by routes both physical and virtual. Such virtual spaces do not simply mirror the essential lack of identity and place that defines cyberspace; if anything, these sites attempt to compensate for that essential lack by emphatically insisting on that which digital culture tends to eradicate. Identity – whether in the form of a wearable pin containing one's preferences or a character with fixed features of race, class, and gender – returns with a vengeance in these two projects. And particularly with *Warcraft*, so does the fantasy of territoriality, located now in the radically deterritorialized realm of networked cyberspace.[25]

The gardens of exile: *Beyond Manzanar*

I would like to conclude by touching on a work of more modest proportions than any we have examined thus far. It is not a networked piece like *Aspects of Gaia* or *World of Warcraft*, it does not have the commercial potential of Gates' wired home, and the VR it utilizes is not so all-encompassing as that of *Osmose*. At least technologically, *Beyond Manzanar* is a comparatively unspectacular virtual world. It is also a world that takes its inspiration from two very real moments in history. Created by digital artists Tamiko Thiel and Zara Houshmand, *Beyond Manzanar* is a virtual-reality installation that reflects on the post-Pearl Harbor internment of Japanese-Americans in camps such as Manzanar (an oasis in the high desert of eastern California), and threats made against Iranian-Americans in the wake of the hostage crisis of 1979–80.[26] The work is an immersive, surreal journey, but it is also a critical reflection on cyberspace and the total work of art. It draws our attention to the longings that are at the center of the digital *Gesamtkunstwerke* we have explored thus far, but it does so in a way that simultaneously acknowledges and estranges their force.

Standing in an enclosed, darkened room before a wall-sized screen, the visitor to *Beyond Manzanar* controls all movements with a simple joystick (Figure 8.3). No virtual paraphernalia (visor, glasses, gloves) are used; as Thiel explains, "if you have a screen that's big enough to present the material life-sized, then the image is

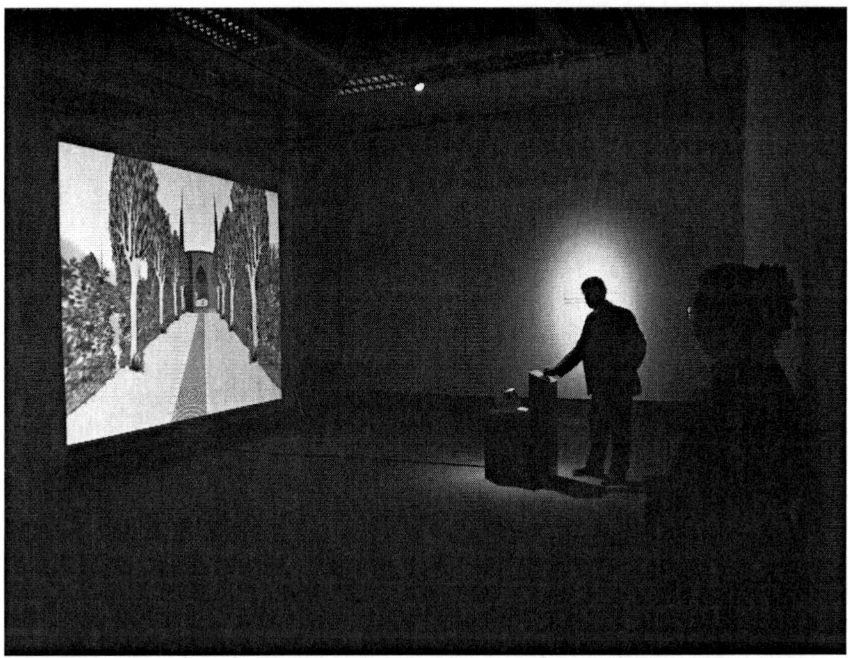

Figure 8.3 Tamiko Thiel and Zara Houshmand, *Beyond Manzanar*, 2000. Spectator at the controls; on the screen, Iranian garden.

already immersive. You see the image in your peripheral vision, and your body reacts to it not as a picture but as a space."[27] Moreover, Thiel wanted the piece to be accessible even to "people who had never touched a computer or never would touch a computer, or veterans who were missing arms and sitting in wheelchairs." The effect is successful: the size of the wall-projection, the accuracy of the three-dimensional recreation, and the use of music and ambient sounds (crunching pebbles, wind, soft voices) palpably simulate the alternate environment without technical accessories. The result is an immersive multimedia experience that consciously draws from the tradition of the total work of art. "I will admit that as a child I had my own fantasies about the *Gesamtkunstwerk*," says Houshmand, who used to "fantasize about what it would be to create a work of art that essentially was a total-immersion virtual reality." "This for me is the excitement of virtual reality," writes Thiel: "it provides an excellent platform for creating gesamtkunstwerke [sic] in which an environment is brought to life by the inclusion of other material such as sound, images, and texts (and for that matter other characters in the form of avatars)" (Thiel 3). VR, according to Thiel, surpasses the stage in its ability to create total artworks. She continues:

Traditional theatre can integrate objects, images, sounds, texts and characters into a gesamtkunstwerk. Virtual reality can go beyond theatre not only by exploiting the irreality of a space with no physical laws, but also by use of a first-person viewpoint to bring the user's own body and personal character into the piece.

(5)

But if *Beyond Manzanar* draws from the tradition of the total work of art, it also deconstructs it in intriguing ways.

At the outset of *Beyond Manzanar*, the visitor finds himself in a reproduction of the internment camp, surrounded on all sides by barbed wire and guard towers. Wandering between the rows of identical barracks, the visitor can see scenes of daily life (taken from period photographs) through the barrack windows. Exploring further, the visitor is taken by surprise to discover the sky clouding over with period newspaper clippings announcing war and rising anti-Japanese sentiment (Figure 8.4). These clippings, like many elements in the world of *Beyond Manzanar*, have a ghostly reality, shifting in and out of our vision; sometimes the sky is clear and bright, at other times it is cluttered with headlines. The effect on first seeing the newspapers filling the sky is unquestionably estranging, bringing the visitor out of the hyper-real simulation of Manzanar and recalling the political and historic context of the event. At the same time that they estrange the visitor from the simulation, they add to the feeling of imprisonment that will be the dominant motif of the work. "The confinement is not only physical," explains Thiel, "it's also a media confinement, a public opinion confinement. You're confined by the hysteria that was provoked." If the visitor explores the site further, a barbed-wire fence eventually materializes in front of the visitor and blocks further movement. Again there is a moment of estrangement from the simulated internment camp: caught between the wires of the camp are the words of poems about exile, longing, and imprisonment, written in English, Japanese, and Farsi. The surprise of finding the barbed-wire poems, like that of the newspaper clippings, furthers the dominant motif of confinement even as it dislocates the spectator from the realistic simulation of the prison camp. *Beyond Manzanar* is rife with such estrangement effects. Unsurprisingly, Houshmand describes Brecht's influence on her work as "profound and all-embracing," and says that she is indebted to the Brechtian techniques of the Iranian playwright Bijan Mofid, with whom she studied.[28]

The Manzanar camp site is only the first of several zones the visitor passes through in *Beyond Manzanar*, and the remainder of the virtual experience furthers the artists' critical engagement with the tradition of the total work of art. While a full analysis of the remainder of the journey – which begins with the lives of Japanese-Americans and ends with those of Iranian-Americans – lies beyond the bounds of this chapter, two further sites should be mentioned. The first is a Japanese garden, which the visitor reaches after passing through one of the barracks of Manzanar. On a historical level, this site (Figure 8.5) refers to an actual Japanese garden that the internees constructed at Manzanar. Reflecting on the inspiration

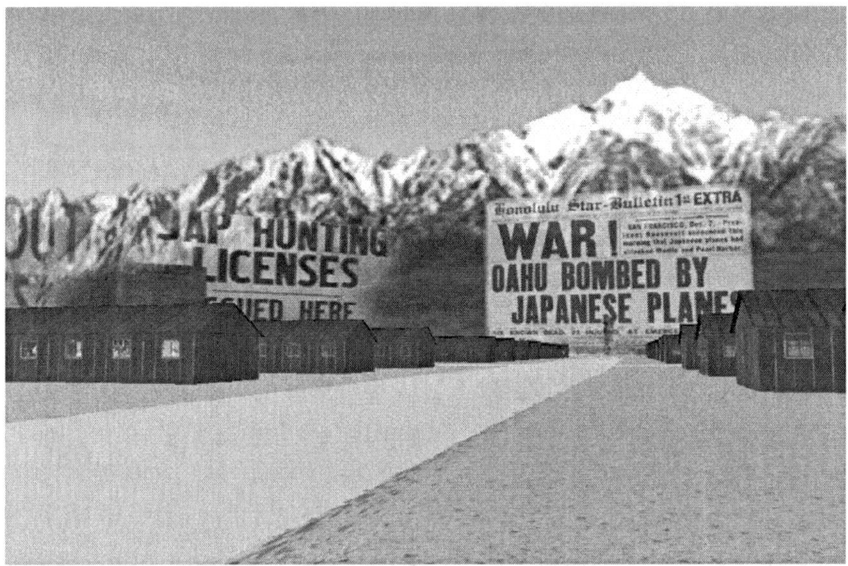

Figure 8.4 Beyond Manzanar: internment camp with newspaper headlines.

for *Beyond Manzanar*, Thiel discusses the recollections of one internee who used the Manzanar garden as a way of mentally escaping the camp.

> She talked about this garden and how she would sit herself very carefully and try not to move for as long as possible. Because as long as she held still, and held only this view, she could pretend she was in paradise of her own accord. But as soon as she moved, she fell out of the garden, because you could see the barracks or see the fence or see the watch-towers. And this was for me the key that said this project has to be done in virtual reality, because only that medium can capture that moment for other people … It was that moment, and all of those associations and also the realization that a garden is an ancient form of *Gesamttheater*, of *Gesamtkunstwerk*, of virtual reality, where you try to create an imaginary world that you can fully inhabit. There were so many cross-associations that we decided that we had to do this.

Thiel's discussion suggests that there is more than the literally historical referent here; the gardens of *Beyond Manzanar* (there are both Japanese and Iranian formal gardens in the piece) are also *Gesamtkunstwerke* themselves. Noting that the "garden is an ancient form of *Gesamttheater*, of *Gesamtkunstwerk*, of virtual reality," Thiel suggests that the garden is a "paradise" (a word with Iranian roots, originally meaning an enclosed garden) that is all too easy to "fall out of." There is a nod here to the Edenic aspirations of the total work of art, to Wagner's desire to recover a

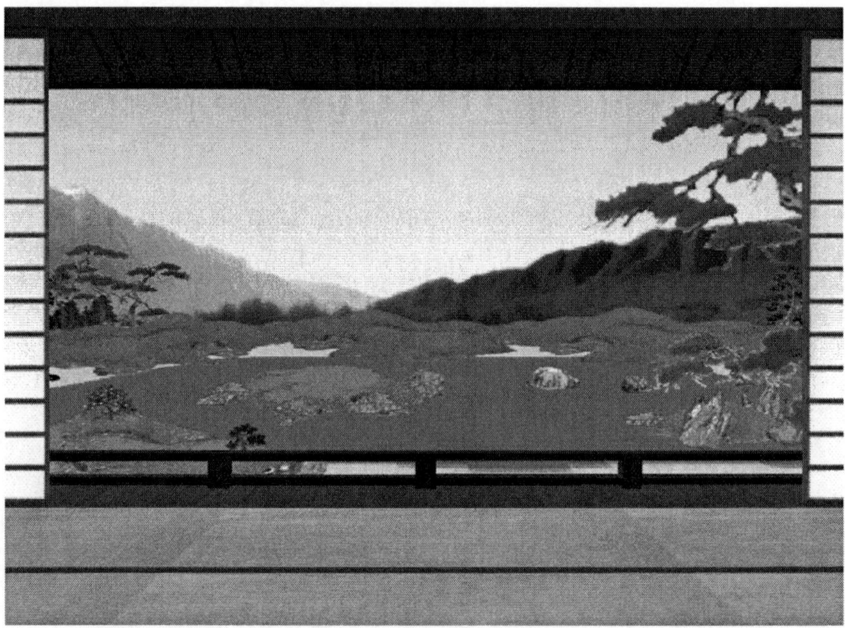

Figure 8.5 Beyond Manzanar: Japanese garden.

lost utopian condition through aesthetic unity. But there is also an awareness that the perfect totality of the *Gesamtkunstwerk* is held only through constant effort. Thiel and Houshmand reflect this precariousness by making the Japanese garden a very transient site; as soon as the visitor starts to explore it, he is thrust out, unable to return. "This sense of unity with nature is deceptive and temporary, a momentary dream in the dull reality of camp life," writes Thiel. "Users are left with the feeling of responsibility, however inadvertently, for having destroyed the dream of the garden" (7). The recurring aspiration of the iconic *Gesamtkunstwerk* to create a work that might reunify nature and humanity is here both celebrated and critiqued. We appreciate the attempt to create utopia (and the Japanese garden is certainly a beautiful, peaceful respite from the more disturbing sites in *Beyond Manzanar*) and yet we are forced to acknowledge, too, its fragility and its impermanence.

The garden motif returns in *Beyond Manzanar,* when the visitor travels through a Persian paradise garden toward the end of the piece. After exploring for a minute or so, the visitor is suddenly thrust from this garden as well, and finds himself flying high above the camp in a fighter plane or bomber (Figure 8.6). The visitor has now lost control of the joystick, and the image on the screen replicates that of a first-person "shooter" game. The work thus culminates in a reference to the origins of virtual reality itself. The ending, says Thiel, "is a subliminal message about our stance on war, that this whole technology was developed in order to train jet fighter pilots and is used mostly now for shooter games. That's how VR technology was

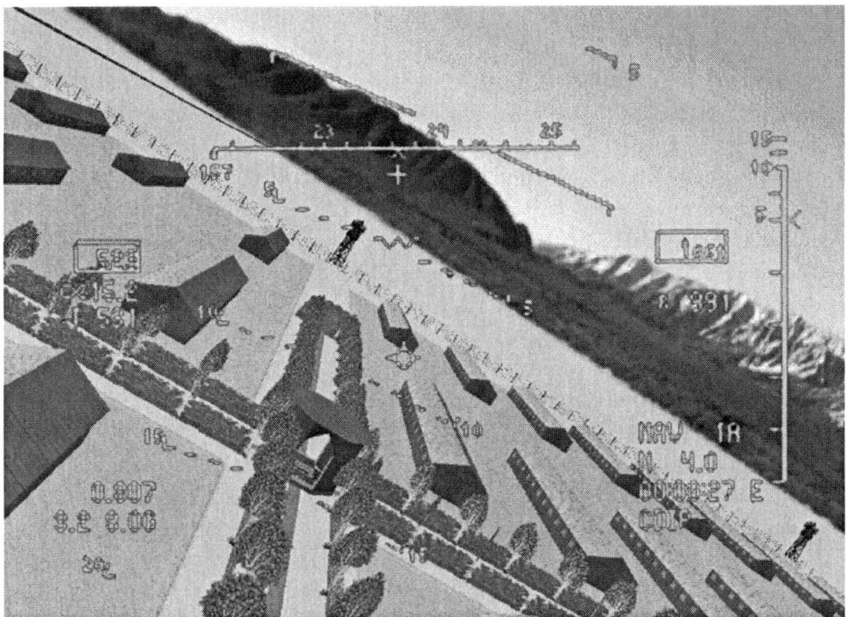

Figure 8.6 Beyond Manzanar: bomber perspective.

developed." The second "fall" from the garden, then, takes the self-reflexive critique one step farther, exposing the ties between VR technology and modern warfare. In their guide to *Beyond Manzanar*, Thiel and Houshmand title this scene "Video/Game/War. The only way out of the garden." But if the paradise garden itself was a sort of *Gesamtkunstwerk*, then it may be more precise to say that these two scenes – the garden and the video game – show two sides of the same aesthetic form, the edenic and the apocalyptic aspects of the total work of art.

This combination of reflexive formal critique with explicitly political content makes *Beyond Manzanar* a rarity among VR artworks. It indicates one Brechtian approach to cyber-arts, a form of dialectical virtuality. At times it exhibits many of the features of the *Gesamtkunstwerk*: full immersion, unity of aesthetic media, longing for utopia. At other times it deconstructs those very features: estrangement effects pull us away from immersion, montage replaces organicism as a principle of unity, and paradise proves precarious and illusory. In the end, it draws our attention to the historical and economic foundations of virtual reality itself, to the uncomfortable relationship between the total work of art, mass media, and the military machine.

The digital dawn

While *Aspects of Gaia*, *Osmose*, the Gates house, and *World of Warcraft* are quite different projects – ranging from VR to networked cyberspace, art installation to mass entertainment – they all participate in a broadly Wagnerian genealogy. They offer themselves as total works of art that seek to recapture a lost harmony with the natural world through the medium of virtual simulacra. All of these four projects stress the unification of media, reliant on mechanics, in order to attain a single, all-encompassing theatre that at once reflects, and helps to achieve, a more perfect social order. All four at times echo the iconic strategies of such artists as Wagner, Riefenstahl, and Disney by hiding the mechanics of their own "organic" spectacle, and at times echo the crystalline strategies of Schlemmer and Moholy-Nagy by attempting to synthesize mechanical and organic elements in a unified "mechanical organism." All four projects, therefore, encourage critical reflection on the medium of their own creation only in order to assuage such reflection, and reincorporate the audience's moments of estrangement (should they occur at all) into the "organic" totality of the whole. The continuation of such iconic and crystalline strategies, both of which hinge on the occultation of labor, suggests that networked digital media alone do not undo ideology. There is nothing about cyberspace, in other words, that necessitates a break with bourgeois aesthetics.

While such visions of restoration as those offered by Gates, Davies, Ascott, and Blizzard Entertainment may hold some promise for the artworks and social constructions of the future, their narratives of estrangement and return sidestep the economic and social realities of the medium. In this light, it is encouraging that some digital artists have begun to reflect critically on the tradition of the *Gesamtkunstwerk*, to introduce estrangement devices that are not ultimately reincorporated back into the totality of the work. Such a Brechtian response to the total work of art is most clearly in evidence in *Beyond Manzanar*. Here, confinement rather than freedom is the subject, and a journey through the historical legacy of ethnic internment in America becomes also a meditation on the promise and danger of the total work of art. *Beyond Manzanar* gives us virtual gardens, but these gardens have weeds: we are given both hope and oppression, rootedness and dislocation. The gardens comfort, but not for long. They provide refuge, but only as stations on a journey that remains as resistant to totality as cyberspace itself.

Conclusion

Film helps Richard Wagner, and Richard Wagner saves film.

(Syberberg 21)

In 1982, precisely one hundred years after the premiere of *Parsifal,* the German director Hans-Jürgen Syberberg opened his *Parsifal* film at the Bayreuth cinema. Syberberg's symbolism was well chosen: here was a work at once for and against Wagner, one that emulated his monumentalism while at the same time confronting it. On one hand, the work's time and place suggested an homage to the master's memory in the fashion of the "centennial tribute." On the other hand, the time and place suggested a challenge to his legacy, echoing Syberberg's notion that film, and not opera, is the *Gesamtkunstwerk* of our age, and that the Bayreuth Festspielhaus has been radically displaced by the Bayreuth moviehouse. Film, according to Syberberg, is now able to realize Wagner's project more fully than ever before. By the same token, Wagner brings to film a return to Romantic mythopoesis that has been degraded in the twentieth century by kitsch both Nazi and Disney. The fruit of this marriage is a rebirth of the *Gesamtkunstwerk* by means of the machine. "A new unity of art as a continuation of life," Syberberg enthuses, "a new metaphysics in the form of mythology mediated by film" (*Hitler* 30).

The irony of Syberberg's myth of a new triumph of art over kitsch is that, by the late twentieth century, the myth had already been reproduced so often as to become a piece of kitsch itself. The *Gesamtkunstwerk* is always suffering a fall, is always being redeemed. The curse is always production, and the balm is always production's fruits. It is necessary, now, to move away from such narratives of burial and resurrection, poison and cure, in order to appreciate the ways in which the *Gesamtkunstwerk* is both less and more than its romanticizers have imagined. It is less than they have imagined because it is irredeemably historical, and cannot transcend the dialectical tensions which gave it birth. It will always be both avant-garde and mass-cultural; it will always be both oppressive and communitarian; it will always be technophiliac and technophobic; it will always be insufficient. Most of all, it will always be internally fractured and condemned to eternal longing for a totality of which it is either the premature realization or a compensatory fantasy. The total work of art is not a solution, not in any form; it is a sublime, telling, and troubling symptom.

And yet the total work of art is also more than has often been supposed. Its influences have been even more varied and profound than studies of lineages from Wagner to Schoenberg, or Wagner to Reinhardt, or Wagner to Hitler would lead one to believe. One of the most important, and most underappreciated, of lineages has been the one that ties the total work of art to developments in technology and mass culture, and that shows the persistent importance of Wagner even to artists and entrepreneurs with whom he is rarely, if ever, associated. Adorno and Horkheimer's provocation, that television "derisively fulfill[s] the Wagnerian dream of the *Gesamtkunstwerk*" (124), at once hits and misses the target. On one hand, to reduce the multiplicities of a mass-cultural medium to a single, totalizing system is to neglect the complexities of such a vast cultural sphere. On the other hand, Adorno and Horkheimer correctly indicate that the ongoing influence of the total work of art is far more central to contemporary mass culture than has generally been acknowledged. I believe that its two most important contemporary manifestations may be found, first, in the proliferation and interlocking of themed environments, and, second, in the virtual creations of cyberspace.

In conclusion, let us return to the *Ring*, and so make our end our beginning. There is a moment toward the end of *Rheingold* when Loge, the trickster god, thinks he's being tricked. Freia has been carried off, and her golden orchards have begun to rot. Without their apples of immortality, the gods suddenly age, wrinkle, weaken. All except for Loge, the fiery half-god who had always been excluded from the regimen of the "true-born" pantheon. Loge, always to one side of the immortals, seems now to surpass them in power. Never fully included in their sacred rites, he also avoids their curse. Watching them decay, Loge cannot believe the evidence of his eyes, imagines himself the victim of some deception. Far from being an illusion, however, the sight is actually a premonition: a vision of the final collapse of the gods amid flood and fire at the end of *Götterdämmerung*. "Am I tricked by mists?" sings Loge, "Am I teased by a *dream*? / Worried and wan, / how quickly you wither."

The catastrophe that ends the *Ring* cycle is not quite universal. The Rhinemaidens triumph as they rise with the waters of the river to reclaim their sacred gold. But only one god still lives: Loge, the half-god whose leitmotif plays as the fire builds to engulf Walhall, and whose fire burns ever higher as the curtain falls. Loge, who threatened to outlast the gods at the beginning of the cycle, now outlasts them indeed at the end.

Of all the gods in Wagner's heaven, it is the trickster alone who survives. The ultimate heir of the gods is not some messianic hero – is not Siegfried, is not Brünnhilde – but rather is the half-blood, the mercurial Loge. Wagner, that master builder who established his own Walhall at Bayreuth, foresaw something important here, though his art outstripped his own comprehension. He foresaw that the consummation of utopian ambition is not catastrophe only, but irony also: the dancing fire that creates as it destroys.

Notes

Introduction

1 The identification of the Arrogance and Crisis motifs I owe to Rudolph Sabor (20, 103).
2 See, for example, Francis Fukuyama, *The End of History and the Last Man* (New York: Free Press, 1992); David Frum and Richard Perle, *An End to Evil: How to Win the War on Terror* (New York: Random House, 2003).
3 I use "total work of art" interchangeably with "*Gesamtkunstwerk*" throughout this study. For the plural of "*Gesamtkunstwerk*," I use the German form, "*Gesamtkunstwerke.*"
4 Alex Ross on the 26 July 2004 premiere: "Christoph Schlingensief's production at the Bayreuth Festival last week gave us ... two dead rabbits, their rotting bodies intertwined, their images projected on a screen above the stage. We then saw a sped-up film of one rabbit decomposing, its body frothing as the maggots did their work."

1 The total work of art in an age of mechanical reproduction

1 Most Wagner quotes in this chapter will include the source in W. Ashton Ellis' translation of Wagner's prose writings, followed by a slash, followed by the volume and page number of the original text. Unless otherwise noted, this text is the Leipzig edition of the *Gesammelte Schriften und Dichtungen*. In many instances I have made minor modifications to Ellis' translations for readability (for example, I have avoided Ellis' practice of capitalizing many of Wagner's nouns). In instances where I have more extensively modified Ellis' translations for accuracy, I have marked the citation with an asterisk. In instances where I have done the translation myself, I have referenced only the original.
2 Though Wagner occasionally expressed discomfort with his notion of communal genius in the Zurich period, he maintained his belief that communal genius alone could revolutionize society. In a letter to Liszt of 8 September 1850, for example, he writes, "Dearest Liszt, was I right when I wrote in the preface of my *Artwork of the Future* that not the individual, but the community alone, could create genuine works of art? See, you've done the *impossible*, – but believe me, *all* must nowadays do the impossible in order to achieve that which is really possible" (*Briefwechsel* 77–8).
3 E.g. Bermbach *passim*; Borchmeyer, *Richard Wagner* 66, 68, 70; Fischer-Lichte *passim*.
4 Andreas Huyssen has persuasively argued that Adorno "never lost sight of" the inseparability of modernism and mass culture (*After* 16–43).
5 Günter Berghaus, for example, holds Wagner's ideas on the *Gesamtkunstwerk* to be a "retrogression" from those of Philipp Otto Runge (Berghaus 15). Hugo von Hofmannsthal, similarly, wrote to Richard Strauss that "[o]pera ... is a *Gesamtkunstwerk*, not just since Wagner, who merely, most boldly and audaciously, gave shape and substance to old universal trends, but ever since its glorious beginning, since the

seventeenth century and by the terms of its fundamental purpose: the rebirth of the *Gesamtkunstwerk* of antiquity. How simple this all is, how easy to understand except by ponderous North-German brains" (quoted in Finger 2–3). See also Neumann *passim*.

6 "The turning point [*Wendepunkt*] seems to have been Schiller, who transformed the transcendental idea of taste into a moral demand and formulated it as an imperative: Live aesthetically!" (Gadamer 82). "Schiller's aesthetic utopia marks a turning point in the history of utopian thinking. The question: 'How could the world be completed?' (Bloch) is no longer answered by a social utopia in the form of a fictional romance of the state, but rather reflected in the experience of art" (Berghahn 272).

7 In Joachim di Fiori's account, human history is divided into three distinct epochs, characterized by the Father, the Son, and the Holy Spirit, respectively. Fiori predicted that the year 1260 would usher in the last of these epochs. This historical periodization would enter German Romantic letters largely through the enthusiasm of Schiller and Lessing for Fiore. In the 1930s and 1940s, it would be used by the National Socialist Party as part of their mystical understanding of the Third Reich.

8 For an excellent study of the influence and development of the idea of the Aesthetic State in modern German thought, see Chytry.

9 A twentieth-century resonance can be found in Vladimir Mayakovsky's *Mystery-Bouffe*, which ends with the depiction of a communist utopia in which tools and machines take the stage as free characters.

10 Wagner's belief in a monarchical republic infuses much of his writing, including that of the Zurich period. While the monarchy emerges unscathed in much of his Zurich writings, the aristocracy comes in for withering attack, second only to the "money-changers" and "merchants" for Wagner's scorn. Later, Wagner advocates on behalf of a strong aristocracy as well, which he hopes, in essays such as *German Art and German Politics*, will be transformed from an idle class into a kind of aesthetic elite. See Borchmeyer, *Richard Wagner* 8–9.

11 Wagner does, however, juxtapose speech and writing elsewhere in *The Artwork of the Future*; in keeping with the Romantic tradition, his preference is for the former. Describing the decline of Greek tragedy, Wagner argues that "[t]he wintry stem of speech, stripped of its summer wreath of sounding leaves, shrank to the withered, toneless signs of *writing*: instead of the ear, it dumbly now addressed the eye; the poet's strain became a *written dialect*, – the poet's breath the *penman's scrawl*" (1:137/3:106).

12 To signify degraded modern culture, Wagner uses a word of French origin: "*die Kultur*." To signify true, organic culture, Wagner uses the Germanic "*Bildung*." *Nachbildung*, based on the root "*Bildung*," thus suggests a truer, more organic sort of imitation than mere *Nachahmung*, which Wagner invariably associates with mechanism (and hence with Jews and the French), and reviles.

13 Levin, *Richard Wagner* 88–95. See also Weiner *passim*.

14 I am thinking particularly of the twelfth section of the 27th letter, in which Schiller writes that the Aesthetic State may be found "like the pure Church and the pure Republic, only in some few chosen circles, where conduct is governed, not by some soulless imitation of the manners and morals of others, but by the aesthetic nature we have made our own." This final paragraph of Schiller's work, with its occultish talk of "chosen circles" where freedom might flourish, contrasts rather sharply with other sections of the treatise, where Schiller demands the "true political freedom" (7) of all people. The ambiguity reflects one of the central contradictions of bourgeois ideology, and it is unsurprising to find Schiller torn in two directions by the issue. On one hand he looks forward to universal emancipation as the culmination of human history, while on the other he fears the "crude, lawless instincts" of "the lower and more numerous classes" (25–7). His final paragraph tries to solve the contradiction by isolating the Aesthetic State to certain small enclaves, and spiritualizing it as a mere matter of "aesthetic" conduct.

15 "With the advent of the so-called second industrial revolution, alienated consumption is added to alienated production as an inescapable duty of the masses. *The entirety of labor sold* is transformed overall into the *total commodity*. A cycle is thus set in train that must be maintained at all costs: the total commodity must be returned in fragmentary form to a fragmentary individual completely cut off from the concerted action of the forces of production." Debord 29.

16 See also Brenkman *passim*.

2 Total stage: Wagner's Festspielhaus

1 The sheer numbers indicate its attraction. In the six months of the Great Exhibition, there were over six million visitors, averaging 43,000 a day (Reeves 16). Over the same period, 4,237,240 people arrived in London, an increase of 50 percent over the previous year; of these, 58,427 were foreigners, an increase of 276 percent (Altick 457).

2 See Musgrave 102, 111 for more on these performances.

3 Ludwig also championed a grand festival theatre in Munich, also designed by Semper, as a permanent site for Wagner's music-dramas. The full story of Ludwig's championing of Munich as a site for the Festspielhaus, the machinations of various Munich politicians to stop both the king and Wagner, and the general abuse of Semper by all sides may be found in Newman 3:409–37.

4 The most important of these was "Science, Industry, and Art: Proposals for the Development of a National Taste in Art," written in 1852 and strongly influenced by Semper's experience of the Crystal Palace.

5 This religious character of Bayreuth reached its apex with the Wagner cult of the Third Reich, but it has by no means passed away – consider Frederick Spotts' recent account, quite typical, of his visit to the Festspielhaus: "There was something oddly religious about the day – a shared experience of deep meaning, like-minded participants, everyone familiar with the ritual and equally moved ... The music and the staging, a long and famous tradition, the theatre itself, the civilized way of doing things, the 'island' atmosphere – do these add up to the mystique that surrounds the Festival and that for a century has drawn millions on what even today retains the character of a pilgrimage?" (Spotts, *Bayreuth* 28).

6 Michel de Certeau offers one of the clearest distinctions between modern and medieval landscapes when he distinguishes between modern maps of "geographic form," which are born "of modern scientific discourse," and medieval maps, which mark out "itineraries (performative indications chiefly concerning pilgrimages)" (120). These two different notions of space also imply two different notions of time. In the modern geographic form, space is mapped separately from time, such that one speaks of "miles" or "kilometers" which may be traversed at varying speeds; the medieval map, on the other hand, was organized around "distances calculated in hours or in days, that is, in terms of the time it would take to cover them on foot" (120). Distance, in the medieval map, was made a unit of travel time and social function of place rather than abstract measurement. Moreover, since the medieval map was largely organized around pilgrimage sites, the diachronic time of travel was inextricably linked to the synchronic time of ritual space. This last point becomes clearer if de Certeau's understanding of the medieval map is read alongside Mircea Eliade's distinction between sacred and profane time. Profane time is the realm of "ordinary temporal duration, in which acts without religious meaning have their setting," whereas sacred time is "*a primordial mythical time made present*," and is particularly associated with festivals and pilgrimage sites (Eliade 68). Medieval mapping, then, organized space according to performative itineraries that particularly stressed the assumption of profane time into sacred time.

7 I borrow Andrew Porter's translation here (Wagner, *Ring* 75).

8 In this case, Wagner's emphasis on harmony rather than sublimity differs from that of

even the most "faithful" of latter-day designers. Take, for example, the ash-tree designed by Günther Schneider-Siemssen for the 1962 production at Covent Garden, in which the tree slammed through the roof like a great phallus, did not branch off until well above the house, and then did so horizontally. This massive, alien tree was itself dwarfed by the hulking vegetation of the 1975 Met production, in which only the base of the trunk was visible, the rest rising up into the gloaming. Such latter-day designs, though hardly radical, evoked the towering redwoods of Bierstadt's California paintings, with their roots as thick as men, more than the aspirations of the Wagnerian landscape. For photographs of these designs, including a model of the original stage design, see Osborne 116, 137, 147.

9 The one exception to this egalitarian seating arrangement was a royal annex, added in 1882 in the hopes of luring Ludwig II to Bayreuth. The exception itself is telling, for it speaks to the populist monarchism (one king, one folk) that becomes particularly pronounced in Wagner's late career.

10 While the Bayreuth Festspielhaus was not quite the first place in which the house lights were ever darkened for performance, it was the first place in which darkened house lights were standard. Experiments had previously been made in darkening the house lights, for example at the 1853 premiere of Verdi's *Il Trovatore* at the Teatro Apollo in Rome, but such experiments had always been one-offs, not regular performance practice. Interestingly, the darkening of the auditorium at Bayreuth was initially the result of an accident: the intent was merely to lower the gas lights in the auditorium, but due to faulty mechanics they went out completely (see Wagner 6:103–4). As with many innovations, this one arose from apparent failure.

11 The premiere of the *Ring* cycle at Bayreuth in 1876 was a financial disaster so serious that Wagner would only witness one more performance in the Festspielhaus during his lifetime: the performance of *Parsifal* in 1882.

12 Fricke describes these troubles in his diary entry for 8 June 1876. For a full history of the creation of steam effects at Bayreuth see Baumann 269–72.

13 While arts, according to Kittler, "entertain only symbolic relations to the sensory fields they presuppose," media "correlate in the real itself to the materiality they deal with" (215). Examples of media include photo plates, which "inscribe chemical traces of light," and photograph records, which "inscribe mechanical traces of sound" (215–16).

14 Examples of this sort may be multiplied. Consider, for instance, Wagner's Preface to the published version of *Der Ring der Nibelungen*, in which he writes: "I next should lay especial stress on the invisibility of the orchestra – to be effected by an architectural illusion quite feasible with an amphitheatric plan of auditorium. The importance of this will be manifest to anybody who attends our opera performances with the notion of getting the true impression of a work of dramatic art; through the inevitable sight of the mechanical movements of the musicians and their conductor, he is made an unwilling witness of technical evolutions which should almost be as carefully concealed from him as the cords, ropes, laths and scaffoldings of the stage decorations – which, seen from the wings, as everyone knows, destroy all vestige of illusion" (5:276–7/6:275).

15 Ernest Newman has written that he considers *Parsifal* "a religious work," but adds that its religious "thesis" may be separated, happily, from its artistic qualities. "[F]or my part I do not know or care how Parsifal is to 'redeem' the world … [B]ut to appreciate a work of art it is not in the least necessary to subscribe to its author's philosophical or religious opinions; a rationalist can be as deeply thrilled by the Matthew Passion as any Christian can be" (*Wagner as Man and Artist* 377). Against this position, Lucy Beckett has argued that the religiosity of *Parsifal* is part of the work's essential dramatic content. The essentially Christian themes are essential to the drama, she argues, adding that this integrity is "both the source and outward form of its power" (263) for those sympathetic

to its general religious stance. Owing much to Nietzsche, Robert Gutman speaks for a third alternative: that the religiosity of the opera is "a rather cheap and cracking veneer of fake Catholicism" (439).

16 For more on *Parsifal* in relation to Wagner's views on race and gender see, e.g. Weiner 185–94, 229–59; Rose 89–102. A contrary opinion is Magee 264–85, 343–80. For a Lacanian interpretation of *Parsifal*'s rhetoric of purification, see Žižek.

17 For more on Kundry's hysteria, see Bronfen *passim*. Much good work has been done on the cultural connections between hysteria, "femininity," and "Jewishness"; see esp. Showalter; Gilman.

18 The "grand united artwork," Wagner wrote in *Religion and Art*, is a unity of "the masculine principle" of "the poet's work" (i.e. the text) and "the feminine" principle of "music" (6:165/10:167). The most important study of Wagner's interest in androgyny is Nattiez.

19 For more on this process in *Parsifal*, see my "Laughing at the Redeemer."

20 In his superb study of Wagner, James Treadwell similarly stresses the importance of incarnation (as opposed to transcendence) in *Parsifal* (Treadwell 220). I hope to complement Treadwell's analysis, which focuses on the Eucharistic mysticism of *Parsifal*, by placing the work in the context of understandings of electrical technology in the 1880s.

21 There was an explosion of texts on electrotherapy in French, German, and English during this period. A partial list would include G. B. A. Duchenne, *A Treatise on Localised Electrisation* (1871), E. N. J. Onimus and Charles Legros, *Traité d'électricité médicale* (1872), Julius Althaus, *A Treatise on Medical Electricity* (1873), Herbert Tibbits, *A Handbook of Medical Electricity* (1873), George Beard, *Medical and Surgical Uses of Electricity* (1874), G. V. Poore, *A Text-book of Electricity in Medicine and Surgery* (1876), Armand de Watteville, *A Practical Introduction to Medical Electricity* (1878), A. Hughes Bennett, *A Practical Treatise on Electro-diagnosis* (1882), and W. H. Erb's third volume (on electrotherapy) of Hugo Wilhelm von Ziemssen's *Handbuch der allgemeinen Theraphie* (1882).

22 Nietzsche may have been the first to advocate this break, with his frequent criticisms of Schopenhauer's influence on Wagner (see, for example, Nietzsche's 1886 Preface to *Birth of Tragedy* and *The Case of Wagner*, 1886). It is this transformation in Wagner's work that supposedly triggered Nietzsche's own split with Wagner. The argument of a profound break between Wagner's pre-and post-Schopenhauerian work continues to be advanced, with some justification, by critics such as Bryan Magee (174–94).

3 Total machine: the Bauhaus theatre

1 The Bauhaus has had a long history, moving from Weimar (1919–25) to Dessau (1925–32) to Berlin (1933) to Chicago (1937–8 as the New Bauhaus; 1939–44 as the School of Design; after 1944 as the Institute of Design). In this chapter, "Bauhaus" should be taken to refer to the Bauhaus of the Weimar and Dessau periods.

2 For an overview of the Wagnerian (and more broadly neo-Romantic) roots of the Bauhaus, especially in the work and theories of Bruno Taut and Adolf Behne, see Franciscono 88–126. Two studies of the Bauhaus and aesthetic totality are Humblet 245–82 and Vitale 62–77. The latter study in particular traces Gropius' evolving relation to the *Gesamtkunstwerk*, an evolution that lies beyond the bounds of the present chapter.

3 Piscator's own conception of "total theatre," which borrowed heavily from Wagner and in turn influenced Brecht, may be found in Piscator, "Theatre of Totality and Total Theatre."

4 Gropius also describes this design in his Introduction to *The Theatre of the Bauhaus*, 13–14.

5 Both Moholy-Nagy and Schlemmer were well aware of Wagner and of the *Gesamtkunstwerk*. Of the two artists, Schlemmer was the more directly influenced by the

Schiller–Wagner tradition, while Moholy-Nagy was the more explicitly involved in the creation of a "total" theatre. The influence of Wagner on Schlemmer can be seen as early as 1915, when Schlemmer writes in his journal of his newfound desire to "merge all styles," and specifically mentions "Wagner, the *Meistersinger*, Nuremberg" as the source of this revelation (13 April 1915). One would not want to overstate the Wagnerian influence, however, as elsewhere Schlemmer expresses a preference for Bach and Handel's music over Wagner's. He expresses his differences with Wagner more forcefully in his journal in 1928, in which he relates a "visionary dream" of "large (architectonic) surfaces (black-and-white lacquer) with little, finely molded figures of great delicacy. Dangers: the 'holy,' angelic, Richard-Wagner-like!" (16 April 1928). Certainly, Schlemmer would not recreate the baroque-ish "Wagner-like" fantasy of his dream. But he would, like Moholy-Nagy, seek to create a new form of artistic organicism by means of the machine.

6 A more precise translation of Schlemmer's "Mensch und Kunstfigur" would be "*Person and Art Figure*," but the translation "Man and Art Figure" was the choice of Arthur Wensinger, the original translator of *Bühne im Bauhaus* into English in 1961. Since the title "Man and Art Figure" has become the standard translation in the English-speaking world, I use it here to avoid confusion.

7 This production may be found on VHS, as *Das triadische Ballett: ein Film in drei Teilen, nach den Tänzen von Oskar Schlemmer* (Bonn: Inter Nationes, 1990).

8 In the 1928 essay "Piscator and the Modern Theatre" ("Piscator und das moderne Theater"), Schlemmer retreats somewhat from his notion of the organic-mechanical "absolute stage." While continuing to argue, now in a more pragmatic vein, that the "all-around application of film, projection, transparencies" are "requirements of the modern stage," Schlemmer raises questions about the ability of such media to stupefy spectators, robbing them of their higher functions. "We do not know," he argues, "to what extent the static-peaceful state of the spectator ought to be disturbed without profoundly disturbing his receptive abilities; we do not know to what extent an accumulation of material effects leaves room for the intellectual [*das Geistige*]" (25). It is a question that Schlemmer's previous theory of the "*absolute Schaubühne*" had never raised, if only because the intellectual (and potentially critical) attitude of the spectator never played a major role. Given the subsequent history of the mass-cultural *Gesamtkunstwerk*, however, it is a prescient concern.

9 Melissa Trimingham draws a similar comparison in her highly illuminating study, "Oskar Schlemmer's Research Practice at the Dessau Bauhaus." Trimingham does not quite claim, however, that the Bauhaus theatre was the birth of this genealogy.

10 On the relationship between the Bauhaus and National Socialism, see esp. Nerdinger. For a study of the relation between the Bauhaus theatre and Italian fascism, see Schnapp, "Border Crossings." For a critique of certain associations of the Bauhaus with "reactionary modernism" and fascism, see Koss.

11 A number of recent studies have stressed this connection; see, for example, Koepnick; Labanyi; Rentschler.

12 Peter Hahn has suggested that Walter Gropius' socialist goals remained throughout his career, despite being forced underground after the early 20s (see Hochman 214). This reading is additionally supported by later writings by Gropius such as *The Scope of Total Architecture*, which continue to exhibit a utopian hope for the potential of total art as late as the 1950s. Still, there is no question that Gropius' attitudes toward the alliance between art and commerce at least become more pragmatic after the early 20s, and never again regain the unabashed utopianism of his early writings.

13 Dessau was more generous than Weimar, but, given the dilapidated state of the Weimar-era economy, neither city could give the school much in the way of public funds.

14 Gropius writes that "[e]ven after the Bauhaus had moved to Dessau [in 1925] it could

only rely on a relatively very small income, which was defrayed by an annual vote from the municipality. Including the salaries of teachers, etc. – of whom there were about 24 to 180–200 pupils – the total grant amounted to some 100,000 Reichsmarks (then slightly under £5000). In addition to this, however, the town had to meet the interest and annual reduction charges on the capital outlay represented by the new buildings and their equipment, which had cost somewhere about 850,000 Reichsmarks (at that time roughly equivalent to £42,450). The royalties from the licenses we granted to various firms for the mass-production of *Bauhaus* models (Furniture, Carpets, Textiles, China, Electric Light Fittings, etc.) contributed a subsidiary source of revenue which steadily increased as time went on ... I was also able to pay pupils for any of their Bauhaus work that proved saleable: an arrangement which assured many of them (necessarily very straitened) means of subsistence during their three-year course of training" (*New Architecture* 95).

15   Ward 83. Janet Ward's superb analysis of the interplay between functionalism and fashion in Weimar Germany has helped to shape my own understanding of the context in which the Bauhaus theatre took root. See esp. Ward 45–91.

16   Friedrich Huth, in Huth 29.

4   Total montage: Brecht's reply to Wagner

1   Most Brecht quotes in this chapter will include the source of the English translation, followed by a slash, followed by the volume and page number of the German text in the *Grosse kommentierte Berliner und Frankfurter Ausgabe*. In instances where I have modified the English translation, I have further marked the citation with an asterisk. In instances where I have not consulted a translation, the appropriate volume and page number in the *Berliner und Frankfurter Ausgabe* appears alone. *BOT* stands for *Brecht on Theatre*, John Willett's edited volume of Brecht essays. *BOF* stands for *Brecht on Film and Radio*, Marc Silberman's edited volume of Brecht essays.

2   Scholars who emphasize Brecht's antithetical relationship to Wagner include, among many others, Esslin 119; Bentley 44, 240; Puchner 139–40.

3   My analysis of the parallels between *Mahagonny* and the *Ring* in this paragraph is indebted to Rowland Cotterill's brief discussion of the same. See Cotterill 197.

4   Brecht's manipulative treatment of his collaborators has been extensively documented in John Fuegi's *Brecht and Company*. Whatever one makes of that book's verdict on Brecht as artist and human being, it now seems clear that Elisabeth Hauptmann, Ruth Berlau, and Margarete Steffin suffered particularly ill treatment at his hands, and that much of Brecht's work was the unacknowledged labor of others.

5   Adorno, "Der dialektische Komponist." In "Negative Philosophy of Music – Positive Results," Ferenc Feher argues convincingly for Adorno's indebtedness to Lukács' dialectical idea of totality.

6   Though Brecht followed Eisenstein's career closely, he also made efforts to separate himself from association with Eisenstein's methods, much as he did from those of Piscator, Meyerhold, and other Marxist artists. To a degree, Brecht's protestations were expressions of real aesthetic and political differences, while to a degree they were expressions of an anxiety of influence. Fuegi discusses this well in Fuegi, *Bertolt* 43–7.

7   More work remains to be done on the connection between Eisenstein and Wagner. Any thoroughgoing analysis of the influence of Wagner on Eisenstein would also trace the influence of Wagner on Eisenstein's compatriot Vsevelod Meyerhold, which remains likewise under-researched despite numerous references to the *Gesamtkunstwerk* in Meyerhold's theoretical writings.

8   Significant differences between Brecht's montage technique and Eisenstein's can also be traced (and, indeed, between Eisenstein's use of montage in, say, *Strike* versus his use of

montage in *Alexander Nevsky*), but an in-depth analysis of the differences between Brecht's use of montage and that of Eisenstein lies beyond the bounds of this chapter. An intriguing if very brief discussion of the similarities and differences between the montage techniques of Brecht and Eisenstein may be found in Laker.

9 In 1950, Brecht changed the title a third time, to *Der Ozeanflug* ("The Ocean Flight"), eliminating Lindbergh's name entirely. This final change was due in large part to Lindbergh's rightist politics and wartime role in the bombing of cities.

10 This passage appears in identical form in two essays of Brecht's from the period: in "An Example of Pedagogics" and "The Radio as an Apparatus of Communication." Both are included in *BOT*.

5 Total state: Riefenstahl's *Triumph of the Will*

1 Recent studies on the influence of the *Gesamtkunstwerk* idea on early cinema include Bordwell; Coates; Paulin; Wyss.

2 The phrase "produced by order of the Führer" appears as one of the opening titles of the film, and appears again on the title page of *Hinter den Kulissen des Reichsparteitag-Films* (1935).

3 Even Hinton allows that Riefenstahl rearranged events for the film, and he provides a useful chronology of actual events side by side with Riefenstahl's film sequence. See Hinton 37.

4 "If you see the film today, you will notice that it doesn't contain a single reconstructed scene. Everything in it is real. And there is no tendentious commentary for the simple reason that there is no commentary at all. It is history. A purely historical film" (Riefenstahl, *Cahiers* 49). She repeated this claim, emphatically, in her interview with Alan Marcus (Marcus, 82). In a 1975 interview with David Hinton, however, she conceded that she restaged and refilmed a short section featuring Julius Streicher (Hinton 46). The fact that this admission blithely contradicts her repeated categorical denials (made both before and after the Hinton interview) is typical of Riefenstahl.

5 The estimate is Richard Barsam's, who breaks down the crew thus: 10 technical staff, 36 cameramen and assistants, 9 aerial photographers, 17 newsreel crew, 12 newsreel crew from Tobis company, 17 lighting crew, 2 still photographers, 26 drivers, 37 watchmen and security force, 4 labor service, and 2 office. See Barsam 23. Different film historians have compiled different estimates, however. Brian Winston, for instance, gives the number of cameramen as at least 49, including newsreel crew, a number he grants is somewhat at odds with Riefenstahl's account and Barsam's estimate (103).

6 See Riefenstahl, *Hinter* 18.

7 In an interview for the German film journal *Filmkritik*, Riefenstahl disavowed authorship of this work, despite the fact that her name appears on the title page. Richard Barsam claims that the book's true author was Ernst Jäger, though he offers no evidence for this claim (79). Though the book's authorship may never be known for certain, whoever wrote *Hinter den Kulissen* seems to have had inside knowledge of precise details of film production on *Triumph of the Will*, and wrote with a voice that sounds remarkably like Riefenstahl's. For its inside knowledge alone, *Hinter den Kulissen* is a valuable historical document regardless of its authorship.

8 See Deleuze, *Cinema 1: The Movement-Image*. Deleuze does mention Riefenstahl, briefly, in *Cinema 2: The Time-Image*, where he connects her with the end of the cinema of the movement-image (164–5). With a gesture toward Paul Virilio's *War and Cinema: The Logistics of Perception*, Deleuze goes on to suggest that Riefenstahl's work indicates an essential connection between the cinema of the movement-image and fascism. But this vastly overstates the case, and needlessly blurs the distinction between fascist and non-fascist film techniques.

9 As no standard classification of the film's scenes exist (each critic numbering them in his or her own way), I have adopted the scene divisions provided on the DVD recording produced by Synapse Films. They are: 1: Overture; 2: Flying to Nuremberg; 3: Motorcade; 4: Night Rally; 5: Youth Encampment; 6: Farmer's March; 7: Labor Front Men; 8: Congress Hall of the NSDAP; 9: Reich Labor Service Review; 10: Viktor Lutze; 11: Hitler Youth Rally; 12: Reichswehr Review; 13: Night Rally of Political Leaders; 14: SA and SS Review; 15: Grand Review of the NSDAP; 16: Leibstandarte Bodyguards; 17: Closing Ceremonies; 18: NSDAP Hymn. In many cases, I have also provided counter numbers from the same DVD recording.

10 Barsam writes that "the lasting impression [of the scene] derives from the awesome size of the massed forces rather than from any cinematic technique or from any aspect of the director's vision" (53).

11 In addition to asserting that *Triumph of the Will* opens with the "swelling sound of the overture from Wagner's *Mastersingers*," Linda Deutschmann adds that "[t]he Wagnerian motif was apparently suggested by Riefenstahl" (28, 30). While the first assertion is incorrect, the second is at least plausible as it pertains to the use of Wagnerian motifs elsewhere in the film. Unfortunately, the second assertion is based on the argument of David Stuart Hull, who writes that "[t]he use of certain excerpts from *Die Meistersinger* was suggested by Miss Riefenstahl herself" (76), but offers no evidence for the claim. On the other hand, David Dennis has correctly refuted the notion that *Triumph of the Will* opens with quotations from *Meistersinger* (98–9).

12 Though this aspect of Hitler's regime has been commented on ever since his rise to power, recent studies have deepened our knowledge of just how extensive Hitler's debt to Wagner was. See, for example, Köhler; Spotts, *Hitler*.

13 For more on Hitler and Goebbels' conception of themselves as Master Artists, with the *Volk* as their raw material, see esp. Jürgens.

14 The Arent-Hitler production reopened the Berlin Opera in 1935, and was revived in Munich in 1936, in Danzig in 1938, at the "Festival of German Youth" in Weimar in 1939, and in Linz in 1941. See Bauer 187. Beyond these revivals, the Arent-Hitler style was widely imitated in other productions throughout Germany. The massed style was also characteristic of the style of the director Heinz Tietjen, whose 1933 Bayreuth *Meistersinger* featured enormous choruses that recalled Nazi rallies.

15 "Reichsminister Dr. Goebbels huldigt Richard Wagner," *Der Angriff* (7 August 1933: 6). Cf. "Dr. Goebbels huldigt Richard Wagner," *Hamburger Fremdenblatt* (28 May 1934); "Das Volk wartet auf das Theater," *Hamburger Fremdenblatt* (1 June 1934).

16 This occurs from 0:15:22 to 0:15:27.

17 The argument has its roots in Adorno and Horkheimer, who write that "[f]rom the outset, there has always been an intimate link between anti-Semitism and totality" (172). For a fuller discussion of totality and antisemitism in Frankfurt School thought, see Jay.

18 Barry Millington, Paul Lawrence Rose, and Marc Weiner, among others, have argued in favor of the reading of Sixtus Beckmesser as an antisemitic stereotype whose expulsion is central to the form and content of the opera. Dieter Borchmeyer, to the contrary, argues that "there are no Jewish characters in [Wagner's] music dramas, still less any anti-Semitic tendencies" ("The Question" 408). Examples on both sides of the debate can be multiplied; see Millington, "Nuremberg Trial"; Rose 112; Weiner 66–72; Borchmeyer "The Question." A recent overview of the controversy may be found in Vaget. After surveying the critical territory, Vaget argues that, "[i]f we look at the entire history of *Die Meistersinger* in Germany ... it becomes evident that anti-Semitism was not a major, let alone a determining factor in [*Meistersinger*'s] political appropriation – not even in the Third Reich" (205). Other scholars, such as David B. Dennis, have reached the same conclusion. Still, Vaget rightly concludes that "the political ramifications of Wagner's treatment of Beckmesser cannot be overlooked. It provided a model for the

marginalization of 'rejects' in general" (208). It is this model that informs my own analysis of the use of *Meistersinger*, and the location of Beckmesser, in *Triumph of the Will*.

19 In her filmed interview with Ray Müller, Riefenstahl says that "[t]here's nothing about anti-Semitism or race theory [in *Triumph of the Will*]. Work and peace are the only messages in *Triumph of the Will*." See *The Wonderful, Horrible Life of Leni Riefenstahl*, Ray Müller, dir., Image Entertainment, 2003.

20 For a fuller discussion of the importance of the Röhm purge for Hitler's total control over the German state, see Kershaw 499–526.

21 The phrase is taken from a letter Röhm wrote to Karl-Günter Heimsoth in 1928: "[n]aturally I fight against the outbreak of morality, above all against Paragraph 175 [the paragraph of the German penal code outlawing homosexuality] ... I fight most keenly with Mr. Alfred Rosenberg, that clumsy moral athlete. His articles are above all directed at my corner, since I make no secret of my inclinations. From this you can gather that even National Socialist circles have had to get used to this criminal peculiarity of mine." Quoted in Hancock 625.

22 Ultimately, an estimated 100,000 male homosexuals were arrested under the regime, of whom 5000 to 15,000 were sent to concentration camps. See Oosterhuis 188, 190, 195.

23 The only point in the film at which Hitler presents himself to women as a group is during a roughly 40-second segment at the conclusion of the "Farmer's March" (Ch. 6; 21:39–22:20), when Hitler shakes hands with select "peasant women" in traditional garb. Though he does not address these women, he does appear to say a few words to a couple of them individually.

24 See Shirer 17–18.

25 The short was inspired by Gregor Ziemer's book of the same title, a bestselling exposé of Nazi techniques for indoctrinating German youth. The short is available on the DVD collection *Walt Disney Treasures: On the Front Lines*, released by Walt Disney Home Video.

26 The short was directed by Clyde Geronimi, who was also the Supervising Director of Disney's *Sleeping Beauty*. It riffs on Disney film as well as Nazi propaganda, though of course to different ends.

27 It is always wise to check Riefenstahl's recollections against the historical record, and in this case there is some supporting evidence in the form of an interview between her and a reporter from *Paris-Midi* on 28 January 1939, which was later reproduced in the *Film-Kurier*. See Storm and Dressler 128.

28 The extent of Disney's antisemitism is a matter of debate: for different views, see Schickel 95; Mosley 207, 221; Eliot 47–51, 129, 208, 236; Gabler 454–8. Disney's views on race and unionization are also a subject of controversy. For a sharply critical view of Disney on these issues, see Mosley 185–97, 207, 221. Others have been less critical. While dubbing him racially "insensitive," Gabler concludes that "Disney was no racist" (433). Thomas (165–71) and Gabler (349f.) also offer somewhat more sympathetic accounts of Disney's stance on labor unions (expecially as exhibited during the 1941 strike of Walt Disney Studios) than that offered by Mosley.

6 Total world: Disney's theme parks

1 All Disney quotes from *The Quotable Walt Disney* will be referenced *QWD*.

2 Attempts by Germans and Austrians to resuscitate the form in recent decades have met with resistance, though several are worth mentioning. Hans-Jürgen Syberberg's film version of *Parsifal* (1982) was an explicit attempt to create a film *Gesamtkunstwerk*, and struggled ostentatiously with the heritage of Wagner (for example, setting the entire opera on an enormous reproduction of Wagner's death mask). Despite the strengths of the film, Syberberg's questionable relationship with the far right, together with his

occasional outbursts of antisemitic obscenities (most notoriously in *Vom Unglück und Glück der Kunst in Deutschland nach dem letzten Kriege*, 1990), have generally made his films unwelcome, and they are almost never shown in Germany. Among recent theatre directors, the performances of the Austrian Hermann Nitsch, especially his "Orgien Mysterien Theater," also recall the *Gesamtkunstwerk*, though less explicitly and less problematically than the films of Syberberg. The German director Hans Neuenfels and the Swiss Christoph Marthaler have also been influenced by the genre in certain of their productions, as have several other more recent artists. Intriguingly, Huyssen encourages us to understand Christo's wrapping of the Reichstag as a way of recovering the monumentality of the *Gesamtkunstwerk* while at the same time deconstructing it (*Present* 46). As such artworks suggest, the German-speaking countries, for better or worse, may be ripe for a renaissance of the form.

3 Karal Ann Marling, *Designing Disney's Theme Parks: The Architecture of Reassurance.*

4 Disney's general manager, for instance, insisted straightforwardly that "culture will kill you" (quoted in Findlay 86).

5 Disney, whose maternal grandmother was German, may have felt some familial connection to Germanic folklore. More importantly, though, Disney's films tapped into a deep and widespread American connection with German culture that was already well established (following several waves of German mass immigration) by the early decades of the twentieth century.

6 While this sequence never got beyond the design-sketch phase, the sketches for it can be seen on *Fantasia Legacy: Supplemental Features* (Walt Disney Pictures, 2000).

7 Susman specifically mentions Reinhold Niebuhr's tragic theology, Arthur Schlesinger's attacks on "historical sentimentalism," Paul Goodman's *Growing Up Absurd*, and 1940s films noirs as examples of a "new collective representation" of America, one "aware of an optimistic world gone wrong" (26, 29). To this list might be added the essays of Clement Greenberg, that central figure in the institutionalization of modernist art in Cold War America, and the figure most instrumental in defining modernism as a movement essentially opposed to mass culture.

8 See also Disney's point that "[a]lthough various sections [of Disneyland] will have the fun and flavor of a carnival or amusement park, there will be none of the 'pitches,' game wheels, sharp practices, and devices designed to milk the visitor's pocketbook" (*QWD* 49). Disneyland, as Susan Willis points out ("Problem" 4) exemplifies the bourgeois domestication of carnival traced by Peter Stallybrass and Allon White in "Bourgeois Hysteria and the Carnivalesque," in *A Cultural Studies Reader*, ed. Simon During (New York: Routledge, 1993).

9 At Walt Disney World, Sleeping Beauty's Castle was replaced by Cinderella's Castle, another Ludwig-esque construction.

10 The anthropologist Margaret King writes that the Disney parks "serve as Meccas, sacred centers, to which every American must make a double pilgrimage, first as a child [and] later as an adult with his own children" (117). King's observation of the cultic nature of Disneyland is expanded upon by anthropologist Alexander Moore, who describes the Magic Kingdom as a "bounded ritual space and playful pilgrimage center" (214). Visitors to the Kingdom, he writes, "come from afar, leave their cars behind, and enter a giant limen, a replica of a baroque capital, whose central avenue is the symbol of the dominant cultural form of nineteenth century America, Main Street. Passage through each attraction takes the form of mini-phases of separation, transition, and reincorporation as the passenger journeys past electronically manipulated symbols evoking well-known myths."

11 See also Haden-Guest 220, where Disney makes similar remarks to the evangelist Billy Graham, who dismissed the park as a "nice fantasy."

12 John Hench describes his experience of this process in Hench 30.

13 Unless otherwise indicated, all employee interviews were conducted by the author. Names have been withheld upon request.

14 For some of these remarks by Disney management, see, for example, Bierman 231, Haden-Guest 243, Apple 167.

15 To date, these parks are Disneyland Paris (formerly EuroDisney) and Tokyo Disney.

16 Developed by the Walt Disney Company and originally run by a subsidiary of the Company, Celebration aims, in the words of its official website, to "take the best ideas from the most successful towns of yesterday and the technology of the new millennium, and synthesize them into a close-knit community that meets the needs of today's families." In addition, it boasts the advantage of "corporate citizenship" rather than real citizenship for its residents, which essentially translates into the elimination of democratic local government in favor of direct corporate control. At least until Disney largely divested itself of the venture, Celebration represented another permutation of the basic strategy of interlocking total performances, and yet went beyond the theme parks in the project of the aestheticization of society. Notable studies of Celebration are Franz and Collins; Roost; Ross, *Celebration*. In 2004, Disney published its own account of the town; see Lassell. The town's website may be found at http://www.celebrationfl.com; all quotations are taken from the site (accessed 2 June 2005).

17 Steve Nelson analyzes EPCOT's relation to the World's Fair expositions in "Walt Disney's EPCOT and the World's Fair Performance Tradition," *The Drama Review* 30.4 (Winter, 1986) 106–46.

18 See, for instance, Michael Wolf, *The Entertainment Economy* (New York: Times Business, 1999); B. Joseph Pine II and James H. Gilmore, *The Experience Economy: Work Is Theatre and Every Business a Stage* (Boston: Harvard Business School Press, 1999); Bernd Schmitt, *Experiential Marketing: How To Get Your Customers To Sense, Feel, Think, Act, and Relate to Your Company and Brands* (New York: Free Press, 1999).

7 Total vacuum: Warhol's performances

1 Riefensthal writes of first meeting Warhol at the Factory in 1974, in her *Memoir* (601–2). While Warhol's *Diary* doesn't begin until 1976, Bob Colacello (the editor of *Interview*) describes the meeting in his book *Holy Terror: Andy Warhol Close Up* (1990). Riefenstahl talked with Warhol about her recently released bestseller *The Last of the Nuba*, "pointing out the 'elegance' of this Nubian's back or the 'strength' of that Nubian's legs." "She's great," Warhol commented after Riefenstahl had left. "She doesn't care about politics. She just cares about beauties." "He could have been talking about himself," adds Colacello (259).

2 Warhol's first "Factory," located at 221 East 47th Street, was his studio (and general headquarters) from 1963 to 1967. At the end of 1967, the Factory moved to 33 Union Square West; it was in the new building that Valerie Solanis attempted to kill Warhol in 1968. Though the Factory continued until Warhol's death, its character changed radically after the attempt on Warhol's life, with much more attention given to security, and much less of an open-door policy. The transformation in the culture of the Factory is one aspect of a larger transformation in Warhol's work, which became much more commercially oriented and less counter-cultural after the Solanis incident.

3 The influence of drugs on the creation, reception, and formal features of multimedia *Gesamtkunstwerke*, especially in the 1960s and 70s, should not be underestimated. In 1966, Sterling Morrison remarked that, under LSD, "[y]ou stop thinking of [the *Exploding Plastic Inevitable*] as a series of lights and movies and music and you start seeing it as one abstract whole" (quoted Bockris and Melanga 56). In their study of the Velvet Underground, Bockris and Melanga note that the proto-punk style of the Velvets "may have had something to do with the fact that a number of the people involved in the production

were on amphetamine, a drug which, among other effects, influences consumers to respond to everything with its mirror, or exactly opposite, image" (29). More explicitly, Timothy Leary's League for Spiritual Discovery (LSD), which met at the Fillmore East, was both directly influenced by the *Exploding Plastic Inevitable* and utterly unimaginable without acid. "He's doing a complete copy of our Exploding Plastic Inevitable show!" shouted Paul Morrissey after attending Leary's production (quoted in Warhol and Hackett 184).

4 Morrissey: "[t]he term 'Exploding Plastic Inevitable' came from sitting around with Gerard and Barbara Rubin thinking of a name [in April 1966]. I picked up a record album with Barbara on the back massaging Bob Dylan's head ('Bringing It All Back Home'). There were some amphetamine Bob Dylan gibberish liner-notes. I looked without reading and saw these words appear: something was 'exploding,' something was 'plastic,' something was 'inevitable.' I said, 'Why not call it *Exploding Plastic Inevitable*, The Velvet Underground and Nico?'" (quoted in Bockris and Melanga 31). Morrissey's recollection differs from that of Warhol, who recollects the original name as being "*Erupting* Plastic Inevitable" in January and February 1966, two to three months before Morrissey's account takes place (Warhol and Hackett 152).

5 Lewis Lapham, for instance, writes that Warhol, along with Robert Rauschenberg, "appointed [McLuhan] to the office of honorary muse" (x).

6 For an account of the origin and development of Happenings in the 1950s and 60s, see Michael Kirby.

7 The phrase is underground film critic Jonas Mekas' description of Warhol's involvement in *Exploding Plastic Inevitable* (quoted in Bockris 247).

8 I share this position with Taylor; see Taylor 198.

9 In so far as it attempted to recapture a less-alienated site of labor, Warhol's work represents a version of the project of art generally within capitalist society. A significant element of the romance of the artist is that he or she pretends to exist outside the sphere of capital relations and is thus supposedly able to labor in a non-alienated fashion. The artist thus represents the possibility of authentic existence even as he or she serves as a public example of the extraordinarily exceptional nature of this authenticity. Presented as rare exotic birds, artists remind the public that non-alienated labor is not a general possibility. Presented as suffering sociopaths, artists remind the public that non-alienated labor may not even be so desirable after all. One paradox of Warhol is that he exposes the rootlessness of this romance even as he (partially) seeks to recover it.

10 Though the expansion of commodity culture to the entire world was already well on its way to becoming a reality by 1960, the expansion of American-style consumerism was not then, nor is likely ever to be, a practical possibility. As Peter Taylor comments: "[i]n its heyday in 1960 the USA with approximately one-fifteenth of the world's population was using about one-third of the world's resources. Obviously this provides no basis for general imitation. In fact, one estimate of the carrying capacity of the world assuming an American standard of living is 600 million people, a figure passed in 1675, before the USA, let alone the American dream, was ever thought of" (283).

11 Opposed to Baudrillard's reading of Warhol are a number of critics. Rainer Crone, for instance, has argued for a Brechtian interpretation of Warhol's work. For Crone, Warhol's avant-garde reproductions of mass-cultural images estrange the viewer and thus provide, at least implicitly, a critique of the commercial world from which these images emerge. In a very different vein, Thomas Crow locates the critical nature of Warhol's art in the "straightforward expressions of feeling" that they evoke, as well as the "nuance and subtlety of response that is his alone" (317). By encouraging empathic identification with such tragic figures of cultural production as Liz Taylor and Marilyn Monroe, Warhol's work, according to Crow, exposes the brutal realities behind "complacent consumption" (322). My aim in this chapter is to develop a reading

between, on one hand, that of Baudrillard, Deleuze, Barthes, and Bürger, and, on the other, that of Crone and Crow. In other words, I want to read Warhol's work, especially in the 1960s and 70s, as neither quite simulacral nor quite critical, but as ambiguous, enigmatic, campy, and sly.

12 With tongue who-knows-how-much in cheek, Warhol repeatedly denied the political import of these images. One instance: speaking to Warhol of his silkscreens of 1960s race riots, Claus Oldenburg said, "When you repeat a race riot, I am not sure you have done a race riot. I do not see it as a political statement but rather as an expression of indifference to your subject." "It is indifference," was Warhol's answer (Lombardo 36).

13 Fredric Jameson's comments in this regard are astute. "Andy Warhol's work in fact turns centrally around commodification, and the great billboard images of the Coca-Cola bottle or the Campbell's soup can, which explicitly foreground the commodity fetishism of a transition to late capital, *ought* to be powerful and critical political statements. If they are not that, then one would surely want to know why, and one would want to begin to wonder a little more seriously about the possibilities of political or critical art in the postmodern period of late capital" (*Postmodernism* 9).

14 "Stated very simply, representation in the system of commerce is that which arises from a singular act; repetition is that which is mass-produced. Thus, a concert is a representation, but so is a meal à la carte in a restaurant; a phonograph record or a can of food is repetition" (Attali 41).

15 Are definitions even possible? Charles Ludlam (who ought to know) dismisses the whole enterprise, saying "I don't think camp can be defined" (227). And Charles, in Christopher Isherwood's *The World in the Evening*, calls *camp* "terribly difficult to define. You have to meditate on it and feel it intuitively, like Laotse's *Tao*" (106). But he then proceeds to divide the term into two categories, Low and High, about which he has a fair bit to say. Similarly, Susan Sontag notes that "[t]o talk about Camp is … to betray it" (275), just before going on to talk about it, campishly, in 58 numbered paragraphs. Beginning in the early 1990s, occasional speculation about the nature and function of "camp" has exploded into the academic version of a Cecil B. DeMille production, complete with papers, panels, articles, anthologies (four, by my count), and book-length studies (five). On this increasingly crowded stage, Matthew Tinkcom's *Working Like a Homosexual: Camp, Capital, Cinema* stands out, and his reading of camp especially influences my own.

16 In 1972, Warhol withdrew most of his films from public circulation, and thereafter left the production of his films to others. Tinkcom notes that the disappearance of the pre-1972 films came at precisely the period of post-Stonewall liberation and identity politics. This unfortunate convergence may account for the lack of attention these films have received in most critical and historical accounts.

17 I am indebted to Annette Michelson for drawing my attention to "Where Is Your Rupture"; see Michelson.

18 *Fear of Music*, once more, comes to mind. "What is happening to my skin?" sings David Byrne in the panicky "Air." "Where is the protection that I needed? / Air can hurt you too."

8 Total immersion: cyberspace and the total work of art

1 The word "cyberspace" originates in a 1982 story entitled "Burning Chrome," which Gibson wrote for *Omni* magazine 72.2. It was popularized, however, by its use in Gibson's cyberpunk novel *Neuromancer* (1984). In a 1994 interview with Dan Josefsson, Gibson emphasized the idea of cyberspace as a realm of electronic communication, including telephone calls, Internet use, and "electronic communication between the world's stock-exchanges" (Gibson, "I Don't"). In *Neuromancer*, cyberspace is both a fully immersive and a massively networked universe.

2 Further information on these installations can be found at: www.immersence.com.

3 Davies's immersant is thus almost the opposite of Donna Haraway's "cyborg." While the immersant in Davies' amniotic cyberspace fits Haraway's conception in certain respects – becoming what Haraway calls "a cybernetic organism, a hybrid of machine and organism" (149) – the immersant is the very antithesis of Haraway's conception of the cyborg as a creature that "has no truck with … seductions to organic wholeness" (150). Haraway's cyborg is a hybrid rather than a synthesis, whose mode is irony rather than organic unity. In this sense, Haraway's "cyborg" is the enemy (though perhaps also the bastard child) of the *Gesamtkunstwerk*.

4 The centrality of breath in *Osmose* brings Wagner's aesthetics once more to mind. As Friedrich Kittler has pointed out, breath is one of Wagner's primary elements, not only a recurring symbol in his libretti but a basic model for his music. Examples of this "respiratory eroticism" include Sieglinde and Siegmund's opening and closing scenes in *Die Walküre*, Kurwenal listening to Tristan's breath in *Tristan and Isolde*, and Isolde's final aria to the "wafting breath" of the world. Indeed, Kittler argues that "[Wagnerian] music-drama as a whole … could be analyzed as the curve of a single, large breath" (262). The revolution of Wagner's music-dramas, according to Kittler, is that they highlighted the physiological source of song in human breath. Wagnerian music-dramas thus exhibit "sound" rather than verbal meaning, and anticipate the techniques of modern mass media.

5 The Internet first came into being in 1969 as ARPANET (an acronym for the Advanced Research Projects Agency, the Pentagon agency that funded it). In its early years, its use was strictly limited to scientific and military communications.

6 "Telematics," as Ascott defines it, "is a term used to designate computer-mediated communications networking involving telephone, cable, and satellite links between geographically dispersed individuals and institutions that are interfaced to data-processing systems, remote sensing devices, and capacious data-storage banks" ("Is" 241). The "Infomedia Notepad System" was developed by French astrophysicist Jacques Vallee. For more on Ascott, see Shanken.

7 Such techno-maternal fantasies, in both their positive and negative forms, saturate contemporary culture, with cyberspace regularly imagined as good and bad mother, the all-embracing spider at the heart of the Web, the Mamma behind the motherboard. This maternal conception of cyberspace is possibly linked to the modernist gendering of mass culture as "Woman." See Huyssen, *After* 44–62; Ronell *passim*.

8 The so-called "digital divide" between digital haves and have-nots has geographic, class-based, and ethnic-based components. Matthew Zook has authored three studies of the geographic divide, and maintains a website on his ongoing research. See also Wheeler *et al.*

9 E.g. Herman and McChesney; McChesney; Barney; Lessing, *Code*; Hardt and Negri 298–300.

10 According to Lévy's definition of "cyberspace," the World Wide Web (a marriage of hypertext technology with the Internet, made widely available to the public in 1993) is a subset of the larger phenomenon of cyberspace. It is, however, a collaborative creation that exhibits many of the traits of cyberspace particularly well. In David Weinberger's understanding, the Web is a "self-organizing, self-stimulated growth of contents and links on a scale the world has literally never before experienced … The result is a loose federation of documents – many small pieces loosely joined" (ix). This description of the Web also bears a number of similarities to Lévy's description of cyberspace.

11 Note that what Lévy calls "cyberspace" is roughly synonymous with what I call "networked cyberspace."

12 On the fundamental difference between networked cyberspace and previous media such as the telephone, radio, and television, Mark Poster is largely in agreement with Lévy. See Poster, "Digital" 101.

13 Lévy's insistence, which I share, on the crucial differences between cyberspace and television is not the same as an insistence on a difference between cyberspace and "the televisual." The televisual, understood as a cultural formation in which television is an "intrinsic and determining element" (Auslander 2), may well be broad enough a category to include both VR and networked cyberspace. Auslander seems to incline toward the view that the televisual includes digitality (and thus, presumably, cyberspace), while Causey explicitly argues for this view. See Auslander 38; Causey 183.

14 Lévy's views are not uncontroversial, however. For a cogent argument contra Lévy, see esp. Cochran. Cochran argues that Lévy's "universality" smuggles "totality" back in through the backdoor, and thus that Lévy's "universality without totality" is at best mistaken and at worst deceptive. I do not agree that Lévy's "universality" is ultimately another form of totalizing discourse, but a full defense of Lévy's theories of cyberspace lies beyond the scope of this chapter.

15 In common usage, the term *avatar* (from the Sanskrit *avatara*) means the earthly incarnation of a god. In VR discourse, it denotes the virtual embodiment in visual form of a networked individual. This latter meaning derives from Neil Stephenson's cyberpunk novel *Snow Crash*.

16 More information on *World of Warcraft* may be found at the game's homepage: www. worldofwarcraft.com.

17 While the sword-and-sorcery genre is most popular, science fiction subgenres ranging from space opera (*Star Wars Galaxies*) to cyberpunk (*EVE Online*) are also common. Other virtual worlds are also available, such as contemporary American life (*The Sims Online*) and a multiplicity of player-created spaces (*Second Life*). These last two worlds are significantly less conflict-oriented than most MMORPGs. *Second Life* has additionally embraced the fluidity of identity in cyberspace by, for example, allowing players to radically alter the appearance of their avatar at any time.

18 "Leveling services" – that is, businesses that play a character for a client until the character reaches a desired level – make the equation between levels and labor time plain in their pricing plans. One such business promises to raise a *World of Warcraft* character from level 1 to level 60 for $450, at an estimated time of 392 hours (Dark Horse).

19 Adorno is eloquent on this collapse; see esp. *Minima* 130–1; "Free Time" *passim*. For an account of the labor involved in leading a *Warcraft* guild, see Butts, "My Second Job."

20 Some of these guilds have numbers in the hundreds of members, and maintain a strong community presence both within the game (where members can communicate on "guild chat" lines) and outside the game (in the form of website bulletin boards and, occasionally, "real-world" get-togethers). The game itself encourages these communal activities by providing services for guilds and by making many quests impossible to complete without group cooperation. Virtual communities similar to those that exist in *Warcraft* have been studied by, for example, Baym; Rheingold; Turkle.

21 While the "human" race often combines this territoriality with crusader spirituality (particularly exemplified in the class of the "paladin"), other races tend more strongly toward nature mysticism. In the realm of the elves, for example, the player is continually reminded of the importance of maintaining nature's "balance." The character class of "druid," similarly, "lives in a state of unparalleled union with nature." In many cases, this nature mysticism is combined with a familiar narrative of tragic savagery. For instance, in the cinematic opening to the "tauren" race (which looks like a cross between humans and buffalo, and is apparently meant to evoke the Plains Indians), we are given a story of their destruction by other races and are told that their "shamen exemplify the primal bond between the savage races and their environment."

22 My own guide through *Warcraft*, Vihanei (aka Erin Snyder), belongs to a guild inspired

by the altruism of Hindu holy men. The website of the guild, "Sadhus of the Smoke," may be found at: http://sadhus.guildportal.com.

23 While much of what Jameson writes about fantasy's deficiencies is indeed true of Tolkien-esque sword-and-sorcery (and thus of *Warcraft*), it would seem to apply nearly as well to Lucas-like space operas, thus disturbing the opposition between fantasy and science fiction. The distinction breaks down even further when one considers sophisticated writers who work between genres, and who combine a taste for the fantastical with an interest in speculative material history. Jameson writes with characteristic brilliance on a few of these writers (notably Ursula Le Guin), but more could be said about the ways in which their genre-crossing work blurs boundaries between fantasy and SF. For a good introduction to some of these writers, see Miéville.

24 If you die in the game then your ghost emerges in a nearby "graveyard," and you have various options about how to bring your character back to life. *Warcraft* is actually most similar, not to the Christian heaven, but to the Valhalla of Norse myth, where dismemberment is only a temporary interruption in a never-ending festive battle.

25 Such totalizing creations threaten to overwhelm the very real potential of the Internet for critique and political emancipation. And yet they are not necessary formations. As Rebecca Schneider and Jill Lane have shown, artist/activist groups such as Critical Art Ensemble and Electronic Disturbance Theatre have made use of the Internet for interventions that combine Web-based performance with a host of other media, including video, film, text, visual art, and live theatre. On a broader scale, virtual political groups such as Daily Kos are exploring the potential of networked cyberspace for purposes of political resistance and social mediation. Though generally referred to as a blog ("web-log"), Daily Kos might be better described as a multidimensional community of networked activists. Averaging roughly half a million visits per day in 2006, organizing its own annual convention (YearlyKos), and sharply influencing political races such as Ned Lamont's 2006 primary challenge to Joe Lieberman, Daily Kos is a forceful exemplar of the power of the Internet for political mediation. At its most promising, Daily Kos suggests that Hardt's concerns about the "withering away of civil society" in "the smooth surfaces of cyberspace" may simply mean the replacement of a pre-digital civil society with a digital one. It also suggests that "netizens" are often most politically effective when the deterritoriality of the Internet is made to serve local or national political ends. Netizenship, in other words, may work most effectively when working in tandem with citizenship, or at least with allegiance to specific local movements. Needless to say, progressives are not the only ones to grasp this concept; for an American conservative virtual community, see: www.redstate.com. See Lane; Schneider; Hardt, "Withering" 32.

26 The installation has shown internationally and is in the permanent collection of the San Jose Museum of Art. A website devoted to the piece may be found at: http://mission.base.com/manzanar.

27 Unless otherwise noted, all quotes from Thiel and Houshmand are from interviews and email exchanges with the artists.

28 Houshmand: "Certainly, when I worked with Bijan Mofid, Brecht was a very, very big influence on me."

Works cited

Adorno, Theodor W. *Ästhetische Theorie*. Ed. Gretel Adorno and Rolf Tiedemann. Frankfurt am Main: Suhrkamp, 1970.

—— "Correspondence with Benjamin." Trans. Harry Zohn. *New Left Review* 81 (1973): 55–80.

—— "Der dialektische Komponist." In *Arnold Schönberg zum 60. Geburtstag* (Vienna 1934). *Impromptus: Zweite Folge neu gedruckter musikalischer Aufsätze*. Frankfurt am Main: Suhrkamp, 1968.

—— "Free Time." *Critical Models: Interventions and Catchwords*. Trans. Henry W. Pickford. New York: Columbia University Press, 2005. 167–76.

—— *In Search of Wagner*. Trans. Rodney Livingstone. New York: Verso, 1981.

—— *Minima Moralia*. Trans. E. F. N. Jephcott. London: Verso, 1978.

—— "On the Score of *Parsifal*." Trans. Anthony Barone. *Music & Letters* 76:3 (1995): 384–97.

Adorno, Theodor W. and Max Horkheimer. *Dialectic of Enlightenment*. Trans. John Cumming. New York: Continuum, 1999.

Altick, Richard. *The Shows of London*. Cambridge, MA: Belknap Press, 1978.

Apple, Michael. "Uncle Walt." *Esquire* (December 1983): 164–8.

Ascott, Roy. "Behaviourist Art and the Cybernetic Vision." *Cybernetica: revue de l'Association internationale de cybernetique*. Part 1: 9:4 (1966): 247–64. Part 2: 10:1 (1967): 25–56.

—— "Beyond Boundaries." In *Art, Technology, Consciousness*. Portland, OR: Intellect, 2000.

—— "Gesamtdatenwerk: Konnektivität, Transformation und Transzendenz." *Kunstform International* 103 (1989): 100–6.

—— "Is There Love in a Telematic Embrace?" *Art Journal* 49 (1990): 241–7.

—— "Technoetic Structures." *Architectural Design* 68:11/12 (1998): 30–3.

AT&T. "AT&T Unveils New World." Press Release, 10 October 2004. Available at: www.att.com/press/0295/950201.csa.html (accessed 1 February 1995).

Attali, Jacques. *Noise: The Political Economy of Music*. Trans. Brian Massumi. Minneapolis, MN: University of Minnesota Press, 1985.

Auslander, Philip. *Liveness: Performance in a Mediatized Culture*. New York: Routledge, 1999.

Barboza, David. "Ogre to Slay? Outsource it to Chinese." *New York Times* 9 December 2005.

Barney, Darin. *Prometheus Wired*. Chicago, IL: University of Chicago Press, 2000.

Barsam, Richard Meran. *Filmguide to Triumph of the Will*. Bloomington, IN: Indiana University Press, 1975.

Barthes, Roland. "That Old Thing, Art … " In *Pop Art: The Critical Dialogue*. Ed. Carol Anne Mahsun. Ann Arbor, MI: UMI Research Press, 1989.

Baudrillard, Jean. *The Consumer Society: Myths and Structures*. London: Sage Publications, 1998.

Bauer, Oswald Georg. *Richard Wagner: The Stage Designs and Productions from the Premières to the Present*. New York: Rizzoli, 1983.

Baumann, Carl-Friedrich. *Bühnentechnik im Festspielhaus Bayreuth*. Munich: Prestel-Verlag, 1980.

Baym, Nancy. "The Emergence of On-line Community." In *Cybersociety 2.0: Revisiting Computer Mediated Communication and Community*. Ed. Steve Jones. Thousand Oaks, CA: Sage, 1998. 35–68.

Beacham, Frank. "Net Loss." *EXTRA!* (May/June 1996): 16.

Beckett, Lucy. "'Parsifal' As Drama." *Music & Letters* 52:3 (1971): 259–71.

Benjamin, Walter. "The Author as Producer." In *Understanding Brecht*. Trans. Anna Bostock. New York: Verso, 1998. 85–103.

—— *Gesammelte Schriften*. Frankfurt am Main: Suhrkamp, 1972.

—— "Paris, Capital of the Nineteenth Century." In *Reflections: Essays, Aphorisms, Autobiographical Writings*. Trans. Edmund Jephcott. New York: Schocken, 1986. 146–62.

Bentley, Eric. *The Brecht Commentaries*. New York: Grove Press, 1981.

Berg, Gretchen. "Andy Warhol: My True Story." In Goldsmith 85–96.

Berghahn, Klaus L. "Nachwort. Ästhetische Utopie und schöner Stil." In Schiller, *Über die ästhetische Erziehung*. 253–86.

Berghaus, Günter. "A Theatre of Image, Sound and Motion: On Synaesthesia and the Idea of a Total Work of Art." *Maske und Kothurn* 32:1–2 (1986): 7–28.

Berlioz, Hector. *Traité d'instrumentation et d'orchestration*. Paris: H. Lemoine, 1925.

Bermbach, Udo. *Der Wahn des Gesamtkunstwerks: Richard Wagners politsch-ästhetische Utopie*. Frankfurt am Main: Fischer Taschenbuch, 1994.

Betsky, Aaron. "The Cutler Edge." *Metropolitan Home* 28:3 (1996): 86–90.

Bierman, James. "The Walt Disney Robot Dramas." *Yale Review* 66 (December 1976): 223–36.

Bloch, Ernst. "Über Wurzeln des Nazismus." In *Politische Messungen, Pestzeit, Vormärz. Gesamtausgabe*. Frankfurt am Main: Suhrkamp, 1970.

Bockris, Victor. *Warhol*. New York: Da Capo, 1997.

Bockris, Victor and Gerard Melanga. *Up-Tight. The Velvet Underground Story*. New York: Cooper Square Press, 2003.

Borchmeyer, Dieter. *Richard Wagner: Theory and Theatre*. New York: Oxford University Press, 1991.

—— "The Question of Anti-Semitism." In *The Wagner Handbook*. Ed. Ulrich Müller and Peter Wapnewski. Trans. Stewart Spencer. Cambridge, MA: Harvard University Press, 1992.

Bordwell, David. "The Musical Analogy." *Yale French Studies* 60.1 (1980): 141–56.

Brecht, Bertolt. *Arbeitsjournal*. Ed. Werner Hecht. Frankfurt am Main: Suhrkamp, 1973.

—— *Bertolt Brecht on Film and Radio*. Ed. and trans. Marc Silberman. London: Methuen, 2000.

—— *Brecht on Theatre*. Ed. and trans. John Willett. New York: Hill and Wang, 1996.

—— *Große kommentierte Berliner und Frankfurter Ausgabe*. 30 vols. Frankfurt am Main: Suhrkamp, 1992.

—— *The Mother*. Trans. Lee Baxandall. New York: Grove, 1965.

—— *"The Rise and Fall of the City of Mahagonny" and "The Seven Deadly Sins."* Ed. John Willett and Ralph Manheim. Trans. W. H. Auden and Chester Kallman. New York: Arcade Publishing, 1996.

Brenkman, John. "Mass Media: From Collective Experience to the Culture of Privatization." *Social Text* 1 (Winter 1979): 101.

Brenner, Hildegard. *Die Kunstpolitik des Nationalsozialismus.* Reinbek bei Hamburg: Rowohlt, 1963.

Bronfen, Elisabeth. "Kundry's Laughter." *New German Critique* 69 (1996): 147–61.

Brontë, Charlotte. Letter of 12 January 1851. In *The Brontës: Their Lives, Friendships and Correspondence.* 4 vols. Ed. Thomas James Wise and John Alexander Symington. Oxford: Blackwell, 1932.

Brown, Tally. Interview, 11 November 1978. In Patrick S. Smith, *Andy Warhol's Art and Films.* Ann Arbor: UMI Research Press, 1986.

Bryman, Alan. *Disney and his Worlds.* New York: Routledge, 1995.

Buck-Morss, Susan. "The City as Dreamworld and Catastrophe." *October* 73 (1995): 2–36.

Bürger, Peter. *Theory of the Avant-Garde.* Trans. Michael Shaw. Minneapolis: University of Minnesota Press, 1999.

Butts, Whitney. "My Second Job." *The Escapist* 56. Available at: www.escapistmagazine. com/issue/56 (accessed 4 November 2006).

Carroll, Lewis. *The Diaries of Lewis Carroll.* 2 vols. Ed. Roger Lancelyn Green. London: Cassell, 1953.

Case, Sue-Ellen. *The Domain-Matrix: Performing Lesbian at the End of Print Culture.* Bloomington, IN: Indiana University Press, 1996.

Casson, Herbert N. "Dramatisieren Sie Ihr Schaufenster!" *Schaufenster – Kunst und Technik* January 1930: 14.

Castells, Manuel. *The Internet Galaxy: Reflections on the Internet, Business, and Society.* Oxford: Oxford University Press, 2001.

Castronova, Edward. "Virtual Worlds: A First-Hand Account of Market and Society on the Cyberian Frontier." CESifo Working Paper No. 618, December 2001.

—— *Synthetic Worlds: The Business and Culture of Online Games.* Chicago, IL: University of Chicago Press, 2005.

Causey, Matthew. "Postorganic Performance: The Appearance of Theater in Virtual Spaces." In *Cyberspace Textuality.* Ed. Marie-Laurie Ryan. Bloomington, IN: Indiana University Press, 1999. 182–201.

Certeau Michel de. *The Practice of Everyday Life.* Trans. Steven Rendall. Berkeley, CA: University of California Press, 1988.

Chytry, Josef. *The Aesthetic State: A Quest in Modern German Thought.* Berkeley, CA: University of California Press, 1989.

Coates, Paul. "Cinema, Symbolism, and the *Gesamtkunstwerk.*" *Comparative Criticism* 4 (1982): 213–29.

Cochran, Terry. "Thinking at the Edge of the Galaxy: Pierre Lévy's World Projection." *boundary* 2:26(3) (Autumn 1999): 63–85.

Colacello, Bob. *Holy Terror: Andy Warhol Close Up.* New York: HarperCollins, 1990.

Conrads, Ulrich. *Programmes and Manifestoes on 20th Century Architecture.* Trans. Michael Bullock. Cambridge, MA: MIT Press, 1970. Original German version: *Programme und Manifeste zur Architektur des 20. Jahrhunderts.* Berlin: Ullstein, 1964.

Cotterill, Rowland. "In Defense of *Mahagonny.*" In *Culture and Society in the Weimar Republic.* Ed. Keith Bullivant. Manchester: Manchester University Press, 1977.

Coyne, Richard. *Technoromanticism: Digital Narrative, Holism, and the Romance of the Real.* Cambridge, MA: MIT Press, 1999.

Crary, Jonathan. *Suspensions of Perception: Attention, Spectacle, and Modern Culture*. Cambridge, MA: MIT Press, 1999.

Croce, Paul Jerome. "A Clean and Separate Space: Walt Disney in Person and Production." *Journal of Popular Culture* 25.3 (1991): 91–103.

Crone, Rainer. *Andy Warhol*. New York: Praeger, 1970.

Crow, Thomas. "Saturday Disasters: Trace and Reference in Early Warhol." In *Reconstructing Modernism: Art in New York, Paris and Montreal, 1945–1964*. Ed. Serge Guilbaut. Cambridge, MA: MIT Press, 1990. 311–31.

"Cyberspace." *Encarta Encyclopedia*. Available at: http://encarta.msn.com (accessed 14 February 2005).

Dark Horse Powerleveling Studio. Available at: www.ilevelu.com (accessed 9 August 2006).

Davidson, George. *Bayreuther Briefe. Augenblicksbilder aus den Tagen der Patronatsaufführungen des "Parsifal"*. Leipzig: publisher unknown, 1882.

Davies, Char. "Changing Space: Virtual Reality as an Arena of Embodied Being." In Packer and Jordan 293–302.

—— "OSMOSE: Notes on Being in Immersive Virtual Space." *Digital Creativity* 9.2: 65–74.

—— "Rethinking VR: Key Concepts and Concerns." Available at: www.immersence. com/publications/char/CDavies-RethinkingVR-N.html (accessed 9 January 2007). Also available in *Hybrid Reality: Art, Technology and the Human Factor*. Ninth International Conference on Virtual Systems and Multimedia. Ed. Hal Thwaites. Montreal: International Society on Virtual Systems and Multimedia, 2003.

Davies, Char and John Harrison. "Osmose: Towards Broadening the Aesthetics of Virtual Reality." *ACM Computer Graphics: Virtual Reality* 33:4 (1996).

Davis, Eric. *Technosis: Myth, Magic + Mysticism in the Age of Information*. New York: Three Rivers Press, 1998.

Deak, Frantisek. *Symbolist Theater: The Formation of the Avant-Garde*. Baltimore, MD: Johns Hopkins University Press, 1993.

Debord, Guy. *The Society of the Spectacle*. Trans. Donald Nicholson-Smith. New York: Zone Books, 1995.

Deleuze, Gilles. *Cinema 1: The Movement-Image*. Trans. Hugh Tomlinson and Barbara Habberjam. Minneapolis, MN. University Minnesota Press, 1986.

—— *Difference and Repetition*. Trans. Paul Patton. Columbia: Columbia University Press, 1968.

—— *Cinema 2: The Time-Image*. Trans. Hugh Tomlinson and Robert Galeta. Minneapolis, MN: University of Minnesota Press, 1989.

Dennis, David. "'The Most German of All German Operas': *Die Meistersinger* through the Lens of the Third Reich." In *Wagner's Meistersinger: Performance, History, Representation*. Ed. Nicholas Vazsonyi. Rochester, NY: University of Rochester Press, 2002.

Deutsche Akademie der Künste zu Berlin, ed. *Erwin Piscator: Political Theatre 1920–1966*. Trans. Margaret Vallance. London: Arts Council, 1971.

Deutschmann, Linda. *Triumph of the Will: The Image of the Third Reich*. Wakefield, NH: Longwood, 1991.

DFC Intelligence. "Online Game Market Is Growing but Making Money is Difficult." Press Release, 25 June 2003. Available at: www.dfcint.com/news/prjune252003.html (accessed 13 December 2005).

Disney, Walt. "The Cartoon's Contribution to Children." *Overland Monthly and the Out West Magazine* 91.8 (1933): 138.

—— *The Quotable Walt Disney*. New York: Disney Editions, 2001.

Disney Institute. *Be Our Guest: Perfecting the Art of Customer Service*. New York: Disney Editions, 2001.

Disney University. "Disney Way I: The Disney Difference." Unpublished training manual. Collection of the author.

"Disneyland Offers 'Pleasure for Children and Adults.'" *Look* 2 November 1954: 82–9.

Ehrler, Hans Heinrich. "Reise nach Berlin." In *Glänzender Asphalt: Berlin im Feuilleton der Weimarer Republik*. Ed. Christian Jäger and Erhard Schütz. Berlin: Fannei und Walz, 1994. 25.

Einem, Gottfried von and Siegfried Melchinger, eds. *Caspar Neher: Bühne und bildende Kunst im XX. Jahrhundert*. Velber bei Hannover: Friedrich Verlag, 1966.

Eisenstein, Sergei. *Film Essays*. Ed. and trans. Jay Leyda. New York: Praeger, 1970.

—— *Film Form*. Ed. and trans. Jay Leyda. New York: Harvest, 1949.

Eliade, Mircea. *The Sacred and the Profane*. New York: Harcourt Brace Jovanovich, 1987.

Eliot, Marc. *Walt Disney: Hollywood's Dark Prince*. Secaucus, NJ: Carol Publishing Group, 1993.

Emery, Elizabeth and Laura Morowitz. *Consuming the Past: The Medieval Revival in Fin-de-siècle France*. Burlington, VT: Ashgate, 2003.

Enzensberger, Hans Magnus. "Constituents of a Theory of Media." In *Electronic Culture*. Ed. Timothy Druckrey. New York: Aperture, 1996.

Enzensberger, Christian. *Smut: An Anatomy of Dirt*. Trans. Sandra Morris. London: Calder and Boyars, 1972.

Esslin, Martin. *Brecht: The Man and his Work*. Garden City, NY: Anchor Books, 1961.

"Father Goose." *Time* 27 December 1954: 42–6.

Feher, Ferenc. "Negative Philosophy of Music – Positive Results." *New German Critique* 4 (Winter 1975): 99–111.

Feild, Robert D. *The Art of Walt Disney*. New York: Macmillan, 1942.

Findlay, John. *Magic Lands*. Berkeley, CA: University of California Press, 1992.

Finger, Anke. "The Poetics of Cultural Unity: Gesamtkunstwerk and the Discourse of National Arts in German and American Cultures." Dissertation, Brandeis University, 1997.

Fischer-Lichte, Erika. "Das 'Gesamtkunstwerk.' Ein Konzept für die Kunst der achtziger Jahre?" In *Dialog der Künste: Intermediale Fallstudien zur Literatur des 19. und 20. Jahrhunderts*. Ed. Maria Moog-Grünewald and Christoph Rodieck. Frankfurt: Peter Lang, 1989. 61–74.

Fjellman, Stephen. *Vinyl Leaves: Walt Disney World and America*. Boulder, CO: Westview, 1992.

Forkel, Johann Nicolaus. "Genauere Bestimmung einiger musikalischer Begriffe." *Magazin der Muzik*. 1 November 1783: 1063–4.

Förster, Bernhard. "Das Bühnenweihfestspiel von Bayreuth." *Zeitschrift für bildende Kunst*. Jahrg. 17 (1882): 325f.

Foster, Thomas. "The Souls of Cyber-Folk: Performativity, Virtual Embodiment, and Racial Histories." In *Cyberspace Textuality*. Ed. Marie-Louise Ryan. Bloomington, IN: Indiana University Press, 1999.

Franciscono, Marcel. *Walter Gropius and the Creation of the Bauhaus in Weimar*. Chicago, IL: University of Illinois Press, 1971.

Franz, Douglas and Catherine Collins. *Celebration U.S.A.: Living in Disney's Brave New Town*. New York: Henry Holt and Co., 1999.

Fricke, Richard. *Bayreuth vor dreissig Jahren: Erinnerungen an Wahnfried und aus dem Festspielhaus.* Stuttgart: Hans-Dieter Heinz–Akademischer Verlag, 1983.

Fuegi, John. *Bertolt Brecht: Chaos, According to Plan.* Cambridge: Cambridge University Press, 1998.

—— *Brecht and Company: Sex, Politics, and the Making of the Modern Drama.* New York: Grove, 1994.

Gabler, Neil. *Walt Disney: The Triumph of the American Imagination.* New York: Knopf, 2006.

Gadamer, Hans-Georg. *Truth and Method.* Second rev. edn. Trans. Joel Weinsheimer and Donald G. Marshall. New York: Continuum, 1996.

Gallo, Max. *The Night of the Long Knives.* Trans. Lily Emmet. New York: Harper and Row, 1972.

Gates, Bill, with Nathan Myhrvold and Peter Rinearson. *The Road Ahead.* Second edn. New York: Penguin, 1996.

Gibson, William. "'I Don't Even Have a Modem': An Interview with William Gibson." Available at: www.josefsson.net/gibson (accessed 16 August 2006).

—— *Neuromancer.* New York: Ace, 1984.

Gilman, Sander L. "The Image of the Hysteric." In *Hysteria Beyond Freud.* Ed. Sander Gilman *et al.* Berkeley, CA: University of California Press, 1993. 345–452.

Goethe, Johann Wolfgang von. *Goethes Sämtliche Werke: Jubiläums-Ausgabe.* 40 vols. Stuttgart and Berlin: J. G. Cotta, 1907.

Goldsmith, Kenneth, ed. *I'll Be Your Mirror: The Selected Andy Warhol Interviews.* New York: Carroll and Graf, 2004

Graham, Cooper C. *Leni Riefenstahl and Olympia.* Metuchen, NJ: Scarecrow Press, 1986.

Grau, Oliver. *Virtual Art: From Illusion to Immersion.* Trans. Gloria Cunstance. Cambridge, MA: MIT Press, 2003.

Gropius, Walter. "Address to the Students of the Staatliche Bauhaus, Held on the Occasion of the Yearly Exhibition of Student Work in July 1919." In Wingler 36.

—— "Baukunst im freien Volkstaat." In *Deutscher Revolutions Almanach für das Jahr 1919.* Ed. Ernst Drahn and Ernst Friedegg. Hamburg: Hoffmann und Campe, 1919. 134–6.

—— "Breviary for Bauhaus Members." In Wingler 76.

—— "Erwin Piscator." In Deutsche Akademie 35–6.

—— "Idee und Aufbau des staatlichen Bauhauses." In *Staatliches Bauhaus in Weimar.* Ed. Walter Gropius. Cologne: Karl Nierendorf, 1923.

—— *The New Architecture and the Bauhaus.* Trans. P. Morton Shand. Cambridge, MA: MIT Press, 1965.

—— "Program of the Staatliche Bauhaus in Weimar." In Wingler 31–3.

—— *Scope of Total Architecture.* New York: Harper and Brothers, 1955.

—— "The Viability of the Bauhaus Idea." In Wingler 51–2.

—— "The Work of the Bauhaus Stage." In Wingler 58.

Gropius, Walter, Bruno Taut, and Adolf Behne. "New Ideas on Architecture." In Conrads 46.

Gropius, Walter and Arthur S. Wensinger, eds. *The Theater of the Bauhaus.* Baltimore, MD: Johns Hopkins University Press, 1996. Original German version: Laszlo Moholy-Nagy, Oskar Schlemmer, and Farkas Molnar. *Die Bühne im Bauhaus.* Mainz: Florian Kupferberg, 1965.

Groys, Boris. *Gesamtkunstwerk Stalin: die gespaltene Kultur in der Sowjetunion.* Trans. Gabriele Leupold. Munich: C. Hanser, 1988.

Gutman, Robert. *Richard Wagner: The Man, his Mind, and his Music.* New York: Harcourt, Brace, and World, 1968.

Habermas, Jürgen. "The Public Sphere: An Encyclopedia Article (1964)." *New German Critique* 3 (Fall 1974): 49–55.

—— *The Structural Transformation of the Public Sphere: An Inquiry into a Category of Bourgeois Society.* Trans. Thomas Burger. Cambridge, MA: MIT Press, 1983.

Haden-Guest, Anthony. *The Paradise Program: Travels through Muzak, Hilton, Coca-Cola, Texaco, Walt Disney, and Other World Empires.* New York: William Morrow, 1973. Published in Great Britain as *Down the Programmed Rabbit Hole.*

Hancock, Eleanor. "Only the Real, the True, the Masculine Held its Value: Ernst Röhm, Masculinity, and Male Homosexuality." *Journal of the History of Sexuality* 8:4 (1998): 616–41.

Hansen, Mark. "Digitizing the Racialized Body, or the Politics of Universal Address." *SubStance* 33.2 (2004): 107–33.

Haraway, Donna. "A Cyborg Manifesto: Science, Technology, and Socialist-Feminism in the Late Twentieth Century." In *Simians, Cyborgs and Women: The Reinvention of Nature.* New York; Routledge, 1991. 149–81.

Hardt, Michael. "The Withering of Civil Society." In *Deleuze and Guattari: New Mappings in Politics, Philosophy, and Culture.* Ed. Eleanor Kaufman and Kevin Heller. Minneapolis, MN: University of Minnesota Press, 1998. 23–39.

Hardt, Michael and Antonio Negri. *Empire.* Cambridge, MA: Harvard University Press, 2000.

Harvey, David. *The Limits to Capital.* Oxford: Oxford University Press, 1982.

—— *Spaces of Hope.* Edinburgh: Edinburgh University Press, 2000.

—— *The Condition of Postmodernity.* Cambridge, MA: Blackwell, 1989.

Hegel, Georg Wilhelm Friedrich. *The Philosophy of History.* Trans. J. Sibree. New York: Dover, 1956.

Hench, John. "Interviewed by Jay Horan." 3 December 1982. Transcript. Walt Disney Archives, Burbank, CA.

Hench, John, with Peggy Van Pelt. *Designing Disney: Imagineering and the Art of the Show.* New York: Disney Editions, 2003.

Herman, Edward and Robert McChesney. *The Global Media.* London: Cassell, 1997.

Hinton, David. *The Films of Leni Riefenstahl.* Second edn. Metuchen, NJ: Scarecrow Press, 1991.

Hirschman, Ruth. "Pop Goes the Artist." In Goldsmith 27–46.

Hitler, Adolf. *Reden und Proklamationen 1932–1945.* 2 vols. Ed. Max Domarus. Munich: Süddeutscher Verlag, 1965.

Hoberman, J. "The Reich Stuff." Review of *Hitler's Hit Parade. Village Voice* 4 January 2005.

Hochman, Elaine S. *Bauhaus: Crucible of Modernism.* New York: Fromm International, 1997.

"How Disney Sells Happiness." *Parade* 26 March 1972: 4–6.

Hull, David Stuart. *Film in the Third Reich.* Berkeley, CA: University of California Press, 1969.

Humblet, Claudine. *Le Bauhaus.* Lausanne: L'Age d'Homme, 1980.

Huth, Friedrich. "Technische Fortschritte." *Schaufenster – Kunst und Technik* December 1930: 29.

Huyssen, Andreas. *After the Great Divide: Modernism, Mass Culture, Postmodernism.* Bloomington, IN: Indiana University Press, 1986.

—— *Present Pasts: Urban Palimpsests and the Politics of Memory.* Stanford, CA: Stanford University Press, 2003.

Imagineers. *The Imagineering Way: Ideas to Ignite your Creativity*. New York: Disney Editions, 2003.

Isherwood, Christopher. *The World in the Evening*. New York: Avon, 1956.

Jäger, Ernst. "How Leni Riefenstahl Became Hitler's Girlfriend." Part 9 (of 11). *Hollywood Tribune* 23 June 1939: 13.

Jameson, Fredric. *Archeologies of the Future: The Desire Called Utopia and Other Science Fictions*. New York: Verso, 2005.

—— *Postmodernism, or, The Cultural Logic of Late Capitalism*. Durham, NC: Duke University Press, 1991.

Jay, Martin. "The Jews and the Frankfurt School: Critical Theory's Analysis of Anti-Semitism." *New German Critique* 19 (Winter 1980): 137–49.

Jürgens, Martin. "Der Staat als Kunstwerk. Bemerkungen zur Ästhetisierung der Politik." *Kursbuch* 20 (1970): 119–39.

Kafka, Franz. *Amerika*. Trans. Edwin Muir. New York: New Directions, 1946.

Kállai, Ernst. "Between Ritual and Cabaret." In *Schrifttanz: A View of German Dance in the Weimar Republic*. Ed. Valerie Preston-Dunlop and Susanne Lahusen. London: Dance Books, 1990.

Kandinsky, Wassily. "Über Bühnenkomposition." *Der blaue Reiter* (1912): 103–13.

Kelly, Kevin. *New Rules for the New Economy: Ten Radical Strategies for a Connected World*. New York: Penguin, 1998.

Kelman, Ken. "Propaganda as Vision – Triumph of the Will." *Film Culture* 56–7 (Spring 1973) 162–6.

Kent, Letitia. "Andy Warhol, Movieman: 'It's Hard to Be Your Own Script.'" In Goldsmith 185–90.

Kershaw, Ian. *Hitler, 1889–1936: Hubris*. New York: W. W. Norton, 1999.

Kindermann, Heinz. *Theatergeschichte Europas*. 10 vols. Salzburg: Otto Müller Verlag, 1957–74.

King, Margaret J. "Empires of Popular Culture: McDonald's and Disney." In *Ronald Revisited: The World of Ronald McDonald*. Ed. Marshall Fishwick. Bowling Green, OH: Bowling Green University Popular Press, 1983. 106–19.

Kirby, E. T., ed. *Total Theatre: A Critical Anthology*. New York: E. P. Dutton, 1969.

Kirby, Michael, ed. *Happenings. An Illustrated Anthology*. New York: E. P. Dutton, 1965.

Kirstein, Lincoln. *Movement and Metaphor*. New York: Praeger, 1970.

Kittler, Friedrich. "World-Breath: On Wagner's Media Technology." In Levin, *Opera*. 215–38.

Kleist, Heinrich von. "Über das Marionettentheater." In *Sämtliche Werke und Briefe*, 4 vols. Munich: Carl Hanser, 1982. 3:338–45.

Koch, Stephen. *Stargazer: The Life, World and Films of Andy Warhol, Revised and Updated*. New York: Marion Boyars, 1991.

Koepnick, Lutz. "Fascist Aesthetics Revisited." *Modernism/modernity* 6:1 (January 1999): 51–73.

Köhler, Joachim. *Wagner's Hitler: The Prophet and his Disciple*. Trans. Ronald Taylor. Malden, MA: Blackwell, 2000.

Koss, Juliet. "Allegorical Procedures, Apocalyptic Threats: Early Weimar Cultural Positions." In *Issues of Performance in Politics and the Arts*. Berkeley, CA: Berkeley Academic Press, 1997. 101–15.

Kostelanetz, Richard, ed. *Moholy-Nagy*. New York: Praeger, 1970.

Kracauer, Siegfried. *From Caligari to Hitler: A Psychological History of the German Film*. Princeton, NJ: Princeton University Press, 1947.

Labanyi, Peter. "Images of Fascism: Visualization and Aestheticization in the Third Reich." In *The Burden of German History 1919–45*. Ed. Michael Laffan. London: Methuen, 1988.

Laker, Graham. "Brecht and Eisenstein: Intellect v. Emotions." *New Welsh Review* 11.4 (Spring 1999): 63–5.

Lane, Jill. "Digital Zapatistas." *TDR* 47.2 (Summer 2003): 129–44.

Lapham, Lewis. Introduction. In Marshal McLuhan, *Understanding Media*. Cambridge, MA: MIT Press, 1997.

Large, David C. and William Weber, eds. *Wagnerism in European Culture and Politics*. Ithaca, NY: Cornell University Press, 1983.

Lassell, Michael. *Celebration: The Story of a Town*. New York: Disney Editions, 2004.

Lenya, Lotte. "Lotte Lenya Remembers *Mahagonny*." The papers of Kurt Weill and Lotte Lenya in the Irving S. Gilmore Music Library, Yale University. Folder 69/22.

Lessing, Julius. "Das halbe Jahrhundert der Weltausstellungen." *Volkswirtschaftliche Zeitfragen* 22:6 (1900): 1–30.

Lessing, Lawrence. *Code and Other Laws of Cyberspace*. New York: Basic Books, 2000.

Levin, David J. *Opera Through Other Eyes*. Ed. David J. Levin. Stanford, CA: Stanford University Press, 1993.

—— *Richard Wagner, Fritz Lang, and the Nibelungen: The Dramaturgy of Disavowal*. Princeton, NJ: Princeton University Press, 1998.

—— "Reading Beckmesser Reading: Antisemitism and Aesthetic Practice in The Mastersingers of Nuremberg." *New German Critique* 69 (Autumn 1996): 127–46.

Lévy, Pierre. *Cyberculture*. Trans. Robert Bononno. Minneapolis, MN: University of Minnesota Press, 2001.

Lissitzky, El. *El Lissitzky: Life, Letters, Texts*. Ed. Sophie Lissitzky-Kueppers. Greenwich, CT: New York Graphic Society, 1968.

Loew, Heinz. "Model for a Mechanical Stage." In Gropius and Wensinger 89.

Lombardo, Patrizia. "Warhol as Dandy and Flaneur". In *Who Is Andy Warhol*. Ed. Colin MacCabe with Mark Francis and Peter Wollen. Pittsburgh, PA: Andy Warhol Museum, 1997.

Ludlam, Charles. *Ridiculous Theatre – Scourge of Folly: The Essays and Opinions of Charles Ludlam*. Ed. Steven Samuels. New York: Theatre Communications Group, 1992.

McChesney, Robert. *Rich Media, Poor Democracy*. New York: New Press, 1999.

McLuhan, Marshall. Interview. *Playboy* March 1969: 53–74.

McLuhan, Marshall, and Quentin Fiore. *The Medium is the Massage*. New York: Random House, 1967.

Magee, Bryan. *The Tristan Chord: Wagner and Philosophy*. New York: Henry Holt, 2000.

Mansbach, Steven A. *Visions of Totality: Laszlo Moholy-Nagy, Theo Van Doesburg, and El Lissitzky*. Ann Arbor, MI: UMI Research Press, 1978.

Marcus, Alan. "Reappraising Riefenstahl's Triumph of the Will," *Film Studies* 4 (Summer 2004): 82.

Marling, Karal Ann, ed. *Designing Disney's Theme Parks: The Architecture of Reassurance*. New York: Flammarion, 1997.

Melanga, Gerard. *Secret Diaries of Gerard Melanga* [excerpts]. In Bockris and Melanga 52–3.

Meyer, Moe. *The Politics and Poetics of Camp*. New York: Routledge, 1994.

Michelson, Annette. "'Where Is Your Rupture?': Mass Culture and the *Gesamtkunstwerk*." *October* 56 (1991): 42–63.

Miéville, China. "Fifty Science-fiction and Fantasy Books that Socialists Should Read."

Available at: www.fantasticmetropolis.com/i/50socialist/full (accessed 3 November 2006).

Miller, Diane Disney. *The Story of Walt Disney, as Told to Pete Martin*. New York: Henry Holt, 1956.

Millington, Barry. "Gesamtkunstwerk." In *The New Grove Dictionary of Opera*. Ed. Stanley Sadie. London: Macmillan, 1992.

—— "Nuremberg Trial: Is There Anti-Semitism in *Die Meistersinger?*" *Cambridge Opera Journal* 3.3 (1991): 247–60.

—— "*Parsifal*: Facing the Contradictions." *Musical Times* 124:1680 (1983): 97–8.

Moholy-Nagy, Laszlo. "Constructivism and the Proletariat." In Kostelanetz 185–6.

—— "Education and the Bauhaus." In Kostelanetz 163–9.

—— *The New Vision*. Fourth rev. edn. New York: Wittenborn, Schultz, 1949.

—— "Theater, Circus, Variety." In Gropius and Wensinger 47–70.

—— "Why Bauhaus Education." *Shelter* 3 (March 1938).

Monk, Egon. "Neher und 'Hofmeister'." In Einem and Mechinger 140–3.

Moore, Alexander. "Walt Disney World: Bounded Ritual Space and the Playful Pilgrimage Center." *Anthropological Quarterly* 53 (1980): 207–18.

Morin, Richard. "How the Game Is Played." *Washington Post* 25 May 2003: B05.

Mosley, Leonard. *Disney's World: A Biography*. New York: Stein and Day, 1985.

Mosse, George L. *The Nationalization of the Masses: Political Symbolism and Mass Movements in Germany from the Napoleonic Wars through the Third Reich*. New York: New American Library, 1977.

Musgrave, Michael. *The Musical Life of the Crystal Palace*. Cambridge: Cambridge University Press, 1995.

Nattiez, Jean-Jacques. *Wagner Androgyne: A Study in Interpretation*. Trans. Stewart Spencer. Princeton, NJ: Princeton University Press, 1993.

Negroponte, Nicholas. *Being Digital*. New York: Vintage, 1995.

Nerdinger, Winifred, ed. *Bauhaus-Moderne im Nationalsozialismus: Zwischen Anbiederung und Verfolgung*. Munich: Prestel, 1993.

Neumann, Alfred. "The *Gesamtkunstwerk* as a Romantic Form." In *Studies in Nineteenth Century and Early Twentieth Century German Literature*. Ed. Norman Binger and A. Wayne Wonderley. Lexington, KY: APRA, 1974.

Newman, Ernest. *The Life of Richard Wagner*. 4 vols. New York: A. A. Knopf, 1941.

—— *Wagner as Man and Artist*. Garden City, NY: Garden City Publishing, 1937.

Nietzsche, Friedrich. The Birth of Tragedy *and* The Case of Wagner. Trans. Walter Kaufmann. New York: Vintage, 1967.

—— *Thus Spoke Zarathustra: A Book for None and All*. Trans. Walter Kaufmann. New York: Penguin, 1954.

—— *Werke*. 9 parts. Ed. Giorgio Colli and Mazzino Montinari. Berlin: Walter de Gruyter, 1969.

Novalis. *Werke und Briefe*. Ed. Alfred Kelletat. Munich: Winkler-Verlag, 1968.

O'Brien, Glenn. "Interview: Andy Warhol." In Goldsmith 233–64.

Oosterhuis, Harry. "Medicine, Male Bonding, and Homosexuality in Nazi Germany." *Journal of Contemporary History* 32.2 (April 1997): 187–205.

Osborne, Charles. *The World Theatre of Wagner*. New York: Macmillan, 1982.

Packer, Randall and Ken Jordan, eds. *Multimedia: From Wagner to Virtual Reality*. New York: Norton, 2001.

Packer, Randall, organizer. "Telematic Manifesto." Available at: www.zakros.com/manifesto/gesamtelewerk.html (accessed 31 October 2005).

Paltridge, Jim. "Andy Out West." In Goldsmith 131–49.

Paulin, Scott. "Richard Wagner and the Fantasy of Cinematic Unity." In *Music and Cinema*. Ed. James Buhler, Caryl Flinn, and David Neumeyer. Hanover, NH: Wesleyan University Press, 2000. 58–84.

Pavis, Patrice. *Dictionary of the Theatre*. Toronto: University of Toronto Press, 1998.

Piscator, Erwin. *The Political Theatre*. Trans. Hugh Rorrison. London: Eyre Methuen, 1980.

—— "Theatre of Totality and Total Theatre." In Deutsche Akademie 64–7.

Polgar, Alfred. *Handbuch des Kritikers*. Zurich: Verlag Oprecht, 1938.

Poore, George Vivian. *A Text-book of Electricity in Medicine and Surgery*. London: Smith, Elder, and Co., 1876.

Poster, Mark. "Digital Networks and Citizenship." *PMLA* 117.1 (2002): 98–103.

—— "The Information Empire." *Comparative Literature Studies* 41.3 (2004): 317–34.

—— *What's the Matter with the Internet?* Minneapolis, MN: University Minneapolis Press, 2001.

Puchner, Martin. *Stage Fright: Modernism, Anti-theatricality, and Drama*. Baltimore, MD: Johns Hopkins University Press, 2002.

Purdum, Todd. "With the Force, in the Movie Line." *New York Times* 29 April 1999: A18.

Ranney, Ambrose L. *Practical Suggestions Respecting the Varieties of Electric Currents and the Uses of Electricity in Medicine*. New York: D. Appleton and Co., 1885.

Reeves, Graham. *Palace of the People*. Bromley: Bromley Library Service, 1986.

"Reichsminister Dr. Goebbels huldigt Richard Wagner." *Der Angriff* 7 August 1933: 6.

Rentschler, Eric. *The Ministry of Illusion: Nazi Cinema and its Afterlife*. Cambridge, MA: Harvard University Press, 1996.

Rheingold, Howard. *The Virtual Community: Homesteading on the Electronic Frontier*. Rev. edn. Cambridge, MA: MIT Press, 2000.

Richards, Thomas. *The Commodity Culture of Victorian England: Advertising and Spectacle, 1851–1914*. New York: Verso, 1991.

Riefenstahl, Leni. *Hinter den Kulissen des Reichsparteitag-Films*. Munich: Zentralverlag der NSDAP., F. Eher Nachf., GmbH., 1935.

—— Interview with Michael Delahaye. *Cahiers du Cinéma* 170 (1965): 42–63.

—— Interview with Ray Müller. *The Wonderful, Horrible Life of Leni Riefenstahl*, Ray Müller, dir. Image Entertainment, 2003.

—— *Leni Riefenstahl: A Memoir*. New York: St Martin's Press, 1993.

—— *Triumph of the Will*. DVD. Synapse Films, 2001.

Ronell, Avital. *The Telephone Book: Technology, Schizophrenia, Electric Speech*. Lincoln, NE: University of Nebraska Press, 1989.

Roost, Frank. *Die Disneyfizierung der Städte: Grossprojekte der Entertainmentindustrie am Beispiel des New Yorker Times Square und der Siedlung Celebration in Florida*. Opladen: Leske und Budrich, 2000.

Rose, Paul Lawrence. *Wagner: Race and Revolution*. New Haven, CT: Yale University Press, 1992.

Ross, Alex. "Nausea." Review of Schlingensief *Parsifal* at Bayreuth. *New Yorker* 9 and 16 August 2004.

Ross, Andrew. *The Celebration Chronicles: Life, Liberty, and the Pursuit of Property Value in Disney's New Town*. New York: Ballentine Books, 1999.

Rühle, Otto. *Karl Marx: His Life and Work*. Trans. Eden and Cedar Paul. London: George Allen and Unwin, 1929.

Runge, Philipp Otto. *Hintergelassene Schriften.* 2 vols. Göttingen: Vanderhöck und Ruprecht, 1965.

Sabor, Rudolph. Commentary. In Richard Wagner, *Das Rheingold.* London: Phaidon, 1997.

Schelling, Friedrich Wilhelm Joseph von. *Sämmtliche Werke.* Ed. K. F. A. Schelling. 14 vols. Stuttgart: J. G. Cotta, 1856–61.

Schickel, Richard. *The Disney Version.* Chicago, IL: Ivan R. Dee, 1997.

Schiller, Friedrich. *On the Aesthetic Education of Man.* German and English edn. Trans. Elizabeth M. Wilkinson and L. A. Willoughby. Oxford: Clarendon Press, 1982.

—— "Über den Gebrauch des Chors in der Tragödie." In *Schillers Werke.* 4 vols. Frankfurt: Insel Verlag, 1966. 241–9.

—— *Über die ästhetische Erziehung des Menschen in einer Reihe von Briefen.* Ed. Klaus L. Berghahn. Stuttgart: Reklam, 2000.

Schiller, Herbert. *The Mind Managers.* Boston: Beacon Press, 1973.

Schlegel, Friedrich. *Lucinde and the Fragments.* Trans. Peter Firchow. Minneapolis, MN: University of Minnesota Press, 1971.

Schlemmer, Oskar. *Briefe und Tagebücher.* Ed. Tut Schlemmer. Munich: Albert Langen and George Müller, 1958.

—— "Das figurale Kabinett – Beschreibung der Neufassung." *Baukunst und Werkform* 8:4 (1955): 212–14.

—— *Letters and Diaries.* Ed. Tut Schlemmer. Trans. Krishna Winston. Middletown, CT: Wesleyan University Press, 1972.

—— "Man and Art Figure." In Gropius and Wensinger 16–46.

—— "Neue Formen der Bühne," *Schünemanns Monatshefte* 10 (1928): 1063–73.

—— "Piscator und das moderne Theater." *Das neue Frankfurt* 2:2 (1928): 22–6.

"The Staatliche Bauhaus in Weimar." In Wingler 65 7.

—— "Theater (Bühne)." In Gropius and Wensinger 81–101.

Schnapp, Jeffrey T. "Border Crossings: Italian/German Peregrinations of the 'Theater of Totality.'" *Critical Inquiry* 21.1 (Autumn 1994): 80–123.

—— *Staging Fascism: 18 BL and the Theater of Masses for Masses.* Stanford, CA: Stanford University Press, 1996.

Schneider, Rebecca. "Nomadmedia: On Critical Art Ensemble." *TDR: The Drama Review* 44.4 (Winter 2000): 120–31.

Sedgwick, Eve Kosofsky. *Tendencies.* Durham, NC: Duke University Press, 1993.

Semper, Gottfried. *Wissenschaft, Industrie und Kunst und andere Schriften über Architektur, Kunsthandwerk und Kunstunterricht.* Mainz: Kupferberg, 1966.

Shanken, Edward A. "Technology and Intuition: A Love Story?: Roy Ascott's Telematic Embrace." *Leonardo.* 10 March 1997. Available at: http://mitpress2.mit.edu/e-journals/Leonardo/isast/articles/shanken.html.

Shapiro, Robert. "Fantasy Economics." *Slate* 4 February 2003.

Shirer, William L. *Berlin Diary.* New York: Galahad Books, 1940.

Showalter, Elaine. *The Female Malady: Women, Madness, and English Culture, 1830–1980.* New York: Pantheon Books, 1985.

Slate, Lane. "USA Artists: Andy Warhol and Roy Lichtenstein." In Goldsmith 79–84.

Smith, Matthew. "Laughing at the Redeemer: On the Bodies of *Parsifal.*" *Modernist Cultures* (Spring 2007): forthcoming.

Smith, R. C. and E. M. Eisenberg. "Conflict at Disneyland: A Root-metaphor Analysis." *Communication Monographs* 54 (1987): 367–80.

Sontag, Susan. *Against Interpretation and Other Essays.* New York: Picador, 2001.

Speer, Albert. *Inside the Third Reich*. Trans. Richard and Clara Winston. New York: Bonanza Books, 1970.

Spotts, Frederic. *Bayreuth: A History of the Wagner Festival*. New Haven, CT: Yale University Press, 1994.

—— *Hitler and the Power of Aesthetics*. New York: Overlook Press, 2004.

Stallabras, Julian. *Gargantua: Manufactured Mass Culture*. London: Verso, 1996.

Stenger, Nicole. "Mind Is a Leaking Rainbow." In *Cyberspace: First Steps*. Ed. Michael Benedikt. Cambridge, MA: MIT Press, 1991. 49–58.

Storm, J. P. and Mario Dressler. In *Im Reiche der Micky-Maus: Walt Disney in Deutschland 1927–1945*. Berlin: Henschel, 1991.

Susman, Warren, with Edward Griffin. "Did Success Spoil the United States?: Dual Representations in Postwar America." In *Recasting America: Culture and Politics in the Age of Cold War*. Ed. Lary May. Chicago, IL: University of Chicago Press, 1989.

Swenson, G. R. "What Is Pop Art? Answers from 8 Painters, Part I." In Goldsmith 15–20.

Syberberg, Hans-Jürgen. *Hitler, ein Film aus Deutschland*. Reinbek bei Hamburg: Rowohlt, 1978.

—— *Parsifal, ein Filmessay*. Munich: Heyne, 1982.

Szeemann, Harald. *Der Hang zum Gesamtkunstwerk: europäische Utopien seit 1800*. Aarau: Sauerländer, 1983.

Tafuri, Manfredo. *The Sphere and the Labyrinth: Avant-Gardes and Architecture from Piranesi to the 1970s*. Trans. Pellegrino d'Acierno and Robert Connolly. Cambridge, MA: MIT Press, 1990.

Talking Heads. "Heaven" and "Air." In *Fear of Music*. The Talking Heads Official Website. Available at: www.talking-heads.net/lyrics_fear.html (accessed 31 October 2005).

Taylor, Mark C. *About Religion*. Chicago, IL: University of Chicago Press, 1999.

Thackeray, W. M. "May-Day Ode." In Christopher Hobhouse, *1851 and the Crystal Palace, Being an Account of the Great Exhibition and Its Contents*. New York: E. P. Dutton, 1937. Appendix 1. 169–73.

Thiel, Tamiko. "Constructing Meaning in Interactive Virtual Reality." Available at: http://mission.base.com/manzanar (accessed 14 December 2005). Originally published in the conference proceedings for COSIGN2001: Computational Semiotics for Games and New Media, Amsterdam, Holland, 11 September 2001.

Thomas, Bob. *Walt Disney: An American Original*. New York: Simon and Schuster, 1976.

Tinkcom, Matthew. *Working Like a Homosexual: Camp, Capital, Cinema*. Durham, NC: Duke University Press, 2002.

"Tomorrowland." Available at: www.disney.com.hk/hkdisneyland/english/tomorrowland.html (accessed 10 February 2004).

Treadwell, James. *Interpreting Wagner*. New Haven, CT: Yale University Press, 2003.

Trimingham, Melissa. "Oskar Schlemmer's Research Practice at the Dessau Bauhaus," *Theatre Research International* 29:2 (2004): 128–42.

Turkle, Sherry. *Life on the Screen: Identity in the Age of the Internet*. New York: Simon and Schuster, 1995.

Urbanitzky, Alfred Ritter von. *Die Elektrizität im Dienste der Menschheit*. Vienna: Pest und Leipzig, 1895.

Vaget, Hans Rudolf. "'Du warst mein Feind von je': The Beckmesser Controversy Revisited." In Vazsonyi 190–208.

Vazsonyi, Nicholas. *Wagner's* Meistersinger: *Performance, History, Representation*. Rochester, NY: University of Rochester Press, 2003.

Vitale, Elodie. "De l'oeuvre d'art à l'oeuvre totale: Art et architecture au Bauhaus." *Les Cahiers du Musée National d'Art Moderne* 39 (Spring 1992): 62–77.

Wagner, Richard. *Briefwechsel zwischen Wagner und Liszt.* Ed. Erich Kloss. Leipzig: Breitkopf und Härtel, 1910.

——*Gesammelte Schriften und Dichtungen.* 10 vols. Leipzig: C. S. W. Siegel, 1907.

—— *Prose Works.* 8 vols. Trans. W. Ashton Ellis. London: Keagan Paul, Trench, Trübner and Co., 1895–6.

—— *Richard Wagner to Mathilde Wesendonck.* Trans. William Ashton Ellis. Boston, MA: Milford House, 1905.

—— *The Ring of the Nibelung.* Trans. Andrew Porter. New York: Norton, 1976.

—— *Sämtliche Schriften und Dichtungen.* 12 vols. Leipzig: Breitkopf und Härtel, 1911–14.

—— *Selected Letters of Richard Wagner.* Ed. and trans. Stewart Spencer and Barry Millington. New York: W. W. Norton, 1987.

Wallace, Mike. "Mickey Mouse History: Portraying the Past at Disney World." *Radical History Review* (1985) 32: 33–57.

Walt Disney Company. "Intercot: Spaceship Earth." Available at: www.intercot.com/edc/ SpaceshipEarth/spscript82.html (accessed 31 October 2005).

—— "Spaceship Earth." Available at: http://disneyworld.disney.go.com/wdw/parks/ attractionDetail?id = SpaceshipEarthAttractionPage (accessed 31 October 2005).

—— "SE Fact Sheet." Available at: www.intercot.com/edc/SpaceshipEarth/spfacts.html (accessed 2 February 2006).

Ward, Janet. *Weimar Surfaces: Urban Visual Culture in 1920s Germany.* Berkeley, CA: University of California Press, 2001.

Warhol, Andy. *THE Philosophy of Andy Warhol.* New York: Harcourt Brace and Co., 1975.

Warhol, Andy and Pat Hackett. *POPism: The Warhol Sixties.* New York: Harcourt Brace and Co., 1980.

Wee, Tommy. "Playing with the Unreal." *Straits Times* 20 May 2003: LIFE!

Weinberger, David. *Small Pieces Loosely Joined: A Unified Theory of the Web.* Cambridge, MA: Perseus, 2002.

Weiner, Marc. *Richard Wagner and the Anti-Semitic Imagination.* Lincoln, NE: University of Nebraska Press, 1995.

Weingartner, Felix. *Lebenserinnerungen.* Vienna: Wiener literarische Anstalt, 1923.

Weininger, Andreas. "The Spherical Theater." In Gropius and Wensinger 89.

Wheeler, David, Susmita Dasgupta and Somik V. Lall. "Policy Reform, Economic Growth, and the Digital Divide: An Econometric Analysis." World Bank Policy Research Paper no. 2567, March 2001.

Wilkinson, Elizabeth M. and L. A. Willoughby. Introduction. In Schiller, *Aesthetic* xi–cxcvi .

Willis, Susan. "Disney World: Public Use/Private State." *South Atlantic Quarterly* 92:1 (1993): 119–37.

—— "The Problem with Pleasure." In *Inside the Mouse: Work and Play at Disney World.* By The Project on Disney. Durham, NC: Duke University Press, 1995.

Wilson, Alexander. *The Culture of Nature.* Cambridge, MA: Blackwell, 1992.

Wingler, Hans M., ed. *The Bauhaus: Weimar, Dessau, Berlin, Chicago.* Trans. Wolfgang Jabs and Basil Gilbert. Cambridge, MA: MIT Press, 1978. Original German version: Hans M. Wingler, ed. *Das Bauhaus, 1919–1933: Weimar Dessau Berlin und die Nachfolge in Chicago seit 1937.* Bramsche: Gebr. Rasch, 1968.

Winston, Brian. "Reconsidering 'Triumph of the Will': Was Hitler There?" *Sight and Sound* 50.2 (Spring 1981): 102–7.

Wong, Herman. "Disneyland: Can it Top 15 Years of Success?" *Los Angeles Times* 12 July 1976: C1, C5.

Woodlawn, Holly. Interview 22 November 1978. In Patrick S. Smith, *Andy Warhol's Art and Films*. Ann Arbor, MI: UMI Research Press, 1986.

Wright, Guy and Glenn Suokko. "Andy Warhol: An Artist and his Amiga." In Goldsmith 333–47.

Wyss, Beat. "*Ragnarök* of Illusion: Richard Wagner's 'Mystical Abyss' at Bayreuth." *October* 54 (Fall 1990): 57–78.

Žižek, Slavoj. "'The Wound Is Healed Only by the Spear that Smote You': The Operatic Subject and its Vicissitudes." In Levin, *Opera* 177–214.

Zola, Émile. *The Ladies' Paradise*. Berkeley, CA: University of California Press, 1992.

Zook, M. A. "Internet Metrics: Using Hosts and Domain Counts to Map the Internet Globally." *Telecommunications Policy* 24:6/7 (2000): 613–20.

—— Internet Geography Research Project. Available at: www.zooknic.com (accessed 22 August 2005).

—— "Old Hierarchies or New Networks of Centrality?: The Global Geography of the Internet Content Market." *American Behavioral Scientist* 44:10 (2001): 1679–96.

—— "The Web of Production: The Economic Geography of Commercial Internet Content Production in the United States." *Environment and Planning A* 32 (2000): 411–26.

Index